Crime Prevention and Security Management

Series Editor
Martin Gill
Perpetuity Research
Tunbridge Wells, Kent, United Kingdom

It is widely recognized that we live in an increasingly unsafe society, but the study of security and crime prevention has lagged behind in its importance on the political agenda and has not matched the level of public concern. This exciting new series aims to address these issues looking at topics such as crime control, policing, security, theft, workplace violence and crime, fear of crime, civil disorder, white collar crime and anti-social behaviour. International in perspective, providing critically and theoretically-informed work, and edited by a leading scholar in the field, this series will advance new understandings of crime prevention and security management.

More information about this series at
http://www.springer.com/series/14928

Randy K. Lippert • Kevin Walby • Ian Warren • Darren Palmer
Editors

National Security, Surveillance and Terror

Canada and Australia in Comparative Perspective

Editors
Randy K. Lippert
Department of Sociology and Criminology,
University of Windsor,
401 Sunset Ave, Windsor, ON, Canada

Kevin Walby
Department of Criminal Justice
University of Winnipeg,
Centennial Hall,
3rd Floor, 515 Portage Avenue,
Winnipeg, MB, Canada

Ian Warren
School of Humanities and Social Sciences,
Deakin University,
Locked Bag 20000,
Geelong, VIC, Australia

Darren Palmer
School of Humanities and Social Sciences,
Deakin University,
Locked Bag 20000,
Geelong, VIC, Australia

Crime Prevention and Security Management
ISBN 978-3-319-82767-4   ISBN 978-3-319-43243-4   (eBook)
DOI 10.1007/978-3-319-43243-4

Cover image © Pixhall / Alamy Stock Photo

Printed on acid-free paper

This Palgrave Macmillan imprint is published by Springer Nature
The registered company is Springer International Publishing AG
The registered company address is: Gewerbestrasse 11, 6330 Cham, Switzerland

Foreword

The social sciences, perhaps especially in the past two decades, are replete with analyses that announce a new sociopolitical order in which familiar institutions, apparatuses and legalities are transformed in form or function. Many of these theories reflect directly on questions of security, surveillance and antiterror initiatives. Perhaps most famously, the Risk Society thesis envisaged an entirely new modernity in which global, unpredictable and catastrophic risks undermined the family, nation states, trades unions and even scientific expertise. A series of security-related spinoff theories foresaw the transformation of police into security-informatic brokers, mapped out the transformation of criminal justice around risk-based mentalities, envisioned the rise of governmental 'precautionary' logics that assumed worst case scenarios and formed themselves around merely imagined disasters. Elsewhere, a new age of exceptionalism has been identified in which a contagion of camps strips human and civil rights from problem people and imposes upon them a regime of bare life. In other writings, national borders as geopolitical places collapse, as the division between internal and external security is undermined and surveillance and militaristic forms once primarily reserved for extra-national security are turned inward. Globalisation, the 'new terrorism,' asymmetrical warfare, the aftermath of 9/11, a clash of civilisations and a myriad other more or less spectacular emergencies and tragedies are found to be root causes of totalised shifts.

These are not just the sensationalist fantasies of ambitious ivory tower academics. Many of them are borrowed or developed from government think-tanks, commissions, policy pronouncements, 'revolutions in military affairs' and so on. As well, no one can doubt that new forms of terrorism have required marked changes in border-security practices; analyses of global warming stimulate programmes for rendering cities and infrastructures 'resilient'; new technologies enable mass surveillance on a hitherto unimaginable scale; and so on. Almost all of these are worthy of concentrated empirical analysis and theoretical attention. The problem lies not in identifying emergent and troubling developments so much as in magnifying these into all-pervasive, unprecedented, irreversible, catastrophic and irresistible sea changes. Sometimes they are mere straws in the wind: police have not been transformed by risk—at least not in ways envisioned. Sometimes they are plain wrong: 'camps,' epitomised by Guantanamo Bay, turn out to be heavily regulated spaces where sovereignty is hide-bound. Sometimes they turn out to be relatively easily controllable: Ebola, Avian Flu and other 'global pandemics' were managed into mainly local epidemics of limited lethality. Sometimes resistance is effective, as in many instances where CCTV cameras have been uninstalled. The future, we might say, is a foreign country and our theories may not work there.

This is why, arguably, analyses of security and securitisation should be progressively insulated from grand conceptions of global or institutional transformation because these later usually become both politically and theoretically problematic. This strategy already has been suggested with respect to that master variable 'neoliberalism' that was used to explain almost every disliked political change since 1970 and which has turned out to be, at best, a kind of greasy, portmanteau term: hard to pin down and carrying a lot of hidden baggage. Such broad concepts and visions may be useful at first, when certain changes need highlighting and outlining, but they become a hindrance once it becomes necessary to focus analysis to gain theoretical and political traction with specific developments. In the domain of security and surveillance, what are no longer necessary are sweeping generalisations backed up by carefully selected examples that ignore or understate complexities and counter-trends. We need more detailed studies that work meticulously in the shadow cast by the grander utterances. That is, theoretical depictions of the risk society, or the state of exception or whatever, may inform analysis, but ongoing research studies should not strive to illustrate or instantiate these 'theories,' nor should they be structured around such accounts. Almost inevitably this will lead to further selection and omissions of convenience to the theoretical account and its advocates, but effectively handicapping a politics that seeks to engage with specific jurisdictions and the formation of what Foucault terms 'strategic knowledge.'

A volume such as this, that focuses on two specific (but comparable) polities and that seeks to explore particular lines of development within and across these, is especially timely and welcome. It develops a form of analysis that should not be understood as 'local' or 'particular' but rather as *precise*. As well, because of the array of 'securitising' techniques, apparatuses and contexts that are explored—from border policing to indigenous politics, from police powers to the 'intelligence community,' from the legislative change to private security—it cannot be dismissed as 'narrow.' It is, collectively, of very considerable *scope*. This is not the 'scope' of grand transnational generalities, but the scope that takes in a range of specific settings, a scope that complements precision. When brought together in one volume the wide ranging but specific and precise studies produce awareness of diversity and complexity while nevertheless recognising broader tendencies—for they are no more than that—that are sheltered under grander pronouncements on sovereignty, securitisation and surveillance.

Pat O'Malley
University of Sydney
Sydney, Australia
November 2015

Series Editor's Introduction

In this volume, Randy K. Lippert, Kevin Walby, Ian Warren and Darren Palmer have put together an impressive range of chapters and marked out new territory in the analysis of the response to terror; you will not find the issues covered in this book available in one volume anywhere else. The book is based on a comparison of the approaches of two countries—Australia and Canada—that have amassed considerable experience on security issues but which until now have received much less attention than the UK and the USA. While Canada and Australia share similar histories, socially and economically, including links to the British Commonwealth and common law traditions, the authors attend to some of the distinct differences that have a bearing on and shape the nature of the response to terror, for example, while Australia is without a *Charter of Rights and Freedoms* or *Bill of Rights* this is not the case in Canada.

More than this though, as the editors note, the book draws on a range of approaches and theoretical frameworks from a wide variety of disciplines, facilitating a more detailed critical analysis than has been undertaken hitherto. This book will walk you through the varying interpretations of the word 'security,' as well as the roles of different security actors at national and local level. You will read about the ways in which these actors sometimes work in harmony to provide a security blanket, and sometimes work in conflict to create security gaps, all of which are rarely acknowledged and much less subjected to scrutiny.

The book is divided into three parts and in each the editors summarise and guide you through the main issues. The first part introduces the issues affecting the expansion of securitisation through, for example, increased partnership work in response to the differing risks to national security. There are many implications and the crucial role of balancing security with people's right to privacy features prominently. The range of ideas covered in the first part of the book is developed in Part 2 with the inclusion of a selection of insightful and empirically based case studies. The expansion of security is reflected here in the examination of Corkill, Brooks and Coole's 'language groups' used by security actors, but also by Walby, Lippert and Gacek in their assessment of the considerable overlaps in behaviour between different security actors through their imaginative use of Freedom of Information requests as a research tool.

The final part focuses on dilemmas in national security, surveillance and terror, looking at accountability, privacy, sovereignty and legitimacy, topics that are common to both countries. You will learn about a security measure that is of increasing importance but only rarely discussed; unmanned aerial devices (UAVs), as well as a specific security programme, the Canadian-US Shiprider programme which seeks to remove a significant barrier—the country border—to law enforcement. There is much that other regions, and authorities at different levels, may learn from this.

This text provides rich insight and new thinking from disciplines that are often seen as marginal to this topic, and in countries that have much to contribute to our need to better understand how the world, locally and nationally, can respond more effectively to the threats posed by terror while remaining true to the principles of freedom and privacy. For students of security, it must be remembered these are not just important democratic rights, but fundamental aspects, perhaps the most important ones, of what constitutes good security practice.

Martin Gill
Perpetuity Research, Tunbridge Wells, UK
May 2016

Acknowledgements

Randy K. Lippert acknowledges support of his amazing partner, Francine, while co-editing this volume. Heartfelt thanks to Heidi Erismann, Heather Leslie and Paul Lippert for quiet moral support from afar. Special thanks to Mathew Zaia, who provided superb assistance with the entire volume and to Martin Gill, series editor, for his solid, enthusiastic support at a crucial juncture. Finally, thanks to Jesse Seary, who first inspired me to think critically and hope for a better world.

Kevin Walby thanks his parents and his brother. Thanks to Joanne DeCosse, Evelyn Mayanja and Melissa Dick for their editorial support.

Ian Warren acknowledges the ongoing support of Dana Bolitho, Remi Bolitho, Brian Warren, Anne Warren, Darren Palmer, Randy K. Lippert, Kevin Walby and the Alfred Deakin Centre for Citizenship and Globalisation for its generous financial assistance on several small-scale research projects related to this volume.

Darren Palmer acknowledges the ongoing support of Katey, Dylan, Jonah and Lila and the research support of the Alfred Deakin Centre for Citizenship and Globalisation at Deakin University.

Contents

Contributors

John Anderson is an associate professor in law at the University of Newcastle, Australia, and an expert on Australian uniform evidence law. He has written widely on criminal law and procedure in Australia and in comparative perspective. He has researched a wide range of issues relating to attributions of fault in arson in Australia, comparative sentencing policy and entrapment by police. His work is also critical of the capacity of current Australian legal frameworks to promote adequate security or crime control objectives.

David Brooks is the Security Science Course Coordinator at Edith Cowan University, Australia. David commenced his career in Military Air Defence, moving into the Electronic Security sector and later, Security Consultancy. His research interests are focused on corporate security, security education and security risk management, having published widely in these areas. He is currently on the Editorial Committee of the *Security Journal*.

Mark Doerksen is a PhD candidate in the Social and Cultural Analysis program in the Department of Sociology/Anthropology at Concordia University. His work explores practices of transhumanism and enhancement of senses through do-it-yourself electronic implants. He has published critical work dealing with courts, peace bonds and policing in Canada. He has studied intensive probation and parole supervision in the North American corrections context. He is co-author of *The Disappearance of Criminal Law* (2015).

Michael Coole commenced his working career in the military, as a Navy Clearance Diver before moving into the Australian justice system working in security and emergency management and also as a private consultant. He now works as a teaching and research scholar at Edith Cowan University, Western Australia with technical interests in physical protection and security decay, along with security social issues including community crime prevention, security deviance, surveillance in society and security professionalism. Michael holds a BSc, MSc (Security Science) and PhD, along with Diplomas in safety and management and is currently on ASIS International's Research Council.

Jeffery Corkill is a lecturer in intelligence and security at Edith Cowan University, Australia. A former army intelligence officer, Jeff acquired his security management experience in the precious minerals industry, before moving into security and intelligence consultancy. Jeff has broad security and intelligence experience within Defence, United Nations, the Resource and Gaming sectors. His research interests are focused on intelligence analysis, surveillance and the role of Resilience in Vetting.

Tia Dafnos teaches in the Department of Sociology at York University, Toronto. Her doctoral thesis examined the policing of Indigenous protests in Canada. Tia's work explores the intersections of power, social ordering and police surveillance as they impact Indigenous land claims, social protest and concepts of emergency in settler-colonial contexts.

Craig Forcese is Associate Professor at the Faculty of Law (Common Law Section), University of Ottawa. He teaches public international law, national security law, administrative law and public law/legislation. Much of his present research and writing relates to national security, human rights and democratic accountability. Craig has also co-authored a recent book on legal issues surrounding recreational and competitive cycling in Canada. Prior to joining the law school faculty, Craig practised law with the Washington DC office of Hughes Hubbard & Reed LLP for two years, specialising in international trade and commercial law. He has a BA from McGill, an MA from the Norman Paterson School of International Affairs, Carleton University, an LLB (*summa cum laude*) from University of Ottawa and an LLM from Yale University. He is a member in good standing of the bars of Ontario, New York and the District of Columbia.

Martin French is Assistant Professor in the Department of Sociology and Anthropology at Concordia University, Montreal. His research examines the social and political dimensions of information processing practices by used by health professionals for both organisational and diagnostic purposes. He has published numerous scholarly articles and book chapters that explore the need for evidence-based policies to inform the use of surveillance in the medical and public health fields, with particular emphasis on emergency pandemic detection and respect for individual privacy.

James Gacek is a lecturer in the Criminal Justice Department at the University of Winnipeg and in the Department of Sociology at the University of Manitoba. His interests span the disciplines of criminology, sociology and geography, and recently his research has taken him into the realm of the relationship between law and society. He is in the process of publishing several works within journals of criminology, media studies and the sociology of punishment.

Erin Gibbs Van Brunschot is Associate Professor and Head in the Department of Sociology at the University of Calgary. Her primary research interests are in the realms of crime, security and risk, with specific interests in how individual, organisation/agency and state orientations to risk both diverge and converge. Erin co-authored *Risk Balance and Security* (Sage 2008) with Les Kennedy and more recently co-authored a second book (with Les Kennedy) entitled *Risk in Crime* (2009 Rowman and Littlefield). Her current research focuses on the concept of offender management and the assessment of various technologies that are used to enhance public security. Her current project focuses most specifically on the use of global positioning systems to electronically monitor offenders and considers the challenges involved with the application of this technology to various types of offending and offender management goals.

Richard Jochelson is Associate Professor at Robson Hall Law School, University of Manitoba, and holds his PhD in law from Osgoode Hall. He has published articles dealing with obscenity, indecency, judicial activism and police powers. He is a member of the Bar of Manitoba and co-authored *Sex and the Supreme Court: Obscenity and Indecency Law in Canada* (2010). His research interests include regulation of sexuality, socio-legal governance of harm, policing and police powers, the criminal and constitutional law jurisprudence of the Supreme Court of Canada, and constitutionalism and the social in Canada.

David Martin Jones is Reader in the School of Political Science and International Studies at the University of Queensland and a fellow of the Australian Institute for Progress and the Institute of Public Affairs. He holds postgraduate degrees from McMaster University (Canada) and the London School of Economics and Political Science and has taught the history of political ideas, political development and the problem of democratisation and state security in Canada, the United Kingdom, Singapore, Malaysia and Australia. He has held visiting professorship positions at the War Studies Department, Kings College, University of London and in the Southeast Asian Studies Department of the University of Malaya as well as a university fellowship at the University of Wales. His books include *Towards Illiberal Democracy in Pacific Asia* (Macmillan/ St Antony's Oxford 1995) with Daniel A Bell, David Brown and Kanishka Jayasuriya, *Political Development in Pacific Asia* (Polity 1997), *Conscience and Allegiance in English Political Thought* (University of Rochester Press 1999), *The Image of China in Western Social and Political Thought* (Palgrave 2001), *ASEAN and the East Asian International Order* (with M.L.R. Smith, Edward Elgar 2007), *The Howard Era* (edited with Keith Windschuttle, Quadrant Books 2009), *The Rise of China and Asia Pacific Security* (with M.L.R. Smith and N. Khoo, Edward Elgar 2013), *The New Counterinsurgency Era in Critical Perspective* (edited with Celeste Ward Gvetner and M.L.R. Smith, London: Palgrave 2014) and *Sacred Violence Political Religion in a Secular Age* (with M.L.R. Smith, London: Palgrave 2014).

Randy K. Lippert is Professor of Criminology and Sociology at the University of Windsor specialising in policing, security and urban governance. He is author or co-author of more than 70 refereed articles and book chapters and is co-editor of several recent interdisciplinary, international collections: *Sanctuary Practices in International Perspective* (Routledge 2014) (with S. Rehaag), *Policing Cities: Urban Securitization and Regulation in a Twenty-first Century World* (Routledge 2013) (with K. Walby), *Eyes Everywhere: The Global Growth of Camera Surveillance* (Routledge 2012) (with D. Lyon and A. Doyle), *Corporate Security in the Twenty-first Century* (Palgrave Macmillan 2014) (with K. Walby) and *Governing Practices: Neo-Liberalism, Governmentality, and the Ethnographic Imaginary* (forthcoming, University of Toronto Press) (with M. Brady). He has co-edited since 2007 five issues of socio-legal, security, migration and surveillance journals. He is author of *Sanctuary, Sovereignty, Sacrifice: Canadian Incidents, Power, and Law* (University of British Columbia Press 2006), and co-author with K. Walby of *Municipal Security in International Context* (Routledge 2015). He is debates editor for the journal *Surveillance and Society.*

Adam Molnar is Lecturer in Criminology at Deakin University, Melbourne, Australia. He completed a Postdoctoral Fellowship in the Surveillance Studies Centre at Queen's University, and attained his PhD in the Department of Political Science at the University of Victoria, where he was a Graduate Fellow at UVic's Centre for Global Studies. Much of his research focuses on contemporary strategies of policing and national security, as they relate to practices of surveillance and privacy. During his PhD work, he examined the security and policing legacies of the Vancouver 2010 Olympics as a raft of technological, inter-organisational, policy and cultural transformations in the areas of urban public safety. He has published journal articles, book chapters, and has commissioned reports for government and civil advocacy organisations. His research has been funded by SSHRC, the New Transparency Project, and the Office of the Privacy Commissioner's contributions programme, the University of Victoria's Centre for Global Studies, and by civil advocacy organisations. His research focuses on surveillance and technology in policing, and security initiatives that consider the associated implications for privacy, civil liberties and social control. Adam is also a Principal at Block G Privacy and Security Consulting and is a board member of the Australian Privacy Foundation.

Benjamin J. Muller is Associate Professor in the Department of Political Science at King's University College. Professor Muller also serves as the current Chair of the KUC Faculty Association and is President of the International Studies Association—Canada (2015–2016). In addition to teaching in the fields of Critical Security Studies and Borderlands Studies, Dr. Muller has published widely on related issues in journals such as *Geopolitics, Citizenship Studies, International Political Sociology*, and *Security Dialogue,* as well as a number of book chapters, and two monographs: *Security, Risk, and the Biometric State: Governing Borders and Bodies* (Routledge 2010); and, with Samer Abboud, *Rethinking Hizballah: Legitimacy, Authority, Violence* (Ashgate 2012). Dr. Muller has provided invited expertise to NATO, Canadian Parliamentary Committees and various stakeholder groups, as well as being an invited guest speaker at Universities throughout North America and Europe. In addition to having held teaching positions in Canada and the UK, Dr. Muller has held Visiting Scholar positions at the Border Policy Research Institute at Western Washington University (2008) and the Confluencenter for Creative Inquiry at the University of Arizona (2014), and was an invited guest of the Department of International Relations and the Ihsan Dogramaci Advanced International Studies Centre at Bilkent University in Ankara, Turkey, in May 2015.

Brendon Murphy is a senior lecturer in law at the University of Newcastle, Australia. His previous work has considered a range of important legal topics, including human rights and euthanasia, comparative sentencing and evidence policy, the role of blood samples in motor accident cases and the role of entrapment in controlled policing operations. His current work examines the relationships among law, surveillance and social theory.

Pat O'Malley is Professorial Research Fellow in Law at the University of Sydney. Previously he was Canada Research Chair in Criminology and Criminal Justice at Carleton University (2002–2006). From 1992 to 2002 he was Professor of Law, Director of the National Centre for Socio-Legal Studies (1990–1992), and Deputy Dean Faculty of Law and Management (1996–2001) at La Trobe University, Melbourne. He has occupied distinguished lecturing appointments at universities in Germany, the United States, Canada, Argentina, Chile, England, Northern Ireland and New Zealand. His principal fields of research have been in criminology and sociolegal studies, with a focus on risk as a technology for governing social and legal problems. This has included research on terrorism and crime prevention, insurance and insurance law, the law of accidents and public health approaches to governing illicit drug use. Currently funded research is focusing on the development and operation of fire protection as a field of urban security, the emergence of resilience as a governmental response to high uncertainty in military and related fields, and the risk-related use of money sanctions in civil and criminal justice. He has published ten books, over 150 articles in international journals and chapters in handbooks and edited collections.

Darren Palmer is Associate Professor in Criminology at Deakin University, Geelong, Australia, with broad interests in policing, security and surveillance. He has conducted collaborative funded research across a range of topics related to policing, social ordering and surveillance and published broadly on these topics, most recently in the *Australian and New Zealand Journal of Criminology*, *Trends and Issues in Crime and Criminal Justice*, *Surveillance and Society* and *Current Issues in Criminal Justice*. He is on the Editorial Committee of *Crime Prevention and Community Safety: An International Journal*. He has also contributed to the edited collections *Policing Cities: Urban Securitization and Regulation in a Twenty-first Century World* (Routledge 2013) and *Corporate Security in the Twenty-first Century* (Palgrave Macmillan 2014) and published comparative research on Canadian and Australian developments in Automatic License Plate Recognition technologies in the Australian Journal *Current Issues in Criminal Justice* (with I. Warren, R. Lippert and K. Walby). He is the co-editor of two books (*The Global Environment of Policing* 2012, and *Crime and Justice* 2011) and co-author of *Global Criminology* (Thomson Reuters 2015, with I. Warren).

Christopher Parsons received his PhD from the University of Victoria. He is currently the Managing Director of the Telecom Transparency Project and a Postdoctoral Fellow at the Citizen Lab, in the Munk School of Global Affairs with the University of Toronto. His research focuses on third-party access to telecommunications data. In addition to publishing in academic journals and presses, he routinely presents findings to members of government and the media. He is also a Privacy by Design Ambassador and a Principal at Block G Privacy and Security Consulting.

Anna C. Pratt is Associate Professor of Criminology at York University. Her interests encompass policing and punishment; law, administration and discretion; borders, risk and security; and national inclusions/exclusions as they relate to immigrants and refugees in Canada. Pratt's research has focused on the intersections of criminal justice and immigration and refugee domains that culminate in detention and deportation (*Securing Borders: Detention and Deportation in Canada,* UBC Press 2005). Her current major study is an SSHRC funded investigation into the culture, organisation and knowledge that shape the policing of borders in Canada.

Scott Thompson is a Postdoctoral Fellow and Adjunct Lecturer in the Department of Sociology, Queens University, Kingston, Ontario. Scott has written extensively on the interrelationship between policing, surveillance and governance, with specific focus on their impacts in producing and reproducing cumulative social disadvantage. His work encompasses both contemporary and historical dimensions of surveillance, including detailed studies of conscription in Canada during World War II, the administrative surveillance of alcohol supply and consumption in Ontario between 1927 and 1975, and more recently the use of special flight operation certificates to regulate unmanned aerial vehicles (UAVs). He is co-author of *Punched Drunk: Alcohol, Surveillance and the LCBO 1927–1975* (Fernwood Publishing, Halifax, 2009 with Gary Genosko).

Kevin Walby is Chancellor's Research Chair and Associate Professor of Criminal Justice at the University of Winnipeg. On the topics of surveillance and security, he has published in *British Journal of Criminology, Criminology and Criminal Justice, Security Journal, Policing and Society, Social and Legal Studies, Crime, Law and Social Change, Law, Culture and the Humanities, Law and Social Inquiry, International Journal of Urban and Regional Research, Urban Studies, Canadian Journal of Law and Society, Canadian Review of Sociology, Qualitative Inquiry, Sociology, Current Sociology, International Sociology, Social Movement Studies* and more. He is author of *Touching Encounters: Sex, Work, and Male-for-Male Internet Escorting* (University of Chicago Press 2012). He is co-author with R. Lippert of *Municipal Corporate Security in International Context* (Routledge

2015). He is co-editor of *Emotions Matter: A Relational Approach to Emotions* with Alan Hunt and D. Spencer (University of Toronto Press 2012) and *Brokering Access: Power, Politics, and Freedom of Information Process in Canada* with M. Larsen (UBC Press 2012). He has co-edited with R. Lippert *Policing Cities: Urban Securitization and Regulation in the Twenty-first Century* (Routledge 2013) and *Corporate Security in the Twenty-first Century: Theory and Practice in International Perspective* (Palgrave Macmillan 2014). He is co-editor of *Access to Information and Social Justice: Critical Research Strategies for Journalists, Scholars and Activists* with J. Brownlee (2015, ARP Books). He is co-editor of the *Journal of Prisoners on Prisons* and book review editor for *Surveillance & Society*.

Patrick F. Walsh is Senior Lecturer, Intelligence and Security Studies. He is responsible for the course coordination of the Graduate Certificate/Diploma/MA (Intelligence Analysis) at the AGSPS, and has academic oversight for all other short intelligence courses offered by the School. He is also consulted widely by federal and state agencies on intelligence reform/capability and bio-security issues. Dr. Walsh has over ten years experience teaching across a range of intelligence analytical subject areas. These include but are not limited to strategic intelligence, comparative national security intelligence issues, intelligence and policy, policing intelligence. Dr. Walsh has also taught widely across Australia and internationally in the USA, New Zealand, India and the Asia Pacific. In addition to leading major reviews of CSU's intelligence programme, he has developed a lot of experience in designing curricula relevant to intelligence agencies with specific learning requirements.

Ian Warren is a Senior Lecturer in Criminology at Deakin University, Geelong, Australia, specialising in international and comparative justice, surveillance and comparative law. He has undertaken several research projects examining surveillance and securitisation practices in various domestic contexts and has co-authored numerous book chapters and refereed articles published in Australian and international sources. His most recent collaborations with Darren Palmer, explore how domestic security practices in Australia are rapidly changing the nature of local law enforcement and governance practices. He has also contributed to the edited collections *Policing Cities: Urban Securitization and Regulation in a Twenty-first Century World* (Routledge 2013) and *Corporate Security in the Twenty-first Century* (Palgrave Macmillan 2014) and published comparative research on Canadian and Australian developments in Automatic License Plate Recognition technologies in the Australian Journal *Current Issues in Criminal Justice* (with R. Lippert, K. Walby and D. Palmer). He is co-author of *Global Criminology* (Thomson Reuters 2015) (with D. Palmer).

List of Figures

List of Tables

1

Interrogating National Security, Surveillance, and Terror in Canada and Australia

Kevin Walby, Randy K. Lippert, Ian Warren, and Darren Palmer

Intelligence agencies collecting email communications, anti-terrorism legislation, biometric technology, drones, building security in national capitals, scooping up citizens' personal metadata, emergency preparedness, sharing intelligence across agencies, cross-border maritime enforcement, state surveillance of Indigenous protest, and framing incidents as terrorism and national interests as security-related are the myriad practices of the vast, complex, growing realm of national security. Citizens are told national security practices in Western countries keep them safe, especially from terrorism, which the Australian prime minister, in his

Randy K. Lippert (✉)
Department of Sociology and Criminology, University of Windsor, 401 Sunset Ave, Windsor, ON, Canada

Kevin Walby
Department of Criminal Justice, University of Winnipeg, Centennial Hall, 3rd Floor, 515 Portage Avenue, Winnipeg, MB, Canada

Ian Warren • Darren Palmer
School of Humanities and Social Sciences, Deakin University, Locked Bag 20000, Geelong, VIC, Australia

© The Author(s) 2016   **1**
R. Lippert et al. (eds.), *National Security, Surveillance and Terror*,
DOI 10.1007/978-3-319-43243-4_1

rhetorical response to November 2015 terrorist attacks in Paris, termed "the work of the devil" (The Guardian 2015). But when probed further the level of safety claimed to be created by these complicated and apparently near divine national security practices more than occasionally turns out to be grossly overstated or inaccurate (e.g. Bronskill 2012; PCLOB 2014) and the practices themselves are revealed as decidedly mortal. It is precisely between the rhetoric and reality of these practices that we find the rightful place for scholarly study and this collection of 14 chapters. Such inquiry is essential if, as noted by various commentators (Petersen 2014; Oriola 2009; Wright 2009; Neocleous 2008), national security is now a key organising principle of government practices and everyday life in the twenty-first century.

Though the history of national security practices is imperative to explore (Hewitt 2002, 1998; Whitaker and Marcuse 1994), the complexity of national security in the early twenty-first century demands empirical research among criminologists, sociologists, political scientists, legal scholars, and others. Focusing on developments in only one country risks missing the similarities and differences that the comparative method provides and which promises to lend greater insight into the trajectories and dilemmas of comparators. Comparing national security practices, policies, and laws in two nations, *National Security, Surveillance, and Terror: Canada and Australia in Comparative Perspective* brings together leading scholars to investigate these issues and raise conceptual questions about the relationship among governments, police and security agencies, and citizens in these two major Western jurisdictions.

National security practices and the surveillance processes they often entail are legitimated through reference to terror policing, critical infrastructure protection, and border security (Walby and Lippert 2015; Warren 2015; Bell and Evans 2010; McCulloch and Pickering 2009; Aradau and van Munster 2009; Palmer and Whelan 2006; Lippert and O'Connor 2003). Resiliency testing and emergency preparedness planning are used to reorganise state practices and the relationship between state and citizens in profound ways (Henstra 2013). Indicative of the extent of these changes and the concerns they raise, the United Nations' Special Rapporteur for counter-terrorism and human rights issued a formal report to the UN General Assembly on 15 October 2014 condemning mass surveillance as violating core privacy rights guaranteed by multiple treaties and conventions. This has direct implications for Canada and Australia, given the significant recalibration of rights and freedoms in relation to deployment of a host of new national security and related surveillance initiatives in both countries.

Our volume provides an analysis of national security and surveillance practices that are legitimated through references to terror policing. With a slate of chapters on national security, surveillance, and terror policing in Canada and Australia, the volume provides a comparative analysis that contributes significantly to international debates currently dominated by US and UK perspectives. Canada and Australia have been traditional comparators in other key realms such as refugee and immigration policy (Adelman et al. 1994) and local government (Brunet-Jailly and Martin 2010) due to similar characteristics and histories but not regarding the complex realms of national security and surveillance. This volume offers empirical investigations of national security practices in two major affluent, technologically advanced Western countries.

During the 1990s, critical scholarship about security cast a wide net, focusing not only on state agencies and national or federal issues, but also a wide range of local and non-state regulatory agencies (Gad and Petersen 2011). The examination of state security and surveillance took a backseat to inquiries into discrete, more localised, and diffused practices of power, especially in governmentality studies (Lippert and Walby 2016). However, 9/11 sparked a resurgence of interest in state surveillance as part of national security strategies and non-state agencies' role in the provision of security services. The revival of a so-called global war on terror in 2014—and recent terror-related shootings in Canada and Australia—has made understanding these issues even more timely, as have the revelations of Edward Snowden on mass surveillance and its relation to national security across the West. On this point it should be made clear that national security is the primary organising concept of the volume and entails some strategies and processes that are not necessarily surveillance-related. As well, surveillance has applications that are not always related to national security or other forms of security. Yet, many chapters that follow in this volume reveal instances of the strong affinities security and surveillance have for one another, how they become realised, and their far-reaching effects.

Surveillance and terror policing are prominent themes in these events above and are key themes in this volume and in what is called surveillance studies (e.g. Monahan and Palmer 2009; Haggerty 2009). Indeed, earlier writings associated with surveillance studies (Higgs 2001; Dandeker 1990; Giddens 1981) proposed that the connection between national security and surveillance is profound and long-standing. Our contributors suggest surveillance should be studied as part of an analysis of power structures, political forces, and social relations. Surveillance is a crucial element of enhancing government security practices, as well as a challenge to civil liberties in both Canada and Australia. To date, the tensions among surveillance, protection, and government transparency are poorly understood in light of the diverse approaches to national security policy development and implementation. The idea of terror policing is often used as a framing device to legitimise legislation or extended policing and security powers, despite the fact that these legal developments almost always raise questions about the erosion of civil liberties and privacy in Commonwealth countries (Oriola 2009). Although the empirical contributions focus on one or the other country, they do not sacrifice depth of critical investigation. For these reasons, *National Security, Surveillance, and Terror: Canada and Australia in Comparative Perspective* is critical and wide-reaching with its focus on national security and terror policing.

National Security, Surveillance, and Terror also addresses how new varieties and practices of national security are reshaping conceptions of sovereignty in the two countries. In much previous scholarship, national security has been depicted as a matter for state agencies to address. However, private entities, such as commercialised mercenary forces, risk mitigation firms, and private security intelligence firms are now not only prominent providers of national security but increasingly operate across 'private' and 'public' lines. New cross-sectoral and cross-jurisdictional national security networks mean the reach of national security practices is expanded. Examination of the pluralisation of agencies responsible for expanded national security and surveillance is another feature of the volume.

Leffler (1990) has remarked that "[e]very year scores of books and hundreds of articles appear on the topic of national security" (143), yet there has been no edited volume on national security, surveillance, and terror policing comparing trends and developments in Canada and Australia. These two contexts have been obscured by near exclusive attention to national security practices in the USA and UK. While sometimes seen as distinct, this volume is among the first to draw together national security, surveillance, and terror policing domains and identify their affinities and overlap. To do so, it draws on multidisciplinary frameworks rather than only one or two disciplines. Many previous contributions in this area of study draw primarily from international relations theory (e.g. Katzenstein 1996; Mangold 1990), focus solely on national security in one country or region, and sometimes lack a critical assessment of associated state power, authority, and sovereignty (see Rubin et al. 2014).

Context

Previous contributions about national security tend to have three key limitations. First, they regularly draw from one theoretical perspective, such as international relations theory. This volume features diverse theoretical positions from criminology, criminal justice, sociology, political science, legal studies, critical security studies, and public administration studies. Contributors refine wide-ranging debates about forms of state surveillance and generate new, innovative concepts. Second, much work on national security lacks a critical focus on issues of power, authority, accountability, and sovereignty. Third, previous volumes tend to examine national security practices only in one country or region rather than in comparative perspective. Skocpol and Somers (1980) argued comparative research is important for parallel demonstration of theories, contrasting empirical contexts, and analytical comparisons. This volume therefore includes analyses of national security practices in two countries with interlocking relations with others in the Global North and South. Examined in chapters that follow are new cross-sectoral and cross-jurisdictional national security networks that are irreducible to one country, though they may be anchored in or steered by Canada or Australia.

The rationale for choosing Canada and Australia deserves elaboration. We have chosen these countries as objects of inquiry not merely because they serve as cases outside the USA or UK and have received relatively scant scholarly attention. We have done so also because they comprise two of the Five Eyes (a long-standing collaborative intelligence-sharing arrangement among these four nations' state agencies and New Zealand (Palmer and Warren 2013)) and, more significantly, both are federations with remarkably similar social, economic, cultural, and political histories. They both feature higher levels of immigration and smaller population densities compared to European countries; increasingly urban populations; similar government, tax, and property structures (Brunet-Jailly and Martin 2010); British Commonwealth and common law traditions; resource-dependent economies with disappearing manufacturing elements; and histories of colonisation of Indigenous peoples, among others. Since 9/11 mostly conservative federal political parties or party coalitions have ruled these two countries, though 2015 marked a possible shift away from this trend. Yet, so far the effects of these political leadership changes on national security and surveillance practices remain unclear. Geographically too they share massive territorial expanses and extraordinarily extensive 'undefended' shorelines and land borders. With increasing globalisation they are both becoming more economically integrated with superpowers, namely the USA and China. We would also point out that both countries are host to many critical academics characterised by an "openness to methodological pluralism and critical disposition" (de Larrinaga and Salter 2014, 14) and who study these issues. It is difficult to imagine two countries more ripe for comparison in the intersecting realms of national security, surveillance, and anti-terrorism. The editors and authors compare these countries across chapters.

Contributors to this volume are leading, critical scholars studying national security, surveillance, and anti-terrorism initiatives as well as related issues of risk, border security, emergency preparedness, and sovereignty. The chapters explore how issues of risk, border security, and terror enable the highly selective exercise of power and authority that often marginalise some communities and justify dismantling of civil liberties in the name of national security.

Our observation of national security literature from the past few decades is that it has little holding it together as a body of work. This is due in part to the security domain's expansiveness. Security is a notoriously difficult concept to define (King and Murray 2001; Baldwin 1997). As Bigo (2002) puts it, "the field is much larger than that of police organizations" (64). It includes police but also intelligence agencies, private security corporations, and even units within corporations (Walby and Lippert 2015). This array of national security players is why a comparative focus becomes crucial—comparison provides some parameters for additional critical inquiry and scholarly dialogue. As noted, when national security is analysed it is often done with practices in one country as the object of analysis (on Canada, see Forcese and Roach 2015; MacDonald 2011; Kinsman and Gentile 2010; Diab 2008; Bell 2006a, b; Kruger et al. 2004; on Australia, see Dupont and Reckmeyer 2012; Michaelsen 2010). Although Canadian national security policy has been compared to similar US policy (see Keating and Murray 2014; Roach 2012a; Sloan 2010; Barry and Bratt 2008), rarely has Canada been compared to Australia (but see Shafqat and Masood 2016; Roach 2007). For these reasons, comparison of national security practices, policies, and laws in Canada and Australia is long overdue.

The domain of national security is one in which rapid changes occurred in the first decade of the twenty-first century. During the first eight years after 9/11, national security became an important policy issue in ways not seen since the occasional flare-ups during the Cold War (see Whitaker and Marcuse 1994). The issue of national security made a tremendous return to policy agendas after 9/11 in Canada, Australia, the USA, and Europe (Shearman and Sussex 2004). In many ways, there was a coordinated response. The War on Terror resulted in forms of surveillance with little or no judicial oversight (Gill 2003; Schulhofer 2002, 66). Such intensification of national security and related surveillance processes continues today. These surveillance initiatives not only erode the distinction among national security practices, intelligence gathering, and law enforcement (Whitaker 2003, 2005; Potter 1998) but also enact a new form of neo-conservatism based on division (Huysmans 2004). Increased surveillance has led to a subtle but pervasive reorganisation of border politics (Biersteker 2003). The resulting location of the border, it is argued, is now two-fold (see also Bigo 2000). First, the border is everywhere (Muller, this volume), such that screening to gain entry to a country like Canada increasingly happens in sites far removed from the actual Canadian border (Lyon 2003, 147). Second, 9/11 has led to a securitisation within (Muller 2004), with more national security operations and surveillance taking place within Canada involving tracking citizens as if they were a type of alien threat (Ahmad 2002). As de Larrinaga and Salter (2014) note, critical security studies predate 9/11, but such inquiry was deepened by the state response to terror and threat discourses in the first decade of the twenty-first century.

In Canada and Australia too, issues of immigration have not only moved to centre stage because of the life and death stakes (Powell et al. 2015; Pickering 2004), but they also have been securitised. Novel forms of monitoring travellers and migrants are being deployed to catalogue and verify identities. Biometric identification measures—face and eye recognition software—are highly touted. In the *U.S.–Canada Smart Border/30 Point Action Plan* enacted by former Homeland Security Secretary Tom Ridge and former deputy Prime Minister John Manley in 2001, the implementation of biometric identification technologies topped the list (The White House 2001). In its first comprehensive statement on national security, *Securing an Open Society* (2004, 44), the Canadian government noted its intention to complete the *Smart Border Action Plan* and to apply these 'smart' border principles, deployed through political rhetoric (what political authority of any nation, after all, would claim to apply 'dumb' principles, even if they were hopelessly unproven and otherwise misconceived), around the world. The post-9/11 intensification of surveillance led to assertions that Canada and the USA were creating a Fortress North America (Bhandar 2004; Biersteker 2003). Although Canadian scholars and lawyers raised questions about the impact of the *Anti-Terrorism Act* (2001) on civil liberties, including the broad definition of terrorism it enacted, the knock-on effects for other laws such as the *Official Secrets Act* which became the *Security of Information Act*, and the lack of real accountability accompanying it (Gabor 2004) remained.

During the mid to late 2000s, the proliferation of national security practices continued in Canada. There were ongoing debates and struggles around security certificates and indefinite detention (de Lint and Bahdi

2012). Immigration and border agencies as well as a specialised branch of the Department of Justice, termed the National Security Group, restricted immigration to Canada (Hameed and Monaghan 2012). The Royal Canadian Mounted Police (RCMP) was not only conducting security intelligence work in Canada but also around the world (Walby and Monaghan 2011a). An inquiry into the actions of the RCMP and Canadian Security Intelligence Service (CSIS) in the post-9/11 period criticised their national security and information sharing practices and the influence an RCMP database had on flagging three Muslim Canadians for rendition to torture in Syria (Iacobucci 2008). The RCMP and CSIS were even involved in surveillance of domestic movement participants such as animal rights activists (Walby and Monaghan 2011b) under the auspices of national security. These two agencies created a massive Integrated Security Unit (of nearly 20,000 police and security intelligence specialists) in the lead up to the Vancouver 2010 Olympics (Monaghan and Walby 2012b). CSIS and the RCMP also contributed to the creation of the Integrated Threat Assessment Centre, renamed the Integrated Terrorism Assessment Centre in 2011. The RCMP and CSIS were heavily involved in security for the 2010 Toronto G20 meetings too (Monaghan and Walby 2012a). Communications Security Establishment Canada (CSEC) had been conducting communications surveillance since 2001, including collection of bulk metadata (Walby and Anaïs 2012) and was also assisting in the so-called War on Terror in numerous ways. Yet with each new law or policy initiative, there has been resistance. Some of the biggest protests in Canadian history were mounted against the War on Terror, including against Bill C-51 that was passed as the Anti-Terrorism Act, 2015. This Bill became a major political issue in the fall Canadian federal election and Trudeau's federal Liberal Party swept to power in the fall of 2015 partially on a promise to introduce more oversight of the intrusive, overly broad arrangements this Act, written by the previous Harper government, had introduced. So far, adapting the words of Canada's Leonard Cohen from *Closing Time*, "the Gates…they budged an inch but I can't say much has happened since." Indeed, Whitaker et al. (2012) and Geist (2015) have argued these new laws reflect the enduring lack of accountability and transparency in Canadian security intelligence that continues today.

In Australia during the 1980s and 1990s, several national security concerns were raised as a result of acts of politically motivated violence against diplomatic posts such as the assassination of the Turkish Consul-General and a bodyguard in 1980, the 1982 bombing of the Israeli consulate, the 1985 bombing of the Turkish consulate, the 1992 attack on the Iranian embassy, the 1995 firebombing of the French honorary consulate, and the 1998 attempted firebombing of a vehicle at the Indonesian consulate (see Australian Government 2010, 9). As the chapter by Palmer and Warren in this volume indicates, this was also a period of ongoing reform of the Australian intelligence community. Yet, it must be recognised that significant legal and institutional reforms unrelated to politically motivated violence were taking place. These were related to organised crime and its perceived threat to national security via the corrupting effects across the Australian community, including the controversial corruption allegation against Lionel Murphy, a member of the High Court of Australia (see Hocking 2004). Organised crime was treated as a fundamental threat to Australian society, or as Findlay (1986, 286) stated rather perceptively at the time: "Organised crime as terrorism." As Hocking (1994) has argued, this period established "a nexus between the traditional criminal justice process and an exceptional response" based on the "increasing use of non-judicial, inquisitorial bodies [and] a significant expansion in and merging of police and national security collections" (220).

In Australia organised crime became central to concerns about national security during the 1980s and 1990s and remains a key part of the deliberations about it. It is equally true that Australian thinking about national security and responses to national security threats were significantly re-shaped by 9/11 and subsequent bombings in Indonesia: the 12 October 2002 Bali bombings that killed 202 people including 88 Australians, 9 September 2004 bombing of the Australian Embassy in Jakarta killing ten people, and the subsequent 10 October 2005 Bali bombing killing 26 people including ten Australians. It was during this period from late 2001 to 2005 that Australia made significant legislative and institutional changes (Palmer and Whelan 2006). For example, there was introduction of the offence of terrorism and related offences, which overcame limits on Federal powers by obtaining state and territory agreements for legislative change, achieved, as Tham (2004, 523) has argued, with "indecent haste." Policing and security now occurs across a "policing continuum" (Palmer and Whelan 2006) that continues to be refined and enhanced today.

As Andrew Goldsmith (2008) argued, Australia and Canada shared some affinities in their respective reforms after 9/11 and in the justifications proffered. Goldsmith suggested that while the *Charter* and the concept of human security shaped the Canadian context for reform, Australia subsequently drew on Canadian notions of human security, particularly the writing of Cotler who became the Canadian Minister of Justice and Attorney General. Both countries also emphasised their responsibilities as global citizens, claiming obligations under various UN treaties and conventions to stress the need for reform. For Goldsmith (2008, 162), while there were limits to the process of law reform, it was not a case of either country reaching 'the doomsday "state of exception."' Rather, according to Goldsmith there are significant opportunities to review and challenge reform proposals, though he also suggested a need to make these more robust, inclusive, and participatory.

The most explicitly political use of the terrorism offences and procedures is the case of Mohamed Haneef who was arrested without charge in 2007 in connection with the bombing of the Glasgow airport. Upon being released the immigration minister used ministerial power to detain Haneef and order his deportation. It was the first time a number of new legislative provisions were used; the communications and intelligence among police, intelligence agencies, and politicians were placed under scrutiny; and legal process was used to disclose government practices (see Pickering and McCulloch 2010). This case captured the Australian public imagination and, while leading to some reforms, fell short of Goldsmith's pluralist reform process, an approach even more distant from the Abbott-led coalition government that had strong ties and national security rhetoric and policies similar to the Harper Government's in Canada. The more recent Lindt Cafe incident in Sydney 15–16 December 2014 in which the hostage-taker and two hostages were killed was used again to ramp up fears about national security, particularly about 'home grown terrorist' and 'radicalised' Muslims. As we write, both leaders have been deposed; Harper via electoral loss and Abbott by loss of internal support within the coalition government. Notwithstanding his comment quoted at the outset, the response of the new Australian prime minister to the 13 November 2015 terrorist attacks in Paris showed a more nuanced and less provocative approach.

As this volume's chapters demonstrate, significant historical events tied to Australia's geopolitical location, and dating back to at least the Cold War in the 1950s, have shaped the approach to national security since 9/11. For example, the gradual expansion of the number of federal security agencies, often working in tandem with state-level police, has amplified counter-terrorism powers that enable questionable forms of surveillance and intelligence gathering. These developments are directly tied to more rigorous border and maritime security arrangements, targeting vessels carrying asylum seekers originating from war torn areas such as Sri Lanka and Iraq, that transit through Indonesia. Australia's mandatory offshore detention arrangements are administered through a combination of public and private agencies that mirror the approach to protecting on-shore critical infrastructure (Palmer and Whelan 2006) and online surveillance (Warren 2015). These highly 'inwardly focused' securitisation measures (Warren and Palmer 2015) have been criticised for their potential to violate the fundamental human rights of asylum seekers and the profound lack of legal or political transparency (Australian Human Rights Commission 2014). They demonstrate too the difficulties Australia has faced in promoting enhanced regional security cooperation, particularly with Indonesia and other Southeast Asian countries.

In addition, neither the array of Canadian nor Australian national security measures documented throughout this volume has adequately grappled with the thorny problem of extraterritoriality, other than via the contentious Five-Eyes partnership, which is widely criticised for lacking transparency. The new cross-sectoral and cross-jurisdictional national security networks and practices that are expanding appear to lack democratic legitimacy or any substantive evidence of their effectiveness. Both the pluralisation of agencies involved and the blurring of purely domestic and transnational securitisation and surveillance measures present fundamental challenges to established notions of sovereignty but have yet to be fully reconciled in each country. This volume highlights the contradictions associated with sovereignty and the inherently extraterritorial character of securitisation, in light of the profound difficulties in determining the effectiveness of these measures. The chapters that follow show that the contemporary approach to national security involves a series of legal and bureaucratic measures that undermine democratic freedom in Australia, while producing few guarantees that an increasing array of terror-related behaviour will be identified before they occur on Australian soil.

Contributions

Canada and Australia are important to examine in comparative perspective for several reasons. First, while these countries share a legal tradition, the organisation of security and policing practices differs markedly. Unlike Canada, Australia is without a *Charter of Rights and Freedoms* or Bill of Rights, although the actual protective value of the Canadian *Charter* in practice remains questionable (see also Jochelson and Doerksen, this volume). Differing legal and structural arrangements that underpin policing, security, and other anti-terrorism processes highlight the need for closer, detailed comparison. The contributions to this volume conceptualise national security links with intelligence agencies and local public police, the work of national security advisors, the oversight of security intelligence agencies, and more. Second, as settler societies, Canada and Australia annually receive large numbers of immigrants and asylum seekers, a fact increasingly framed in national and border security terms. This distinguishes these two countries from, for example, many European nations such as the UK. Third, these countries form part of a broader Western security intelligence network (The Five Eyes) meaning that some security agencies in Canada and Australia regularly coordinate closely with each other and with UK and US agencies, thus potentially lending insight into how this key network operates and is legitimated in the name of enhanced transnational security. Fourth, there is evidence of policy transfer across security and policing domains, immigration/border controls, and intelligence gathering among leading security agencies of these two countries. Contributors have permitted comparison of similarities and differences of these processes to provide an insightful and captivating account of the convergences and divergences of national security policies in the early twenty-first century. The chapters were not matched to provide one-to-one comparison about specific topics in the respective countries. Rather, the empirical focus is delimited to Canada and Australia across the entire volume to create common ground for editors and authors to engage in comparison, debate, and discussion while providing freedom for authors to make unique conceptual and methodological contributions.

This raises the question of disciplinary formations and influences reflected in the works of our authors. Many examinations of national security post-9/11 have been doctrinal legal studies. A consideration of black letter law is important to include in this collection since some of the most prescient analyses of national security come in this form (e.g. Forcese and Roach 2015). For example, Kent Roach (2007) has compared Canadian and Australian anti-terrorism laws, examining their content as well as the citizen protections and police powers contained in each. He argues the differences between the two countries "cannot solely be attributed to the courts and the Charter" (ibid., 85). Elsewhere Roach has examined entrapment in comparative perspective (Roach 2011), terrorism prosecutions in Canada (Roach 2014) and in the USA (Roach 2012a), and anti-terrorism practices inside and outside Canada (Roach 2012b). While such legal scholarship is essential to include in any volume focused upon national security, socio-legal scholarship and inquiries from criminology, sociology, political science, critical security studies, and public administration are equally enlightening. Indeed, their inclusion in this volume provides more comprehensive analyses, deeper critiques, and a rich plurality of methodological and conceptual tools and insights. *National Security, Surveillance, and Terror* offers readers interdisciplinary scope to critically explore and appraise these issues in light of the insights that each chapter provides.

National Security, Surveillance, and Terror is significant for the field of national security for an additional reason. The chapters provide an empirical view of national security practices that is international. As Pat O'Malley explains in his foreword, the empirical comes first here. Thus we have avoided making contributors conform to, for example, international relations theory, the Copenhagen School with its focus on security as speech act, the Paris School with its focus on security as practice, the pacification model with its neo-Marxist underpinnings, or what de Larrinaga and Salter (2014) refer to as the Canadian critical school of security studies (also see Cox 2014) characterised by theoretical and methodological heterogeneity, a focus on First Nations, immigration, refugees, and human security. These theoretical models have their place (Williams 2011) and some authors draw from them here, but this volume does not seek to tout some conceptual approaches as *the only way* to understand these pressing matters of global concern. Instead, we show that the "epistemological community that shares…an openness to methodological pluralism and critical disposition" (de Larrinaga and Salter 2014, 14) extends to Australia too.

Overview

The purpose of this volume is to reflect on national security, surveillance, and terror policing in Canada and Australia in comparative perspective. The collection is organised in three sections, which are described in greater detail in each section introduction. All sections include a balanced slate of chapters on national security, surveillance, and terror policing in Canada and Australia. The first section offers four chapters that elaborate on or refine legal approaches to analysis of national security and terror laws in Canada and Australia. The second section includes four empirically driven chapters on national security, surveillance, and terror policing in Canada and Australia. Authors explore national security, surveillance, border security, terror policing, and protection of critical infrastructure in each of the two countries. The third section comprises chapters that focus on the issues and dilemmas of national security, surveillance, and emergency management. These include crucial issues relating to accountability, transparency, ethics, privacy, sovereign responsibility, and legitimacy. All sections include perspectives from more than one discipline. Some chapters address practices in both countries, such as chapters by Adam Molnar and Craig Forcese, while others assess in greater depth practices in one or the other country but discuss their broader comparative implications. Specific details on each chapter can be found in the section introductions.

References

Adelman, Howard, Allan Borowski, Meyer Burstein, and Lois Foster. 1994. *Immigration and Refugee Policy: Australia and Canada Compared.* vol. 2. Toronto, ON: University of Toronto Press.

Ahmad, Muneer. 2002. Homeland Insecurities: Racial Violence the Day After September 11. *Social Text* 20(3): 101–115.

Aradau, Claudia, and R. van Munster. 2009. Exceptionalism and the 'War on Terror': Criminology Meets International Relations. *British Journal of Criminology* 49(5): 686–701.

Australian Government. 2010. *Counter-Terrorism White Paper.* Canberra: Australian Government Printer.

Australian Human Rights Commission. 2014. The Forgotten Children: National Inquiry into Children in Immigration Detention. Canberra ACT: Australian Human Rights Commission.

Baldwin, David. 1997. The Concept of Security. *Review of International Studies* 23(1): 5–26.

Barry, Donald, and Duane Bratt. 2008. Defense Against Help: Explaining Canada-U.S. Security Relations. *American Review of Canadian Studies* 38(1): 64–84.

Bell, Colleen. 2006a. Surveillance Strategies and Populations at Risk: Biopolitical Governance in Canada's National Security Policy. *Security Dialogue* 37(2): 147–165.

———. 2006b. Subject to Exception: Security Certificates, National Security and Canada's Role in the 'War on Terror'. *Canadian Journal of Law and Society* 21(1): 63–83.

Bell, Colleen, and B. Evans. 2010. From Terrorism to Insurgency: Re-Mapping the Post-Interventionary Security Terrain. *Journal of Intervention and Statebuilding* 4(4): 371–390.

Bhandar, Davina. 2004. Renormalizing Citizenship and Life in Fortress North America. *Citizenship Studies* 8(3): 261–278.

Biersteker, Thomas. 2003. The Rebordering of North America: Implications for Conceptualizing Borders After September 11. In *The Rebordering of North America: Integration and Exclusion in a New Security Context*, eds. Peter Andreas and Thomas Biersteker, 153–167. New York: Routledge.

Bigo, Didier. 2000. When Two Become One: Internal and External Securitisations in Europe. In *International Relations Theory and the Politics of European Integration: Power, Security, and Community*, eds. Morten Kelstrup and Michael C. Williams, 171–205. London: Routledge.

———. 2002. Security and Immigration: Toward a Critique of the Governmentality of Unease. *Alternatives* 27(1): 63–92.

Bronskill, Jim. 2012. Flying the Secret Skies: Difficulties in Obtaining Data on Canadian Airport Screening Tests Following 9/11. In *Brokering Access: Power, Politics and Freedom of Information Process in Canada*, eds. M. Larsen and K. Walby, 97–114. Vancouver: University of British Columbia Press.

Brunet-Jailly, E., and J. Martin. 2010. Local Government in a Global World: Australia and Canada in Comparative Perspective. In *Local Government in a Global World: Australia and Canada in Comparative Perspective*, eds. E. Brunet-Jailly and J. Martin, 3–34. Toronto, ON: University of Toronto Press.

Cox, Wayne. 2014. Canadian Critical Security Studies as a Non-American Social Science: A Rejoinder To de Larrinaga and Salter. *Critical Studies on Security* 2(1): 35–38.

Dandeker, Christopher. 1990. *Surveillance, Power, and Modernity: Bureaucracy and Discipline from 1700 to the Present Day.* New York: St. Martin's Press.

de Larrinaga, Miguel, and Mark Salter. 2014. Cold CASE: A Manifesto for Canadian Critical Security Studies. *Critical Studies on Security* 2(1): 1–19.

de Lint, W., and Reem Bahdi. 2012. Access to Information in an Age of Intelligencized Governmentality. In *Brokering Access: Power, Politics and Freedom of Information Process in Canada*, eds. M. Larsen and K. Walby, 115–141. Vancouver: University of British Columbia Press.

Diab, Robert. 2008. *Guantanamo North: Terrorism and the Administration of Justice.* Fernwood: Halifax.

Dupont, Alan, and William Reckmeyer. 2012. Australia's National Security Priorities: Addressing Strategic Risk in a Globalized World. *Australian Journal of International Affairs* 66(1): 34–51.

Findlay, Mark. 1986. Organised Crime as Terrorism. *The Australian Quarterly* 58(3): 286–296.

Forcese, Craig, and Kent Roach. 2015. *False Security.* Irwin Law Inc: Ottawa.

Gabor, Thomas. 2004. *The Views of Canadian Scholars on the Impact of the Anti-Terrorism Act.* Ottawa: Research and Statistics Division, Department of Justice Canada.

Gad, U., and Karen Petersen. 2011. Concepts of Politics in Securitization Studies. *Security Dialogue* 42(4): 315–328.

Geist, Michael. 2015. Why Watching the Watchers Isn't Enough: Canadian Surveillance Law in the Post-Snowden Era. In *Law, Privacy and Surveillance in Canada in the Post-Snowden Era*, ed. M. Geist, 225–256. Ottawa: University of Ottawa Press.

Giddens, Anthony. 1981. *A Contemporary Critique of Historical Materialism: Vol. 1 Power, Property, and the State*. London: The Macmillan Press Ltd.

Gill, Peter. 2003. *Democratic and Parliamentary Accountability of Intelligence Services After September 11th* (Working Paper No. 103). Geneva Centre for the Democratic Control of Armed Forces.

Goldsmith, Andrew. 2008. The Governance of Terror: Precautionary Logic and Counterterrorist Law Reforms After September 11. *Law & Policy* 30(2): 141–167.

The Guardian. 2015. Paris Attacks Condemned by World Leaders as the 'Work of the Devil'. http://www.theguardian.com/world/2015/nov/14/paris-terror-attacks-world-leaders-condemn-the-work-of-the-devil. Accessed 15 Nov

Haggerty, Kevin. 2009. 'Ten Thousand Times Larger…' Anticipating the Expansion of Surveillance. In *New Directions in Surveillance and Privacy*, eds. B. Goold and D. Neyland, 159–177. Cullompton: Willan.

Hameed, Yavar, and Jeffrey Monaghan. 2012. Accessing Dirty Data: Methodological Strategies for Social Problems Research. In *Brokering Access: Power, Politics and Freedom of Information Process in Canada*, eds. M. Larsen and K. Walby, 142–168. Vancouver: University of British Columbia Press.

Henstra, Dan. 2013. Multilevel Governance and Canadian Emergency Management Policy. In *Multilevel Governance and Emergency Management in Canadian Municipalities*, ed. D. Henstra. Montreal: McGill-Queen's University Press.

Hewitt, Steve. 1998. Intelligence at the Learneds: The RCMP, the Learneds, and the Canadian Historical Association. *Journal of the Canadian Historical Association* 8: 267–286.

———. 2002. *Spying 101: The RCMP's Secret Activities at Canadian Universities, 1917–1997*. Toronto, ON: University of Toronto Press.

Higgs, Edward. 2001. The Rise of the Information State: The Development of Central State Surveillance of the Citizen in England, 1500–2000. *Journal of Historical Sociology* 14(2): 175–196.

Hocking, Jenny. 1994. First the Verdict then the Trial. *Policing and Society* 4(3): 219–236.

Hocking, Jenny. 2004. *Terror Laws: ASIO, Counter-Terrorism and the Threat to Democracy*. Sydney: University of New South Wales Press.

Huysmans, Jef. 2004. Minding Exceptions: The Politics of Insecurity and Liberal Democracy. *Contemporary Political Theory* 3(3): 321–341.

Iacobucci, The Honourable. 2008. *Inquiry into the Actions of Canadian Officials in Relation to Abdullah Almaki, Ahmad Abou-Elmaati and Muayyed Nureddin*. Ottawa: Queen's Press.

Katzenstein, Peter, ed. 1996. *The Culture of National Security. Norms and Identity in World Politics*. New York: Columbia University Press.

Keating, Tom, and Robert Murray. 2014. Mutual Constitution or Convenient National Interest? The Security Strategies of Canada and the United States since 1991. *Canadian Foreign Policy Journal* 20(3): 247–258.

King, Gary, and Christopher J. Murray. 2001. Rethinking Human Security. *Political Science Quarterly* 116(4): 585–610.

Kinsman, Gary, and Patrizia Gentile. 2010. *The Canadian War on Queers: National Security as Sexual Regulation*. Vancouver: UBC Press.

Kruger, Erin, Marlene Mulder, and Bojan Korenic. 2004. Canada After 11 September: Security Measures and 'Preferred' Immigrants. *Mediterranean Quarterly* 15(4): 72–87.

Leffler, Melvyn. 1990. National Security. *Journal of American History* 77(1): 143–152.

Lippert, Randy K., and Daniel O'Connor. 2003. Security Assemblages: Airport Security, Flexible Work, and Liberal Governance. *Alternatives* 28(3): 331–358.

Lippert, Randy K., and Kevin Walby. 2016. Governing Through Privacy: Authoritarian Liberalism, Law, and Privacy Knowledge. *Law, Culture, and the Humanities* 12(2): 329–352.

Lyon, David. 2003. *Surveillance After September 11*. Cambridge: Polity Press.

MacDonald, N. 2011. Parliamentarians and National Security in Canada. *Canadian Parliamentary Review* 34(4): 33–41.

Mangold, Peter. 1990. *National Security and International Relations*. London: Routledge.

Michaelsen, Christopher. 2010. Reforming Australia's National Security Laws: The Case for a Proportionality-Based Approach. *University of Tasmania Law Review* 29(1): 32–48.

Monaghan, Jeffrey, and Kevin Walby. 2012a. '… They Attacked the City': Security Intelligence, the Sociology of Protest Policing, and the Anarchist Threat at the 2010 Toronto G20 Summit. *Current Sociology* 60(5): 653–671.

———. 2012b. Making up 'Terror Identities': Security Intelligence and Canada's Integrated Threat Assessment Centre. *Policing & Society* 22(2): 133–151.

Monahan, Torin, and Neal Palmer. 2009. The Emerging Politics of DHS Fusion Centers. *Security Dialogue* 40(6): 617–636.

McCulloch, Jude, and Sharon Pickering. 2009. Precrime and Counter-Terrorism: Imagining Future Crime in the 'War on Terror'. *British Journal of Criminology* 49(5): 626–645.

Muller, Benjamin J. 2004. (Dis)Qualified Bodies: Securitization, Citizenship and Identity Management. *Citizenship Studies* 8(3): 279–294.

Neocleous, Mark. 2008. *Critique of Security*. Montreal: McGill-Queen's University Press.

Oriola, Temitope. 2009. Counter-Terrorism and Alien Justice: The Case of Security Certificates in Canada. *Critical Studies in Terrorism* 2(2): 257–274.

Palmer, Darren, and Ian Warren. 2013. Global Policing and the Case of Kim Dotcom. *International Journal for Crime, Justice and Social Democracy* 2(3): 105–119.

Palmer, Darren, and Chad Whelan. 2006. Counter-Terrorism Across the Policing Continuum. *Police Practice and Research* 7(5): 449–465.

PCLOB (Privacy and Civil Liberties Oversight Board). 2014. Report on the Telephone Records Program Conducted under Section 215 of the USA Patriot Act and on the Operations of the Foreign Surveillance Court. Washington, DC. https://www.pclob.gov/library/215-Report_on_the_Telephone_Records_Program.pdf. Accessed 15 Nov 2015.

Petersen, Karen. 2014. The Politics of Corporate Security and the Translation of National Security. In *Corporate Security in the 21st Century: Theory and Practice in International Perspective*, eds. K. Walby and Randy K. Lippert, 78–96. London: Palgrave Macmillan.

Pickering, Sharon. 2004. The Production of Sovereignty and the Rise of Transversal Policing: People Smuggling and Federal Policing. *Australian & New Zealand Journal of Criminology* 37(3): 362–379.

Pickering, Sharon, and Jude McCulloch. 2010. The Haneef Case and Counter-Terrorism Policing in Australia. *Policing and Society* 20(1): 21–38.

Potter, Evan, ed. 1998. *Economic Intelligence and National Security*. Ottawa: Carleton University Press.

Powell, Rebecca, Leanne Weber, and Sharon Pickering. 2015. Every Death Counts: An Argument for Counting Deaths in Immigration Custody in the National Deaths in Custody Collection. *Current Issues in Criminal Justice* 27(1): 114–121.

Roach, Kent. 2007. A Comparison of Australian and Canadian Anti-Terrorism Laws. *UNSW Law Journal* 30(1): 53–85.

———. 2011. Entrapment and Equality in Terrorism Prosecutions: A Comparative Examination of North American and European Approaches. *Mississippi Law Journal* 80(4): 1455–1490.

———. 2012a. Uneasy Neighbors: Comparative American and Canadian Counter-Terrorism. *William Mitchell Law Review* 38(5): 1701–1803.

———. 2012b. Counter-Terrorism In and Outside Canada and In and Outside the Anti-Terrorism Act. *Review of Constitutional Studies* 16(2): 243–264.

———. 2014. Be Careful What You Wish For? Terrorism Prosecutions in Post-9/11 Canada. *Queen's Law Journal* 40(1): 99–140.

Rubin, David, Kim Lynch, Jason Escaravage, and Hillary Lerner. 2014. Harnessing Data for National Security. *SAIS Review of International Affairs* 34(1): 121–128.

Schulhofer, Stephen J. 2002. *The Enemy Within: Intelligence Gathering, Law Enforcement, and Civil Liberties in the Wake of September 11*. New York: Century Foundation Press.

Shafqat, Narmenn, and Ashraf Masood. 2016. Comparative Analysis of Various National Cyber Security Strategies. *International Journal of Computer Science and Information Security* 14(1): 129–136.

Shearman, Peter, and Matthew Sussex. 2004. America and Europe After 9/11. In *European Security After 9/11*, eds. Peter Shearman and Matthew Sussex, 51–68. Aldershot: Ashgate.

Skocpol, Theda, and Margaret Somers. 1980. The Uses of Comparative History in Macrosocial Inquiry. *Comparative Studies in Society and History* 22(2): 174–197.

Sloan, Elinor. 2010. *Security and Defence in the Terrorist Era: Canada and the United States Homeland*. 2nd ed. Montreal: McGill-Queen's University Press.

Tham, Joo-Cheong. 2004. Casualties of the Domestic 'War on Terror': A Review of Recent Counter-Terrorism Laws. *Melbourne University Law Review* 28(2): 512–531.

Walby, Kevin, and Seantel Anaïs. 2012. Communications Security Establishment Canada (CSEC), Structures of Secrecy, and Ministerial Authorization After September 11. *Canadian Journal of Law and Society* 27(3): 363–380.

Walby, Kevin, and Randy K. Lippert. 2015. The Difference that Homeland Security Makes: Municipal Corporate Security in Canada and the United States Compared. *Security Dialogue* 46(3): 238–255.

Walby, Kevin, and Jeffrey Monaghan. 2011a. 'Haitian Paradox' or Dark Side of the Security-Development Nexus: Canada's Role in the Securitization of Haiti, 2004–2009. *Alternatives* 36(4): 273–287.

———. 2011b. Private Eyes and Public Order: Policing and Surveillance in the Suppression of Animal Rights Activists in Canada. *Social Movement Studies* 10(1): 21–37.

Warren, Ian. 2015. Surveillance, Criminal Law and Sovereignty. *Surveillance and Society* 13(2): 300–305.

Warren, Ian and Darren Palmer. 2015. *Global Criminology*. Pyrmont, NSW: Law Book Company/Thomson Reuters.

Whitaker, Reginald. 2003. After 9/11: A Surveillance State? In *Lost Liberties: Ashcroft and the Assault on Personal Freedom*, ed. Cynthia Brown, 52–74. New York: New Press.

———. 2005. A Faustian Bargain? America and the Dream of 'Total Information Awareness'. In *The New Politics of Surveillance and Visibility*, eds. Kevin Haggerty and Richard V. Ericson, 141–170. Toronto, ON: University of Toronto Press.

Whitaker, Reginald, and Gary Marcuse. 1994. *Cold War Canada: The Making of a National Insecurity State, 1945 1957*. Toronto, ON: University of Toronto Press.

Whitaker, Reginald, Gregory Kealey, and Andrew Parnaby. 2012. *Secret Service: Political Policing in Canada From the Fenians to Fortress America*. Toronto, ON: University of Toronto Press.

The White House. 2001. U.S.–Canada Smart Border/30 Point Action Plan Update. https://2001-2009.state.gov/p/wha/rls/fs/18128.htm

Williams, Michael. 2011. The Continuing Evolution of Securitization Theory. In *Securitization Theory: How Security Problems Emerge and Dissolve*, ed. T. Balzacq, 212–222. London: Routledge.

Wright, Katie. 2009. Redefining Development for National Security: Implications for Civil Society. *Development in Practice* 19(6): 793–798.

Part I

Introduction: Thinking About National Security, Surveillance and Terror

The four chapters in this section reveal several commonalities in the Canadian and Australian approaches to national security since 9/11, despite differences in legal approaches in each jurisdiction. These contributions highlight the array of agencies, legislative reforms and judicial decisions that point to an incremental expansion of securitisation validated by formal law. Frequently, these measures are reactive political responses to domestic incidents classifiable as terror-related activities or more profound data security breaches such as the whistle blowing of Julian Assange and Edward Snowden. Whether operating with law enforcement agencies, or simply undertaking blanket surveillance to collect intelligence to pre-emptively target discernible risks, chapters in this volume explore these approaches to enhancing national security in both jurisdictions, even though these are moderated by distinct historical, geopolitical, legal and procedural underpinnings.

In the first chapter, Craig Forcese provides a consolidated review of his extensive research into laws and practices of Canada's two major national security organisations, the Canadian Security Intelligence Service (CSIS) and the Communications Security Establishment (CSE). Here technological developments are increasingly blurring the distinction between domestic and foreign surveillance. This chapter's specific emphasis is the problematic issue of extraterritorial surveillance activities that impact on Canadian citizens who are physically located or communicating with other people outside Canadian territory. This is troublesome in light of CSE's mandate, which is specifically confined to 'foreign intelligence' activity that is not directed at Canadians at home or abroad. However, Forcese emphasises a Canadian Supreme Court decision that enables Canadian enforcement and security agencies to collect admissible evidence offshore, without extending the reach of the *Canadian Charter of Rights and Freedoms* on foreign soil. The legal justification for this decision is to preserve international good will and national sovereignty where surveillance is undertaken. Subsequent legislative reforms and judicial decisions are then outlined, current anomalies in the legislative mandates of Canada's two major national security agencies, and incremental creep of extraterritorial surveillance authorised by revised warrant requirements and their authorisation by the Canadian federal judiciary. These developments represent the increasing 'judicialisation' of facets of Canadian extraterritorial intelligence activity. Forcese posits several avenues for future reform of extraterritorial surveillance, including a discussion of the mandates of the Australian Security Intelligence Organisation (ASIO) and related agencies in the other three Five Eyes nations.

Patrick Walsh shifts the focus to examine the gradual evolution of Australia's counter-terrorism laws, which have rapidly expanded since the death of 88 Australian citizens in the Bali bombing in October 2002. Walsh's chapter discusses how global shifts in terrorist activity have forged greater concern over national security, emergency preparedness and prevention of identifiable terrorist risks in Western nations. As with Forcese, he suggests these developments collapse the historical distinction between domestic and extraterritorial security initiatives. Walsh then documents the incremental expansion of reforms to Australia's counter-terrorism and surveillance laws in three key political phases. These comprise reforms introduced by the Howard Government between 1996 and 2007, which focused primarily on early intervention and pre-emption; the introduction of enhanced Parliamentary oversight and cooperation among multiple agencies under the Rudd/Gillard Labor leadership between 2007 and 2013; and the more recent enhancement of domestic security and digital surveillance reforms under the conservative Abbott Government between 2013 and 2015. For Walsh, recent expansion of the surveillance of Australian citizens at home and abroad, particularly in recognised conflict zones, is only understandable by examining incremental legislative developments in each political context since the Bali bombings. Through a comparison of related Canadian developments during this time frame, this chapter concludes by highlighting the volume and speed of reforms to Australia's national security landscape that underscores practical difficulties in implementation of appropriate oversight mechanisms and streamlined cooperation amongst Australia's intelligence and policing agencies.

The chapter by Richard Jochelson and Mark Doerksen shares synergies with Forcese's argument too by questioning whether judicial interpretations of the *Canadian Charter* temper the incremental expansion of constitutionally authorised mass surveillance. Rather than promoting a guardianship role, Jochelson and Doerksen suggest the history of judicial decisions examining the unreasonable search and seizure provision in Sect. 8 of the *Charter* actively support an expanded bureaucratic and legal structure that normalises various contentious forms of police surveillance. These developments are attributed to the nature of judicial methodology that divorces specific constitutional claims from where alleged *Charter* violations are ultimately forged, and which has increasingly legitimised conservative rulings that favour expanded warrantless police searches in a growing array of circumstances. Rather than upholding reasonable expectations of privacy, recent jurisprudence tends to justify warrantless search powers in an expanded range of locations, such as schools, where privacy expectations are considered less worthy of legal protection. This starting point has also expanded the array of policing and non-policing agencies authorised to conduct warrantless searches of mobile phones and personal belongings, as the reasonable expectation of privacy gradually shifts within a broader pre-emptive securitisation framework. This chapter concludes by revealing the Supreme Court's tendency to create new powers by providing constitutionally enshrined guidelines for police to follow, which works in tandem with legislative measures identified by Forcese that legitimise forms of surveillance for national security purposes. The legal status of *Charter* decisions, combined with the 'justification-based' approach to the judicial authorisation of expanded law enforcement surveillance at the expense of the right to privacy, is critically examined in light of the prevailing Australian approach involving blanket legislative authorisation of police searches, which is customarily interpreted in individual court cases that lack an equivalent constitutional authority. The authors end by suggesting how the Canadian approach facilitates a growing range of 'surveillant incursions' to promote public safety and national security, in a way that undermines the initial protective libertarian principles.

This section concludes with a chapter by Brendon Murphy and John Anderson that also adopts the notion of 'counter-law' to explore surveillance in Australia. Contemporary law enforcement in Australia relies heavily on surveillance and investigations that depend on legal architectures deployed to authorise, prohibit, control and often legitimate those activities. The authors examine the current Australian legal architecture of covert surveillance. The history of Australian surveillance legislation, a discussion of the regulatory framework at the state and federal level, and consideration of the justification for strategic targeted surveillance comprise this chapter.

These four contributions highlight a wide range of national security and surveillance procedures that are intrusive and lack judicial and bureaucratic oversight. However, these deficits are by no means reducible to the most obvious structural legal difference between the two nations, namely Australia's lack of a constitutionally enshrined *Charter of Rights and Freedoms*. Both Canadian chapters demonstrate the 'flexibility and elasticity' of judicial interpretations of the *Charter* that raise questions about how the prevailing methodological approach by the Canadian Supreme Court effectively balances citizen rights, in a broader national and transnational milieu of increased securitisation. This suggests the incremental ratcheting of Australian federal legislation, which is overseen through a more bureaucratic 'managerial rationalist' framework, is perhaps no more or less intrusive on individual liberty and democratic freedom. However, in Australia the political willingness to gradually expand the array of laws that legitimise enhanced mass surveillance by national security and law enforcement agencies seems geared towards pre-empting *any* conceivable activity deemed to threaten the sanctity of the state and public safety. As Pat O'Malley alludes to in his foreword, the empirical richness of each chapter highlights structural, political, and legal similarities and divergences that open up many new understandings of the respective localised, national and extraterritorial dimensions of national security governance collectively and in each country.

2

One Warrant to Rule Them All: Reconsidering the Judicialisation of Extraterritorial Intelligence Collection

Craig Forcese

Introduction

States spy. They spy on each other, and they spy on people they perceive as threats or (in the world of economic espionage) opportunities. There is nothing new in any of this. What is new is how states spy. Technology has not erased borders, but it has created a new place for spying: cyberspace. Increasingly, the substance of spying travels or is stored in the electronic realm, which changes the 'how' of spying. Changing the 'how' also complicates the question of 'where' states spy and on whom. More than that, the changed 'how' confounds the question of 'when,' and specifically the extent to which spying is wrapped into the orbit of privacy rules. In the result, spying is much more complicated than it used to be, certainly from a legal perspective and probably also operationally.

C. Forcese (✉)
Faculty of Law, University of Ottawa, Ottawa, ON, Canada

© The Author(s) 2016
R. Lippert et al. (eds.), *National Security, Surveillance and Terror*,
DOI 10.1007/978-3-319-43243-4_2

The complexity is evident in Canada, where security intelligence practices have been in the cross-hairs of controversy for more than a decade. Commissions of inquiry and judicial decisions have dragged many practices out of the nether region of operations and into the world of legal checks and balances (see Canada 2006, hereafter Arar Inquiry; Canada 2008, hereafter Iacobucci Inquiry; Canada 2010, hereafter Air India Inquiry). The consequences have been uncomfortable for intelligence agencies, which have needed to adjust to what former senior Canadian Intelligence Chief Jim Judd has labelled "the judicialisation of intelligence" (Global Futures Forum Conference 2008). But those consequences also have been uncomfortable for law as a system of governance geared towards transparency has been swept into a world allergic to it. The resulting clash of cultures has provoked unexpected controversies and various workarounds that risk the worst possible outcome: making spying less useful as a legitimate national security tool and making law less principled as it tries to mitigate this risk. This result stems in part from a regular Canadian tendency to let the chips fall as they may in the world of national security law: the government rarely legislates proactively to cure foreseeable problems, and when it does legislate, it prefers a minimalist approach that often creates more headaches than it resolves.

This chapter explores these assertions, focusing specifically on the question of extraterritorial surveillance by Canadian intelligence services, along with occasional comparative notes of relevance to an international audience. I begin by examining the role and jurisdiction of Canada's two chief intelligence services. I then highlight recent controversies, before describing the legal questions they have provoked. Finally, I propose several steps for remedying a growing incoherence in Canadian spying law.

CSIS's Security Intelligence Functions

Canada's chief intelligence service is the Canadian Security Intelligence Service (CSIS). An analogue to the Australian Security Intelligence Organization (ASIO), CSIS is charged with several functions, the historically most important of which is collecting, analysing and retaining information and intelligence on "threats to the security of Canada" (*CSIS Act* R.S.C. 1985, c. C-23, ss. 2 and 12). It is, therefore, principally a 'security intelligence' organisation. While it can compile more purely foreign intelligence unconnected to threats, it is not a true foreign intelligence service: it may collect foreign intelligence only within Canada (ibid., s. 16).

Unlike its counterpart in Australia (Jones this volume; Walsh this volume), though, CSIS operates in a legal system with a constitutionalised bill of rights. As a result, only judges (and not executive officials) may issue search warrants.

In the course of its intelligence-gathering activities, CSIS may invade privacy in a manner that would transgress the *Canadian Charter of Rights and Freedoms* Sect. 8 warrant requirement if a court does not properly authorise its surveillance activities. Accordingly, CSIS's governing statute instructs CSIS to apply for a judicial warrant if, among other things, it "believes, on reasonable grounds, that a warrant…is required to enable the Service to investigate a threat to the security of Canada" (ibid., s. 21).

CSIS warrants are adjudicated secretly, with only the government party present, although judges occasionally retain the services of *amicus curiae*. Unlike police-intercept warrants, CSIS warrants are almost never disclosed in subsequent proceedings. And unlike with police intercepts, the target is never notified that they were surveilled (*Criminal Code* R.S.C. 1985, c. C-46, Part VI).

Because of this secrecy, it is impossible to say definitively what CSIS warrants cover. But extrapolating from past practice and the structure of the governing law, it seems likely that CSIS warrants are narrowly tailored and meet specificity standards: that is, they identify with precision the target, location and nature of the invasive surveillance. While the CSIS law does empower a judge to issue warrants for 'classes of persons' it is difficult to imagine a CSIS warrant being used for mass surveillance purposes. Put another way, CSIS warrants are much less likely to reach surveillance of entire computer networks (e.g. the internet) than are the enhanced computer access ministerial warrants at issue in recent amendments to ASIO's law (*ASIO Act* 1979, Part III, Division 2, Subdivision C, as amended by *National Security Legislation Amendment Act* 2014).

CSE's Foreign Intelligence and CSIS Assistance Mandate

Canada also has a signals intelligence service, the Communications Security Establishment (CSE). A core member of the famous Five Eyes consortium that links the signals intelligence services of the USA, the UK, Australia, New Zealand and Canada, CSE's mandate includes: acquiring and using "information from the global information infrastructure for the purpose of providing foreign intelligence" ("Mandate A") and providing "technical and operational assistance to federal law enforcement and security agencies in the performance of their lawful duties" ("Mandate C") (*National Defence Act* (*NDA*), R.S.C. 1985 c. N-5, s. 273.64). These mandates are similar in focus to those assigned to CSE's Australian counterpart, the Australian Signals Directorate (ASD) (*Intelligence Services Act* 2001, s. 7).[1]

Like ASD, CSE is principally an electronic eavesdropping agency. More than that, it is obliged to orient its Mandate A activities outward, away from Canada. CSE's rules insist that its foreign intelligence activities "not be directed at Canadians or any person in Canada; and…shall be subject to measures to protect the privacy of Canadians in the use and retention of intercepted information" (*NDA* 1985, s. 273.64). Under Mandate C, meanwhile, CSE can spy on Canadians, but here it is simply acting as a technological proxy for agencies like CSIS. Legally, therefore, the assisted agency itself must possess legal authority for the spying.

As this discussion suggests, CSIS and CSE can and do work together, although in doing so, they must square their different roles and reconcile their different legal operating environments. For example, under a secret 2012 Memorandum of Understanding, the two agencies agreed to:

> cooperate to the greatest extent practicable within their respective legal authorities and mandates on the collection and sharing of information

---

[1] CSEC also provides "advice, guidance and services to help ensure the protection of electronic information and of information infrastructures of importance to the Government of Canada." This Mandate 'B' does not, however, figure in this chapter.

or intelligence, without compromising intelligence assets, sources or methods, while recognizing the legal rights of Canadians inside an outside Canada, as well as those of any person in Canada. (CSIS 2012)[2,3]

The reference in the MOU to "recognizing the legal rights of Canadians inside and outside Canada, as well as those of any person in Canada" sounds straightforward in principle, but has proven awkward in practice.

Legal Rights of Persons in Canada

Until comparatively recently, spying on people in Canada was a simple legal issue. Section 8 of the *Canadian Charter of Rights and Freedoms* guards against 'unreasonable searches and seizures.' An 'unreasonable' search is generally one that invades a protected zone of privacy without first being authorised by judicial warrant (see *Hunter v. Southam Inc.* 1984; *R. v. Duarte* 1990; *R v. Tse* 2012). For instance, police wiretaps have, since the inception of the *Charter* (and before), enjoyed privacy protection, and must therefore almost always be blessed in advance by judicial authorisation (*Criminal Code* 1985, Part VI; see also Jochelson and Doerksen, this volume).

Conventional Domestic Spying

When CSIS was created in 1984, its legislation built on this set of legal principles and superimposed a warrant requirement on certain CSIS activities. The statute did not prescribe a precise threshold at which point a CSIS investigation would trigger a warrant obligation. However, the warrant trigger was implicitly any circumstance where Sect. 8 of the *Charter* would require such a warrant, or would otherwise violate certain

---

[2] A copy of this document has been released under Access to Information and is on file with the author.

[3] Memorandum of Understanding between CSIS and CSE received by Access to Information request #CSIS 117-2014-345, released Apr 29 2015. For more information contact Craig Forcese.

special criminal restrictions on intercepting electronic communications (see *R. v. Atwal* 1988, para. 36). CSIS is governed by legal privacy expectations very similar to those observed by police, and there is nothing particularly novel about domestic CSIS surveillance operations that could not be addressed by extrapolating from conventional privacy law expectations.

CSE, for its part, operated largely in the shadows. Its existence was not officially acknowledged until 1983, and its mandate was not codified in law until 2001. As noted, its legal mandate after 2001 included assisting CSIS, which raised no new legal questions distinct from those existing for CSIS itself.

Technological Development and the Blurring of Domestic and Foreign Spying

However, CSE's 'Mandate A' focus on 'foreign intelligence' and the proviso that it not direct its foreign intelligence activities at persons in Canada or Canadians abroad has proven more complex. In 2001, the apparent government expectation was that if CSE was operating purely internationally (and did not target persons in Canada or Canadians wherever they were), the *Canadian Charter* was simply inapplicable, or could be interpreted in a more forgiving manner.

Webbed Communication and Incidental Domestic Spying

That 2001 law was not blind to the possibility that the compartmentalisation of 'foreign' and 'Canadian' might fail. For this reason, CSE's law recognises that "there may be circumstances in which incidental interception of private communications or information about Canadians will occur" (Government of Canada/Attorney General of Canada 2014, hereafter "GoC Response," para. 5).[4] The law permits the Minister of National Defence to issue a 'ministerial authorization' permitting CSE

---

[4] This document is on file with the author.

to collect 'private communications.' The minister may issue this authorisation only where satisfied, among other things, that the interception is directed at foreign entities outside of Canada and privacy-protecting measures are in place in the event that Canadian communications are captured (*NDA* 1985, s. 273.65(2)).

In practice, ministerial authorisations have since been issued on a 'just in case' basis. That is, because one can never be sure that the communications intercepted will lack a Canadian nexus, authorisations are sought regularly to make sure CSE remains within the scope of the law. Compared to warrants issued by judges in police investigations (and those in investigations by CSIS) where the target, location and nature of surveillance practices are specified, ministerial authorisations are general, lacking the details normally associated with warrant-based authorisations. As described by the commissioner charged with review of CSE in his 2011–2012 annual report, ministerial authorisations "relate to an 'activity' or 'class of activities' specified in the authorizations…the authorizations do not relate to a specific individual or subject (the whom or the what)" (Commissioner of the Communications Security Establishment 2012; GoC Response 2014, paras. 7 and 8).

Right from its inception, however, this ministerial authorisation process departed from conventional Canadian constitutional expectations that independent judges, and not members of the political executive, would issue warrants. More than this, the neat compartmentalisation between foreign and Canadian collapsed to a degree impossible for legislators in 2001 to anticipate. In a world where telecommunications systems are webbed together, even 'foreign intelligence' may have a Canadian nexus. For instance, it may be that a telephone call sent to or originating in Canada might be intercepted. Similarly, CSE surveillance may capture the communication of a Canadian located overseas. As the government acknowledges, "the complexity of the global information infrastructure is such that it is not possible for CSE to know ahead of time if a foreign target will communicate with a Canadian or person in Canada, or convey information about a Canadian" (GoC Response 2014, para. 5). Since 2001, this webbing has accelerated, and the global information infrastructure is even more complicated. Of particular note has been controversy over 'metadata' collection.

Pervasive Metadata as a New Source of Intelligence

In a 2013 report, the Privacy Commissioner of Ontario defined 'metadata' as:

> information generated by our communications devices and our communications service providers, as we use technologies like landline telephones, mobile phones, desktop computers, laptops, tablets or other computing devices. It is essentially information about other information, in this case, relating to our communications. (Cavoukian 2013, 3)

The Commissioner compared metadata to "digital crumbs" that reveal "time and duration of a communication, the particular devices, addresses, or numbers contacted, which kinds of communications services we use, and at what geolocations" (Cavoukian 2013, 3).

Starting in at least 2004, CSE has been collecting metadata pursuant to one or other secret ministerial policy directives. It seems clear from records released through access to information that some portion (presumably a relatively modest part) of the metadata sucked up by CSE foreign intelligence operations is Canadian. Nevertheless, not even a 'ministerial authorization' blesses this metadata collection, presumptively because the government does not regard metadata as a form of personal communication. Nor does CSE collect metadata pursuant to judicial warrant (Forcese 2015). For this reason, a prominent Canadian civil liberties group has sued CSE, urging that this practice is a constitutional breach (BCCLA 2014).

That lawsuit awaits resolution, but its very existence illustrates the doubtfulness of dividing spying into hermetically sealed quadrants to be governed by different legal standards. Technological change blurs once distinct spying activities, blending (in this case) the foreign with the domestic and leading to new expectations that domestic privacy rules will govern operations.

Legal Rights of Persons Outside of Canada

Just as Canada's signals intelligence service's activities implicate more domestic content, so too do developments in the threat environment necessitate new thinking about foreign spying by CSIS. The events of 9/11 sparked an understandable preoccupation with terrorism, and with Canadians who might be members of (or inspired by) international terrorist entities like Al-Qaeda and now ISIS. This threat was not cleanly compartmentalised into domestic and international threats. Footloose Canadians travelling overseas to Afghanistan, North Africa, Somalia and now, especially, Syria and Iraq, constitute a potential security threat. CSIS, whose mandate clearly centres on understanding the threats these people may pose, risks being blinded if its investigations stop at Canada's border (see also Pratt, this volume; Muller, this volume). More than that, these people journey to places where CSIS cannot always rely on cooperation with local authorities. Indeed, even alerting local authorities in some of these countries of the Canadian interest might be controversial: Canada spent the better part of the last decade striking judicial inquiries examining the knock-on effect of this sort of security flagging on Canadian victims of torture in overseas jails (see Arar Inquiry 2006; Iacobucci Inquiry 2008).

But CSE has legal competence under its 'Mandate C' to act as a technological proxy for CSIS. Often CSE, and not other security services, will have the technological capacity to intercept foreign communications by these potentially dangerous Canadians. In these circumstances, one obvious solution is for CSIS to deploy CSE's capacities and continue its threat investigation even as the targets leave the country.

Extraterritorial spying of this sort has, however, been uncommon and so raises murky new legal issues. Beginning at least by 2005, CSIS confronted a key new legal question: in what circumstance might a warrant be required authorising CSIS intrusive surveillance outside of Canada (whether done alone, or by CSE under its Mandate C)?

The Hape Headache and the CSIS Aftermath

One possible answer was: 'never,' because the *Charter* does not reach outside of the country's borders, and therefore, a warrant requirement is never triggered under CSIS's governing law. To some extent, a 2007 Supreme Court of Canada case supports this view. In *Hape* (2007), the RCMP conducted an overseas criminal investigation with the express consent of the foreign authorities, and in partnership with them. Mr Justice LeBel, for a majority of the Court, looked to international law and the principle of the comity of nations to conclude that Sect. 8 of the *Charter* did not reach the RCMP's conduct in this context. Summarised succinctly, LeBel J. reasoned:

- Sovereign equality of states is a bedrock principle of customary international law, and includes the doctrine of non-interference in the sovereign affairs of other states;
- International comity, or the deference one sovereign state owes to the actions another legitimately takes on its own territory, means that states seeking the cooperation of a territorial sovereign must respect the manner in which the latter provides that assistance;
- Absent some other permissive rule of international law or state consent, international law precludes the exercise by one state on the territory of another of "enforcement jurisdiction" or "the power to use coercive means to ensure that rules are followed, commands are executed or entitlements are upheld" and;
- The extension of *Charter* Sect. 8 exterritorialy without the consent of the territorial state would be intrusive invasion of state sovereignty and would necessarily "entail an exercise of the enforcement jurisdiction that lies at the heart of territoriality" (ibid., paras. 52, 58, 65 and 87).

Transposed to the CSIS context, this holding sparked an unexpected chain of events culminating in a stern rebuke of CSIS by a federal court judge, and a new piece of legislation. This sequence of developments began with Federal Court Justice Blanchard's holding in an initial warrant application (*Re CSIS Act* 2008). There, CSIS sought a warrant to engage in intrusive surveillance activities outside of Canada of persons regarded as possible terrorist threats, urging that *Hape*'s applicability to this operation was unclear, and that a warrant was necessary to guard against violation of the *Charter* (ibid., para. 57). In response, Blanchard J. concluded:

- Without express statutory permission, CSIS did not have legislative authority under its governing statute to engage in extraterritorial intrusive surveillance that presumptively impinged on the territorial sovereignty of foreign states;

- Federal Courts had no authority to authorise activities inconsistent with and likely to breach international law (ibid., paras. 39 and 52) and;
- While not strictly necessary for its holding, *Hape* required that Sect. 8 of the *Charter* cannot apply to intrusive investigations conducted in a foreign state, without its consent (ibid., para. 62).

Subsequently, in authorising what came to be called "30–08 warrants" for extraterritorial surveillance, a second federal court judge distinguished Blanchard J.'s judgement (Re CSIS Act 2008 FC 301). Mosley J. authorised the communications intercepts on the basis that while they might involve overseas communications, the intercept would be done *within* the territory of Canada. It was this fact, and this fact alone, that appeared to satisfy him that he had jurisdiction to issue the warrants and that the CSIS conduct would comply with international law, and specifically the prohibition against violations of foreign territorial sovereignty (ibid., paras. 64–66).

It was never entirely clear from the limited public record in this case as to how an intrusive intercept of a foreign communication could be done within Canada, without reaching out (electronically) and hacking communications overseas, in presumptive violation of some foreign law. More significantly, subsequent controversy stemmed from CSIS's non-observance of this Canadian territorial expectation. In coordination with the CSE, CSIS outsourced the intercept function to (unnamed) Five Eye partner intelligence agencies. Intrusive surveillance was not, therefore, confined to the territory of Canada, and was instead conducted by Five Eyes partners (*Re X* 2014, para. 6). Moreover, this intrusive surveillance was not confined to Five Eyes territories, and involved intrusive surveillance in third-party states (*Re X* 2013, para. 102).

This had the effect of rendering Blanchard J.'s holding directly material to the warrants at issue in this case. Put another way, the grounds on which Mosley J. distinguished this prior decision dissolved, and the Blanchard J. position on the reach of the *CSIS Act* became immediately applicable. After Blanchard J.'s decision, CSIS apparently developed a legal theory about its powers under its governing Act allowing it autonomous authority to seek, without warrant, extraterritorial intrusive surveillance assistance through CSE from Five Eyes partners, including where this would involve a breach of international law (ibid., para. 94).

This government position, it seemed, depended on an interpretation of Blanchard J.'s holding to the effect that the *Charter* did not apply to the outsourcing of intrusive surveillance. However, Mosely J. and then the Federal Court of Appeal ultimately dismissed this particular construction (ibid., para. 30, and affirmed in *Re X* 2014, paras. 82 and 88).

A Legislative Solution that Fails to Fix

In direct reaction to this sequence of events, the government finally tabled a legislative response in Parliament in late 2014. Introduced as Bill C-44, and duly enacted without any amendments by Parliament (Statutes of Canada 2015, c. 9) the law responded to Blanchard J.'s decision, in part, by confirming the competence of the Federal Court to issue a warrant for extraterritorial surveillance, even in violation of foreign or international law. This constitutes the only circumstance of which I am aware in which a democratic state has so emphatically and clearly legislated an authority for its courts to authorise foreign law-breaking by a clandestine service.

However, in a striking omission, the legislation includes no clarifying language on when CSIS must seek such a warrant to begin with (Forcese 2014). The absence of a clear statutory trigger leaves intact the implied requirement that a warrant is required where the *Charter* would otherwise be violated. As already noted, doubt on the extraterritorial reach of the *Charter* is what sparked the dispute culminating in the legislation. So in a striking lack of foresight, the new law responds to a controversy without curing the uncertainty that sparked it in the first place. That is, Bill C-44 clarifies the Federal Court's warrant powers, without answering the underlying question of when CSIS must actually ask the Federal Court to exercise those powers. This then remains a question ripe for litigation and new controversy.

Uncertain Legality and Applicability

One obvious aspect of the likely controversy will be the viability of the Federal Court's new warrant powers. Politically, it will be awkward for Federal Courts to bless violations of foreign law and foreign state sovereignty. Each judge must be acutely aware of the personal and institutional reputational consequences of a CSIS foreign operation that goes wrong, complete with revelations of an undergirding warrant.

More than this, the constitutionality of the new competency is not entirely clear. It is indisputable that in the Canadian system of parliamentary sovereignty, Parliament may emphatically legislate a departure from international law (see *Hape* 2007, paras. 53 and 68). But such departures are permissible only to the extent that the international principle in question is not also part of Canadian constitutional law, which serves as a check on parliamentary sovereignty.

The Supreme Court's holding in *Hape* created unexpected murkiness on this question. In a puzzling exegesis (Currie 2008, 317–21), it suggested without any reference to positive law that the exercise of "enforcement jurisdiction"—that is, enforcing Canada's laws on the territory of another state—without the consent of the territorial state, will be beyond the legal competency of any Canadian agency, regardless of whether that conduct is authorised by the legislation: "Neither Parliament nor the provincial legislatures have the power to authorize the enforcement of Canada's laws over matters in the exclusive territorial jurisdiction of another state" (*Hape* 2007, para. 105, and see also paras. 68 and 69). This may mean that in no circumstance could any Canadian agency partake in invasive surveillance in violation of foreign law without the consent of the territorial sovereign. Under this construal, the *CSIS Act* simply cannot constitutionally authorise intrusive foreign surveillance in violation of foreign law, whether done directly by Canadian agencies or outsourced to foreign partners. But even if this rather perplexing language from the Supreme Court is disregarded and the new Federal Court's warrant competency is lawful, the necessary subsidiary question is 'where must it be exercised,' that is, what is the trigger for the warrant? This is left unaddressed by the legislation.

Extending the Charter Privacy Protections to Foreign Operations

This lacuna invites jurisprudence filling the gap. Having failed to offer up its own statutory answer, the government now confronts the prospect of a judicially constructed response. It may not like the outcome.

One possible response would be for the courts simply to distinguish the *Hape* ruling and conclude that the standard *Charter* Sect. 8 trigger is applicable to overseas surveillance of Canadians. There are powerful arguments favouring extraterritorial *Charter* reach in this kind of CSIS surveillance case. For one thing, none of *Hape*'s preoccupations with international comity apply: there is no question of respecting the activity of a foreign sovereign on its own territory if the CSIS operation is done without its consent and in violation of its law.

In these circumstances, international comity and the state sovereignty concern in international law that animated the *Hape* holding have already been disregarded. Having abandoned these principles for the purpose of authorising assertive use of state power, it would be incongruous for the government to invoke these concerns to stave off careful judicial control and safeguards concerning the use of its own state power.

Not least, if Canadian agencies can directly (or through proxies) ignore foreign law, but the *Hape* holding then denies the reach of the *Charter* to the covert, invasive surveillance operation, there is no prospect of *any* law filling the resulting legal accountability gap. Unless a Federal Court warrant is 'triggered' by the invasive extraterritorial surveillance, neither foreign nor Canadian privacy law is brought to bear on the operation. As a result, whatever safeguards exist do so entirely at the discretion of the Canadian executive government. The result would be a 'legal black hole.'

As a further argument, the Supreme Court held in *Hape* that the *Charter could* reach overseas conduct by a Canadian agency where at issue was compliance with Canada's international obligations: "The principle of comity does not offer a rationale for condoning another state's breach of international law" (*Hape* 2007, para. 51, and see also paras. 52, 90, and 101). The Court has since commented on this *Hape* exception: "the Court was united on the principle that comity cannot be used to justify Canadian participation in activities of a foreign state or its agents that are contrary to Canada's international obligations" (*Khadr v. Canada* 2008, para. 18; *Khadr v. Canada* 2010, para. 14).

The Court has applied the *Hape* 'exception' to extend the *Charter* overseas where Canadian state actors are in violation of Canada's international human rights obligations (ibid.). International human rights law is, however, underdeveloped in the area of privacy, and it is not at all clear that even intrusive extraterritorial surveillance by CSIS would transgress Canada's obligations under, for example, the International Covenant on Civil and Political Rights (Forcese 2011).

Surveillance conducted without the territorial state's consent may raise, however, sovereignty preoccupations, at least where foreign law is violated. No application of the *Hape* exception has involved a circumstance in which the Canadian state agent acts covertly without the consent of the foreign sovereign. For this reason, the Court has never ruled on whether Canada's violation of international law in the form of breaching the sovereignty of another state falls within that exception.

But nothing in the *Hape dicta* confines its exception strictly to violations of international human rights norms. Restricting its reach to this cadre of international principles would be highly formulistic. This is not a formalism that the Court has observed. In *Khadr*, the Court concluded that Canada was in violation of the *Geneva Conventions* of 1949, and "that participation in the Guantanamo Bay process which violates these international instruments would be contrary to Canada's binding international obligations" (*Khadr v. Canada* 2008, para. 25). The *Geneva Conventions* are, technically, international humanitarian law, a branch of international law distinct from international human rights law. Put another way, the Court has already reached beyond human rights law to identify the other circumstances in which non-compliance with international law triggers the *Hape* exception. It might reasonably follow that a violation of a foreign state's sovereignty is another breach of Canada's international obligations that triggers the extension of the *Charter* extraterritorially.

This new trigger would necessitate an arcane review of just when, exactly, a CSIS operation offends foreign sovereignty. This analysis is not as clear cut as may be assumed: whatever the soft law sparked by the recent Snowden revelations (see UNGA 2014), international law is creatively ambiguous on the legal propriety of extraterritorial spying (Forcese 2011; Deeks 2016). Suffice to say that the more invasive and intrusive the spying—e.g. hacking systems or breaking into facilities—the more likely it amounts to the illicit exercise of enforcement jurisdiction on foreign soil.

This 'breach of sovereignty' trigger could be enough, then, to bring the matter before the Court. But what then would the Court do in issuing a warrant? In a conventional Sect. 8 context, the Court imposes conditions that render the invasion of privacy 'reasonable' and therefore compliant with the *Charter*. Here, the *Charter* may apply because Canada's international obligations are in play. But the Court then is instructed by Bill C-44 to issue a warrant that may violate these obligations, so 'reasonableness' does not include 'complying with international law.'

One response from the Court could be to hold that this new warrant power violates the *Charter*, and is of no force and effect. Or the Court could hold that it violates the *Charter*, but is saved because it is reasonable in a free and democratic state, per the *Canadian Charter*'s Sect. 1 justification. But the bottom line is that exactly what a court would do if it concludes the *Charter* is applicable to extraterritorial intrusive surveillance in violation of foreign law is utterly unclear, and without any precedent.

So in the minimalist way C-44 was crafted, the government has opted to let judges do what judges do, and it will need to live then with that consequence. At the very least, it seems likely that judges will resort to the sort of oversight they deploy for conventional warrants, perhaps with added wariness and prudential conditions because of the risk that an operation gone wrong will produce an international incident.

Moreover, Federal Court judges will reasonably be preoccupied by collaboration with Five Eyes partners, given past scandals concerning information sharing from Canada then contributing to maltreatment of Canadians by foreign governments (Arar Inquiry 2006; Iacobucci Inquiry 2008). In a recent Supreme Court case addressing international information sharing, all seven justices suggested that the *Charter* may preclude information sharing where the risk of resulting mistreatment cannot be mitigated (*R. v. Wakeling* 2014, paras. 76, 80, 95, 104; see also *Re X* 2013, para. 115). This approach counsels, at minimum, strict conditions as part of warrants permitting collaboration with foreign partners in extraterritorial surveillance.

Using a Breach of International Law as the Trigger for a Warrant

Even if a court chooses not to go down the *Charter* path, there are other possible outcomes on this trigger question, dependent on careful parsing by both CSIS lawyers and the court. After C-44, CSIS's governing law now emphatically specifies that CSIS may perform its security intelligence investigations "without or outside Canada" (*CSIS Act* 1985, s. 12(3)). It does not, however, go on to specify that CSIS may do so in violation of foreign and international law. Parliament has not, in other words, authorised CSIS to breach international law unilaterally. And Canadian statutory interpretation presumptions provide that, in the absence of express language, Parliament is presumed to legislate compliance with international law (*Hape* 2007, para. 53). The aspect of Blanchard J.'s decision denying CSIS's unilateral capacity to act in violation of international law remains, therefore, intact.

The only place where Parliament now has anticipated actions in violation of foreign or international law is in relation to the new competency of Federal Court judges to issue warrants for overseas CSIS investigations. In this manner, the Federal Court warrant becomes the only gateway to any international law violation. Passing through this gateway is, therefore, the only conceivable manner in which CSIS's mandate can be construed as reaching violations of international law.

It follows that the trigger for the warrant under the new C-44 regime is each circumstance where CSIS believes on reasonable grounds that international law might be violated. If it acts in these circumstances without warrant, it acts outside its jurisdiction, and therefore unlawfully. A more straightforward approach than the *Charter* outcome, this trigger possibility still requires a careful consideration of when international law is violated, which is not always a simple assessment. It again provides little guidance on what courts would then do once the warrant question was before them.

A Third Way

The highly technical nature of the last part illustrates a key point: spying questions have become legally complex to an unprecedented degree, and the 'judicialisation of intelligence' is in full bloom in Canada. The risk is that it is developing in an episodic, uneven and unpredictable manner, driven by events and not in command of them. CSIS extraterritorial surveillance standards are now propelled by court cases, and half-hearted legislative responses. CSE's foreign intelligence collection is now also wrapped into predictable constitutional law disputes.

As the title of this chapter proposes, the net outcome may be a system of 'one warrant to rule them all,' or an undifferentiated swing towards the judicialisation of all intelligence. As much as such a development appeals to an academic lawyer acculturated to expect much from courts and little from government, it is probably bad from an operational security perspective. It is also bad for law, to the extent that efforts to make law reach novel situations create new, unforeseen knock-on effects. The *Hape* case, and its second-order impacts on CSIS, is a case in point.

It is worth considering, therefore, whether a premeditated, predesigned alternative might prove more advantageous, as compared to the crisis-response system of law-making exhibited in this area by Canada. Here, it is worth looking at developments in other Five Eye jurisdictions.

A Pure Foreign Intelligence Organisation

Like New Zealand, but unlike Australia, the USA and the UK, Canada does not have a purely international intelligence service. While CSE performs a foreign signals intelligence function, Canada has not conducted other forms of covert purely foreign, as opposed to security, intelligence collection outside of its borders.

Setting aside the uncertainty raised by the Blanchard J. decision, CSIS has construed its mandate to investigate threats to the security of Canada as reaching threats located outside Canada. Until recently, its international operations have been modest. As noted, internationalisation has been driven in large measure by the transnational terrorist threat. As this chapter suggests, this has prompted efforts to fit the square peg of CSIS's domestic legal architecture into the round hole of redoubled international operations.

Tracking developments in multiple foreign jurisdictions is challenging. But it would appear that close allies have not struggled with the sorts of issues analogous to those raised by the Blanchard J. decision and its aftermath. In part, this may reflect the fact that in Australia and the UK, the executive and not the judiciary authorises intercepts, presumably making the process less legalistic but also perhaps more arbitrary and less trans-parent than even the secretive CSIS warrant process.

In part the differences between Canada and its partners may stem from the reality that in other Five Eye states, other than New Zealand, overseas surveillance may be conducted by specialised foreign intelligence agen-cies such as MI6, the Australian Secret Intelligence Service (ASIS) and the United States Central Intelligence Agency. These organisations, in turn, are generally governed by a fairly permissive legal structure because of their exclusively international orientation. The UK's MI6 law provides, simply, that the Secretary of State may exonerate via prior authorisation international conduct by MI6 that would render someone civilly or criminally liable in the UK (*Intelligence Services Act* UK 1994, c. 13s. 7). ASIS's law contains no warranting requirement even roughly analogous to that governing CSIS or ASIS's domestic counterpart, ASIO, and indeed requires ministerial authorisations for its conduct only in limited cir-cumstances (*Intelligence Services Act* 2001, ss. 8-9B). In recent Australian developments, ASIO's own overseas intelligence collection abilities have been increased, but are still confined to collection activities in Australia (*ASIO Act* 1979, s. 17(1)(e)).

As these examples suggest, allies have not struggled to twin the cul-ture of strict domestic law checks and balances and the murkier world of overseas spying. Presumably, for this same reason, the legislatures of these countries have not been forced by developments in their courts to legis-late quite as frankly as Canada has and emphatically authorise warranted surveillance in violation of foreign law.

It follows that one solution for Canada is to replicate this pattern: confine CSIS to domestic operations, and stand-up a separate foreign intelligence service competent to take carriage of international operations. Caution is, however, warranted. There may be good reasons for pursuing this approach, but easing surveillance strictures in anti-terror cases should not be one of them. De-legalising or de-judicialising anti-terror surveillance risks under-mining counter-terrorism strategies. Anti-terror has many ingredients, but one important element is prosecution and incarceration. Convictions depend on fair trials, which in turn depend on disclosable evidence. Likewise, administrative proceedings tied to anti-terrorism are increas-ingly gravitating towards demanding evidentiary standards. De-legalising extraterritorial surveillance may make it impossible for Canada to use these legal tools. It would risk creating new intelligence products that can never be converted into evidence supporting convictions or administrative remedies. Put another way, de-legalisation may make it easier to watch people, but it will not make it easier to stop them (c.f. Air India Inquiry 2010).

For exactly this reason, intelligence reforms should favour a greater investment by intelligence agencies in collecting information to evidential standards that is readily convertible into evidence for prosecutorial or administrative law purposes. In the Canadian legal environment, warranted intercepts are a step in this direction, at least in anti-terror investigations or any investigation that might reasonably culminate in criminal or administrative proceedings.

A Typology of Investigations

This distinction between intelligence gathering in cases that may culminate in legal proceedings versus all others suggests a different point of departure for reconceiving Canada's surveillance laws. Here, the ASIO approach may prove instructive. Setting aside minor differences for subversion investigations, CSIS warrants are designed on a 'one size fits all' template: there is one warrant process for all CSIS investigative activities, for all security threat types. This approach has largely withstood the test of time, to the extent that it has created a system generic enough to accommodate changes in technology and the evolution of the threat environment. However, relatively few of CSIS's investigations address threats that reasonably could lead to criminal prosecutions, or even administrative proceedings. Indeed, until the refocus on anti-terror, virtually none did.

One objection to the judicialisation of intelligence is not so much that it impairs an intelligence agency's anti-terror investigations, although there are those who will make this argument, but instead that it superimposes a judicial model on other intelligence operations far removed from the subject matter that courts deal with and that are very unlikely to end up anywhere near a subsequent court or tribunal case.

While it does so for its own purposes and in relation to special powers other than surveillance, Australia's ASIO legislation does distinguish between sorts of intelligence operations. That is, it creates different powers for anti-terror investigations than for the other security matters that might implicate the organisation (*ASIO Act* 1979, Part III, Division 3). There are lessons to be learned from this bifurcated 'different sizes for different purposes' approach.

As an academic lawyer, I am professionally predisposed to view 'more judicialisation' as better, in part as a guarantor of civil liberties. On the other hand, I accept it might be worth debating whether Canada should distinguish between different forms of surveillance, with the effect of recreating a less legalistic approach to surveillance oversight for broad, non-criminal or non-administrative law connected security concerns. Specifically, it might be tolerable for CSIS extraterritorial surveillance operations unconnected to prospective court or administrative proceedings to be conducted without judicial warrant. Would it be necessary or even desirable, for example, for a CSIS intrusive extraterritorial investigation into Chinese cyber espionage implicating no Canadian person, and with no prospect of criminal proceedings, to be authorised by a Federal Court warrant? On the other hand, for those investigations with more obvious criminal (or administrative) law implications (usually anti-terror) warranted surveillance should be the norm, along with collection procedures meeting evidential standards.

While the issue is much more complex with CSE because it is only peripherally, and perhaps less predictably, involved in collection activities that implicate downstream legal proceedings, similar expectations might also be grafted onto that organisation's foreign intelligence mandate. The government now runs the serious risk that recalcitrance in the face of calls for reform will culminate in constitutional findings that judicialise much CSE activity, without clear distinctions between types of operations. A judicial warrant process may become a requirement for all of CSE's Mandate A activities, whenever that collection activity might incidentally collect Canadian information, which may be almost always. Subjecting CSE to a judicial warrant in these sorts of circumstances is a position with which I am personally perfectly comfortable. Still, the government might usefully have blunted this constitutional clash by applying the filtered, bifurcated process proposed above for CSIS: a judicial warranting process applicable where there is some prospect a foreign intelligence operation might have implications for a domestic criminal or administrative proceeding.

Conclusion

I am conscience that the bifurcated approach to judicialisation raised in this chapter is not entirely responsive to the privacy issues raised by surveillance. It instead uses 'administration of justice' implications, rather than privacy, as the driver for robust judicialisation. I am more comfortable taking this approach for international surveillance than I would for domestic surveillance, if only because there is so little positive international law governing international privacy and little reason to believe it reaches all forms of surveillance.

I am also aware that this proposal does not pay full heed to the sovereignty concerns of other countries raised earlier in this chapter. On the other hand, I see little policy reason for Canada always to be peculiarly sensitive to sovereignty preoccupations, in an international legal system where spying is commonplace and the illegality of extraterritorial spying is a disputed question (Forcese 2014). Finally, I am also cognisant that my bifurcated proposal requires agencies to prognosticate on the downstream criminal or administrative law implications of their activities. This does not, however, seem beyond their capacity, especially since Canadian courts have effectively already insisted on such prognostication by CSIS in other contexts (*Charkaoui v. Canada* 2008).

Whatever its shortcomings, the proposal set out in this chapter does seem more balanced than the current blind alley down which Canada risks travelling: initial resistance to judicialisation; half-baked legislative responses that fail to cure existing problems or anticipate new ones; and then an ultimate capitulation imposed by constitutional case law after government positions prove unsustainable. It would be far better to instead craft legislation addressing preemptively all of the foreseeable issues I raise in this chapter in a coherent and logical fashion. This may not stave off all constitutional objections. But by speaking first and addressing inevitable legal issues coherently, Parliament may preempt more unpredictable and perhaps idiosyncratic judicial responses.

In sum, spying in Canada is the stuff of courts and litigation lawyers, in a way it never was before. This is exciting for courts and lawyers. Whether it produces the best possible system for squaring national security with liberty is quite another question. It is long past time for the Canadian Parliament, and the government that tables bills in it, to start taking national security law-making seriously.

References

British Columbia Civil Liberties Association (BCCLA). 2014. Statement of Claim, Federal Court of Canada. https://bccla.org/wp-content/uploads/2014/12/20141027-CSEC-Statement-of-Claim.pdf.

Canada. 2006. *Commission of Inquiry into the Actions of Canadian Officials in Relation to Maher Arar: A New Review Mechanism for the RCMP's National Security Activities* (Arar Inquiry). Ottawa: Public Works and Government Services Canada.

———. 2008. *Internal Inquiry into the Actions of Canadian Officials in Relation Abdullah Almalki, Ahmad Abou-Elmaati and Muayyed Nureddin* (Iacobucci Inquiry). Ottawa: Public Works and Government Services.

———. 2010. *Commission of Inquiry into the Investigation of the Bombing of Air India Flight 182, Air India Flight 182: A Canadian Tragedy* (Air India Inquiry). Ottawa: Public Works and Government Services Canada.

Cavoukian, Ann. 2013. A Primer on Metadata: Separating Fact from Fiction. Ontario: Information and Privacy Commissioner, July.

Commissioner of the Communications Security Establishment. 2012. 2011–2012 Annual Report. http://www.ocsec-bccst.gc.ca/ann-rpt/2011--2012/5_e.php.

Currie, John H. 2008. Khadr's Twist on Hape: Tortured Determinations of the Extraterritorial Reach of the Canadian Charter. *Canadian Yearbook of International Law* 46: 307–335.

Deeks, Ashley. 2016. Confronting and Adapting: Intelligence Agencies and International Law. *Virginia Law Review* 102: 599–685.

Forcese, Craig. 2011. Spies Without Borders: International Law and Intelligence Collection. *Journal of National Security Law & Policy* 5(1): 179–210.

———. 2014. The Judicialization of Extraterritorial Spying: Gaps and Gap-Fillers in the World of CSIS Foreign Operations. *Criminal Law Quarterly* 61(4): 440–450.

———. 2015. Law, Logarithms and Liberties: Legal Issues Arising from CSE's Metadata Program. In *Law, Privacy and Surveillance in Canada in the Post-Snowden Era*, ed. M. Geist. Ottawa: University of Ottawa Press.

Global Futures Forum Conference. 2008. Remarks by Jim Judd, Director of
  CSIS. Vancouver, April 15.
Government of Canada/Attorney General of Canada. 2014. *Response to Civil
  Claim*, in *BC Civil Liberties Association v. AG of Canada* (GoC Response).
  Supreme Court of British Columbia, no. S137827, January 20.
United Nations General Assembly (UNGA). 2014. Resolution A/RES/68/167.
  The Right to Privacy in a Digital Age, December 18.

Legislation

ASIO Act (Commonwealth of Australia). 1979.
Bill C-44. 2015. Statutes of Canada.
Criminal Code. 1985. Revised Statutes of Canada.
CSIS Act. 1985. Revised Statutes of Canada.
Intelligence Services Act (Commonwealth of Australia). 2001.
Intelligence Services Act (United Kingdom). 1994.
National Defence Act, R.S.C., 1985. c. N-5.
National Security Legislation Amendment Act (No. 1) (Commonwealth of
  Australia). 2014.

Cases

Charkaoui v. Canada. 2008. SCC 38.
Hunter v. Southam Inc. 1984. 2S.C.R. 145.
Khadr v. Canada. 2010. SCC 3.
———. 2008. SCC 28.
R. v. Atwal. 1988. 1F.C. 107.
R. v. Duarte. 1990. 1 SCR 30.
R. v. Hape. 2007. SCC 26.
R. v. Tse. 2012. SCC 16.
R. v. Wakeling. 2014. SCC 72.
Re CSIS Act. 2008. FC 301.
Re X. 2014. FCA 249.
Re X. 2013. FC 1275.
Re X. 2009. FC 1058.

3

Australian National Security Intelligence Collection Since 9/11: Policy and Legislative Challenges

Patrick F. Walsh

Introduction

The World Trade Centre disaster in New York (9/11) was a paradigm shift in the global security environment (see also Muller, this volume). During the Cold War, there had been a suite of threats from non-state actors, including terrorism, arms trading and drug trafficking, though these were partially hidden by the dominant security paradigm of the day involving the bipolar struggle between the USA and the Soviet Union. From the 1960s to 1980s, transnational terrorism was primarily motivated by a range of political ideologies associated with nationalism, separatism, Marxism and nihilism (Wilkinson 2001; Hoffman 2002). Jihadist terrorism existed, but usually entailed hostage taking and assassination rather than large-scale bombings. Additionally, until the Cold War's end,

P.F. Walsh (✉)
Australian Graduate School of Policing and Security, Charles Sturt University, Manly, NSW, Australia

© The Author(s) 2016
R. Lippert et al. (eds.), *National Security, Surveillance and Terror*,
DOI 10.1007/978-3-319-43243-4_3

terrorism was also largely a state-sponsored threat. For example, Ghadafi's Libya in the 1970s and 1980s supported terrorist groups by providing training and funding for attacks in European countries. Similarly, after the 1979 Islamic Revolution, Iran became the chief sponsor of international terrorism with Hezbollah and other groups (Lacqueur 1999, 156–183). This 'old terrorism' was more structured and targeted than its current manifestation and large-scale terrorist attacks were uncommon in Five Eyes countries.[1] The Five Eyes countries include: Australia, Canada, New Zealand, the UK and the USA.

The rise of a different 'brand of Islamic terrorism' was much less reliant on state sponsors and diffusely structured. This 'brand' from the late 1990s onwards trumpeted a manifesto of targeting both Middle East regimes and Western countries. Bin Laden's Al Qaeda surpassed earlier Islamic terrorism by suggesting it was legitimate to cause mass civilian casualties: in his mind it was every Muslim's duty to do so. The globalisation of transport and finances gave Al Qaeda the reach to carry out such attacks. The 9/11 attacks also showed this new Al Qaeda strategy had both foreign and domestic dimensions. A subsequent franchising of Al Qaeda across Africa and Middle East (e.g. Al-Shabaab (Somalia) and AQIM (Algeria/West Africa)) occurred. Even more recently, the development of diffuse groups such as Islamic State of Iraq and the Levant (ISIL) and the lone wolf phenomenon further complicated understanding of terrorist threats in the Middle East and the West amongst Five Eyes intelligence countries. In particular, what constitutes 'foreign' or 'domestic' terrorism became blurred. The greying of this line in turn raised a question after 9/11 about whether it was still helpful to distinguish between foreign and domestic intelligence in responding to terrorist threats (Walsh 2011a, 16; Lowenthal 2012, 5).

The 9/11 Commission Report addressed impacts of this pre-9/11 foreign and domestic siloing of intelligence collection by suggesting the attacks went undetected because there was insufficient information sharing between, for example, the Central Intelligence Agency (CIA) and

---

[1] In Canada there were some early periods of terrorism primarily perpetrated by groups such as the Sons of Freedom Doukhobors, a Russian religious sect, and the Front de Liberation Quebec (FLQ)—the violence of the latter peaking in the mid-1970s. In the main, Canada was used as a base to support terrorism groups planning attacks elsewhere in the world such as the Air India Flight 182 bombing by Sikh separatists. See Mullins 2013.

Federal Bureau of Investigation (FBI), and inadequate integration and coordination of their foreign and domestic intelligence collection efforts (The 9/11 Commission Report 2004, 353–360). Lessons were learned about how the US intelligence community could shift its policy, legal, cultural, structural approaches to better integrate intelligence collection and meet the new foreign and domestic manifestations of global terrorism.

Post-9/11, the US intelligence community was extensively reformed. The establishment of the Department of Homeland Security (DHS) in 2003 represented an attempt to better coordinate collection efforts of both the foreign and domestic elements of the US intelligence enterprise. In addition, the new *Intelligence Reform and Terrorism Prevention Act (IRTPA)* 2004 included significant changes, such as creation of the Office of the Director of National Intelligence (ODNI) and sanctioned a new information sharing environment (ISE) involving major security organisations. In contrast, other Five Eyes countries such as Australia and Canada underwent less dramatic reform (but see Forcese, this volume). The policy and legislative reform agenda of national security intelligence collection in Australia compared to the USA was more evolutionary than revolutionary, though the changes since 9/11 have been nonetheless profound.

This chapter has two objectives. First, it surveys the key post-9/11 policy and legislative landmarks underpinning counter-terrorism intelligence collection and the key challenges faced by the Australian intelligence community. Second it assesses these challenges, including briefly how they compare to the Canadian experience. In doing so, the chapter raises several issues discussed in other chapters concerning expanding surveillance, intelligence gathering, police powers and public legitimacy.

Before proceeding, some clarification is required about what follows. First, I only refer to 'intelligence collection' as it relates to electronic surveillance (i.e. interception of emails, wiretapping, data bases and social media), and not to human intelligence gathering involving physical surveillance (see Brooks et al., this volume) or undercover agents (but see Walsh 2011a, 196; SSCI 2014). Second, I examine the policy and legislative counter-terrorism changes in Australian national security intelligence collection since 9/11 together because both dimensions are inextricably linked. Third, analysis is organised chronologically around the four Australian prime ministers since 9/11.[2] Fourth, I focus only on counter-terrorism legislation and policy that substantially changed the collection capabilities of Australian intelligence agencies. Finally, this chapter discusses how key counter-terrorism legislation has impacted intelligence collection and the underlying policy environment at the time.

Policy and Legislative Landmarks

The Howard Government (1996–2007)

The first Howard Government between 1996 and 1998 was not overly focused on national security. 9/11 of course focused the remaining Howard years rendering national security and counter-terrorism major policy priorities. While Australia had provisions within its criminal law to prosecute terrorism offences, the Howard Government argued terrorism needed to be treated differently from other standard criminal offences.

Central to this change of approach was the idea of early intervention: whereas someone would normally be prosecuted after an offence, terror-ism necessitated (from the government's perspective) police and security agencies having the powers to intervene much earlier in the evolution of the offence in order to prevent catastrophic damage after a terrorist attack. The government's sentiment was reflected in amongst the first amendments to existing counter-terrorism arrangements post-9/11, the *Security Legislation Amendment (Terrorism) Bill* 2002 *(Cth)*. The Act wid-ened the meaning of the commission of terrorism offences to include several preparatory actions such as the preparing of documents for the engagement of a terrorist attack (Sect. 101.5(2) (b)). This provided a legal framework for Australian law enforcement and intelligence agencies to intervene earlier in the planning stages of a terrorist attack.

---

[2] While writing this chapter, Prime Minister Tony Abbott was deposed in a Liberal Party leadership challenge by his Communications Minister, Malcolm Turnbull. In September 2015 Mr Turnbull became the fifth prime minister since 9/11. It is still early days for the new Turnbull Government and there has been no major departure on counter-terrorism and intelligence policy or legislation from his predecessor to date.

Other early legislative changes included amendments to the *Commonwealth Crimes Act* on what constituted a terrorist act, amendments to the national *Criminal Code*, passing of the *Anti-Terrorism Act 2004 (Cth)*, and the *Australian Anti-Terrorism Act (No. 1)* 2005. In particular, under the Howard Government there were several early clarifying amendments made in Division 100.1 of the *Criminal Code Act* 1995 *(Cth)* about the definition of a terrorist act. Definitions were similar to those drafted for the *Security Legislation Amendment (Terrorism) Bill* 2002, and included new offences such as providing or receiving training with terrorists even if a terrorism act does not occur. Other new amendments to the *Criminal Code* included terrorist financing offences (Division 103), speech offences (i.e. urging violence) (Part 5.1), as well as new powers to allow the Attorney General to prescribe a terrorist organisation (Division 102). Although *Criminal Code* amendments were important, additional legislation allowed more coercive powers for police and security organisations. For example, the *Anti-Terrorism Act* 2004 *(Cth)* underscored how the Howard Government post-9/11 intended to interpret terrorism offences differently from other offences in terms of the length of time police or security agencies could question someone under arrest. The normal extended questioning provision of 12 hours was extended to 20, which increased the overall intelligence gathering capabilities of agencies under Division 2 (Sect. 23E) of the *Crimes Act* 1914 *(Cth)*. These provisions also allowed police and security agencies to suspend or delay questioning of a suspect up to one week if they were waiting on additional information from overseas or if information required translation.

These reforms proved a concern to the legal rights community as it extended the time someone could be questioned without a formal charge and were legally tested in the *Haneef* case in 2007. Mohamed Haneef, an Indian born medical doctor working in Australia, was arrested in July 2007 and detained for questioning for 12 days before being charged for intentionally providing resources to a terrorist organisation. The Australian Federal Police (AFP) used the provisions in the 2004 Act to extend their questioning of Haneef and allow time to receive relevant information from the UK Metropolitan Police. The AFP thought he was involved in an attempted terrorist attack at Glasgow Airport, though he was later acquitted of these charges (Walsh 2011a, 219–221). The application of these new provisions in the *Haneef* matter was troubling and became the subject of an inquiry sponsored by the succeeding Rudd Labor Government in November 2008.

Another early and specific response to enhance intelligence collection capabilities post-9/11 was the *Australian Security Intelligence Organisation Legislation Amendment (ASIO) (Terror) Act* 2003 *(Cth)*, which amended the previous *ASIO Act* 1979 *(Cth)* by introducing a questioning and detention warrant scheme. ASIO is Australia's domestic security intelligence agency (also see Jones, this volume). The amendments to Part III of the original 1979 *ASIO Act* allowed ASIO officers to detain and question persons not yet formally charged of a terrorism offence for a period of 24 hours when this could substantially assist in the collection of intelligence that is important in relation to a terrorism offence. Additionally, a person could be detained up to one week for questioning if there were reasonable grounds he or she may alert another person about an ASIO investigation, was a risk of not appearing for questioning, or could obstruct or destroy material that might be requested under warrant. These amendments proved controversial, with legal and human rights scholars claiming them to be potentially unconstitutional (Williams 2011). The amendment was due to expire three years after their introduction but was extended until July 2016.

The other significant intelligence collection and counter-terrorism response during the Howard years were control and preventative detention orders. Division 104 of the *Criminal Code* now allowed control orders against individuals not suspected of any criminal offence that may be subjected to restrictions (equivalent to house arrest). These measures were thought to be reasonably necessary to protect the public from terrorism. Views on the need for control orders varied at the time these reforms were introduced (see for example, McDonald 2007, 106; White 2012, 116–125). The preventative detention measures under Division 105 of the *Criminal Code* allowed for an individual to be detained for up to 48 hours if there was a reasonable expectation this would prevent imminent terrorist acts or assist in preserving evidence relating to a recent terrorist act. The initial 48-hour period could be further extended under state law by 14 days.

The initial focus on enabling more proactive security intelligence collection through either new or amending legislation would soon shift for the Howard Government with the US-led coalition invasion of Iraq in 2003. As widely known, the invasion's rationale was principally due to the alleged presence of Weapons of Mass Destruction (WMD) in Iraq. The post-invasion and occupation of Iraq period raised several additional intelligence policy dilemmas for the USA not solely related to security intelligence collection including the quality of intelligence assessments, politicisation of intelligence and the role of coercive interrogation (Walsh 2011a). The quality of Australian intelligence assessments and the perception of the politicisation of intelligence also got the attention of policymakers in Canberra and resulted in the 2004 Flood Inquiry into Australian intelligence agencies (Walsh 2011a). The fallout from the Iraq invasion, the 2005 London bombings and the rise of Southeast Asian jihadist groups leading to the Bali bombing dominated the remainder of the Howard Government's national security policymaking and legislative response.

Like the US Bush Administration, the Office of National Assessments (ONA), which is the leading intelligence assessment agency in Australia, came to the same incorrect assessments about the presence of WMD in Iraq. This led the Howard Government to implement the Flood Review in March 2004, which looked at how the WMD issue was assessed by Australia's intelligence community and the level of coordination amongst multiple agencies, the contestability of intelligence analysis, resourcing and accountability (Flood 2004). In the background, other transnational threats such as illegal maritime people smuggling contributed significantly to the policy and legislative responses to counter-terrorism, national security and the use of criminal intelligence by Australia's law enforcement agencies.

The Rudd/Gillard/Rudd Governments (2007–September 2013)

The first Rudd Government came into power in 2007 and promptly initiated a review of Australia's national security and intelligence arrangements. The key early policy initiative was the Smith Review in 2008, which examined whether the coordination of national security and intelligence was adequate across government agencies. The Smith Review was never made public, although some findings were later released in government policy statements. Smith's key recommendation was to avoid creation of a US style homeland security agency for Australia, because Australian intelligence agencies had a good history of cooperation and sharing intelligence. His other main recommendation was to further improve coordination amongst members of the Australian intelligence community.

Echoing the findings of the Smith Review, the prime minister called for a greater coordinating role for the Department of Prime Minister and Cabinet, the installation of a National Security Adviser and the establishment of more coordination of intelligence collection and analytical efforts via the National Intelligence and Coordination Committee (NICC). The NICC became the leading body outside the National Security Committee of Cabinet responsible for setting strategic direction of Australia's expanding intelligence community. Its key functions included developing national intelligence priorities and eliminating barriers to optimal coordination and sharing of intelligence across government. Its other important function was to combine disparate domains of intelligence, including military, foreign, domestic and policing intelligence, so that the Australian government developed a broad and integrated view of national security issues (Walsh 2011b, 121). The Rudd Government's policy perspective broadened the meaning of 'national security' (see Walby et al., this volume) and this was to include peripheral issues such as organised crime (see Pratt, this volume).

A second major initiative under the Rudd Government was establishing in March 2008 an official inquiry into the circumstances leading to the wrongful arrest and detention of Dr. Haneef in 2007 (Clarke 2008). The government inquiry exonerated Haneef and in 2010 he was awarded a substantial compensation settlement from the Commonwealth Government. The Hon. Mr Clarke QC led the inquiry and he made two recommendations relevant to this chapter. One was that dead time provisions in the *Crimes Act* 2014 *(Cth)* should be amended to reduce the total period a person can be held in police custody regardless of whether they are being questioned or not. This was followed by the government in Schedule 3 of the *National Security Legislation Amendment Act* 2010 *(Cth)*. The other was that an independent monitor be established to review Australia's increasing number of counter-terrorism laws. This latter issue was addressed with enactment of the *Independent National Security Legislation Monitor Act 2010 (Cth)*, which created an independent reviewer of Australia's counter-terrorism legislation. While Rudd's amendments implemented many recommendations arising from the Clarke Inquiry, it also gave new powers enabling police and ASIO's intelligence collection capabilities. For example, Schedule 4 allows police or intelligence officers to enter a premise without a warrant in an emergency related to a terrorism offence, where material is located that is believed to present a risk to public health and safety. In Schedule 3, ASIO was given the power to detain and interrogate individuals who may be suspected of involvement in any terrorism offence for up to seven days to collect unspecified intelligence.

In June 2010, Julia Gillard became prime minister. The Gillard Government soon became pre-occupied with other security issues such as illegal maritime immigration and organised crime (see Pratt, this volume). There were no new counter-terrorism/intelligence-related laws passed during her tenure, but in 2009 the Organized Crime Strategic Framework strongly extended Kevin Rudd's expanded approach to declaring organised crime was a significant threat to national security like terrorism or WMD. The Organized Crime Strategic Framework was also focused on improving coordination of national criminal intelligence collection across federal and state agencies, which remains incomplete (Walsh 2012).

After Rudd replaced Gillard as prime minister prior to the 2013 election, there were no new significant legislative or changes to national security policy and intelligence collection. This was largely because the Labor Government was distracted by political survival and migrant smuggling via Indonesia. The Rudd/Gillard/Rudd Governments were also marked by slight reductions in expenditure on national security and intelligence following the 2008 global financial crisis (Maley 2013). The other significant intelligence policy issue unfolding during the Rudd/Gillard years was WikiLeaks (Walsh 2011a, 210–218), which at the time involved the largest disclosure of classified information on the internet. WikiLeaks helped raise public, policy and political debates on what is legitimate intelligence collection, surveillance and secrecy in ways not previously seen in Australia.

The Abbott Government (September 2013–September 2015)

In September 2013 the conservative-liberal Abbott Government came to power. One of its main election slogans was to 'stop the boats' referring to the growing number of boats with asylum seekers coming via Indonesia. It was initially unclear how the new government's national security and intelligence policy, particularly on counter-terrorism, would differ from the former Labor Government's. However, the Abbott Government's policy and legislative national security and intelligence agenda soon became characterised by three significant pieces of federal legislation: the *National Security Legislation Amendment Act* 2014, the *Counter Terrorism Legislation Amendment (Foreign Fighters) Act* 2014 and the *Telecommunications (Interception and Access) Amendment (Data Retention) Act* 2014. Although each piece of legislation has been aimed at slightly different objectives they all represent a significant enhancement of Australia's national security and intelligence collection capabilities—arguably not seen since the Howard Government in 2007. These acts represent the continuation of the common legislative theme running since the Howard Government of building a more proactive intelligence collection capability. More importantly, they represent greater powers granted across all intelligence agencies, including ASIO, the AFP, the Australian Signals Directorate (ASD) and the Australian Secret Intelligence Service (ASIS).[3]

As discussed earlier, WikiLeaks had already precipitated a greater political and community debate in Australia about the role of intelligence, surveillance and privacy. The June 2013 Snowden leaks also had a catalytic effect on this debate, particularly when it was revealed the Australian intelligence community was spying on the wife of the president of

---

[3] The ASD or Australian Signals Directorate is Australia's sigint collection agency. Until May 2013, it was known as DSD or the Defence Signals Directorate. The government changed its name to reflect a desire to see it have a more 'whole of government' function in Australia's national security beyond the defence portfolio. Its Canadian counterpart is the Communications Security Establishment Canada (CSEC). ASIS or the Australian Secret Intelligence Service is Australia's foreign intelligence collection agency. It does not have an exact equivalent in the Canadian intelligence community.

Indonesia and on behalf of the National Security Agency (NSA) during US-Indonesian trade talks. Three major bills were introduced against an increased public awareness of Australia's intelligence capacities and extensive debate over the scope of legally sanctioned surveillance activity. In the background, the growth in lone wolf terrorist threats posed by the Islamic State significantly challenged the Abbott Government, and drove the implementation of several additional legislative measures to further the intelligence collection capabilities of key Australian law enforcement agencies.

More people are interested in the privacy/human rights impacts of new national security and intelligence measures than ever before (Walsh and Miller 2015). Against this increased interest in the activities of intelligence agencies, the government has had mixed success 'selling' the need for new legislative measures, including the enhanced retention of online data by internet service providers. One of the many controversial inclusions in both the national security legislation amendment and the data retention legislation has been the increase of penalties from two to ten years of imprisonment for the use of communications by whistleblowers and journalists. For example, Schedule 6 (Protection of Information) of the *National Security Legislation Act* sought to enhance the protection of intelligence from future insider leaks like Snowden, by creating two new offence provisions and updating existing ones, including increasing penalties already stipulated in other acts such as the *Intelligence Services Act* 2001 and the *ASIO Act* 1979.

Similarly, earlier drafts of the new data retention laws raised concerns from journalists over warrantless access to their metadata by police and ASIO. Journalists became concerned about freedom of the press and particularly protection of sources leaking national security information for publication. The government yielded a little on journalists as a special case under the bill, by requiring ASIO and policing agencies obtain a journalist information warrant before accessing a journalist's metadata. Though the provisions will not allow a journalist to have forewarning that a warrant has been sought, media companies will only be able to appeal via a public interest advocate appointed by the prime minister and not by formal legal representation or an independent court examining the merits of the warrant application (Hurst 2015).

The *National Security Legislation Amendment Act* 2014 also increased the powers of ASIO to issue warrants independently of the minister and Director-General of ASIO, if it is reasonably suspected a person is engaged in activities prejudicial to national security. ASIO can also issue warrants if it is considered the collection of intelligence will substantially assist national security. This is a lower threshold for issuing a warrant than under the general criminal law and underscores a greater emphasis on enhancing the flexibility of ASIO to proactively collect intelligence. Schedule 3 of the legislation (Protection for Special Intelligence Operations) also allows limited liability against civil actions or criminal prosecution against ASIO personnel involved in special intelligence conduct that might involve criminal activity.

The *Foreign Fighters Act* 2014 is also significant for amending multiple counter-terrorism, intelligence, law enforcement and security laws. The chief extension of intelligence collection capabilities is located in Division 2, which deals with delayed notification of search warrants. These powers enable the AFP to covertly enter premises for a search without producing a warrant, which can be extended for up to 12 months. Other key parts of the legislation strengthen the government's counter-terrorism policy rather than the specific roles of intelligence agencies.

The *Foreign Fighters Act* gives the foreign minister the authority to list 'declared areas' (e.g. war zones within foreign countries such as Syria, but not the entire country). It is an offence to enter or remain in one of these areas unless for prescribed reasons outlined in the legislation, including a bona fide family visit, representing the Australian Government, journalism or working for a humanitarian aid agency. The other controversial inclusion is the additional provision for 'advocating terrorism,' which includes the somewhat vague term of being 'reckless' in inciting or advocating terrorism. The government had in mind radicalised individuals, who use religious gatherings or the internet to incite others to advocate violence. This section raises considerable civil liberty concerns as to how it will be applied to free speech more broadly.

Finally, the *Telecommunications (Interception and Access) Amendment (Data Retention) Act* 2014 is a significant strengthening of the Australian intelligence community's proactive intelligence collection capabilities. It requires telecommunications providers to retain data for a mandatory two-year period. The Act stipulates that intelligence agencies would still require a warrant to access the content of phone calls, internet browsing content or social media postings, though clearly there remain concerns over the privacy implications associated with personally identifiable information that can be obtained through metadata.

An Overview of Canadian Policy and Counter-Terrorism Legislation Since 9/11

Detailed comparisons of Australian and Canadian counter-terrorism laws and policy relating particularly to intelligence collection can be found elsewhere (see Rudner 2007; Farson and Teeple 2014). However, a cursory review of Canada's legislative approach shows some broad similarities to policy and legislative measures adopted in Australia. After 9/11, Canada also made a substantial fiscal commitment to public safety and intelligence. The December 2001 federal budget committed CAD $7.7 billion over five years to counter-terrorism, critical infrastructure protection and internal security (Rudner 2007, 473–490). Interestingly, Ottawa devolved most domestic security intelligence and coordination functions away from the Privy Council Office down to the Department of Public Safety and Emergency Preparedness Canada, while in Australia security intelligence functions and coordination were strengthened at the national level through the Department of Prime Minister and Cabinet.

Shortly after 9/11 Canada broadly followed the same legislative response as the Australian Government to the increased threat from terrorism. Canada also enacted and amended legislation that clearly defined the act of terrorism, criminalised such acts and proscribed groups involved in terrorism. Additionally, Canada's *Anti-Terrorism Act* 2001 compelled those with information about possible terrorist offences to cooperate with authorities by introducing compulsory investigative hearings without protection against self-incrimination. Under this provision an individual summoned before an investigative hearing cannot refuse to appear or refuse to answer questions. Failure to do so results in a penalty of up to one-year imprisonment. While Canada had earlier introduced control orders in the *Criminal Code* 1985, Ottawa adopted extended detention with a preventative purpose in the *Criminal Code* via the *Anti-Terrorism Act* 2001. However, these provisions expired under a sunset clause in March 2007 (McDonald 2007, 113) unlike Australia's powers conferred on ASIO that were extended to 2016. While preventative detention under reasonable suspicion has expired under Canadian law, the *Anti-Terrorism Act* 2001 still contains a provision "whereby a provincial judge can impose a control order on someone for a 12-month period if there are reasonable grounds to fear that the person will commit a terrorism offence" (Roach 2007, 72).

Canada has also enacted a process akin to 'control orders' through its immigration security certificate. This procedure has used intelligence collection (sometimes not well as seen in the *Charkaoui* and *Harkat* cases) to apprehend and detain people suspected of involvement with terrorism pending their deportation (Walsh 2011a, 221). Most people detained under security certificates were approved for release by the Supreme Court of Canada though in some cases have been released under strict conditions.

Another broad common theme between Australian and Canadian intelligence and counter-terrorism laws has been a modernisation of 'old acts,' which were drafted largely in the Cold War era (e.g. *ASIO Act* 1979, *CSIS Act* 1984) with very different threats in mind. This modernisation has been incremental, albeit somewhat reactionary rather than systematic. The other major similarity was the development in Canberra and Ottawa of an early threat detection philosophy. This has resulted in the proactive application of legislation and policy to facilitate early intelligence collection, analysis and disruption of threats. However, in both capitals the policy response to 9/11 and the growing terrorism threat thereafter was often political, reactive and not always proportionate to the actual threats in each homeland.

A key difference between Australia and Canada's counter-terrorism legislative response is the volume and speed of enacting legislation since 9/11. Roach argues:

> the degree of legislative activism is striking compared even to the UK active agenda and much greater than the pace of legislation in the US and Canada. Australia's hyper-legislation strained the ability of the parliamentary opposition and civil society to keep up let alone provide effective opposition to the relentless legislative output. (Roach 2011, 301)

Large majority governments and a sympathetic electorate after the 2002 Bali bombing and 2004 Australian Embassy bombings in Jakarta facilitated the volume and speed in which counter-terrorism legislation could be passed in Australia by successive Howard Governments (1996–2007). In contrast, in the first five years after 9/11 Canadian citizens were largely unaffected by large-scale terrorist attacks and successive minority governments in both 2004 and 2006 elections did not have the political capital to pursue the degree of legislative and policy activism seen in Australia (also see Forcese, this volume). However, more recent signs following two lone wolf terrorism attacks in Ontario and Quebec in 2014 indicate Canada's counter-terrorism policy and legislative agenda is heading for major change not seen since the *Anti-Terror Act* of 2001. The conservative Harper Government introduced a major revamp of anti-terrorism laws partly in response to these attacks. For example, in 2015 a new C-51 bill was passed in the House of Commons that amends several of Canada's intelligence and security-related acts including the *CSIS Act*, the *Secure Air Travel Act*, the *Criminal Code* and the *Immigration and Refugee Protection Act*.

Part 1 of the 2015 amendments enhances existing information sharing arrangements amongst Canadian government departments in order to protect against activities that may undermine national security. Part 2 of the *Secure Air Travel Act* seeks to enhance security relating to transportation and to prevent air travel for the purpose of engaging in acts of terrorism. Part 4 amends the *CSIS Act* permitting CSIS to take measures within and outside Canada to reduce threats to national security, including measures authorised by the Federal Court. Part 4 also outlines enhanced reporting measures for CSIS on operational activities to reduce specific threats to Canada, including a requirement to report on the number of warrants issued and a description of measures taken under warrants during a specified reporting period.

The emphasis on information sharing in C-51 is somewhat vague and concerning as information sharing protocols and coordination issues were arguably largely resolved immediately after 9/11. It is difficult to know just how this legislation will further improve any outstanding information sharing and coordination issues. In some respects, legislation alone cannot fix organisational systems, including information communication technology and cultural issues (Walsh 2011a). Information sharing cannot be resolved by legislation alone and this remains an issue in other Five Eyes countries despite enacting legislation. Former Canadian Supreme Court Judge John Major has suggested that a national security adviser might be necessary to intelligence sharing and coordination. This would be similar to the proposal adopted in Australia under the previous Rudd Labor Government's appointment of a national security advisor to more centrally coordinate national security policy and intelligence processes.

Other parts of C-51 mirror legislative changes enacted recently by the Abbott Government in Australia. For example, the *Secure Air Travel Act* provisions of C-51 relating to preventing air travel for the purpose of engaging in acts of terrorism are similar to Schedules 1 and 3 of Australia's *Foreign Fighters Act*. Similarly, amendments to the *CSIS Act* detailed in Part 4 (C-51) include similar provisions on warrants and reporting requirements found in amendments of the *ASIO Act* made through both the *Foreign Fighters* and *Data Retention Acts*. Finally, Part 3 amends the *Criminal Code* to lower the threshold of how terrorism offences are now defined under Canadian law including the provision of "knowingly advocating or promoting the commission of terrorism offences in general" (Canada *Criminal Code* 1985, 96). This enables a judge to order the seizure of terrorist propaganda. Such provisions are similar to advocating terrorism through 'reckless speech' that results in another conducting a terrorism offence under amendments to the *Australian Criminal Code Act* 1995 enacted through the *Foreign Fighters Act*.

Australian National Security Intelligence Challenges

This section identifies major legislative and policy challenges faced by Australian and Canadian policymakers as they attempt to provide intelligence agencies with a more flexible intelligence collection tool kit, while upholding privacy and human rights of their citizens.

The first challenge for intelligence agencies remains ensuring all personnel fully understand how to use the new suite of legislative powers and intelligence processes including those related to information collection and sharing during terrorist investigations. Looking back at the

Haneef (Australia), *Arar* and *Charkaoui* (Canada) cases, agencies in both Australia and Canada since 9/11 have clearly not always understood how to operationalise new powers and procedures, leading to a failure to use legislation correctly.[4] This in turn results in insufficient intelligence to support admissible evidence in court or the wrongful arrest and detention of suspects. As the legislative and policy response for intelligence collectors becomes more complex, being able operationalise new powers effectively, legally and ethically presents an ongoing challenge for Australian and Canadian intelligence and law enforcement agencies.

The second challenge arising from Canberra and Ottawa's counterterrorism responses has been the ad hoc approach to reviewing legislation. In Australia, in particular, parliamentary, judicial and independent review of specific legislation, while improving, has been patchy and needs addressing as the legislative and policy environment for intelligence collection becomes more complex. The parliamentary extension of sunset clauses and the overall judicial and operational effectiveness of legislation require a more strategic and independent (from parliament) review approach. Additionally, regular independent policy and legal review mechanisms will need to consider on an ongoing basis how the principle of proportionality is being applied by intelligence agencies to ensure that intelligence collection methods allowed under legislation remain proportionate to the offence.

Similarly, reviewers need to evaluate how legal requirements such as 'reasonable suspicion' and 'probable cause' are being used by intelligence and law enforcement agencies under the suite of new, more flexible and

---

[4] There is insufficient space to provide detailed discussion of both the *Arar* and *Charkaoui* cases. In brief, Maher Arar was detained in the USA on his way home to Canada in 2002 based on information provided to US officials from Canadian authorities. The USA then renditioned Arar back to Syria (the country of his birth), where he was again detained and tortured for a year by the Syrian Military Intelligence Agency. The *Arar* case demonstrated several procedural problems during Arar's investigation in Canada particularly with sharing intelligence and its accuracy (see Walsh 2011, 154–155). Adil Charkaoui's case related to an adverse security finding against him under Canada's security certificate legislation (*Immigration and Refugee Protection Act* 2001), which enables usually the Ministers for Public Safety and Immigration to arrest, detain and eventually deport a person named in a security certificate, if the ministers have reasonable grounds to believe a person is a danger to national security. In 2009, a federal court declared the security certificate against Charkaoui null and void as the government failed to meet its burden of proof once it removed disputed material gathered by wiretaps (see Walsh 2011, 230–231).

proactive intelligence collection methodologies which are enshrined in legislation discussed earlier. The examination of both legal requirements combined with ethical considerations of the right to life and privacy are also important considerations for a comprehensive approach to review (Walsh and Miller 2015).

The issue of intelligence oversight and accountability transcends assessments about whether specific legislation is appropriate, effective, proportionate or safeguards human rights. A strengthened approach to reviewing intelligence-related counter-terrorism legislation is insufficient to gauging the extent to which the Australian and Canadian intelligence agencies are working effectively in the post-9/11 environment. For example, the growing reliance on data mining and analytics by intelligence agencies needs to be assessed on an ongoing basis given some of the more invasive aspects of data retention acts passed in Australia, the UK and the USA (Walsh and Miller 2015). However, since 9/11 much has been written about how intelligence agencies in Australia and Canada are effectively responding to new security threats (see Walsh 2011a; Farson and Teeple 2014). The same question can be posed about whether the multiple oversight and accountability institutions and mechanisms established many decades ago in both countries remain equipped to deal with recent legislative and policy activism surrounding intelligence collection (Walsh 2011a; Walby and Anais 2012).

Australia's oversight mechanisms have grown relatively slowly since the end of the Cold War, though now include a number of important institutions, including the Inspector-General for Intelligence and Security (IGIS), the Commonwealth Ombudsman, the Parliamentary Joint Committee of Intelligence and Security (PJCIS), ad hoc independent inquiries and various forms of ministerial oversight. The IGIS typically has been the backbone of independent review of the Australian intelligence community, though increasingly amendments or new legislation have brought to the forefront the role of other oversight and accountability mechanisms.

Most recently, the PJCIS has become more effective and bipartisan in its analysis of new counter-terrorism bills (e.g. the foreign fighters and data retention bills) as demonstrated by government and opposition party members collaborating to develop workable recommendations. The Rudd Government also appointed an independent national security legislation monitor in April 2011 to review counter-terrorism legislation. However, in Australia most existing oversight and account-ability mechanisms are legacies of history and developed in a pre-9/11 security world where threats were less diffuse and transnational in nature. Without a major review of existing oversight and accountability mecha-nisms, Australia could end up with a similar fragmented approach like in the USA, where oversight and accountability seem to be at every level across intelligence agencies and communities yet ironically does not lead consistently to good oversight (Walsh 2011a).

For example, the increased role of the Commonwealth Ombudsman to inspect agencies accessing, storing, using and destroying metadata under the enhanced data retention laws supplements the role of the IGIS in reviewing intelligence activity. The increased overlap of discrete oversight processes appears to demonstrate little reflection by successive governments of whether such institutions amount to an enhanced or fragmented oversight capability.

A final point arising from Australia's counter-terrorism legislative agenda is the impact this may be having on the broader capacity of agen-cies within the intelligence community to collect and share the greater volumes of intelligence. Further investigation is required to assess the impact on the capabilities of agencies being monitored centrally by governments in Canberra and Ottawa. In Australia such an investiga-tion could be conducted by IGIS to evaluate what issues may arise from increasingly proactive intelligence collection legislation and how are they being managed and coordinated along with the broader national security policymaking processes of government.

The Snowden leaks made clear that both Australia's and Canada's signal intelligence (signit) agencies (ASD, CSEC) have spied on friendly coun-tries such as Indonesia and Brazil for economic intelligence/espionage (Walsh and Miller 2015; Farson and Teeple 2014, 63). Several similar revelations from Snowden about the NSA intercepting communications of the leaders of close allies such as German Chancellor Angela Merkel's cell phone also show poor judgement. Some of the leaks from Snowden suggest that Canberra and Ottawa may need to reinvigorate their national security and intelligence coordination by strengthening institutions and the remit of national security advisors. In Australia, this would mean strengthening the National Intelligence Coordination Committee and elevating the influence, role and remit of the national security advisor to monitor and coordinate security intelligence collection policies and procedures across the intelligence community.

It is unlikely that Canberra and Ottawa would ever categorically rule out spying on other allies and their leaders for either economic or national security matters. However, governments do need to develop stricter policy and risk management guidelines, including cabinet authority for future communication interceptions of political leaders who are close allies (Walsh and Miller 2015, 20). The biggest difference between Australia and Canada's oversight and accountability system has been the absence in Canada of a dedicated parliamentary capacity to scrutinise the security and intelligence functions of government including one with access to classified information. In 2015, a private member's Bill C-622 to establish an intelligence and security committee of parliament was rejected by the government.[5] Nevertheless, Canada's Security Intelligence Review Committee (SIRC) is almost the equivalent to Australia's Inspector-General of Intelligence and Security (IGIS).[6]

While it seems the Canadian public has been relatively supportive of C-51, there is concern that the new Bill highlights gaps in oversight mechanisms. For example, respected Canadian intelligence scholar Wesley Wark has suggested the reestablishment of the independent committee on intelligence and security that existed from 2005 to 2012 to advise the prime minister on how to learn from intelligence failures and monitor future trends (Wark 2013). Wark also notes that Canada's last national security statement was in 2004. A new national security statement by the Trudeau Government could address concerns about the impact of the *Anti-Terrorism Act* (Bill C-51) on Canada's intelligence community and how this will be managed, coordinated and overseen.

---

[5] In June 2016, however, the new Trudeau Government introduced Bill C-22 into parliament to create a new national security and intelligence committee.

[6] There are some differences in the mandate and operations of Canada's SIRC and IGIS in Australia. SIRC only has review and audit responsibilities for CSIS while Australia's Inspector-General is responsible for reviewing all agencies in the Australian Intelligence Community. SIRC tends to do historical, 'retrospective' reviews while IGIS does regular inspections seeking to remedy an issue before it requires a more major intervention.

While the administrative, judicial and human rights impact of Australia's *Foreign Fighters Act* and Canada's *Anti-Terrorism* Act 2015 remain unclear, previous counter-terrorism legislation suggest these issues will present numerous challenges to intelligence agencies and the community once they become operationalised. However, it is also clear some of the new provisions will encounter judicial and political difficulties once operationalised. For example, in the no-fly provisions contained in the *Foreign Fighters Act* and in C-51, the governments of Canada and Australia give considerable scope to reject appeals from people placed on a no-fly list. In C-51 ministers and judges may draw on any confidential intelligence or evidence without disclosing this information to the person's legal counsel if it is deemed injurious to national security or endangered the safety of any person.

Similarly, Part 2 (Appeals 16(6) (e)) of C-51 shows that anything can be received as evidence that in the judge's opinion is reliable or appropriate even if it is inadmissible in a conventional trial. This suggests that intelligence can be used as untested evidence in formal judicial decisions, which could result in miscarriages of justice. It is unclear whether or how an independent body would review such decisions outside the conventional legal appeals process. It is likely such forms of review would remain confidential to preserve the value of such intelligence.

While the *Anti-Terrorism Act* 2015 has the tripwire of Canada's *Charter of Rights* (see Jochelson and Doerksen, this volume), Australia does not have an equivalent protection. In contrast, relevant international law, such as the International Covenant on Civil and Political rights, is often cited in Australia in new counter-terrorism laws, though it is obviously less binding. As Australian constitutional lawyer George Williams suggests, a bill of rights may arguably provide a 'yardstick' against which to assess the making of anti-terror laws, particularly providing human rights protection by post-enactment analysis (Williams 2011, 1170). However, the now former Abbott conservative Government started to recognise growing concern in some sectors of the community about the additional intelligence collection and counter-terrorism powers of its three key legislative reforms. For example, the *Foreign Fighters Act* specifically includes a role for the Independent National Security Legislation Monitor to review key amendments to various acts (*ASIO Act*, *Crimes Act* and *Criminal Code*) by September 2017.

Conclusion

This chapter discussed how the flurry of counter-terrorism and intelligence-related reform legislation post-9/11 has impacted on intelligence collection by the Australian intelligence community. The cumulative impact of such a hyper-reform environment on both Australia's intelligence agencies and the broader community remains to be seen. The critical questions are: whether Australia is building a more 'fit for purpose' intelligence community for the evolving threat, and the potential impacts this is having on Australia's liberal democratic values and institutions. As the threat environment and the policy response to it only becomes more complex, one measure that might help address these questions may be a systematic 'root and branch' review of Australia's intelligence overview and accountability mechanisms given that many of these are artefacts of history—developed in a pre-9/11 security world where threats were less diffuse and transnational. At this stage, it remains unclear whether the re-elected Turnbull-led Government will see such a review as a policy priority.

References

Clarke, John. 2008. *Clarke Inquiry into the Case of Dr Mohamed Haneef*. Canberra: Attorney-General's Department.

Farson, Stuart, and Nancy Teeple. 2014. Increasing Canada's Foreign Intelligence Capability: Is it a Dead Issue? *Intelligence and National Security* 30(1): 47–76.

Flood, Philip. 2004. *Report of the Inquiry into Australian Intelligence Agencies*. Canberra: Commonwealth of Australia.

Hoffman, Bruce. 2002. Rethinking Terrorism and Counter Terrorism Since 9/11. *Studies in Conflict and Terrorism* 25(5): 305–316.

Hurst, Daniel. 2015. Australia's New Improved Data Retention Laws: How Will They Work? *The Guardian* (Australian Edition), March 19.

Lacqueur, Walter. 1999. *The New Terrorism*. London: Phoenix Press.

Lowenthal, Mark M. 2012. *From Secrets to Policy*. 5th ed. Thousand Oaks, CA: CQ Press.

Maley, Paul. 2013. Austerity for Spies a 'Disgrace' says Labor MP Anthony Byrne. *The Australian*, May 28.

McDonald, Geoff. 2007. Control Orders and Preventative Detention-Why Alarm is Misguided. In *Law and Liberty in the War on Terror*, eds. A. Lynch, E. MacDonald, and G. Williams, 106–115. Annandale: The Federation Press.

Mullins, Sam. 2013. 'Global Jihad': The Canadian Experience. *Terrorism and Political Violence* 25(5): 734–776.

Roach, Kent. 2007. A Comparison of Australian and Canadian Anti-Terrorism Law. *University of NSW Law Journal* 30(1): 53–85.

———. 2011. *The 9/11 Effect: Comparative Counter-Terrorism*. Cambridge: Cambridge University Press.

Rudner, Martin. 2007. Canada's CSE, Signals Intelligence and Counter-Terrorism. *Intelligence and National Security* 22(4): 473–490.

The Commonwealth of Australia. 1995. *Criminal Code Act*. Canberra.

The Parliament of Canada. 1985. *Canada Consolidation Criminal Code. RSC., c. C-46*. Ottawa.

The US Senate Select Committee on Intelligence. 2014. *Committee Study of the Central Intelligence Agency's Detention and Interrogation Program*. Washington, DC.

The 9/11 Commission Report. 2004. *Final Report of the National Commission on Terrorist Attacks Upon the United States*. Washington, DC: US Government Printing Office.

Walby, Kevin, and Seantel Anais. 2012. Communications Security Establishment Canada (CSEC), Structures of Secrecy, and Ministerial Authorization after September 11. *Canadian Journal of Law and Society* 27(3): 363–380.

Walsh, Patrick F. 2011a. *Intelligence and Intelligence Analysis*. Abingdon: Routledge.

——— 2011b. Intelligence and National Security Issues. In *Policing in Practice*, eds. V. Herrington and P. Birch, 109–127. South Yarra: Palgrave Macmillan.

——— 2012. *Submission and Testimony to Inquiry into the Use of Criminal Intelligence* (Joint Parliamentary Committee on Law Enforcement). Canberra: Australian Parliament.

Walsh, Patrick F., and Seumas Miller. 2015. Rethinking 'Five Eyes' Security Intelligence Collection Policies and Practice Post Snowden. *Intelligence and National Security* 31: 1–24.

Wark, Wesley. 2013. How To Reclaim the National Security Agenda. *The Globe and Mail*, October 11, A15.

Wilkinson, Paul. 2001. *Terrorism vs. Democracy: The Liberal State Response*. London: Frank Cass.

Williams, George. 2011. A Decade of Australian Anti-Terror Laws. *Melbourne University Law Review* 35(3): 1137–1151.

White, Margaret. 2012. A Judicial Perspective—The Making of Preventative Detention Orders. In *Law and Liberty in the War on Terror*, eds. A. Lynch, E. MacDonald, and G. Williams, 116–127. Annandale: The Federation Press.

4

The Supreme Court of Canada Presents: The Surveillant Charter and the Judicial Creation of Police Powers in Canada

Richard Jochelson and Mark Doerksen

Introduction: Creating Police Powers, the Canadian Judicial Way

Instead of understanding the *Canadian Charter of Rights and Freedoms* as a document of fundamental rights and freedoms, one can view the text as a framework for administering surveillance in service of social conditions at a moment in time. Its flexibility and elasticity in the hands of the Canadian judiciary provide ample opportunities for liberal legal conceptions of rights to be challenged. Over time, this elasticity can be seen in judicial interpretations that seem to have moved further away from the

R. Jochelson (✉)
University of Manitoba, Winnipeg, MB, Canada

M. Doerksen
Department of Sociology and Anthropology, Concordia University, Montreal, QC, Canada

© The Author(s) 2016
R. Lippert et al. (eds.), *National Security, Surveillance and Terror*,
DOI 10.1007/978-3-319-43243-4_4

positivistic conception of idealised rights claimed by the *Charter's* most passionate supporters. In this chapter, we discuss how the Supreme Court of Canada has become one of the principal instruments of administering police powers in Canada since the advent of the *Charter*. Indeed, the Supreme Court has produced a multitude of decisions over the last few decades that have generated police powers, using the *Charter* as support for its decision-making. The reframing of the Court's role as generative of police powers suggests that understanding policing and deployment of security by the state in Canada necessarily requires a study of the Canadian judiciary, a study that is overdue. A secure state includes a commitment to surveillance, and in turn understanding state surveillance practices provides insight into the nature of security within a nation (Jochelson et al. 2014). This in turn provides insight into the nature of security by unpacking the sweep of information-gathering techniques used by the government and its agents. If surveillance is the means by which civil liberties are given content, one can hypothesise that a state makes security a priority in its domestic policy in addition to its obvious genesis as a reaction to foreign-policy concerns (Jochelson et al. 2014).

We draw from the surveillance studies literature to help identify the proliferation of police surveillance projects in recent years (Bloss 2008; Jochelson 2009a, b). The judiciary acts in concert with this proliferation and in some contexts contribute to it (Bloss 2008; Jochelson 2009a, b; Wilkinson 2009). The rationales that underlie surveillance are risk-averse and precautionary logics; these in turn foster the development of an infrastructure and bureaucracy that supports surveillance (Agamben 2005; Rasmussen 2004). Studies emerged which focused on the extra-legal spaces of securitisation, focusing on municipal workspaces and corporate policing (Lippert and Walby 2012). Haggerty and Ericson (2000, 606) identify a quantitative increase in surveillance in the Western world, technologies that coalesce into a meta-system of surveillance practices known as a surveillant assemblage (see also Murphy and Anderson, this volume). If one envisages a surveillant assemblage on a broad scale (as a meta-assemblage, especially given the intermeshing of security responses by nation states, for example, to precautions against threats of terror), it seems clear that assemblages traverse nation states, especially when their governance structures are similar and their fears of insecurity apposite.

This chapter explores surveillance through juridical countenancing of police powers in Canada, though clearly other jurisdictions have also seen expansion of police powers, through more traditional means. In Australia, police powers are delineated by an amalgamation of exhaustive legislative powers and to a lesser extent, some implicit conceptions of due process related to the role of the judiciary in the *Australian Constitution* (Title III). The *Australian Constitution* contains little in the way of a bill of rights to limit police powers. It does contain some provision for due process to a limited extent though. It contains, for example, express rights for a jury trial for serious offences (*Australian Constitution* 1900, Sect. 80). Constitutionalism in Australia connotes a limited sense of due process in comparison to the delineated protections contained within the Canadian *Charter* (McHugh 2001). Though some of the Australian states have enacted due process statutes (e.g. Victoria's *Charter* 2006), their effect is not as a "supreme laws of the land"; these statutes are not given the same primacy as constitutional documents. If one is seeking out constitutional supremacy for civil liberties in Australia, one finds limited protections in the *Australian Constitution*; for example, the *Constitution* includes implicit rights to legal representation. More particular substantive protections from police powers have yet to be accepted by the High Court although conceptions of natural justice colour Australian constitutional interpretation (McHugh 2001). Implicit in conceptions of fundamental justice, the High Court has begun to crystallise some protections against arbitrary state power. McHugh writes that cases such as *Chu Kheng Lim v. Minister for Immigration* 1992 and *Kruger v. Commonwealth* 1997 provide:

> a foundation for the conclusion that, except in limited circumstances, the detention of citizens against their will may be constitutionally permissible only when determined by a court and only when the *determination conform*s to the traditional procedures and safeguards of the judicial process. (McHugh 2001)

Yet, the majority of police powers in Australia are delineated in state-specific legislation such as the *Law Enforcement (Powers and Responsibilities) Act* 2002 (NSW, hereafter LEPRA). This legislation saw significant expansion in the passing of the *Law Enforcement (Powers and*

Responsibilities) Amendment (Arrest without Warrant) Act 2013 (Dennis and Chambers 2014; Sanders 2015). These legislated powers reflected an expansion of police use of technologies and precautionary practices (e.g. sniffer dog searches, investigative detention, reasonable suspicion standards for detention, and lower arrest standards) as well as codification of more traditional police powers (arrest protocols, investigative powers, search powers). What distinguishes these powers and the protections from police powers in Canada is the absence of constitutionalism in most instances. The LEPRA, for example, provides that if its terms conflict with other legislation, the LEPRA shall be paramount (LEPRA, Sect. 6). Yet, this conflict provision has less effect than due process protections in supreme constitutional documents such as the *Canadian Charter*. Interestingly, police powers in Canada, while found in legislation and cases, have not been subject to an exhaustive legislative effort like in Australian states. Instead, in many cases, the Supreme Court of Canada has been left to interpret the limits of police powers using the wording of the *Charter*, and, in some cases, the Court has created police powers within the lacunae of the written and common law. While the proliferation of police powers in Canada seems to have developed at a similar pace to Australia in recent years, Canada is unique in the way its Supreme Court has created and simultaneously constitutionalised police powers.

We argue that the Supreme Court of Canada's decisions in the area of police powers have been generally supportive of expanded police powers and that these decisions have coalesced into the skeletal infrastructure of a surveillant assemblage. Further, this body of decisions indicates a Supreme Court that sees the *Charter* as generative of police powers. Viewed this way, the *Canadian Charter of Rights and Freedoms* can be viewed as a charter of surveillance. A surveillant charter is supportive of Canadian security practices, because inherent in approaches to keeping nations secure are conceptions of large- and small-scale information-gathering operations. Approaches to policing that adopt such practices may be reflective of a nation state that has internalised security as an organising logic, and may provide a counterargument to the suppositions that civil liberties are protections for those who reside within the nation (Jochelson et al. 2014).

To make this argument, in this chapter we examine claims principally in the search and seizure case law that the Supreme Court has developed during the life of the *Charter*. The search and seizure jurisprudence of the Supreme Court of Canada interrogates the scope of Sect. 8 of the *Charter*—the right to be free from unreasonable search and seizure. There are four jurisprudential techniques that the Court has used to expand surveillant possibilities we investigate. First, the Court has developed extensive threshold legal tests to police which citizens may have access to protection under Sect. 8 of the *Charter*. Second, the performance of the accused on these threshold tests determines the degree of protection an accused is provided under the *Charter*. Related to our second claim, the degree of protection provided in these cases of underperformance on threshold issues results in a newly articulated standard of 'protection' created by the Court. Finally, in cases where the Court is unable to use this existing framework to resolve constitutionality of search and seizure problems it faces, it resorts to its common law authority to generate new police powers that it constructs as constitutional and *Charter* proof. One can see the surveillant effects of these Court decisions in the sheer number of adjudications reported over the last ten years. The discussion leads one to deduce that the *Charter* serves a surveillant purpose as opposed to providing protection from the state's long arm.

Theorising Surveillance, the State, and the *Charter*

Haggerty and Ericson move beyond Foucault by drawing from the work of Deleuze and Guattari (1987) to describe an assemblage which consists of a "multiplicity of heterogeneous objects, whose unity comes solely from the fact that these items function together, that they 'work' together as a functional entity" (Haggerty and Ericson 2000, 607). It is in this claim, however, that we encounter a difficulty with assessing law as part of the assemblage.

According to Haggerty and Ericson (2000, 607), assemblages are "part of the state form" but that one should not confuse this form with those "traditional apparatuses of governmental rule studied by political scientists." Rather, the state form seeks to create "bounded physical and cognitive spaces and introduces processes designed to capture flows to 'striate the space over which it reigns'" (Haggerty and Ericson 2000, 608; Deleuze and Guattari 1987, 385).

Judge-made law under the *Charter* might be seen as a traditional apparatus of the state form, but for reasons below, we view them as worthy of study as state forms (distinct from traditional apparatuses nonetheless). This is largely because the implementation of the *Charter* in Canada did more than create the myth of rights held against the government in Canada. Enactment of the *Charter* created hegemonic discourse, but it was left to the Court to account for both this discourse and competing social discourses brought before it. Thus, a type of parallel and independent sovereignty for the Supreme Court became part of the Canadian legislative landscape in 1982 at the inception of the *Charter*. The Court was tasked with guarding the *Constitution*, and the delegated function created something in the way of a novel development of more than the usual judicial independence, which most Western nations assert. Rather, a type of judicial sovereignty emerged, charged with governing an ever-changing social realm via strategies of rights implementation (Jochelson et al. 2014, 17).

This guardianship amounts, in the criminal procedure area, to be the policing of policing. In cases where enumerated rights are contested between an individual and the state police, the Court must determine the boundaries of police powers in these interstitial spaces. These cases where previous law does not govern due to lack of precedent provide a moment of contact between the Court and the social world, as the Court attempts to (re)iterate its vision of the appropriate balance between police powers and a citizen's freedom from state intrusion. Indeed, it is within these spaces where rights, which an average Canadian would assume were guaranteed, are reproduced and reassembled into something contingent and unpredictable. This destabilising of the 'promises' made by the *Charter* document creates a 'rights holder' (an ideal liberal subject) who is no longer equivalent with the individual who was charged at the case's inception. The individual's protections are more opaque and citizens facing the state in future instances are left with alternatively constructed rights in these situations. Moreover, these new iterations of rights discourses are dispersed amongst various governmental techniques, such as the day-to-day duties of police officers. Indeed, there is tremendous striation in these instances of the space over which the state can reign when rights are rearticulated by the delegated sovereignty of a Supreme Court. We suggest these judicial striations coalesce "into systems of domination" that are "less stable," are "asymmetrical," and which "direct or govern the actions of others" (Haggerty and Ericson 2000, 609).

The study of judicio-mentalities (Jochelson et al. 2014) is an integral yet often subtle node of this interlinking, dynamic network of surveillance. As we study the rights discussed below, we remain aware that these judicio-mentalities hybridise the human body, divorcing it from territorial settings, and reassembling a rights holder into something other than what a Canadian citizen might expect. We see this reconstitution in cases involving privacy rights, and search and seizure, amongst others. The spread of this reconstitution through such vast and diverse (and, to some, mundane) fundamental civil liberties suggests a certain rhizomatic expansion is in place (Haggerty and Ericson 2000, 614). The rhizome is an analytic metaphor developed by Deleuze and Guattari (1987) and expanded upon by Haggerty and Ericson (2000, 614). Analogising surveillance as rhizomatic suggests its growth works like roots of a weed that are part of a connected but decentralised network. The removal of one set of roots does not disrupt the functioning of the assemblage. Rather, gaps are filled with new offshoots springing up elsewhere (this is salient in the context of the administration of police powers by the Court). This dynamic facet to surveillance suggests that for each of phenomenon discussed, and across different surveillance technologies we see concomitant surveillance events. The rhizome metaphor seems to work on a microscopic level in the development of legal tests that Courts develop for constitutionalised police powers. Since 9/11, significant deviations from the baseline of the promises made by the *Charter* have appeared across a variety of moments of contact between citizen and state. Since the text of the judiciary's decisions seems to largely meet the approval of what Parliament views as necessary, the infestation of these ideas, which troubles civil liberties, seems to have increased and spread at accelerated rates. Indeed, in one study of judicial rhetoric in the area of police search powers, the Supreme Court was found to have used more conservative interpretations of civil liberties and governed in the direction of police latitude more in the post-9/11 epoch than it had during the period spanning the *Charter*'s inception through to 9/11 (Jochelson et al. 2012). The study examined how the Supreme Court spoke of its own restraint or activism in respect of its use of the *Charter*—its conservatism was indicated by the use of more language of judicial restraint in interpreting the *Charter*. Interestingly, restrained language seems to occur even in decisions that provide more latitude to policing, suggesting that what the Court says about its own judicial restraint may not curtail the development of police powers by the judiciary (Jochelson et al. 2012).

Analysing police powers jurisprudence of the Court has obvious links to notions of surveillance and security. As the Court administers these powers, it makes choices, which fundamentally change the nature of police powers. Below are some methods the Court uses to generate new police powers. When policing is apprised of Court decisions that provide the function with greater latitude, the ancillary effects are less than obvious. The notion that courts can generate or alter police powers presents grey zones of surveillance, which represent opportunities for state actors to gather more information and undertake innovative police practices in their investigations. This expansion has links to the capacity of the state to respond to wide-scale security threats or events. Simply put, the jurisprudence of surveillance in areas of police powers is unpredictable and benefits any state actor seeking to gather information on citizens, permanent residents, foreign nationals, and visitors to Canada. Below, we interrogate the development of search and seizure jurisprudence in Canada to demonstrate the considerable expansion of police power through the Court's decisions.

Threshold Issues

The high watermark for search and seizure protections occurred early in the *Charter* era. In 1984, in *Hunter v. Southam*, a case involving a search by non-police administrative investigators, a corporation, Southam Newspapers, was able to assert Sect. 8 *Charter* protections against Combines Investigation Officers. The Court noted that when a reasonable expectation of privacy existed, and where feasible, a search could only be reasonable (i.e. constitutional) when it occurred on prior authorisation (i.e. a warrant) and was based on reasonable and probable grounds

(*Hunter v. Southam* 1984, paras. 25, 29, 43). The case was important because it provided strict protections against state incursions even in the context of administrative as opposed to criminal investigations.

The phrase 'reasonable expectation of privacy' was not explicated in the *Hunter v. Southam* case and was left for future development. It seemed that the absence of a reasonable expectation of privacy might give the state permission to search. This intuition gave rise to what is commonly accepted as a threshold issue of access to Sect. 8 protections—the existence of a reasonable expectation of privacy in the thing or place to be searched.

This intuition became the fundamental legal question in cases that followed. In 1996, in *R. v. Edwards*, the accused, a suspected drug dealer, was storing his merchandise in his girlfriend's apartment. The police obtained the cooperation of the girlfriend and discovered cocaine at the dwelling. The Court asked whether Edwards enjoyed a reasonable expectation of privacy in his girlfriend's apartment. The Court noted that this expectation depended on a totality of circumstances, including the accused's relationship to the property (presence at the search, control, ownership, use, and regulation of the property) as well as the accused's subjective expectation of privacy and the objective reasonableness of that expectation (*Edwards* 1996, para. 45). The Court could not find that Edwards was able to control and expect control of the property searched and he thus had no reasonable expectation of privacy. As a result, the police required no warrant or grounds for the search.

At this point in the development of Sect. 8 of the *Charter* jurisprudence, the reasonable expectation of privacy analysis seemed to be a zero sum game. If one possessed this expectation, then one experienced the protections of warrant and reasonable, probable grounds. Without this possession, the police were free to engage in searches relatively unencumbered. Noteworthy is that the language in the *Charter* itself says nothing about the section being contingent on a reasonable expectation of privacy. The notion was interpreted by the Court and its own assessment of the development of search and seizure law in other jurisdictions, most notably, the USA. In later cases, the analysis of reasonable expectation of privacy would become more contextual still and provide shades of different protections for different accused persons.

Degrees of Privacy Protection and the Sliding Scale

In 1998, in the *R. v. M.(M.R.)*, the analysis of reasonable expectation of privacy became more complicated because the searchers in this case were public school officials. One could argue that non-police search jurisprudence had already been settled earlier in *Hunter* (1984), yet the Court considered a case that involved what it considered to be a diminished expectation of privacy outside of the public policing context. *M.(M.R.)* involved public school officials searching students suspected in possession of drugs. The Court viewed the school context as one in which the expectation of privacy was diminished. For example, a student would not expect to have as high degree of privacy in their school locker as in a bedroom (*M.(M.R.)* 1998, para. 33). Given that schools were to be secured consistent with provincial law, which called for public order in schools, the Court noted the diminished expectation of privacy called for different constitutional standards of search. Notably, such searches could be conducted without warrants and on the standard of reasonable belief of contraband possession.

   M.(M.R.) clarified that when an accused was entitled to lower expectations of privacy, the accused would also receive reduced constitutional protections. This seemed most relevant to cases involving searches by state actors who were not police. This assumption was troubled in 1999, in *R. v. Monney*, where the search powers of border customs officials were at issue. The Court was considering the searches that transpired at a drug loo facility where bodily emissions were surveyed to determine whether drugs were being transported across borders. The passive nature of the vigils indicated customs agents would wait for drugs to pass through the system in the absence of physiological inducements. Given the itinerant status of travellers, the importance of national security and that the passive vigil was embarrassing but not fundamentally an affront to human dignity, the search in such instances could be conducted without warrants but with a reasonable cause to suspect the ingestion of illicit substances. The search standards required of state officers were reduced from the *Hunter* standards (Mackinnon 2007, 48).

The constellation of factors that the Court assessed in establishing a reasonable expectation of privacy continued to be reorganised in various cases, but in each instance the Court noted the contextual nature of the assessment. Famously, in *R. v. Tessling*, in 2004, the Court, using a modified *Edwards* analysis, concluded that forward-looking infrared (FLIR) cameras (that could image heat waves and provide a thermal image of people and places) overflying a suspected marijuana grow operation did not constitute a search at all because the material that FLIR revealed was 'informational' with no connection to an accused's biographic core, and also because the accused could not contain or control the heat waves (*Tessling* 2004, paras. 27, 62–63). A similar analysis was conducted in *R. v. Patrick*, 2009, where police were permitted to search garbage on an accused's property within the property line because the bag contained mere 'information' about the accused that had been essentially 'abandoned' (ibid., paras. 26–27, 30, 44, 62).

In 2008, in the 'sniffer dog' cases of *R. v. Kang Brown* and *R. v. A.M.*, the Court had to assess whether the sniff of a police dog constituted a search. The former case took place at a bus depot in the context of policing the drug trade; the latter case took place at a school. While the Court's rulings in these cases were complex with multiple written decisions, the majority of the Court articulated a new standard for sniffer dog searches, which it viewed as constitutional. Sniffer dog searches could occur in both case contexts because of the diminished expectation of privacy in the situations. The searches could be conducted without a warrant, and upon reasonable suspicion of criminal activity (*Kang Brown* 2008, para. 140; *A.M.* 2008, paras. 68, 136, 138, 140). The use of the reasonable suspicion standard was not used routinely in previous legislation, though, for example, customs legislation had previously spoke of searching travellers when the searcher had a reasonable reason to suspect that illicit activity was occurring. The use of the phrase reasonable suspicion or reasonable grounds to suspect has proliferated as a result of Supreme Court cases countenancing the standard. Notably in *R. v. Mackenzie* and *R. v. Chehil* (2013), the Court upheld the constitutionality of the reasonable suspicion standard in the sniffer dog context. The Court noted that the reasonable suspicion standard was appropriate due to the 'minimal intrusion' of the dog sniff (*Chehil* 2013, para. 24). Reasonable suspicion is "based on objectively discernible facts, which can then be subjected to independent judicial scrutiny" (ibid., para. 26), but is a lower standard than reasonable and probable grounds because "it engages the reasonable possibility, rather than the probability of crime" (ibid., para. 27) though its scope cannot be 'generalized' to a "particular activity of location rather than to a specific person" (ibid., para. 28). A reviewing court would need to consider the reliability of the sniffer dog *ex post facto* using accepted judicial tools of reasonableness (ibid., para. 53). The majority of the Court endorsed using sniffer dogs for vehicle searches (*Mackenzie*) and unanimously approved their use for airport security (*Chehil*). The Supreme Court was thus instrumental in generating lower thresholds for the deployment of police powers of surveillance. This is a departure from the liberal legal role of constitutional guardianship by the judiciary, where the judiciary stands firmly in favour of civil liberties. The motivations for easing police power deployment were the threat of a mass security event or the alleged insidiousness of the drug trade; these are conceptions variously invoked throughout the development of this jurisprudence.

Common Law Expansion

The Court has also used the common law in concert with the *Charter* to create new police powers. The literature on this point is well established (Jochelson et al. 2014; Jochelson 2013), and has its roots in British case law (*R. v. Waterfield* 1963). The legal test that the Court posits in these situations is generative of new police powers on the basis of a justification-based analysis. In situations where heretofore unknowable police conduct takes place, the Court asks whether police conduct falls within the statutory or common law police duties, and second whether the police conduct pursuant to the duty was unjustifiable (early examples include *R. v. Knowlton* 1974 and *R. v. Dedman* 1985). In the *Charter* era, the use of the test by the Court when successful is also iterative of essentially *Charter* proof police powers (hence it is known as the ancillary powers approach). There never has been a case where the Court discovers a new common law police power and declares it unjustifiably unconstitutional. The Court generates the new power and then ensures its constitutionality. This approach can be contrasted with the Australian model of passing sweeping legislative police powers, which are then subjected to judicial review (Jochelson 2009a). The advantage of the latter legislated model is not only the possibility of fresh judicial review but also that the main source of police power is available for public scrutiny in a more centralised form rather than secreted within the thousands of pages of legal decisions. After a somewhat slow beginning to the judicial creation of common law police powers (*R. v. Knowlton* 1974), the Court began to gain traction in generating new police powers more rapidly in the *Charter* era. The ancillary powers doctrine begat judicial creation of check stop powers, and drunk-driving stops (*R. v. Dedman* 1985; *R. v. Orbanski and Elias* 2005); police search and entry powers in response to 911 calls (*R. v. Godoy* 1999); stop, detain, and frisk powers in response to dispatch calls (*R. v. Mann* 2004); roadblock powers in response to dispatch calls (*R. v. Clayton* 2007); and sniffer dog searches in airports, bus depots, streets, and schools (*R. v. Chehil* 2013*; R. v. Kang Brown* 2008*; R. v. Mackenzie* 2013*; R. v. A.M.* 2008). The creation of these powers was not without controversy, even within the Court itself, but the use of the police power-generating mechanism is now well established (Jochelson 2009a).

Interestingly, the Court has found high expectations of privacy in digital devices such as computers and cell phones in relatively recent cases, as well as upholding Sect. 8 protections regarding electronic interceptions, and third party service provider investigations (*R. v. Spencer* 2014; *R. v. Telus Communications Co* 2013; *R. v. Tse* 2012; *R. v. Vu* 2013; *R. v. Cole* 2012; *R. v. Fearon* 2014). Geist (2014) has written that the Court has been somewhat persistent in protecting electronic information. But this conclusion may be problematic. In most cases where the proceedings before the Supreme Court of Canada involved police officer *Charter* breaches, the evidence was included by the Court due to its reliability and the importance to the Court of adjudicating the case on merits (here the Court uses s.24(2) of the *Charter* to argue that the exclusion of reliable evidence would bring the administration of justice into disrepute: see *R. v. Cole* 2012; *R. v. Vu* 2013; *R v. Spencer* 2014; *R. v. Fearon* 2014 for cogent examples); in *R. v. Morelli*, 2010, the majority excluded the digital evidence because the electronic information was on a home computer and was based on an irredeemable information to obtain (a fatally flawed document that the police relied upon to justify their initial warrant).

R. v. Fearon, 2014, is another example of how the Court is able to use the common law and *Charter* in concert to generate new police powers. The majority ruled that the power to search, incident to arrest, could include permission to search accused persons' cell phones or other devices. In this case, Fearon had allegedly been involved in armed robbery of items, including jewellery, and part of the evidence against him was texts sent using his cell phone. The texts were found during an arrest pat-down search and were inculpatory. Frisk searches incidental to arrest had been established in earlier cases (*Cloutier v. Langlois* 1990; *R. v. Golden* 2001; *R. v. Beare* 1988; *R. v. Debot* 1989). The Court in *Fearon* relied on previous case law and its analytics to answer the question of the legality of the cell phone search (*R. v. Caslake* 1998; *R. v. Golden* 2001; *R. v. Nolet* 2010). The analysis used two questions:

> the first is whether the search here falls within the general common law parameters for searches incident to arrest. If it does, the second issue is whether, having regard to the appropriate balance between the need for effective law enforcement and the suspect's privacy interests, some further restrictions must be imposed and if so, what they should be. (*Fearon* 2014, para. 26)

The majority answered the first question in the affirmative because "the search was directed at public safety (locating the handgun), avoiding the loss of evidence (the stolen jewelry) and obtaining evidence of the crime (information linking Mr. Fearon to the robbery and locating potential accomplices)" (*R. v. Fearon* 2014, para. 33). In delineating restrictions for cell phone searches, the majority noted as follows:

> a search will comply with s. 8 where: (1) The arrest was lawful; (2) The search is truly incidental to the arrest in that the police have a reason based on a valid law enforcement purpose to conduct the search, and that reason is objectively reasonable. The valid law enforcement purposes in this context are: (a) Protecting the police, the accused, or the public; (b) Preserving evidence; or (c) Discovering evidence, including locating additional suspects, in situations in which the investigation will be stymied or

significantly hampered absent the ability to promptly search the cell phone incident to arrest; (3) The nature and the extent of the search are tailored to the purpose of the search; and (4) The police take detailed notes of what they have examined on the device and how it was searched. (ibid., para. 83)

Once again, and outside the ancillary powers context, the Supreme Court of Canada has generated new search powers, this time regarding searches incidental to arrest. In doing so, it has enacted the new powers and attempted to insulate them from constitutional scrutiny by providing guidelines for police to meet should they undertake incident to arrest searches of digital devices. The majority in *Fearon* found a breach of Fearon's s. 8 rights but ultimately included the evidence since the police were acting in a 'grey area' of the law, in good faith, the evidence was 'reliable' and its exclusion would undermine the 'truth-seeking function' of the courts (ibid., paras. 94, 97). The exclusion of evidence rules of Canada are instantiated in Sect. 24(2) of the *Charter* and have been the subject of vigorous debate and refinement; its most recent interpretation does away with automatic exclusionary rules and considers the totality of the circumstances of the evidence in light of due process implications, the repute of the administration of justice, the good faith of police officers, and reliability of the evidence (Jochelson et al. 2014). This calculus seems to hearken back to common law exclusionary rules that were concerned with reliability of evidence and truth as opposed to the human dignity of the person under investigation.

Empirical Estimations

Regardless of the proliferation of search powers that the Supreme Court has generated or expanded, more search-related information is coming before the courts than ever before. Whether or not courts ultimately exclude this information, the materials before the courts are still subject to the surveillant gaze of the state. The materials at issue in exclusion of evidence *voire dires* may form the impetus for future investigations or scrutiny of the accused individuals (Tables 4.1 and 4.2).

Table 4.1 Reported cases dealing with sects. 8 and 24(2) analysis since the Charter

Era	Reported cases (with search terms) $N = 1257$
Charter 1982–1 January 1993	135
2 January 1993–1 January 2004	370
2 January 2004–14 May 2015	752

Table 4.2 Yearly reported cases dealing with sect. 8 and 24(2) analysis since 2004

Years	Reported cases (with search terms) $N = 752$
2004–2005	49
2005–2006	65
2006–2007	58
2007–2008	51
2008–2009	65
2009–2010	72
2010–2011	87
2011–2012	68
2012–2013	78
2013–2014	69
2014–2015	70

A LexisNexis Quicklaw search for the terms 'Sect. 8' within a paragraph of 'Sect. 24(2)' and the word 'Charter' indicates that 1257 cases were reported with these search terms between the *Charter* coming into force in 1982 and 14 May 2015—roughly 33 years. In 11-year increments, 135 reported cases appear between 1982 and 1 January 1993; 370 cases are reported between 2 January 1993 and 1 January 2004; last, 752 reported cases appear between 2 January 2004 and 14 May 2015. There are mediating reasons to decipher why the rampant increase in reported cases that contain these search terms is occurring. Jurisprudential changes in Sect. 24(2) analysis in 2009 (*R. v. Grant*) might have contributed to the recent growth in reported cases, but the last ten years of reported case numbers suggest a somewhat consistent high yield of cases annually. More justices and more decisions are yielding more reported cases. Regardless of remediating explanations, however, it is clear that more material is increasingly under scrutiny by courts. More accused conduct is subject to the judicial gaze with respect to Sects. 8 and 24(2) analysis of the *Charter.*

A Charter of Surveillance

The development of search and seizure jurisprudence since the *Charter's* inception suggests the *Charter* is not in a 'tug of war' with security but rather is working broadly in concert with security and surveillance (Jochelson et al. 2014, 110). This observation and these case data suggest a rethinking of the constitutional document. The protection under Sect. 8 of the *Charter* speaks of a 'right' to be 'free' from 'unreasonable search and seizure' from the state (Jochelson et al. 2014, 110). If we understand the Supreme Court as the administrator of this section, rather than as the 'guardian of the constitution' and in light of the foregoing evidence, the constitutional document and its interpretation begins to be seen as supportive of a surveillant assemblage.

The most protection the *Charter* provided in the way of search and seizure law was at its coming into force, and in the high watermark of *Hunter v. Southam*. Since then, cases reveal a diffusion of the relatively strong protections of that early case. The Supreme Court's guardianship of the *Constitution* allowed it the means to not merely adjudicate police power, but to expand it and in the process, declare the newly generated power in conformity and cohesion with constitutional standards.

These changes in on-the-ground police powers work act in concert with broader security approaches undertaken by the state. Some argue that after 9/11 the state has been empowered in a type of permanent emergency, which has given rise to legislative and political antiterror expansion (Diab 2015). At work in an insidious way, microscopically, is the expansion of police powers countenanced and created by the Court in written decisions which prove inscrutable to the lay reader. The resultant police power creep in the area of search and seizure law provides a supportive environment in which legislative impetuses for greater surveillance and security can safely be proffered. For example, the recent passing of Bill C-51 in 2015 in Canada is a wide-scale legislative attempt to survey subjects, share information intra- and intergovernmentally through intelligence agencies, and to criminalise terror-related offences on the basis of, in some cases, mere suspicion, reasonable fear, or reasonable grounds to suspect anti-security or terrorist-related activity (see Forcese, this volume). One could ask whether such sweeping legislation would have been passed were the

Supreme Court's record replete with decisions that limited police powers and required that *Hunter v. Southam* standards be upheld.

It would be easy to lay responsibility at the hands of the judiciary for changes in police powers jurisprudence. The jurisprudence stands in stark contrast to the role of the Court imagined by some civil libertarians since the *Charter's* inception. This vision imagines a "Court will stand with the vulnerable" and "protect the person against the long and intrusive arm of the law" (Jochelson et al. 2014, 111). The reasons for the expansion of police powers might have to do with 'fear of harm' and the 'risk of harm' and their normalisation as justifications for legal interventions (ibid.; Diab 2015).

Also noteworthy is that the architecture of the *Charter* itself mandates judicial intervention through words like 'unreasonable' and through equivocation clauses such as Sects. 1 and 24(2) of the *Charter*. The former is the leading provision of the *Charter* and guarantees rights only insofar as the violations are not reasonably necessary in a free and democratic society; discretion is left to the courts to determine the occasions when violations are permissible, and the Court developed its own such calculus for making those calls in the *R. v. Oakes* (1986) case. Similarly, in response to police malfeasance, Sect. 24(2) of the *Charter* gives courts power to exclude or include evidence when a *Charter* breach by police has occurred depending on whether the administration of justice is brought into disrepute. The latest calculus for making this determination was delivered by the Supreme Court in *R. v. Grant* (2009). This discussion is meant to demonstrate that from its inception the *Charter* could have been read as a charter of equivocation as opposed to a charter of rights and freedoms. Given that the Court has used these written equivocations to provide police with more information-gathering tools, the development of police powers jurisprudence in Canada is pivotal in the development of a surveillant charter.

The Ripening of Surveillance

The development of police powers since the *Charter* went into force is a story of drift, a move away from conceptions of protection from the state and the high watermarks of the earliest cases. It is also a narrative of diffusion. New search powers develop in novel circumstances: upon detention, upon arrest, because of the common law, because of the context surrounding the search, and because of the police officer's belief that they were acting according to the law. These developments also allowed for different standards to apply to different searches. Sometimes no warrant was required, and rather than reasonable and probable grounds of the commission of crime, some searches became allowable on the basis of possibility of crime, on a reasonable suspicion standard. The lower standard was intimately tied to the Court's conception of how much privacy protection an accused was entitled to in a given case, and thus a sliding scale of protections on the basis of reasonable expectation of privacy developed.

The architecture of the *Charter* is equivocation—it is a *Charter* of possibilities. In the context of police powers, the courts administer these possibilities. Rather than providing robust protections against legislative and state affronts to civil liberties, the Supreme Court has administered a different kind of charter—a charter that looks for ways to countenance police conduct in investigations of high importance, to create police powers if necessary in these areas, and to declare its pronouncements the *Charter*-proof law of the land. Thirty years after the defiant prose of *Hunter v. Southam*, steeped in its language of civil liberty protection, the Court has deployed a body of work more consistent with a charter of surveillance. In the wake of recent legislative shifts, in seems apparent that the legal context is ripe for surveillant incursions in the name of public safety and security. The *Charter* has been flexible enough to allow such incursions in traditional policing and possesses the same surveillant potential in investigations of offences and threats that trouble national security interests. Recent anti-security legislation (Bill C-51) contains 44 instances of offences and investigative permissions to proceed in state action in the context of reasonable suspicion, belief, and fear of anti-security or terrorism-related activity. The pathway for the constitutionality of such legislation may well have been paved by the Supreme Court's own jurisprudence in the context of police powers.

Regrettably, the development of Canadian search and seizure Supreme Court jurisprudence has squandered some of the protections that inure when constitutional supremacy is at play. One conception behind constitutional supremacy is that parliamentarians should not play fast and loose with civil liberties because judicial guardianship of the *Constitution* will act as a check on unfettered civil liberty incursion. In Australia, where constitutional supremacy is relatively limited to jurisdictional matters relating to federalism, there is less room for judicial guardianship of civil liberties by virtue of constitutional supremacy. Interestingly, a judiciary that has abandoned its constitutional stewardship, as we have suggested is the case in the context of search and seizure law in Canada, is logically analogous to the nation state where civil liberties do not hold constitutionally supreme status (as we suggest is the case in Australia). Thus, both models seem to be influenced by risk aversion, precaution, and provide a supporting architecture for a surveillant assemblage. Despite quite different constitutional approaches to civil liberties, both countries find themselves with similar standards in the context of search and seizure law, and thus in the ways in which states gather information. It would seem then that constitutional infrastructure alone does not resist the pull of surveillance when sociolegal conditions call for security.

References

Agamben, Giorgio. 2005. State of Exception. Trans. K. Atell. Chicago, IL: University of Chicago Press.

Bloss, William. 2008. Escalating U.S. Police Surveillance After 9/11: An Examination of Causes and Effects. *Surveillance & Society* 4(3): 208–228.

Deleuze, Gilles, and Félix Guatarri. 1987. *A Thousand Plateaus*. Minneapolis, MN: University of Minnesota Press.

Dennis, Mark and Forbes Chambers. 2014. What the Fuck's Happening: A Discussion Paper on Sections 99, 105 and 20 of the *Law Enforcement (Powers and Responsibilities) Act* 2002 (NSW). http://www.criminalcle.net.au/main/page_cle_pages_police_powers.html. Accessed 23 June 2015.

Diab, Robert. 2015. *The Harbinger Theory: How the Post-9/11 Emergency Became Permanent and the Case for Reform*. Oxford: Oxford University Press.

Geist, Michael. 2014. The Spencer Effect: No More Warrantless Access to Subscriber Info with Five Minutes of Police Work. www.michaelgeist.ca/2014/11/spencer-effect-warrantless-access-subscriber-info-five-minutes-police-work/. Accessed 27 June 2015.

Haggerty, Kevin, and Richard Ericson. 2000. The surveillant assemblage. *British Journal of Sociology* 51(4): 605–622.

Jochelson, Richard. 2009a. Multidimensional Analysis as a Window into Activism Scholarship: Searching for Meaning with Sniffer Dogs. *Canadian Journal of Law and Society* 24(2): 231–249.

———. 2009b. Trashcans and Constitutional Custodians: The Liminal Spaces of Privacy in the Wake of *Patrick*. *Saskatchewan Law Review* 72(2): 199–222.

———. 2013. Ancillary Issues with Oakes: The Development of the Waterfield Test and the Problem of Fundamental Constitutional Theory. *Ottawa Law Review* 43(3): 355–376.

Jochelson, Richard, Kirsten Kramar, and Mark Doerksen. 2014. *The Disappearance of Criminal Law: Police Powers and the Supreme Court*. Halifax: Fernwood Publishing.

Jochelson, Richard, Michael Weinrath, and Melanie Janelle Murchison. 2012. Searching and Seizing After 9/11: Developing and Applying Empirical Methodology to Measure Judicial Output in the Court's Section 8 Jurisprudence. *Dalhousie Law Review* 35(1): 179–213.

Lippert, Randy K., and Kevin Walby. 2012. Municipal Corporate Security and the Intensification of Urban Surveillance. *Surveillance and Society* 9: 310–320.

MacKinnon, William. 2007. Tessling, Brown and A.M.: Towards a Principled Approach to Section 8. *Alberta Law Review* 45: 79–115.

McHugh, Justice. 2001. Does Chapter III of the Constitution Protect Substantive as Well as Procedural Rights? *Australian Bar Review* 21: 235–239.

Rasmussen, Mikkel Vedby. 2004. 'It Sounds Like a Riddle': Security Studies, the War on Terror and Risk. *Millennium: Journal of International Studies* 33(2): 381–395.

Sanders, Jane. 2015. Arrest Without Warrant in New South Wales (March 2015 update). http://www.criminalcle.net.au/main/page_cle_pages_police_powers.html. Accessed 23 June 2015.

Wilkinson, Lori. 2009. Are Human Rights Jeopardized in Twenty-First-Century Canada? An Examination of Immigration Policies post-9/11. In *Anti-Terrorism: Security and Insecurity After 9/11*, ed. Sandra Rollings-Magnusson, 102–124. Nova Scotia: Fernwood Publishing.

Legislation

Bill C-51. *Anti-terrorism Act.* 2015. 2nd Session, 41st Parliament 62-63 Elizabeth
II, 2013-2014-2015. http://www.parl.gc.ca/HousePublications/Publication.
aspx?DocId=6932136&File=32&Col=1. Accessed 8 Aug 2015.

Canadian Charter of Rights and Freedoms, s. 2, Part I of the Constitution Act,
1982, *being Schedule B to the* Canada Act, 1982 *(UK), c 1.*

Charter of Human Rights and Responsibilities Act. 2006. Act No. 43/2006
(Victoria).

Constitution Act, 1982, *being Schedule B to the* Canada Act, 1982 *(UK),
1982, c 11.*

Commonwealth of Australia Constitution Act, 1900 *Title III.*

Criminal Code of Canada, *RSC* 1985, *c C-46, s 745.*

Law Enforcement (Powers and Responsibilities) Act 2002 No. 103 (LEPRA).

Cases

Chu Kheng Lim v. Minister for Immigration (1992) 176 CLR 1; 110 ALR 97.

Cloutier v. Langlois, [1990] 1 SCR 158.

Dedman v. R., [1985] 2 SCR 2, 20 DLR (4th) 321.

Hunter v. Southam, [1984] 2 SCR 145.

Knowlton v. R., [1974] SCR 443.

Kruger v. Commonwealth (1997), 190 CLR 1; 146 ALR 126.

R. v. A.M., 2008 SCC 19.

R. v. Beare, [1988] 2 SCR 387.

R. v. Caslake, [1998] 1 SCR 51.

R. v. Chehil, 2013 SCC 49.

R. v. Clayton, 2007 SCC 3.

R. v. Cole, 2012 SCC 53, [2012] 3 SCR 34.

R. v. Debot, [1989] 2 SCR 1140.

R. v. Edwards, [1996] 1 SCR 128.

R. v. Fearon, 2014 SCC 77, [2014] SCR 621.

R. v. Godoy, [1999] 1 SCR 311.

R. v. Golden, 2001 SCC 83, [2001] 3 SCR 679.

R. v. Grant, 2009 SCC 32, [2009] 2 SCR 353.

R. v. Kang-Brown, [2008] 1 SCR 456, 2008 SCC 18.

R. v. M. (M.R.), [1998] 3 SCR 393.

R. v. MacKenzie, 2013 SCC 50.

R. v. Mann, [2004] 3 SCR 59.

R. v. Monney, [1999] 1 SCR 652.

R. v. Morelli, 2010 SCC 8, [2010] 1 SCR 253.

R. v. Nolet, [2010] 1 SCR 851.

R. v. Oakes, [1986] 1 SCR 103, 53 OR (2d).

R. v. Patrick, 2009 SCC 17.

R. v. Orbanski; R v Elias, [2005] 2 SCR 3.

R. v. Spencer, 2014 SCC 43, [2014] 2 SCR 212.

R. v. Telus Communications Co., [2013] SCC 16.

R. v. Tessling, [2004] SCR 432.

R. v. Tse, 2012 SCC 16, [2012] 1 SCR 531.

R. v. Vu, 2013 SCC 60, [2013] 3 SCR 657.

R. v. Waterfield; R. v. Lynn, [1963] 3 All ER 659, [1964] 1 QB 164 (CA).

.

5

Assemblage, Counter-Law and the Legal Architecture of Australian Covert Surveillance

Brendon Murphy and John Anderson

Introduction

Ever since the publication of Haggerty and Ericson's 'Surveillant Assemblage' (Haggerty and Ericson 2000) article (see also Jochelson and Doerksen, this volume), contemporary forms of surveillance have generally been understood as a complex network of loosely connected practices involving state and private actors, a diversity of purposes and a complex interaction of knowledge systems. The concept of assemblage allows us to conceive how diverse surveillance practices, institutions and knowledge systems enter into relationships and interact to make visible and knowable many aspects of social life, while simultaneously installing mechanisms of governance and identity. Assemblage is characterised by relations of exteriority, by which independent components join and interact, but also exist independently, separate and destabilise over time (Deleuze and Guattari

B. Murphy (✉) • J. Anderson
Law School, University of Newcastle, Callaghan, NSW, Australia

© The Author(s) 2016
R. Lippert et al. (eds.), *National Security, Surveillance and Terror*,
DOI 10.1007/978-3-319-43243-4_5

1987; DeLanda 2006).[1] Ericson (2007) subsequently argued that surveillant assemblages have connections with law, both in the organisation and facilitation of surveillance practices, and also in the architecture of law itself. The precautionary logic that is pervasive in surveillant assemblages mobilises an evolution of both surveillance practices and forms of law. Ericson reasoned that this dynamic was part of a single development: the emergence of counter-law (also see Molnar and Parsons, this volume).[2] While surveillance studies continue to explore the contours of surveillant assemblage, the relationship between surveillance and law is a neglected aspect of scholarship. This chapter contributes to understanding how surveillance and law may be understood as assemblages.

Drawing on the concepts of assemblage and counter-law, this chapter begins by proposing the question: what roles does law play in surveillant assemblage? This is a complex question. As Lippert (2009) has explained, because of the diverse character of surveillant assemblages, law operates in dexterous ways in different contexts, affecting institutional practices, information and the character of surveillance in diverse ways. Law is influenced by a multiplicity of elements and, in turn, stabilises and destabilises elements of surveillant assemblages. The combination of surveillance and law is both a rationality of governance and a technology

---

[1] Assemblage is a complex theory, and not without its problems. While it is not the purpose of this chapter to dwell on the contours of assemblage, it is worth noting some key elements. Assemblages are composed of physical actants, institutions, processes, technologies and knowledge formations. These components can be identifiable and discrete, but also obscure, composed of overlapping, multiple parts. The elements of assemblage interact with one another in equally complex ways. They are organic, in the sense of evolving, growing, receding, and in some cases ending and mutating. Power is endemic, but dispersed, with it rarely the case that any one component has complete power over the totality of its arrangements. The connectivity between components is also highly variable, in terms of speed, impact and resistance. At its simplest, Deleuze and Guattari (1987, 8) conceived of assemblages as 'multiplicities.' DeLanda (2006) subsequently extended the concept.

[2] Counter-law emerged in the opening years of this century in Ashworth's (2000) work, but more fully in Ericson (2007, 24–31). Ericson argued that counter-law has two limbs. The first relates to "the form of laws against law" (Ericson 2007, 24). The second relates to "the form of surveillant assemblage" (ibid.). 'Laws against law' are characterised by the tendency in recent decades for an increasingly punitive use of criminal law, in the form of increasing sentences, new law and alterations of due process standards to facilitate prosecution. The broad dynamic is a policy imperative based on precaution that is based on logic of exception. The second limb of counter-law is the surveillant assemblage itself: the tendency for surveillance, policing and information collection to form and proliferate.

that permits interventions, encourages disciplinary self-regulation and crystallises locations in which power is deployed and deployable.

Assemblage invites debate into the distinction between law and norms, between hard and soft law, and is further coloured by jurisdictional differences and the division between public and private systems of regulation. Nevertheless, it is clear that surveillant assemblages are saturated with legalities that operate at multiple levels, including formal laws that evolve over time, knowledge systems in and around law, and distinct discourses about security, privacy and necessity. Understanding this system requires isolating exemplars. In this case, the focus of examination is concerned with the regulation of covert investigation in Australia. While Harfield and Harfield (2010) have explored some of the doctrinal and accountability models governing covert investigation, the present chapter deploys assemblage and counter-law as its theoretical foundations in order to explore the discursive formation of surveillance law.

To this end, this chapter considers those architectures regulating the surveillance activities of law enforcement. Australian legal architecture regulating the surveillance activities of the executive presents a complex array of concurrent federal and state laws. However, unlike those jurisdictions that vest exclusive national power to make laws regulating crime and investigation, such as Canada,[3] the Australian Commonwealth has no specific powers arising under its Constitution to make laws for criminal investigation. Such matters are generally recognised as being incidental to some other head of power, such as customs or external affairs (Brown et al. 2010, 35–38; Bronitt and McSherry 2010, 103–109). Most criminal law in Australia is located in state laws. Unlike many comparable legal systems, such as the USA, the UK and Canada (see Forcese, this volume), Australian law is without universal human rights instruments outside the common law, except where those rights have been specifically recognised in a limited range of statutes (Gans et al. 2011).[4] In this respect, surveillance laws are normally the only source of public protections against surveillance activities, although private remedies (such as trespass to land

---

[3] Arising under s. 91(27) of *The Constitution Act* 1867 (UK) 30 & 31 Vic c.3.
[4] Notably, the *Human Rights Act* 2004 (ACT) and the *Charter of Human Rights and Responsibilities Act* 2006 (Vic).

and goods) have been used. This chapter aims to map the contemporary Australian surveillance and regulatory landscape (see also Molnar and Parsons, this volume), understand some historical undercurrents (see also Palmer and Warren, this volume) and consider the character of the core public policy imperatives that inform and challenge this field of regulation. Flowing from these imperatives is an array of distinct and persistent discourses concerned with risk, investigation and security that have a direct impact on the legal architecture of surveillance.

To explore these issues, this chapter is presented in four parts. Part I considers a historical perspective on Australian surveillance law. It maps out some of the broad historical themes present in the emergence and evolution of this field of public law. Part II identifies and considers the foundation typologies of investigative regulation, aiming to synthesise the comparative characteristics of surveillance law. Part III explores the policy discourses that inform and shape Australian surveillance law. Part IV concludes with a discussion about the linkages and identity of actants in surveillant assemblages in the present exemplar.

Historical Perspectives on Australian Surveillance Law

Australian surveillance laws are characterised by three principal legal categories: private, public and national security. These laws are normally characterised as either specific laws governing categories of surveillance, or laws that have the *effect* of regulating surveillance, but not necessarily directed to that end, such as general privacy statutes (see also Molnar and Parsons, this volume).[5] Private surveillance laws tend to be concerned with regulating the actions of private individuals, employers, businesses, incorporated entities and non-government agencies. Workplaces are a prime example.[6] Public surveillance laws tend to be concerned with

---

[5] The extent to which privacy legislation in Australia may be understood as 'general' is doubtful. Australian privacy legislation is primarily concerned with the availability, use and exchange of information between and by agencies collecting information. See, for example, *Privacy Act* 1988 (Cth); *Privacy and Personal Information Protection Act* 1988 (NSW).

[6] For example, *Workplace Surveillance Act* 2005 (NSW).

the regulation of the executive branch of government. Within the broad category of public surveillance law can be found mechanisms that have the effect of regulating surveillance (such as general privacy statutes), and specific laws regulating government in its law enforcement capacity. Conversely, this body of law also tends to prohibit the general public from engaging in a range of intrusive covert surveillance practices, effectively ensuring state monopolies of specific investigative practices. In this respect 'public' law is characterised by the regulation of public authorities or executive surveillance only. The third category, national security, overlaps with public surveillance law, but is a specialist class of executive regulation, deployed in specific instances by a limited number of federal agencies.[7]

There is no standard legal definition of 'surveillance' in Australian law. Generally, it retains its ordinary meaning of purposeful observation. For example, the Victorian Law Reform Commission's 2010 *Surveillance in Public Places* report used Lyon's (2007) definition of 'surveillance': "the deliberate or purposive observation or monitoring of a person, object or place" (Victorian Law Reform Commission 2010, 21). Most surveillance practices in Australia are linked to technologies that enable an investigator to, often invisibly, observe, monitor, track and listen to individuals, objects and communications in both public and private locations. However, since most 'public' surveillance does not require formal authorisation, a dichotomy exists in Australian law between covert and overt surveillance. Most Australian surveillance law is covert in orientation, and mainly concerned with the collection of information about specific targets or groups, although with the advent of accessible telecommunications 'metadata' the size of the group able to be examined is effectively the entire population. Covert surveillance, in this context, reflects the English statutory conceptions of 'directed' and 'intrusive' techniques, found in the *Regulation of Investigatory Powers Act* 2000 (UK) (Harfield and Harfield 2008a). In the law enforcement environment the information collected has two primary orientations. The first is intelligence. The second is evidence capable of supporting further investigation or crimi-

---

[7] In Australia those organisations include the Australian Security Intelligence Organisation (ASIO), the Australian Secret Intelligence Service (ASIS) and the Defence Signals Directorate (DSD).

nal prosecution. The information collection aspect of investigation is a general function of law enforcement. What makes directed and intrusive surveillance unique is that it tends to be directed towards activities that are normally resistant or impervious to ordinary investigation, particularly consensual crimes, and those activities involving secretive behaviour, such as drug trafficking, prostitution and criminal conspiracies (Bronitt and McSherry 2010, 930). These kinds of crimes may be understood as taking place in a 'private' space, outside of the reach of ordinary investigative activity. 'Surveillance law' is therefore best understood as exclusive executive laws regulating directed and intrusive covert investigations into secretive unlawful activity.

General 'Surveillance' Law Landscape

Australia, like much of the Western world, has undergone a surveillance revolution over the last 40 years. Legally, this revolution has been gradual, ad hoc, and complicated by the federal structure of the Commonwealth. The result is a system of regulation governing criminal investigation and surveillance operating in six states, two territories and an overarching federal structure (see also Jones and Walsh, this volume). Although the legal architecture tends to regulate similar areas of practice, resulting in taxonomies of surveillance and investigations law, the diversity within the Australian framework means that surveillance law is best conceived as jurisdictionally specific, requiring precise attention to detail when legalities are at issue, but with sufficient commonalities to allow for comparative analysis and synthesis of principle.

Historically, Australian surveillance practices generally have been unregulated. The common law position is that a police officer is limited by the same general law as a civilian (Secretary of State for the Home Department (UK) 1929; Alderson 2001),[8] except where special powers incidental to their function as a peace officer are required, or otherwise extended by legislation. As 'citizens in uniform,' police are able to engage in any surveillance practice that is not otherwise an offence or a tort.

---

[8] For example, *Enever v. The King* (1906) 3 CLR 969.

Consequently, a great deal of overt and covert law enforcement surveillance activity remains unregulated because it is generally lawful to engage in unobtrusive public observation, including photography, listening to conversations and even talking to people without disclosing the investigator's status or purpose.

Difficulty arises when there is a need to enter 'private spaces' for law enforcement. Two well-known competing interests appear to conflict in this environment. The first is the legitimate need for investigators to penetrate the 'veil of privacy' to obtain and assess information related to crime and national security. The second is the equally legitimate expectation that a citizen should be free from undue state interference. This competition of interests lies at the heart of the legal architectures that both limit and authorise investigators to conduct intrusive forms of surveillance. The public policy imperative forms the fulcrum of the common law limits to intrusive surveillance: the 'king's men' have the right and power to engage in conduct that would otherwise be unlawful only in the face of a warrant or present and demonstrable necessity.[9]

The common law has historically provided little protection for privacy. Australia, like Canada, relies primarily on the general law of torts (notably trespass),[10] the general limits of the criminal law and those statutory provisions that either specifically regulate surveillance, or extend a limited range of privacy and control over personal information held by government agencies.[11] Attempts to regulate surveillance practices are ongoing and complicated by the federal distribution of legislative power

---

[9] The jurisprudence crystallised as early as 1572 in *Semayne's Case* (1604) 5 Co Rep 91a. *Semayne's* case has been accepted as authority in Australia and Canada. For example, *Plenty v. Dillon* (1991) 171 CLR 635 and *Eccles v. Bourque* [1975] 2 SCR 739.

[10] For example, *Kuru v. State of New South Wales* (2008) 236 CLR 1.

[11] The common law position on privacy in Australia is complex. Some intermediate courts have held there is a common law right to privacy, but there has yet to be a definitive authority from the High Court of Australia. The most recent significant decision was in *Australian Broadcasting Corp v. Lenah Game Meats* (2001) 208 CLR 199. There appears to be substantial resistance to proposals for the recognition of a cause of action for breach of privacy, despite recommendations from Australian Law Reform Commissions (see Australian Law Reform Commission 1983; Australian Law Reform Commission 2008; Victorian Law Reform Commission 2010). In Canada, the Ontario Court of Appeal has recently recognised a right to personal privacy, enforceable through a new tort of 'intrusion upon seclusion.' See *Jones v. Tsige* [2012] ONCA 32.

and political economy. In practical terms, this has meant that covert surveillance was (and is) largely confined to the activities of a suspect in public places, unless an undercover operative can effectively infiltrate private spaces legally through extant powers or authorisation (e.g. warrants). This does not, of course, prevent officers from acting unlawfully during an investigation by engaging in unauthorised covert activities, or from engaging an informant to do the same. In practical terms, this might only become apparent during a criminal trial. Since the position at common law was generally permissive of relevant and probative evidence even if improperly obtained (Australian jurisdictions do not automatically exclude illegally obtained evidence),[12] activities that might be considered improper or unlawful were not necessarily a problem for the prosecution, and no barrier to the collection of relevant criminal intelligence. On one hand, there were important limitations on the ability of investigators to access 'hard targets' located within closed networks in the private sphere. On the other hand, the potential for evidence to be admitted in the face of impropriety, and the utility of information that was otherwise not subject to scrutiny, has meant that breaches of law are not necessarily fatal to prosecution cases.

Telecommunications Surveillance

As with Canada, Australian law has followed the English legal tradition and shifted towards a complex set of legislative provisions, ordinarily based on a system of *prospective authorisation*. Australian governments responded to international and domestic pressures to both regulate and enable investigation of crime and corruption. Australian covert surveillance law is characterised by a system of warrants (both judicial and senior officer), record-keeping and retroactive inspection. Historically, this transition began during the Cold War (1950–1989) (see also Jones as well as Palmer and Warren, this volume), but gained particular momentum following public inquiries into drugs, criminal investigation, procedure

---

[12] See *R. v. Sang* [1980] AC 402; *Bunning v. Cross* (1978) 141 CLR 54; see also Bronitt and Roche 2000; Presser 2001.

and police corruption (1975–1995),[13] and the Royal Commission on Intelligence and Security (1974–1977).[14]

The first clear shift was the move to regulate telecommunications interception. The Australian federal government introduced the *Telephonic Communications Interception Act* in 1960 with prohibitions for unauthorised wiretaps but concurrently providing a system of warrants enabling the Attorney General to authorise interception of personal communications. This Act was intended to augment the national security powers of the Australian Security Intelligence Organisation (ASIO) and was controversial in the Cold War period, attracting considerable debate about the fear of communism on the one hand and an emerging police state on the other. The Second Reading Speech demonstrates, however, that telephone interception had been taking place for more than a decade through executive authorisation without any explicit legislative authority. From 1950 until 1960, the Director General of ASIO had power delegated by the prime minister to engage in 'wiretapping.' By 1960, in the wake of Parliamentary concerns (notably the 'Petrov' Royal Commission into Espionage in 1955), and the political battle between the Menzies Government and the Australian Labour Party in this period, government policy shifted to place telephone intercepts on a legislative footing, primarily to import some 'safeguards' into their authorisation and use. Despite the appearance as a recent phenomenon, Hansard confirmed, however, that telecommunications interception began almost as soon as telecommunications technology appeared at the turn of the century, and was always a feature of military intelligence gathering. As the availability of telecommunications expanded, and the power itself began to be deployed in the civilian context of perceived national emergencies in the

---

[13] Australian Law Reform Commission 1975. Report No. 2: An Interim Report : Criminal Investigation. Canberra, Australian Law Reform Commission, Commonwealth of Australia, New South Wales Government, Queensland Government and Victorian Government (1983). Royal Commission of Inquiry into Drug Trafficking. Canberra, Australian Government Publishing Service, Stewart, D. 1986. Royal Commission of Inquiry into Alleged Telephone Interceptions. Canberra, Australian Government Publishing Service, Wood, J. J. 1997. Report of the Royal Commission into the NSW Police Service. Sydney, New South Wales Government.

[14] The Royal Commission on Intelligence and Security published eight volumes between 1976 and 1977. These documents are declassified, some as recently as 2008, but there remains a substantial amount of material that is redacted. The materials are now available through the National Archives of Australia.

1950s and 1960s, the regulation and authorisation of telephone interception materialised.[15]

These early legislative provisions were characterised by a small number of clauses within a more general legal architecture. They were
replaced with a more detailed and expansive set of powers in the
Telecommunications (Interception) Act 1979, introduced concurrently
with the expansion of powers and reorganisation of ASIO.[16] These powers were subsequently extended at the state level in the 1980s through
the passage of relatively uniform legislation that succeeded through an
unusual degree of state and federal cooperation.[17] The effect of these
reforms was to centralise telecommunication interceptions regulation at
the federal level. This did not, however, prevent state law enforcement
agents from using wiretaps. In 1986 the Stewart Royal Commission into
telephone interception was presented with clear evidence that a num-

---

[15] The Second Reading Speech and associated debate illustrates a classic dilemma governments face
in balancing privacy with security, and establishing appropriate accountability measures while also
ensuring operational utility. The *Telephonic Communications (Interception) Bill* 1960 intended to
shift the authority to grant wiretaps from a delegated power in the hands of the Director General
of ASIO (granted by the then Prime Minister Chifley in 1950), to a requirement for applications
to be made to the Attorney General. See Australian Commonwealth, *Parliamentary Debates*, House
of Representatives, 5, 11 and 12 May 1960. Notably, there had been existing statutory authority
under the *Telegraph Act* 1909 (Cth) s. 3 to 'take control' of telegraph communication in cases of
'emergency' and telecommunications had been regularly intercepted by both military and civilian
authorities, with an unfettered right to do so during war time—see Australian Commonwealth,
Parliamentary Debates, Australian Senate, 16 August 1905 (Senator Keating) 963 concerning
amendments to the *Wireless Telegraphy Bill* 1905.

[16] The Second Reading Speech and associated debate illustrates a classic dilemma governments face
in balancing privacy with security, and establishing appropriate accountability measures while also
ensuring operational utility. The *Telephonic Communications (Interception) Bill* 1960 intended to
shift the authority to grant wiretaps from a delegated power in the hands of the Director General
of ASIO (granted by the then Prime Minister Chifley in 1950), to a requirement for applications
to be made to the Attorney General. See Australian Commonwealth, *Parliamentary Debates*, House
of Representatives, 5, 11 and 12 May 1960. Notably, there had been existing statutory authority
under the *Telegraph Act* 1909 (Cth) s. 3 to 'take control' of telegraph communication in cases of
'emergency' and telecommunications had been regularly intercepted by both military and civilian
authorities, with an unfettered right to do so during war time—see Australian Commonwealth,
Parliamentary Debates, Australian Senate, 16 August 1905 (Senator Keating) 963 concerning
amendments to the *Wireless Telegraphy Bill* 1905.

[17] *Telecommunications (Interception) Amendment Act* 1987 (Cth), s. 21 inserted a new Part into the
TI Act that permitted the Commonwealth to authorise state agencies to apply for warrants. Each
State legislature enacts its own laws to nominate and declare specific agencies empowered to use
these provisions. See, for example, *Telecommunications (Interception) (New South Wales) Act* 1987
(NSW); *Telecommunications (Interception) (State Provisions) Act* 1988 (Vic).

ber of specialist police officers in New South Wales (NSW), Victoria, the Federal Narcotics Bureau and the Australian Federal Police had been involved in systematic wiretapping for many years (Stewart 1986, 81–226). The justification presented to the Commission was that the legal framework was preventing effective law enforcement, and creating an environment where corruption could take hold. The surrounding controversy resulted in recommendations for a national framework giving each Australian state law enforcement authority the capacity to obtain telecommunication interception warrants (Stewart 1986, 354). This legislation has been amended primarily in response to emergent communications technology over time, and also the growing international character of digital communication. Australia is now a signatory to the European *Convention on Cybercrime*.[18] That Convention includes requirements for domestic telecommunications law to retain and share data with other signatory law enforcement agencies. To that effect Australian telecommunications law has recently been extended by the requirements of telecommunications providers to store 'metadata' for at least two years for possible retrieval for intelligence and law enforcement purposes pursuant to a 'stored communications warrant.'[19] Interception warrants now cover traditional eavesdropping, the collection of electronic data, email and images whether 'live' or stored. Any form of 'communication' transmitted over an electronic device is within the remit of current legislation.

Personal Surveillance

The first raft of personal surveillance legislation emerged in the late 1960s, authorising use of listening devices by law enforcement and

---

[18] The treaty came into effect through the Council of Europe in Budapest on 23 November 2001, coming into general operation on 1 July 2004. Canada was an immediate signatory, but did not ratify the treaty until 8 July 2015. By contrast, Australia ratified the treaty on 30 November 2011, with the treaty coming into effect in Australia on 1 March 2013. See *Australian Treaty Series* [2013] ATS 9.

[19] *Telecommunications (Interception and Access) Amendment (Data Retention) Act* 2015 (Cth) assented to 13 April 2015 and commencing operation on 13 October 2015.

national security agencies.[20] With the expansion of technologies that allowed for optical recording and surveillance in the 1990s, legislation governing listening devices began to merge with optical surveillance, and by the early 2000s was replaced with broader, generic 'surveillance device' statutes. Most Australian jurisdictions now have concurrent listening and surveillance 'device' statutes operating at the state level, augmented by the uniform Commonwealth telecommunications interception provisions.[21] In New South Wales (NSW) this went one step further with the introduction of real-time in-car video cameras in police vehicles directed to recording interactions between police and the public.[22] More recently, this has expanded to include police officers wearing personally fitted digital cameras or 'body cams.'[23] The trend is that legislative provisions tend to track with the available technology, but only after the technology is publicly and commercially available.

Intrusive Covert Investigations

The most sophisticated undercover operations involve the personal insertion of investigators directly into a suspect's local ecology. In many cases such investigations simply involve a plainclothes operative attending a location and talking to or observing people. Australian law does not provide a statutory governance structure for cases of simple observation and consensual discussion in public places. Such investigations are generally lawful and require no regulation, being left to the professional judgement of the investigators, but are often governed by an internal organisational code of conduct. In more intricate operations, which might involve an

---

[20] For example, *Listening Devices Act* 1969 (NSW), *Listening Devices Act* 1984 (NSW), *Listening Devices Act* 1972 (SA), *Listening Devices Act* 1969 (Vic), *Listening Devices Act* 1978 (WA) and *Invasion of Privacy Act* 1971 (Qld).

[21] *Surveillance Devices Act* 2007 (Vic); *Surveillance Devices Act* 2007 (NSW); *Surveillance Devices Act* 2008 (WA); *Crimes (Surveillance Devices) Act* 2010 (ACT); *Surveillance Devices Act* 2007 (NT); *Police Powers and Responsibilities Act* 2000 (Qld); Chap. 13; *Police Powers (Surveillance Devices) Act* 2006 (Tas).

[22] *Law Enforcement (Powers and Responsibilities) Amendment (In-car Video Systems) Act* 2004 (NSW).

[23] *Surveillance Devices Amendment (Police Body-Worn Video) Act* 2014 (NSW).

investigator infiltrating a closed network, officers may find themselves engaging in various trespass or unlawful activities, as well as having to construct one or more false identities. In these cases, Australian jurisdictions began to construct legislative frameworks from the mid-1990s to regulate such activities. These laws enabled intrusive investigations by establishing statutory frameworks for assumed identities[24] that permitted deceptive and invasive undercover investigations, including a limited range of authorised unlawful conduct.[25]

The new legislative schemes were linked to at least three developments. The first was a High Court decision (*Ridgeway v. The Queen* (1994)) that found a particular undercover operation was unlawful, and rejected as inadmissible compelling evidence of narcotic importation because it was unlawfully obtained.[26] The absence of a clear statutory foundation for this kind of covert investigation in Australian law meant law enforcement agencies were basically authorising themselves to engage in unlawful activity. The result was the acquittal of a convicted drug trafficker,[27] and similar cases were cast into doubt. In addition, the case suggested that investigators themselves were potentially civilly and criminally liable for their actions during an otherwise successful sting operation, a result which the Court recognised was manifestly unsatisfactory for ordinary law enforcement. Consequently, recommendations were made

---

[24] *Crimes (Assumed Identities) Act* 2009 (ACT); *Crimes Act* 1914 (Cth), Part IAC; *Law Enforcement and National Security (Assumed Identities) Act* 2010 (NSW); *Police (Special Investigative and Other Powers) Act* 2015 (NT), Part 3; *Police Powers and Responsibilities Act* 2000 (Qld), Chap. 12; *Crime and Corruption Act* 2001 (Qld), Part 6B; *Criminal Investigation (Covert Operations) Act* 2009 (SA), Part 3; *Police Powers (Assumed Identities) Act* 2006 (Tas); *Crimes (Assumed Identities) Act* 2004 (Vic); *Criminal Investigation (Covert Powers) Act* 2012 (WA), Part 3.

[25] *Crimes (Controlled Operations) Act* 2008 (ACT); *Crimes Act* 1914 (Cth), Part 1AB; *Law Enforcement (Controlled Operations) Act* 1997 (NSW); *Police (Special Investigative and Other Powers) Act* 2015 (NT), Part 2; *Police Powers and Responsibilities Act* 2000 (Qld), Chap. 11; *Crime and Corruption Act* 2001 (Qld), Part 6A; *Criminal Investigation (Covert Operations) Act* 2009 (SA); *Police Powers (Controlled Operations) Act* 2006 (Tas); *Crimes (Controlled Operations) Act* 2004 (Vic); *Criminal Investigation (Covert Powers) Act* 2012 (WA), Part 2.

[26] *Ridgeway v. The Queen* (1995) 184 CLR 19.

[27] Note, however, that the offender in this case, John Anthony Ridgeway, was subsequently charged and convicted of being in possession of a traffickable quantity of heroin under South Australian law. See *R. v. Ridgeway* [1998] SASC 6963.

for legislative intervention[28] and ultimately for legislation that addressed these concerns by authorising what have become known as 'controlled operations.'[29]

The second development related to corruption findings in Queensland, NSW and Victorian Police Forces (Queensland Fitzgerald Commission of Inquiry 1989; Wood 1997; Office of Police Integrity 2007). The Wood Royal Commission in NSW specifically recommended the regulation of covert investigative activities, not only for the purposes of facilitating undercover investigations but also corruption enquiries (Wood 1997, 2: 407–431). These developments were fundamental to an expansion of public sector and internal agencies restricting and regulating covert surveillance, through an emphasis on accountability and integrity. While Australian police have long maintained an 'internal affairs' branch, the 1980s and 1990s saw the expansion of independent agencies tasked with ensuring the integrity and absence of corruption within government departments, including the National Crime Authority,[30] the NSW Independent Commission Against Corruption,[31] the Victorian Inspectorate[32] and the Australian Commission for Law Enforcement Integrity.[33] These organisations share the statutory investigative powers

---

[28] *Ridgeway v. The Queen* (1995) 184 CLR 19 at [38] per Mason CJ, Deane and Dawson JJ:

[I]n the context of the fact that deceit and infiltration are of particular importance to the effective investigation and punishment of trafficking in illegal drugs such as heroin, it is arguable that a strict requirement of observance of the criminal law by those entrusted with its enforcement undesirably hinders law enforcement. Such an argument must, however, be addressed to the Legislature and not to the courts. If it be desired that those responsible for the investigation of crime should be freed from the restraints of some provisions of the criminal law, a legislative regime should be introduced exempting them from those requirements. In the absence of such a legislative regime, the courts have no choice but to set their face firmly against grave criminality on the part of anyone, regardless of whether he or she be a government officer or an ordinary citizen. To do otherwise would be to undermine the rule of law itself.

[29] See above n. 19.

[30] The National Crime Authority was established pursuant to the *National Crime Authority Act* 1984 (Cth). Following a number of controversies about its powers and the focus of its investigations, the NCA was decommissioned in 2003, and replaced by the Australian Crime Commission.

[31] A statutory corruption investigation authority located in New South Wales. See *Independent Commission Against Corruption Act* 1998 (NSW). Refer also to www.icac.nsw.gov.au.

[32] A statutory compliance and monitoring organisation based in Victoria. See *Victorian Inspectorate Act* 2011 (Vic) and www.vicinspectorate.vic.gov.au.

[33] ACELI is a Federal law enforcement integrity and compliance-monitoring agency. See *Law Enforcement Integrity Commissioner Act* 2006 (Cth) and www.aclei.gov.au.

of other law enforcement agencies, but specifically investigate crime and corruption within the executive.

The third development was the reaction to 9/11. This was significant because it crystallised a national approach to more proactive investigation, which was a particular problem in a federal system where there were no explicit national constitutional powers to create criminal laws and jurisdictionally complicated in cross-border cooperation between law enforcement agencies. The resulting *Report on Cross Border Investigation* (Standing Committee of Attorneys-General and Australasian Police Ministers Council Joint Working Group on National Investigation Powers 2003) was a landmark in recommending a range of model laws that have strongly influenced covert investigation laws during the last decade.

In summary, Australian surveillance laws have been shaped by a combination of developments introduced mainly between 1985 and 2010, but with much earlier origins. There were various environmental factors at play, including advances in technology, changes to police investigative practices and the associated behaviour of target populations. The nature of certain kinds of crimes, notably those involving large profits, conspiracies between willing participants and the general absence of operational scrutiny and accountability, has created an environment extremely difficult to regulate, while the potential for corruption remains substantial. Technological advances necessarily augmented the practices within a closed criminogenic location. Demands for enhanced regulation intersect with a complex range of security and law enforcement requirements, and the competing call for the control and limitation of those practices in an ostensibly liberal democracy that expects meaningful respect of privacy and lawful conduct by law enforcement agents. The result is a legislative design in which law enforcement powers are augmented within strict accountability frameworks. The shift towards the regulation of undercover investigations is often linked to public scandal, particularly official findings of police misconduct and corruption. These complex discourses created a set of principles that provide a typology of investigative regulation (Murphy 2014), but also serve to identify the character and identity of elements within surveillant assemblages and provide insights into the array of forces that crystallise, stabilise and destabilise those elements.

Typologies of Investigative Regulation

Although the timing and nature of surveillance laws in Australia vary, there are important common elements and guiding principles in the regulatory framework (see also Walsh, this volume). The identification and characterisation of principles provides a useful foundation for comparative analysis, particularly those federal common law jurisdictions such as Australia and Canada (see Forcese, this volume). Theoretically, these typologies also provide important elements of the knowledge systems that constitute the surveillant assemblage. As epistemological components, the elements of these typologies serve multiple purposes, ranging from organising concepts to literal statements of law, through to lines of visibility that attach to individual and institutional actors. They form conceptual parts of the embedded rationalities of governance and identity that characterise assemblages, and also serve as concepts integral to the formation of counter-law. These elements arguably function as epistemic threads that provide cohesion and stability, reinforcing the linkage between legal structures and surveillance practices.

Authorisation Requirements

Generally, all forms of lawful intrusive surveillance require authorisation. This classification is important because legal consequences attach to unauthorised surveillance activities, especially when those activities include criminal behaviour. For example, soliciting and purchasing narcotics from a suspect without a warrant would likely result in misconduct proceedings and/or criminal charges against the investigator. Typically, authorisation is both prospective and sourced from a specified senior officer within the organisation, or through a judicial or an administrative authority. In most cases the authorising officer must be independently satisfied of the need for authorisation, which is ordinarily demonstrated through information that the target is a valid suspect. At this stage, the threshold requirement of that information will vary according to the legislation, but usually involves establishing reasonable grounds for suspicion. The authorisation requirement provides a significant control mechanism over a range of intrusive surveillance activities because it requires sufficient evidence to satisfy the authorising officer of the need for the warrant. This immediately makes the investigator visible to one or more executive or judicial agencies. At the same time the authorisation itself empowers the investigator to penetrate closed environments to conduct invasive and directed surveillance.

Controlled Activity

While surveillance and investigation warrants empower agents to act in ways that might otherwise be unlawful, such warrants also limit activity. An investigator is required to act in a controlled manner during the life of a warrant. The character of these controls will vary according to the nature of the investigation and warrant. A telecommunications interception warrant, for example, would normally provide authorisation to covertly record and listen to telephone conversations, but not physically enter the person's home. As the regulation of covert investigation has expanded, this has meant that complex covert investigations have come to rely on multiple warrants to extend the time required, authorise different techniques and authorise cross-border collaboration. One result of this administrative complication is the gradual appearance of 'multifunction' covert investigation authorities that permit both entry to premises and some other activity. For example, telecommunications interception warrants may also authorise entry to premises, installation and retrieval of devices in addition to the interception of communications.[34] The scope of a warrant is further qualified, in most instances, by a time limitation, which may limit the operation to a matter of hours, days or weeks. As a matter of practical law enforcement, this often means a complex investigation may involve several warrants being issued for multiple purposes and actors. The governing principle here is that regulation typically limits both the time and scope of surveillance.

---

[34] For example, *Telecommunications (Interception and Access) Act* 1979 (Cth), s. 48; *Criminal Investigation (Covert Operations) Act* 2009 (SA).

Immunities

A major practical effect of a warrant is to identify a specific investigator as possessing conditional immunity from various causes of action for their conduct during a legitimate investigation. The immunity offered by a warrant is generally *conditional* on the officer acting *within the scope of the warrant* during the investigation. Exceeding the mandate has substantial consequences as it may expose the officer to legal and/or professional sanction, and may compromise prosecution of the suspect.

Prosecution Evidence

In Australian law there are significant controls over the admissibility of evidence during a trial,[35] particularly relating to questions of relevance, probative value, reliability and unfair prejudice. In undercover investigations a vast amount of information is typically gathered about the social networks of the suspect, and while much of this information has no direct legal purpose and will be irrelevant or inadmissible, it often can be significant for criminal intelligence (Harfield and Harfield 2008a, b; Stelfox 2009; Brodeur 2010). The focus in actual prosecutions is upon the specific elements of a criminal charge that must be satisfied beyond reasonable doubt.[36] One practical problem investigators face is ensuring a sufficient degree of evidence capable of sustaining a prosecution against a suspect given the high standard of proof. Unlawfully or improperly obtained evidence infringes numerous rules in Australian evidence law and may be excluded from trial.[37] Consequently, investigators collecting evidence through covert surveillance often monitor the issuing, character and execution of any warrant, particularly in controlled operations because these normally involve the investigator

---

[35] See *Evidence Act* 1995 (Cth), particularly ss. 135–8. This Act is largely mirrored as uniform legislation in a number of Australian jurisdictions, including NSW, Victoria, Tasmania, ACT and NT.

[36] For example, *Smith v. R.* (2001) 206 CLR 630 at 654.

[37] For example, *Bunning v. Cross* (1978) 141 CLR 54. In those states where Uniform Evidence law applies, section 138 provides a statutory presumption against admissibility, but entrenches the discretionary power of the judicial officer to admit that evidence if it is desirable to do so.

engaging in technically unlawful conduct, which could arguably taint all evidence obtained from an operation. One notable effect of controlled operations law, and surveillance law broadly, is to provide some legal protections for the admissibility of prosecution evidence.[38] The existence of a warrant that authorises intrusive surveillance practices will mean evidence obtained from the investigation is ordinarily admissible, while simultaneously providing opportunities for collecting criminal intelligence which, as Harfield and Harfield have observed, these are the primary purposes of covert investigation, a dynamic common to both Australian and Canadian criminal justice and surveillance laws (Harfield and Harfield 2010, 777).

Accountability Structures

At one level, the legal architectures regulating investigation operate as an accountability structure. This structure facilitates a multilayered apparatus with both vertical and lateral systems of account. The investigation itself is intended to hold individuals and networks to account for corrupt and criminal conduct. Detailed record-keeping and administrative supervision is intended to hold the investigator and the executive agency to account for its surveillance activities, while the lateral supervision of the courts and the investigating agency similarly function to assess an agency's conduct. This accounting involves mechanisms of documentation that permit retrospective and temporal examination of conduct. Individuals involved in the investigation know their actions may come under close examination in the future. Records, identification, scrutiny and comparative normative assessment function as key accountability technologies. Surveillance, in this respect, is internalised to encourage legality, which is a powerful technology to direct conduct and establish operational norms. The investigator and those that authorise the operation are subject to systems of vertical and lateral surveillance themselves, which provide a major system of accountability.

---

[38] For example, *Law Enforcement (Controlled Operations) Act* 1997 (NSW), s. 3A.

Theorising Principles of Governance

These guiding principles provide a regulatory structure that serves several purposes. Individual accountability is achieved through mechanisms that function to identify specific individuals in particular moments in time, and allows for both present and retrospective analysis of conduct. The surveillance technology allows for observation during an event that has been recognised as criminogenic. In this way the surveillance technology allows for transformation from clock time to event time (Adkins 2009), for the specific purpose of legal and normative evaluation. In this respect, close examination of an individual or a place allows collection of general and specific intelligence, as well as the capacity to directly observe and record unlawful conduct. Segments of history may thus be captured and examined.

Harfield and Harfield (2010) also highlight two key principles of effective governance of covert investigation: the presence of internal governance structures through internal management processes and structures, and the presence of external governance structures in the form of legislation and the audit practices of executive government. These governance structures are intended to restrict and control the potential for abuses and deviance by the investigating agency itself. Harfield and Harfield imply that a key aspect of covert investigation governance involves a double movement: the simultaneous investigation of crime and corruption, and the control of deviance within law enforcement.

While much attention on surveillance has been concerned primarily with the empowerment and limitation of law enforcement agents in the investigation of crime, this is only one element of surveillant assemblage. Assemblage is not restricted to a single flow or line of observation; surveillance operates as a technology that captures the investigators as much as the suspect. Not only does surveillance provide the opportunity to identify criminal conduct and pursue criminal charges against individuals, the mechanisms of covert surveillance are deployed internally through record-keeping, audit, identification and examination of conduct. Surveillance is deployed in ways designed to contain and control the conduct of the investigating authority, as much as to observe the civilian population. The reason is that the purpose of surveillance technology and regulation is for the surveillance of suspect populations. Here the apparatus of state is itself a suspect population.

Policy Discourses

At the highest level of abstraction, law is linked to a range of public policy discourses about political and theoretical dimensions of managing social life. Policy discourses not only engage the political debate; they constitute and mobilise normative and theoretical discourses about the composition and functioning of social order and directly shape the legal and regulatory framework. Arguably, discourse can function to not only form distinct components of assemblage, but also mobilises distinct forces that shape, reshape and disrupt those components. The discourses that flow through and shape the intersections between law and surveillance are affected not only by what is said, but how it is said, and who is speaking.

For surveillance, many discourses shaping policy involve the intersection of ethical, legal and security themes. The intersection itself is complicated, and it is unwise to assume the governing policies concerning surveillance law are addressed to any one specific issue, such as terrorism. Marx, for example, identified no less than 21 justifications and objections concerning the ethics of undercover surveillance, including respect for privacy, the requirement for the state to act lawfully when using its investigative and coercive powers, and the notion of 'ethical equilibrium': that when a citizen behaves in questionable ways to achieve their goals, the state is justified in doing the same (Marx 1988, 89–107).

There are, however, dominant themes within the complex of policy discourses. As previously outlined, surveillance laws normally enliven two well-known, oppositional arguments. The first is a concern for the privacy and protection of the citizen against the power of the state. Law responds and attends to this by constructing specific frameworks regulating state power, typically expressed as rights. In Western liberal democracies, privacy is often cited as a treasured right that allows individuals and families to go about their business, free from the intrusion of their neighbours and state authorities. Consequently, privacy is enshrined in apex human rights instruments.[39] Individuals move between the private and the public, a boundary that is necessary to permit and protect healthy social and psychological functioning within a community.[40] For individuals to enjoy quiet anonymity, they must be free from others' scrutiny, including, or especially, from government. Thus, privacy is necessary for at least a part of daily life. The deployment of mass surveillance represents a threat to the privacy of ordinary citizens, particularly where state law enforcement exercises a monopoly over using extraordinary investigative powers, manufacturing false realities, intrusion into private spaces and property, and prosecution reliant upon sensitive evidence. The utility of this power for law enforcement is undeniable, but it is also highly invasive. Accordingly, legal theorists, such as Herbert Packer, have long argued that a core element of any legal system aiming to balance the competition of interests is to construct and maintain architectures that both facilitate and, at times, obstruct executive action (Packer 1964, 1968).

The second major theme relates to the concept of necessity. The capacity to conduct surveillance is often presented as a necessary and valuable instrument for law enforcement, governance and public security. Without the ability to conduct surveillance, two central pillars of good government are less effective: accountability and security. Accountability is mobilised as a discourse that provides mechanisms of control over state action, and for the observation, evaluation and prosecution of citizens and groups behaving unlawfully or who present a manifest threat. This overlaps with security discourse, which presents surveillance as an effective and powerful instrument in the identification of unlawful, deviant and increasingly dangerous behaviours within the population. The capacity for government to provide security to its people is made more effective when the government has information about the activities of specific individuals and groups. Such information is mobilised both at the level of political rhetoric and justification, as well as the allocation of executive resources and the adjustment of legal architectures.

---

[39] *International Covenant on Civil and Political Rights* 1966, Art 17; *Universal Declaration of Human Rights* 1948, Art 12; *Convention for the Protection of Human Rights and Fundamental Freedoms* 1950, Art 8.

[40] Feminist scholars have challenged the distinction between the private and the public for some time. See, for example, Pateman (1989) and Lacey (1993).

The interaction of these two discourses is fundamental to the legal architectures that govern surveillance. It is characterised by a balancing rhetoric, in which the legislature, the courts and the law itself aim to preserve privacy via the protection of individuals from arbitrary interference, while at the same time insisting upon accountability and the suppression of crime and violence. The mechanism is the investigative and surveillance apparatus, while the goal is providing security for the population being governed. In this respect the combination of accountability and security functions as a categorical imperative, where demands for security have the potential to trump rights-based claims. In this environment the rhetoric of security appears frequently in policy statements that justify legislative changes to existing law.[41] It is a utilitarian logic in which the ends justify the means, and the individual's demands for respect of privacy and protection from the interference of state is subject to the expectations of accountability and the provision of security. This imperative is, however, not necessarily controversial, as civil society has always, to some extent, operated on the basis that an individual's conduct must fall within the reasonable limits of public law. If a person behaves in a manifestly unlawful manner, it is not unreasonable for state law enforcement to displace that person's claim of privacy and protection, or for the public at large to expect intervention for the purposes of investigating crime or ensuring security. In this respect, the accountability discourse provides a powerful legitimising force for legal mechanisms that otherwise override rights-based claims or legal protections and to concerns about arbitrary use of state power. The system of warrants and accountability ensures that law enforcement is not arbitrary. Similarly, even at the level of constitutional and international law and relations between nations, there has always been present a 'safety valve' within law: the power to derogate from commitments otherwise operative as the essence of 'ordinary law.' Indeed, derogation is a power routinely exercised by Australia, Canada and many other nations to promote national security (De Londras and Davis 2010; Hafner-Burton et al. 2011).

---

[41] The Prime Minister of Australia, the Hon. Tony Abbott gave a speech on 22 September 2014, in which he outlined an array of legislative changes intended to maximise security and augment domestic law enforcement and intelligence gathering. He began the speech by stating "protecting our people is the first duty of government" (Hansard, House of Representative 22/9/2014, 9957).

Australian surveillance laws contain a binary dynamic, purporting on the one hand to protect the individual and the public from arbitrary interference, but also entrenching surveillance and the investigations monopoly. Each statute imports a mechanism for prohibition and authorisation to engage in intrusive surveillance practice as exclusive powers of specified state instrumentalities. Authorisation is recognised as playing an important role in the containment of state power and operational risk, concurrently within the scope of the warrant (Mulgan 2003; Prenzler 2013; Murphy 2015). Operational risks include the conduct of the investigator and the investigated, unexpected events, the admissibility of evidence and state liability for the investigator's conduct. In addition to being a powerful investigative tool, surveillance architectures are characterised by complex mechanisms of accountability and exception that rests upon the identification of specific individuals, decision-makers and conduct. The investigative limb serves the intelligence gathering and prosecution arm of the state. The accountability limb aims to govern and stabilise the activities of state and the civilian population, while the exception limb aims to stabilise legal interference with the prosecution of individuals and state investigators.

Investigations, Assemblage and Counter-Law

There is a powerful link between surveillance, legal architectures, risk and uncertainty. These are, in fact, actants within surveillant assemblage, brought together and constituted by the combination of historical forces, technology, practices and legal architecture. The linkages and heterogeneous elements are a part of surveillant assemblage. As is well known, crime plays a major role in the political economy of risk and uncertainty (Ericson 2007; Garland 2001). As Ericson (2007) correctly argued, part of the response to the nexus between risk, crime and uncertainty is the mobilisation of law and surveillance. Ericson, drawing on earlier observations by Ashworth (2006) and Agamben (1998, 2005), argued that the mobilisation of law and surveillance is based on a political imperative grounded in precautionary logic. This logic involves legislative activity by states that result in laws that not only expand the categories of crime and facilitate prosecution but also facilitate and entrench surveillant assemblages. These two dynamics—precautionary law and surveillance—are part of the counter-law dynamic. The surveillant assemblage is necessarily connected to legal architectures (itself an independent and complex assemblage), because both assemblages form part of a whole. In the present study, we may observe both.

In Australian surveillance laws we observe a clustering of powers that facilitate various techniques that enable a comprehensive apparatus of investigation. There are mechanisms that not only collect a vast amount of important social and criminal intelligence but also provide a vehicle for powerful and unprecedented examination of a suspect. This examination is rendered possible by a distinct array of legal architectures designed to facilitate and legalise that examination and are directed towards the twin goals of prosecution and domestic security. In effect, surveillance laws and practices can function as an apparatus of power, allowing strategic and tactical management of populations, which are directed as much internally into the agencies that deploy such mechanisms, as to the outward examination of suspect populations. The investigator is therefore captured by the same technology as the suspect.

The counter-law thesis involves the idea of laws operating against law itself. In this respect surveillance laws operate in distinct and open-ended dimensions. Legal architectures provide authority for the investigator to lawfully engage in surveillance activities ordinarily considered unlawful. The same architecture converts surveillance evidence usually considered unlawful into admissible evidence. In both instances the unlawful is transformed into the lawful. In these cases, the law is directed to two imperatives. The first is to ensure that activities of the investigator are notionally immune from criminal prosecution or civil action. The second, as far as possible, aims to ensure that evidence obtained for use in a criminal trial is admissible and of probative value. In both cases, there is a real risk that the investigator is compromised by the absence of formal legal protections.

Laws can be mobilised in ways that aim to control external and internal sources of risk and uncertainty. This is achieved through containment of operational risks associated with specific surveillance and accountability practices, and through the direct structural alterations of the ordinary rules of law through the medium of exceptions. Arguably, this characteristic of regulation provides controls over the conduct of the investigative agency of government, and in this respect is a net public good. The difficulty here is that surveillance operates invisibly, and tends to generate a great deal more information about the suspect than is required to prosecute (Bronitt and Kinley 1996; Bronitt 1999; Bronitt and Roche 2000).

Returning to the idea of assemblage introduced at the chapter's outset, Haggerty and Ericson conceptualise surveillant assemblages as concerned with the actual practices and the knowledge systems these practices both rely on and produce. Central to surveillance practice is the process of producing knowledge about known individuals for the specific purpose of governing them. This combination of knowledge, power and discourse lends itself to a deeper consideration of intrusive intervention beyond the legal architectures that capture and orchestrate the practice. Understanding covert surveillance legal architectures therefore requires a multilateral conception of purpose. To some extent, the discourses that shape covert surveillance law are mutually exclusive and tend to follow disciplinary interests and boundaries. The investigator and the lawyer are primarily concerned with understanding whether or not the investigation is warranted, properly conducted, and within law's scope. They will be interested in the results of the investigation, which typically involves the arrest and successful prosecution of the suspect. The theorist, on the other hand, will be interested in how the intersection, clustering and impact of distinct surveillance rationalities shape the legal architecture. The assemblage of law, power, risk and security mobilise important questions of public policy that go to the heart of surveillance as a social practice, the preservation of security and the preservation of rights, freedoms and legitimate expectations in liberal democracies.

Acknowledgements The authors are grateful for the energy and vigorous review of the editors. Brendon extends sincere thanks to Dr Jay Anderson for his insights into assemblage.

References

Adkins, Lisa. 2009. Sociological Futures: From Clock Time to Event Time. *Sociological Research Online* 14(4): 8.

Agamben, Giorgio. 1998. *Homo Sacer: Sovereign Power and Bare Life*. Stanford, CA: Stanford University Press.

———. 2005. *State of Exception.* Chicago: University of Chicago Press.

Alderson, Karl. 2001. *Powers and Responsibilities: Reforming NSW Criminal Investigation Law.* Ph.D Thesis, University of New South Wales, Sydney.

Ashworth, Andrew. 2000. Is the Criminal Law a Lost Cause? *Law Quarterly Review* 166: 225–256.

———. 2006. Four Threats to the Presumption of Innocence. *South African Law Journal* 123(1): 63–97.

Australian Law Reform Commission. 1975. Report No. 2: An Interim Report: Criminal Investigation. Canberra: Australian Law Reform Commission.

———. 1983. *Privacy.* Canberra: Australian Government Printing Service.

———. 2008. *For Your Information: Australian Privacy Law and Practice.* vol. 3. Canberra: Commonwealth of Australia.

Brodeur, Jean-Paul. 2010. *The Policing Web.* New York: Oxford University Press.

Bronitt, Simon. 1999. Entrapment, Human Rights and Criminal Justice: A Licence to Deviate? *Hong Kong Law Journal* 29(2): 216–239.

Bronitt, Simon, and David Kinley. 1996. Undercover Policing: Detection or Deception? In *Tomorrow's Law*, ed. H. Selby. Sydney: Federation Press.

Bronitt, Simon, and Bernadette McSherry. 2010. *Principles of Criminal Law.* Sydney: Lawbook Co.

Bronitt, Simon, and Declan Roche. 2000. Between Rhetoric and Reality: Sociolegal and Republican Perspectives on Entrapment. *International Journal of Evidence and Proof* 4(2): 77.

Brown, David, David Farrier, Sandra Egger, Luke McNamara, Alex Steel, Michael Grewcock and Donna Spears. 2010. *Criminal Laws: Materials and Commentary on Criminal Law and Process in New South Wales.* 5th ed. Sydney: Federation Press.

Commonwealth of Australia, New South Wales Government, Queensland Government and Victorian Government. 1983. *Royal Commission of Inquiry into Drug Trafficking.* Canberra: Australian Government Publishing Service.

De Londras, Fiona, and Fergal F. Davis. 2010. Controlling the Executive in Times of Terrorism: Competing Perspectives on Effective Oversight Mechanisms. *Oxford Journal of Legal Studies* 30(1): 19–47.

DeLanda, Manuel. 2006. *A New Philosophy of Society: Assemblage Theory and Social Complexity.* London: Continuum.

Deleuze, Gilles, and Félix Guattari. 1987. *A Thousand Plateaus.* Minneapolis, MN: University of Minnesota Press.

Ericson, Richard V. 2007. *Crime in an Insecure World.* Cambridge: Polity Press.

Gans, Jeremy, Terese Henning, Jill Hunter, and Kate Warner. 2011. *Criminal Process and Human Rights.* Sydney: Federation Press.

Garland, David. 2001. *The Culture of Control: Crime and Social Order in Contemporary Society*. Chicago: University of Chicago Press.

Hafner-Burton, Emilie, Laurence R. Helfer, and Christopher J. Fariss. 2011. Emergency and Escape: Explaining Derogations from Human Rights Treaties. *International Organization* 65: 673–707.

Haggerty, Kevin D., and Richard V. Ericson. 2000. The Surveillant Assemblage. *British Journal of Sociology* 51(4): 605–622.

Harfield, Clive, and Karen Harfield. 2008a. *Covert Investigation*. New York: Oxford University Press.

———. 2008b. *Intelligence: Investigation, Community and Partnership*. Oxford: Oxford University Press.

———. 2010. The Governance of Covert Investigation. *Melbourne University Law Review* 34(3): 773–804.

Lacey, Nicola. 1993. Theory into Practice: Pornography and the Public/Private Dichotomy. *Journal of Law and Society* 20(1): 93–113.

Lippert, Randy K. 2009. Signs of the Surveillant Assemblage: Privacy Regulation, Urban CCTV, and Governmentality. *Social and Legal Studies* 18(4): 505–522.

Lyon, David. 2007. *Surveillance Studies: An Overview*. Cambridge: Polity Press.

Marx, Gary T. 1988. *Undercover: Police Surveillance in America*. Berkeley, CA: University of California Press.

Mulgan, Richard. 2003. *Holding Power to Account: Accountability in Modern Democracies*. Basingstoke: Palgrave Macmillan.

Murphy, Brendon. 2014. Retrospective on Ridgeway: Governing Principles of Controlled Operations Law. *Criminal Law Journal* 38(1): 38–58.

———. 2015. *Zone of Impeachment: A Post-Foucauldian Analysis of Controlled Operations Law and Policy*. Ph.D Thesis, University of Newcastle.

Office of Police Integrity. 2007. *Ceja Task Force: Drug Related Corruption*. Melbourne: Victorian Government Printer.

Packer, Herbert. 1964. Two Models of the Criminal Process. *University of Pennsylvania Law Review* 113(1): 1–64.

———. 1968. *The Limits of the Criminal Sanction*. Palo Alto, CA: Stanford University Press.

Pateman, Carole. 1989. Feminist Critiques of the Private/Public Dichotomy. In *Public and Private in Social Life*, eds. S. Benn and G. Gaus. London: St. Martin's Press.

Prenzler, Tim. 2013. *Ethics and Accountability in Criminal Justice*. Toowong: Australian Academic Press.

Presser, Bram. 2001. Public Policy, Police and Interest: A Re-Evaluation of the Judicial Discretion to Exclude Improperly or Illegally Obtained Evidence. *Melbourne University Law Review* 25(3): 757–785.

Queensland Fitzgerald Commission of Inquiry into Possible Illegal Activities and Associated Police Misconduct. 1989. Report of a Commission of Inquiry Pursuant to Orders in Council. Brisbane: Queensland Government Printer.

Secretary of State for the Home Department (UK). 1929. Report of the Royal Commission on Police Powers and Procedure. London: H. M. Stationery Office.

Standing Committee of Attorneys-General and Australasian Police Ministers Council Joint Working Group on National Investigation Powers. 2003. *Cross-Border Investigative Powers for Law Enforcement Report*. Canberra: Leaders Summit on Terrorism and Multijurisdictional Crime.

Stelfox, Peter. 2009. *Criminal Investigation: An Introduction to Principles and Practice*. Collompton: Willan Publishing.

Stewart, Donald. 1986. *Royal Commission of Inquiry into Alleged Telephone Interceptions*. Canberra: Australian Government Publishing Service.

Victorian Law Reform Commission. 2010. *Surveillance in Public Places*. Melbourne: Victorian Law Reform Commission.

Wood, James. 1997. *Report of the Royal Commission into the NSW Police Service*. vol. 3. Sydney: New South Wales Government.

Part II

Introduction: Case Studies in Comparative Perspective

Part II includes five empirically driven chapters on national security, surveillance, border security and intelligence, and terrorism in Canada and Australia. The section begins with a chapter by Corkill, Brooks and Coole that addresses a familiar surveillance technology: CCTV. They avoid a rehearsal of well-established arguments about the role of CCTV in expanding surveillance capacities and questions about CCTV effectiveness. Instead, Corkill et al. use CCTV 'talk' to explore the extent that there is a national security continuum operating from the national level to the individual level incorporating state, private and corporate security actors in Australia. They raise queries about the existence of such a unity of purpose and functionality by exploring how diverse surveillance language is used as we traverse the differently located security service agencies and providers. They discern seven 'language groups' used by security actors. They suggest two alternative readings that follow recognition of different language groups, namely that this produces 'security gaps,' particularly as the security practice becomes more abstract, or that such language groups act as a bulwark against an overbearing monocultural framing that inadequately accounts for the different locations of security actors along the security continuum.

Whereas Corkill and Brooks focus on the Australian security continuum across state and non-state actors, Walby, Lippert and Gacek focus more directly on corporate security provision in national security settings in Canada. Walby, Lippert and Gacek explore different security actors operating within the national security domain and argue that there is often an epistemological divide between researchers examining national security and those examining corporate security, a situation which needs to be corrected to enrich our understanding of the range of security actors and practices. They explore these issues through an emergent, underused method of accessing data through freedom of information laws. This approach provides insights into the routine, mundane corporate security practices of six national departments in Canada. Two key findings follow. First, these national security actors practice security in ways more often associated with 'corporate' and 'private security.' Second, while much of the literature focuses on the concepts of 'responsibilising' corporate and private security to provide national security needs or the idea of state outsourcing or privatisation of state function, neither accounts are sufficient to explain security practices and arrangements. Instead, it is the institutional structures (distinct departments) that locate security actors in domains of practice that, in turn, shape how they go about their work. Rather than pre-ordaining security practices and actors as 'national' or 'corporate security,' researchers should pay closer attention to what these actors actually do, and one key means to consider is the use of FOI as a research tool to enable greater insights into everyday security work in government.

While the two previous chapters identify the need to question the idea of a continuum of national security or clear delineations between national and corporate security in Australia and Canada, Palmer and Warren examine how the idea of an 'intelligence community' was established in Australia. Palmer and Warren use open source reports and reviews to explore the historical development of national security and intelligence arrangements and practices. They start by taking the reader back to the formative 'moment' in the 1970s when considerable reform to security and intelligence was occurring globally. This was when the Australian 'intelligence community' was brought into being, a process of 'making up' a governmental object. They use the governmentality approach based on Rose's analysis of shifting government rationalities from governing *through* the social to governing *through* community. Palmer and Warren adapt this analytic to how the idea of an intelligence community is formed and opens up intelligence and security arrangements to a series of governing technologies. Beginning with the transformative Hope Royal Commission on Intelligence and Security (1976–1978), they identify how existing intelligence and security arrangements were problematised as lacking a coherence and fitness for purpose in a changing world. Hope identified the need to shift from the focus on defence and protection from external threats to other internal needs. The naming of this community enabled several steps to occur, including bringing into being new community members (new agencies) and acknowledging formerly hidden agencies and practices; formalising existing agencies through new legislation and the key problematic of community coordination. What they identify is that the governmental object of the community and the technology of 'coordination' are continually problematised from this time as identified in subsequent inquiries and reviews. They end their chapter with the most recent 2015 Review of intelligence, which led to the introduction of a 'Coordinator of coordination' for the intelligence community based on the Operation Sovereign Borders model of stopping the boats, a single authority of authority on intelligence coordination.

In the final chapter of Part II, Van Brunschot raises questions about how security and intelligence are framed in Canada. Whereas Palmer and Warren focus on the development of the intelligence community, Van Brunschot identifies key coordinates in national security and antiterror campaigns and how events are framed as being indicative of the 'reality' of the terrorist threat to Canadians at home and the need for more resolute efforts against global terrorism and the involvement of Canada in the fight against ISIL and the need for further enhancements in domestic antiterrorism mechanisms and practices. Van Brunschot uses two "terrorist" events to explore the framing of national security and anti-terrorism measures. The first involved a person known to the RCMP attempting to leave Canada for Turkey to join ISIL. He was arrested but then released and subsequently drove a motor vehicle into two soldiers, killing one. Two days later, on 22 October 2014, another 'terrorist' attack occurred at the National War Memorial on Parliament Hill in Ottawa, where a gunman shot and killed a soldier standing guard at the Memorial. Van Brunschot explores how framing an event as terrorism-related displaces other potential explanations (such as mental illness and addiction).

Van Brunschot proceeds by providing an account of the post 9/11 antiter-rorism reforms and the role of Canada in Iraq and Syria before focusing in more detail on the second 'terrorism' event, providing a biographical account of the offender that renders the 'terrorism' label highly problem-atic. The conflation of both offences shaped the antiterrorism discourse and led to further reforms to the legislative antiterrorism framework including proposed new offences, dramatically enhanced powers for CSIS at home and abroad undercutting the *Charter of Rights and Freedoms* pro-tections, new detention power and increased capacity for information sharing and limits on international travel. These amendments passed in May 2015. Van Brunschot suggests much closer examination of cases that shape how political responses are framed is required and that more attention should be given to the diversity of factors underpinning any act of violence rather than accepting more simplistic explanations.

6

The Australian Security Continuum: National and Corporate Security Gaps from a Surveillance Language Perspective

David Brooks, Jeffery Corkill, and Michael Coole

Introduction

Surveillance is undertaken for a multitude of reasons, often in the pursuit of security. However, security is a diverse term that is multidimensional and practiced across a broad spectrum by many entities and actors. Consequently, surveillance as a concept and in the name of security has diverse meanings, applications, techniques and cultural actors (see also Muller as well as Pratt, this volume). Today, the contemporary security domain encompasses many contexts, such as traditional security with concerns towards safeguarding sovereignty and territorial integrity in the pursuit of national interests, framed as national security, to nontraditional security concerns, stemming from environmental and human

D. Brooks (✉) • J. Corkill • M. Coole
School of Science, Edith Cowan University, Joondalup, Western Australia,
Australia

© The Author(s) 2016
R. Lippert et al. (eds.), *National Security, Surveillance and Terror*,
DOI 10.1007/978-3-319-43243-4_6

security down to corporate security (see Walby, Lippert and Gacek, this volume) and private security functionalities, to name a few.

Such diversity makes it difficult to provide a single encompassing definition for these many contexts, as definition is dependent on applied context and perspective (Bourne 2014, 1; Brooks and Corkill 2014). For example, Zedner (2009) uses the term 'layers of meaning' (26) to articulate the concept of security and integrate its contexts towards a unified whole as a pursuit. However, it is suggested that the concept of security within applied context is not truly understood or has been inadequately considered across the broad security spectrum.

The public discourse on security in the post-9/11 world suggests a dangerous and fractured security environment, one dominated by extreme threats from terrorists and organised criminal syndicates. Politicians and public servants actively preach a mantra of security singularity in the national interest, and at the cost of an open and frank discourse on the security strengths and weaknesses of a nation. Perhaps, more important is the discussion concerning the balance of personal freedoms against appropriate security measures, such as surveillance. Furthermore, the exposure of national intelligence secrets and cover-ups by WikiLeaks and the more recent disclosures by Snowden have reinforced the perception of the security singularity. Whereas the disappearance of commercial flight MH370 demonstrates clearly that security singularity is a myth, rather than a reality.

Has modern security evolved into a singular, fully integrated continuum or is it in fact a continuum punctuated by a variety of gaps? This chapter presents the concept of surveillance as embedded in the Australian security continuum (also see Walsh, this volume; Jones, this volume) and its many agencies and actors, arguing that there are still challenging gaps in surveillance capabilities impeding the security singularity. These gaps are argued to stem from a cultural disconnection across surveillance actors' discourse, impeding functional efficacy. To support such a position, this chapter identifies security areas and draws on variations in the language of surveillance to highlight its cultural disconnection across discourses and ultimately states of security. We use the example of closed-circuit television (CCTV) technology to illustrate our argument. The language of surveillance provides the opportunity to highlight the changing views, needs and applications amongst the many security continuum practice areas and their actors in surveillance discourse.

Surveillance and Its Role in the Pursuit of Security

The Oxford dictionary (2015) defines surveillance as "close observation of a spy or criminal." The practice of surveillance has become a staple within criminal justice systems in the pursuit of a safer society (Zedner 2009). However, in the present day surveillance has come to mean more broadly the observation or monitoring of anyone or anything usually by a range of electronic means (Sarre and Prenzler 2011) that may include CCTV, satellite tracking and dataveillance along with the capture of biometrics and DNA profiling. Such technological developments are subjecting more and more people, both citizens and non-citizens, to social sorting (Lyon 2007; Zedner 2009, 74), which determines that some people require further, more intensive monitoring. Consequently, it is this broadly held perception that as a community we are constantly being monitored and observed by all manner of electronic technologies that gives rise to the view of a fully integrated security continuum, a security singularity.

For security actors, surveillance is a tool, directed to achieve a goal and best understood as a tactic. In articulating the tactics of conflict, Sun Tzu (1971) explained that "in battle, there are not more than two methods of attack, the direct attack and the indirect attack; yet these two in combination give rise to an endless series of manoeuvres" (62). The same can be said for surveillance: there are not more than two types of surveillance, active (direct) and passive (indirect). Nevertheless, in combination, often through layers of participants, there exists an endless series of surveillance in the name and pursuit of security.

Furthermore, indirect methods of surveillance are inexhaustible and can draw in all actors. The direct and indirect methods of surveillance become a vortex. Consequently, surveillance in the security society relies on the combined energy of its many actors, focused on either a general problem such as national security in a broader sense, or a specific concern embodying concentrated types of crime or its perpetrator. Within the notion of the security continuum, surveillance, including its strengths and weaknesses, can be likened to a mosaic; however, unlike a mosaic the picture is often never complete. For instance, within a nation's boundaries the gaps in the surveillance picture are less, with more collective or discernable detail facilitating analytical interpretation. In contrast, when looking externally (internationally) in the name of security the surveillance picture gaps are larger, with less collective detail, unless plugged into a foreign nation's internal detail. In the security society, the surveillance actors can be considered and embedded within the security continuum.

In today's security environment, surveillance is often considered to be a third entity, government or corporation that has the

> ability to monitor, observe and record what, where and when someone does something … designed to control or influence the behaviour of the subject of the surveillance. Of great interest today are its manifestations and the rapid growth in technological innovations that makes surveillance more accessible, more covert and thus more insidious. (Sarre et al. 2014, 329)

Nevertheless, surveillance can be an aid to allow us to better understand the security continuum.

The Australian Security Continuum

The Australian security continuum, like most other nations, encompasses many domains and actors. Such a continuum extends from national security functionary, with actors who look both inwards and outwards to protect and defend a nations' interest, down to shopping centre security guards, who look inwards with internal and bounded interests, and finally the broader citizenry as legitimate users and observers. The approach of security is defined by why, how and where it may be applied. As Button (2008, xv) argues, security needs to be developed for various contexts, where at one end of the continuum from a housing estate and shopping centre up to the national level at the far opposite end of the security continuum.

We argue that security is divided into two prominent streams: traditional security and nontraditional security. Traditional security concerns are of nation-state sovereignty and stability of external foreign threats, pursued politically and through militarily actions (Smith and Brooks

2013, 12–13). Nontraditional security is broader, and considers risks across many societal concerns at the international or national community, or within the functioning of a nation (Coole 2015, 1). However, many of the problems with security involve scholars, policy makers and practitioners often considering security within their own area of experience and with detachment (Zedner 2009, 3). Adding to these problems are the perceptions of security by the general public. Public perceptions of security are skewed, as many see or focus on security only when it directly concerns or impacts them.

Security is an assemblage of contextual nodes (Button 2008), overlapping in parts, discrete in other parts, equal but considered different and the same but distinct. As Tow and Taylor (2008) indicate, security can "comprise of different layers that address different aspects of regional security" (3). Furthermore, security "is used to cover a much wider range of conditions than the most salient examples relating to crime" (Button 2008, 4). For example, there is in general understanding of a nation-state's military and its role in security; however, the use of corporate security to protect critical military bases is not so clear.

Such diversity leads to difficulty in not only defining security but having clear boundaries between its parts. In practice, security can be displayed along a continuum, with distinct overlaps at times in responsibility along this continuum (Fig. 6.1). Although in many ways such a continuum oversimplifies a complex domain; therefore, a more accurate reflection would be as a matrix. For example, the Australian Security and Intelligence

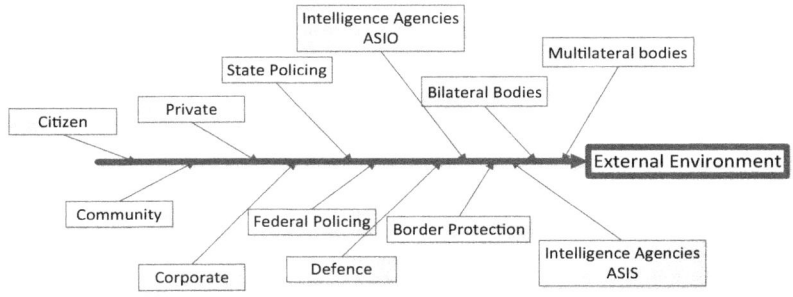

Fig. 6.1 The Australian Security Continuum

Organization (ASIO) provides national security and surveillance, but as an organisation it also has internal corporate security and private security actors. These actors are integral to what is in essence a national security organisation, but they provide corporate security functions.

Such diffusion of security and surveillance functionality can be seen further in private security firms that provide national security protection, such as Critical Infrastructure. As Petersen (2013) suggests, a key driver of twenty-first century corporate security growth is 'responsibilisation' and the embracing of the corporate environment by government as a whole of community response to national security threats, such as terrorism and transnational organised crime. Such an approach further dilutes the ability to provide clear and articulated responsibilities, allowing gaps in the security surveillance continuum to develop, remain and perhaps be exploited.

Understanding the Actors in the Security Surveillance Continuum

The security continuum (Fig. 6.1) is a topology of practice areas and actors, made up of many sectors ranging down from national security to private security roles and functionalities. Such a continuum can be extended, as shown in Fig. 6.1, from global and regional, to border protection (see Muller this volume; Pratt this volume). Furthermore, many of these sectors, such as private security, extend from explicit occupations such as guards, technicians and locksmiths, to practice areas such as physical security, security management, risk management and crisis response (Brooks 2013). Given such diversity and complexity, the focus of the following discussion will be restricted to the national, corporate and private security sectors.

National Security

National security is a state's defensive and offensive capability to protect its citizens, interests and organisations. To achieve such protection, there is a mandate for surveillance. Nevertheless, the concept of protection and resulting surveillance varies, contingent on the context of the organisation or citizen who seeks or is offered such protection. The current Australian national security discourse in relation to surveillance is a case in point. Whilst the government and for the most part, those agencies tasked with keeping the nation secure, are convinced of the need for metadata collection and retention, large swathes of the community see such activity not as a means of protection but rather one of suppression.

The reasons for these widely divergent views are not easily reduced to singular answers; however, we argue that one element that contributes to this divergence is the choices of language. Language does not simply divide communities along political and ethnic lines or community from government, nor is it simply the glue that binds disparate communities. Language both binds and divides at the macro-level the glue, whilst at the micro-level the crack. It is for this reason one should be sceptical of accepting a concept of a singular unified continuum of security, as the agencies and organisations lying along this continuum represent a broad range of language groups accordant with their contextual interests.

National security epitomises both the integration of disparate security functions across the continuum and the gaps that emerge as a result of integration. In many cases, the integration in reality consists only of small discrete elements in an agency, yet the perception created is one of the agencies being an integral part of the national security function. For example, Table 6.1 presents portfolio departments and agencies that constitute the national security actors according to the Guide to Australia's National Security Capability (Australian Government 2013, 3–4).

These 17 departments and agencies all possess unique primary functions, and whilst for some that function is specifically national security, for others this is not the case, even though they have a national security function embedded. Nevertheless, all of these agencies may have a primary national security function depending on how broadly national security is defined. However, each of these agencies is possessed of its own agency values, culture and language, and whilst these differences may not be significant amongst some—there is or will be a high degree of commonality shared by the intelligence agencies and their portfolio departments—it would be expected that there would be far less between the intelligence agencies and the Department of Agriculture, Fisheries

Table 6.1 Australian national security actors

Australian government national security actors		
Portfolio departments	Intelligence agencies	Law enforcement agencies
Attorney-General's Department (AGD)	Australian Security Intelligence Organisation (ASIO)	Australian Crime Commission (ACC)
Department of Foreign Affairs and Trade (DFAT)	Australian Secret Intelligence Service (ASIS)	Australian Customs and Border Protection Service (ACBPS)
Department of Defence (Defence)	Australian Signals Directorate (ASD)	Australian Federal Police (AFP)
Department of Health and Ageing (DoHA)	Office of National Assessments (ONA).	
Department of Immigration and Citizenship (DIAC)	Australian Geospatial-Intelligence Organisation (AGO)	
Department of Infrastructure and Transport (DIT)		
Department of the Prime Minister and Cabinet (PM&C)		
Department of Agriculture, Fisheries and Forestry (DAFF)		
Australian Agency for International Development (AusAID)		

and Forestry. Each of these differences, regardless of how subtle, creates a crack in the concept of seamless surveillance integration.

If this view is accepted, that language and culture within organisations and agencies create gaps in the integrated national security function of the federal government, then it must be also accepted that such gaps will exist or emerge as the continuum extends into state and local government agencies, and continues as it integrates into the private and social sector. One driver of security's growth is a greater reliance on the private sector for protection against crime and violence (Sarre and Prenzler 2011, 5–6), which extends to corporate protection of national interests. This does not mean that national security is ineffective, nor agencies ineffective in their tasks, but rather, it should alert the policy and decision maker to the potential factors that may contribute to systems failures due to language differentiation.

Corporate Security

Corporate security is a discrete portion of the security continuum, with distinct drivers and skills. It is a sector that provides internal security services and functions for either a public or private enterprise in the protection of assets (Brooks 2013, 2). Corporate security exists to provide self-protection of the corporation and its actors; it is not part of the private security sector (Brooks 2013). As Cubbage and Brooks (2012) claim "corporate security is a unique part of the general security domain … a support function that for efficacy aligns with its corporation and assists in its success" (xiii). However, the corporate security sector is the least understood and quantified sector within the security continuum (see also Walby, Lippert and Gacek, this volume).

Nevertheless, corporate security is embedded within the many parts of the security continuum. As a sector, it is a part of its parent organisation, exploiting as required the private security sector. For example, corporate security from time to time will employ the services of private security for guarding and response services. In addition, they may use the electronic security sector for the maintenance of CCTV surveillance and access control. Corporate security operates across diverse areas of practice, such as national security departments, public municipal government departments and private corporations, from small to large (Brooks and Corkill 2014). Potential for gaps to emerge in this domain comes from the primary function, being one of protection of the interests of the organisation which may put the function at odds with the national or community interest.

Private Security

Private security is a service-orientated function, in general, with a narrow focus to provide goods and service to a third party. For example, private security providers include operational roles such as surveillance, investigations, crowd control, prison escorts and court security, guarding and patrolling, along with proactive crime prevention, risk management and assessment, weapons training, crime scene examination, information technology, technology systems development and communications support (Prenzler et al. 2009, 1) and locksmiths. The private security sector, at a commercial level, has had a rapid expansion (Sarre 2015, 45), with CCTV surveillance being the most significant in growth, size and value. Such diversity and growth has reached a point where private security personnel outnumber sworn police by more than two to one (Prenzler et al. 2009, 1).

The Surveillance Language in the Security Continuum

Closed-circuit television (CCTV) technology has become a common form of surveillance, infused into many parts of daily life including public, private, work and social environments. Whether CCTV is used to track likely or actual offenders in crime prevention, by the media in a voyeuristic mode for reality shows or in public transport to reduce assaults and improve safety, the technology is essentially the same. For example, from a technological perspective the most simple to complex CCTV systems include common elements of illumination, lens, camera and communication medium to the monitor and system operator. However, as Taylor and Gill (2014, 705–706) point out, CCTV systems are not homogenous as developments have led to a more complex technology integration with such functions as facial recognition, number plate recognition and thermal imaging. Nowadays, all actors along the security surveillance continuum use CCTV; however, just because the technology elements are somewhat common does not necessarily result in a consensual CCTV understanding across this continuum.

On 19 April 2011, a major security incident occurred at Sydney Airport, Australia. A power failure allowed a number of passengers to pass through a security screening point, without being deemed appropriately screened. In response, the airport was evacuated and all passengers rescreened. Airport management and the political ministers described this event as evidence of the effectiveness of the airport security and its supporting surveillance function. Nevertheless, what did this mean in relation to the significant CCTV surveillance capacity deployed across the airport and its many security actors? Such actors ranged from private airport security to Australian Customs and Border Protection, to the Australian Federal Police, all having a security function and a level of CCTV surveillance capability.

Such an event represents a gross failure of CCTV surveillance beyond whether CCTV is an effective means of surveillance. Within such a controlled and regulated environment, with diverse security actors, questions have to be raised as to why non-screened passengers could not be identified, their movements traced and their whereabouts accounted for? However, in context, this event can be judged in the disunified language of CCTV surveillance.

What are the languages of CCTV surveillance actors and how does language differentiation influence the perceptions and understanding of surveillance more broadly, and CCTV more specifically in terms of how it may be employed? Past studies have investigated the effectiveness of CCTV surveillance, particularly public systems (Brooks 2005; Gill and Spriggs 2005; Welsh and Farrington 2009); however, the discussion has not addressed the question of what people believe CCTV surveillance is. As Sarre et al. (2014) note, "despite the ubiquity of surveillance, our knowledge of it and its purpose is in relatively short supply" (327). More important, what do the actors who employ CCTV surveillance— in the most part, the security actors—think it is? It is a question that commentators and researchers need to ask themselves; otherwise, how do they know what is really being applied, used and measured?

The Language of CCTV Surveillance

The language of CCTV surveillance explores how and in what context we understand this concept. For example, is surveillance used to protect, is it to monitor people or make them safer, or is it a tool for warning? Through such understanding of the broader language of surveillance, we can begin to understand the similarities and differences across the secu-

Fig. 6.2 Languages of CCTV surveillance

rity continuum. Brooks and Corkill (2012, 57) suggested that CCTV can be divided into five distinct languages; however, this chapter argues that there are seven distinct language groups of CCTV surveillance (see Fig. 6.2).

1. *CCTV as a Technology*

CCTV first developed as a technology and as such, the technology of CCTV will continue to evolve. Technology evolution will include high-frequency cameras, the increasing use of smart algorithms and artificial intelligence (Smith and Brooks 2013, 237–239) to name just a few. The technological group is assessed to be the dominant language driver for CCTV. This group is comprised of manufacturers, engineering research and development, and the private sales sector, primarily because of its simplistic application. That is not to suggest that CCTV is technically simple; rather, that the mechanics of integrating a system requires a technical approach.

This group uses terms including solutions, bit rates, bandwidth, pixels, algorithms and costs to communicate its message. For example, in a recent industry article Wine (2015) used surveillance in terms of business intelligence, being the use of information technology, software and physical sources to build a 'picture' (24–25). The current drive to develop government and industry standards, and to train and licence CCTV technicians, is somewhat limiting, as for the most part such a discourse is a limiting language of technology. However, CCTV surveillance is not just about its technological attributes and such language has the potential to exclude those actors not familiar or fluent in such technical language.

2. *CCTV as Evidence*

The value of CCTV as a source of evidence has been known for some time; in fact, it was the role of CCTV in post-event reconstruction that cemented its value as an evidence tool. Most significant was the 1993 James Bulger murder. Later, the 2005 London subway bombing is another example of the power of this vocabulary. Police generally support CCTV, demonstrated by initiatives such as Blue Iris (Western Australia Police 2015) or guidelines which state "a CCTV system becomes a powerful investigative tool for police" (ANZPAA 2014, 2). In contrast, events such as the Jill Meagher case in Melbourne (2012) where CCTV failed to capture admissible evidence has not generally reduced CCTV language as a source of evidence.

Governments around the world supported significant expansions of CCTV capacity across their mass transit sectors based on the successful gathering of evidence from the London system. Law enforcement's embrace of CCTV is in a large part due to potential access to images as evidence. As evidence is the primary focus of this CCTV discourse, words such as conviction, apprehension, admissibility, image quality, storage and retrieval (Brooks and Corkill 2012, 58) are dominantly used.

3. *CCTV as Deterrence*

For many in the security community and the general public, the value of CCTV is often believed to be its ability to deter potential deviance. CCTV surveillance, in particular public space CCTV, is procured and promoted on a law enforcement or political mandate (Brooks 2005). Deterrence is the language of the security sector and political agendas, and as a secondary language of law enforcement. Words common to this discourse include behaviour, identification, safety, visibility, observation, conviction, privacy and statistics. The discourse of deterrence is often used to persuade the general community of the value of CCTV surveillance and support its prevalence across parts of the security continuum. However, it also implies a direct security utility when in fact it may not be.

4. *CCTV as Situational Awareness*

Situational awareness is one area of the CCTV surveillance discourse that receives restricted attention outside of its operational community. The contextual application of CCTV for the provision of situational awareness is one of the most effective applications. For example, CCTV can be used to provide operational awareness in the manufacturing, process, factory or mining sectors, or monitor highway traffic flow. An example from Perth, Australia, was the 2011 Commonwealth Heads of Government Meeting (Premier of Western Australia & Cabinet Ministers 2011), where many CCTV systems from fixed and mobile assets were transmitted to a centralised Western Australian Police control room. The state police controlled security resources, traffic flow and monitored the passage of dignitaries' en route, providing operational commanders with situational awareness as part of a broader security operation. The discourse of situational awareness includes words such as control, visibility, safety, management and response.

5. *CCTV as Surveillance*

The surveillance function of CCTV is perhaps how most laypeople understand CCTV, whether in the public or commercial environment (both public and pseudo-private) or on transportation systems, to name a few. It is suggested that the surveillance function is also the least understood function of CCTV by both the lay community and security actors, partly due to the dichotomy or interplay between active and passive typologies. The surveillance discourse tends to be dominated by words such as observation, active, operators, targets, tracking and privacy (Brooks and Corkill 2012, 57).

6. *CCTV for Warning*

The use of CCTV for warning is perhaps the most implicit, as it extends beyond just the technology of CCTV to imply intervention action. CCTV may be used to monitor people and their actions, seeking those that may display indications of, or actual deviant behaviour. Today, the rapid growth in CCTV technology makes surveillance far more accessible and covert (Sarre et al. 2014, 329) for use by many more actors than have traditionally had such access. Similar to surveillance, the warning discourse is dominated by words such as big data, records, national security, intelligence, terrorism and counter-terrorism.

7. *CCTV as a Research Language*

CCTV research tends to focus on three distinct areas: (1) its crime prevention effectiveness, (2) public perception in whether people feel safer with CCTV and, finally, (3) technological advancement. Technology advancement seeks to improve CCTV technology, such as camera imaging devices and wide-spectrum devices, to a strong research drive to develop smart CCTV surveillance using algorithms to predict, detect, alert and respond to deviant behaviour. The research discourse is dominated by words such as effectiveness, perception, video analytics and intelligent CCTV.

Understanding the CCTV Surveillance Language Effect

The language discourse may be framed in many ways depending on the environmental context, realised event and its stakeholders across the security continuum. Therefore, a singular incident may be framed in many ways depending on the context actors and their language. For example, on 19 April 2010 Carl Williams died after being repeatedly bludgeoned with a part of an exercise bike in the high-security correctional unit at Barwon Prison in VIC, Australia. It was almost half an hour before correctional officers discovered Williams's body. Such an event, when framed in the languages of surveillance or deterrence, situational awareness or warning, can only be described as a failure; however, when framed in the language of evidence the role of such surveillance becomes a success (Brooks and Corkill 2012). Consequently, there are significant implications on the resulting deployment and employment of CCTV surveillance systems when various security actors are unaware of the many different languages (Table 6.2) being used and how they alter the narrative.

Table 6.2 Vocabulary of CCTV

CCTV language group	CCTV vocabulary	Indicative actor
Technology	Crime prevention, consultants, solutions, integration, bit rates, networks, bandwidth, storage, analytics	Private security
Evidence	Apprehension, admissibility, image quality, court, conviction, storage, retrieval, prosecution	Police
Deterrence	Criminology, behaviour, safety, visibility, conviction, privacy, statistics, response, police-private, antisocial, community values	Police, private security, corporate
Situational awareness	Monitor, detect, control, safety, process, manage, response	Corporate, border protection
Surveillance	Public, community, local government, crime reduction, antisocial behaviour, observation, active, passive, intelligence, operators, targets, perception, privacy, tracking, pre-emptive, security	Intelligence agencies, border protection
Warning	Government, police, security intelligence services, monitor, track, covert, regulation	Intelligence agencies
Research	Effectiveness, perception, privacy, research and development	

Source: Adjusted from Brooks and Corkill (2012, 58)

Why is CCTV effective in some contexts but has only a limited or no effect in others? (Taylor and Gill 2014, 711). As CCTV surveillance becomes more explicit in its application, it also becomes more effective in crime prevention. For example, research suggests that CCTV reduces crime by up to 51 per cent in car parks and by 23 per cent on public transport (Welsh and Farrington 2009). In a Western Australian Auditor General's report (2011, 6), the Perth Transport Authority reported a 50 per cent reduction in assaults on trains due to CCTV. However, such CCTV systems are applied within a defined environmental context with explicit surveillance objectives, whereas public space CCTV surveillance systems reduce crime by less than 7 per cent; why is this so? Gill and Loveday (2003) argued that from a deterrent aspect unless an offender has been caught by CCTV it offers little deterrence with no effect on non-emotive crime.

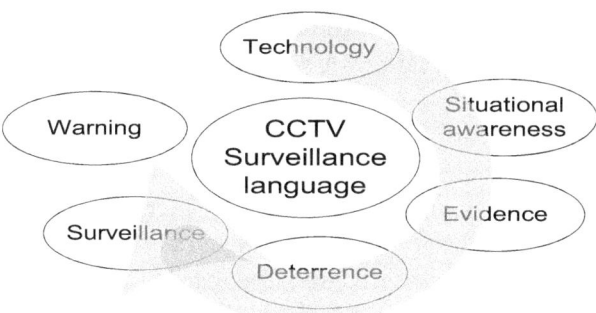

Fig. 6.3   Language diversification and CCTV surveillance effectiveness?

The capacity of CCTV surveillance to be more or less effective is directed by its context and explicit objectives. For example, such contextual surety in the language discourse is generally restricted to the technology, evidence and situational awareness language groups. Nevertheless, the arrow shown in Fig. 6.3 indicates that as the context and application becomes more abstract, the less-effective CCTV surveillance becomes more important, the diverseness of its group's language.

Australian Security Surveillance Gaps

The security continuum and its actors are multidimensional in both concept and application (Smith and Brooks 2013, 6). Many such actors will use CCTV surveillance; however, they will use quite differing language. Each actor is seated within culturally different views and understanding of CCTV, resulting in conflict in what is largely a difficult tool to apply well. As Sarre et al. (2014) argue, the "advances in technology have largely legitimated surveillance as a multi-purpose policing tool that is not only available to police and regulatory agencies, but also to individuals and organizations" (329; but see also Jochelson and Doerksen, this volume).

It is argued that when a nation uses, and in today's environment, relies on nontraditional security actors, the security continuum is exposed to gaps. As Button (2008) notes, "Governments often take a limited interest in enhancing security in the private sector and even in much of the public sector" (xv). In this continuum, each actor will have a differing culture, intent and application of surveillance resulting in variations of scene coverage.

Some national security and nontraditional security agencies language may align, but others may not. Therefore, the language of surveillance between actors and along the continuum alters to some degree. For example, in the context of border protection the Australian Customs and Border Protection Service, the Department of Transport and the Australian Federal Police, language aligns closely, whereas the Department of Health and Ageing when compared to the Department of Defence, surveillance language will differ significantly.

CCTV surveillance has efficacy in some crime reduction areas, where such efficacy further supports the misinterpretation of language. For example, the language group of technology will often use CCTV to mitigate a threat. Consequently, private security from a crime reduction view and policing from an evidence perspective both support and maintain such language. However, in general, CCTV cannot physically treat threats, as it does not truly target harden or deter. Therefore, those who require CCTV surveillance to provide mitigation against threats may not be protected.

Language may be further blurred in the many functional surveillance actors within a single agency. ASIO will have both a corporate security surveillance function and covert national security surveillance monitoring role. Furthermore, in respect to surveillance and its language, are there differences between such primary and ancillary functions of agencies? For example, both ASIO and Australian Secret Intelligence Service (ASIS) have clearly identified security functions, as a primary function in each case; however, this is not the case for agencies such as Department of Health and Ageing and Department of Infrastructure and Transport.

Where policy or legislation has been introduced, it only exists to address societal risks. Such risks are directed at the vocational elements of the security continuum, such as private security or security-regulated adjective sectors such as aviation or maritime security. Policy or legislation generally does not address the language issue.

The benefit of articulating clear language groups within the security continuum will lead to a more informed design, application and management of surveillance systems in all their operational applications. Such different language emphasis is dependent on many factors, one such factor being the diversity of the continuum and their contextual function. One way to better understand the security surveillance continuum is to gain a better understanding of how each actor uses and applies their discourse of surveillance. Bourne suggests that as security moves towards *hybridity*, rather than focusing on the binaries, a better understanding will prevail (Bourne 2014, 295). Such a view is misguided, as security actors will be unable to resolve many of their own gaps, overlaps or misunderstanding due, in part, to mandate and cultural language. Nevertheless, a counter-narrative is that gaps in the security continuum are beneficial. Such gaps in the continuum have, by default, represented weakness in surveillance. However, differing language supports unique cultural actors along the continuum, supporting both explicit and implicit differences that ensure complacency or 'blind' trust does or cannot develop. Familiarity could breed such complacency, even in the most robust and conscientious organisation. Therefore, does maintaining differing language and having subsequent gaps benefit the security continuum to provide strength and perhaps, resilience?

There are many questions that have not been fully addressed within this chapter, with many requiring further research. For example, what does surveillance mean to these disparate agencies and their actors that make up the security continuum? How is surveillance understood and how is it practiced? How does surveillance practice and target focus influence language?

Conclusion

Security and the function of surveillance are undertaken by a diverse group of entities across a broad continuum, ranging from international security to private security to an individual citizen. Consequently, the security continuum is not seamless; rather, it is a mosaic that has many overlaps which is punctuated by many gaps. Such gaps may be narrow or wide, and exist because of differences in language, culture, philosophy, ownership and stakeholder engagement. There appears to be a widely held perception that in the post-9/11 security environment, the security continuum has evolved into a *singularity* with the national security function fully integrating with corporate and private security. This chapter has challenged that assumption through an examination of the concept of CCTV surveillance language.

Surveillance is considered to be the observation and monitoring of anyone or anything that may be undertaken actively (direct) or passively (indirect), which combines to become a vortex or mosaic of surveillance. Surveillance, in today's digital environment, has become a primary tool of many security actors within their security continuum. One particular method of surveillance is CCTV, which has become infused into our everyday lives. By understanding the language of CCTV surveillance, we can better understand the broader security continuum.

Language explores how and in what context we understand CCTV surveillance. For example, is surveillance used to protect, monitor, make safe, for warning or to investigate persons or things? Through such understanding of the broader language of CCTV surveillance, we can begin to better understand the similarities and differences across the security continuum. We argue that there are seven distinct language groups of CCTV surveillance (see Fig. 6.2), namely technology, evidence, deterrence, situational awareness, surveillance, warning and research. Security actors will use one or some of these language groups depending on their position, function or role within the security continuum.

Security actors will use CCTV surveillance; however, they will use quite different language that is seated within culturally different views and understanding of CCTV. These differing views result in conflict in what is largely a difficult tool to apply well. Where language aligns with the security actors across the continuum, there is commonality of understanding and therefore fewer security gaps. Where the actors have differing language, there may be misalignment and resulting security gaps. Where legislation or policy has been developed, as a method to align language, this is generally at the lower end of the security continuum to control societal risk.

A counter-narrative is that such language gaps are beneficial, as it supports unique cultural actors along the continuum. These differences ensure trust does or cannot develop, resulting in complacency.

Nevertheless, there are many questions that have not been fully addressed within this chapter. For example, what does surveillance mean in the language groups of the security continuum, and how does surveillance practice influence the language that is used to describe corporate and national security?

References

ANZPAA. 2014. *Australian New Zealand Police: Recommendations for CCTV Systems*. Melbourne: Australian New Zealand Policing Advisory Agency.

Australian Government. 2013. *Guide to Australia's National Security Capability*. Canberra: Australian Government.

Bourne, Mike. 2014. *Understanding Security*. Basingstoke: Palgrave Macmillan.

Brooks, David J. 2005. Is CCTV a Social Benefit? A Psychometric Study of Perceived Social Risk. *Security Journal* 18(2): 19–29.

———. 2013. Corporate Security: Using Knowledge Construction to Define a Practising Body of Knowledge. *Asian Journal of Criminology* 8(2): 89–101.

Brooks, David J., and Jeffery Corkill. 2012. The Many Languages of CCTV. *Australian Security Magazine ASM*, 57–59.

———. 2014. Corporate Security and the Stratum of Security Management. In *Corporate Security in the 21st Century: Theory and Practice in International Perspective*, eds. K. Walby and R.K. Lippert, 216–234. New York: Palgrave Macmillan.

Button, Mark. 2008. *Doing Security: Critical Reflections and an Agenda for Change*. Basingstoke: Palgrave Macmillan.

Coole, Michael Patrick. 2015. Physical Security Professional's Body of Knowledge: A Cultural Domain Analysis of Physical Security's Knowledge Structure. Doctor of Philosophy, Curtin University of Technology, Perth.

Cubbage, Christopher J., and David J. Brooks. 2012. *Corporate Security in the Asia Pacific Region: Crisis, Crime, Fraud and Misconduct*. Boca Raton, FL: Taylor and Francis.

Gill, Martin, and Karryn Loveday. 2003. What Do Offenders Think About CCTV? *Crime Prevention & Community Safety* 5: 17–25.

Gill, Martin and Angela Spriggs. 2005. Assessing the Impact of CCTV. Home Office Research Study 292: Home Office Research, Development and Statistics Directorate.

Lyon, David. 2007. *Surveillance Studies: An Overview*. Cambridge: Polity Press.

Petersen, Karen L. 2013. The Corporate Security Professional: A Hybrid Agent Between Corporate and National Security. *Security Journal* 26(3): 222–235.

Premier of Western Australia & Cabinet Ministers. 2011. CHOGM 2011. https://www.premier.wa.gov.au/Pages/CHOGM2011.aspx. Accessed 26 May 2015.

Prenzler, Tim, Karen Earle, and Rick Sarre. 2009. Private Security in Australia: Trends and Key Characteristics. *Trends and Issues in Crime and Criminology* 374: 1–6.

Sarre, Rick. 2015. Private Security in Australia: Some Legal Musings. *Journal of the Australasian Law Teachers Association* 3(1/2): 45–54.

Sarre, Rick, and Tim Prenzler. 2011. *Private Security and Public Interest: Exploring Private Security Trends and Directions for Reform in the New Era of Plural Policing*. Caberra: Australian Research Council.

Sarre, Rick, David J. Brooks, Clifton Smith, and Rick Draper. 2014. Current and Emerging Technologies Employed to Abate Crime and to Promote Security. In *The Routledge Handbook of International Crime and Justice Studies*, eds. H.Y. Bersot and B. Arrigo, 327–349. Abington: Routledge.

Smith, Clifton, and David J. Brooks. 2013. *Security Science: The Theory and Practice of Security*. Waltham, MA: Elsevier.

Taylor, Emmeline, and Martin Gill. 2014. CCTV: Reflections in Its Use, Abuse and Effectiveness. In *The Handbook of Security*, 2 edn, ed. M. Gill, 705–726. Basingstoke: Palgrave Macmillan.

Tow, William, and Brendan Taylor. 2008. *What Is Regional Security Architecture?* Paper presented at the ISA 2008 Annual Convention, San Francisco.

Tzu, Sun. 1971. *The Art of War*. Stepney, SA: Axiom.

Welsh, Brandon C., and David P. Farrington. 2009. Public Area CCTV and Crime Prevention: An Updated Systematic Review and Meta-Analysis. *Justice Quarterly* 26(4): 716–745.

Western Australia Auditor General. 2011. *Use of CCTV Equipment and Information*. Perth: Author.

Western Australia Police. 2015. *Blue Iris CCTV Registration*. Perth: Author.

Wine, Kevin. 2015. Smarter Surveillance: Managing Risk with Business Intelligence. *Australian Security Magazine*, April/May, 24–25.

Zedner, Lucia. 2009. *Security: Keys Ideas in Criminology*. London: Routledge.

7

Securitising 'National Interests': Canadian Federal Government Departments, Corporate Security Creep, and Security Regimes

Kevin Walby, Randy K. Lippert, and James Gacek

Recent scholarship suggests that corporate security work is unique and multifaceted, insofar as it operates as an inescapable form of regulation in both private and public organisations (Brooks 2013; Petersen 2014; Walby and Lippert 2015a,b). Yet studies of corporate security models and practices in private and public sectors remain few. One notable study has explored corporate security in the private sector (Dalton 2003). More recent research has examined corporate security in municipal governments (Lippert and Walby

K. Walby (✉)
Department of Criminal Justice, University of Winnipeg, Winnipeg, MB, Canada

R.K. Lippert
Department of Sociology and Criminology, University of Windsor, Windsor, ON, Canada

J. Gacek
Law/Criminology, University of Edinburgh, Edinburgh, Scotland

© The Author(s) 2016   **155**
R. Lippert et al. (eds.), *National Security, Surveillance and Terror*,
DOI 10.1007/978-3-319-43243-4_7

2012, 2014; Lippert et al. 2013; Walby et al. 2014). But such inquiry must be expanded to corporate security at federal levels of government. Despite the penchant for examining national security practices in North America after 9/11, there remains a need to study the intersection of corporate security and national security. National security and corporate security are typically thought of as distinct realms; security scholars in one do not typically acknowledge or debate those in the other (see Petersen 2013, 2014). This chapter explores the elective affinity between these two security domains in Canada at the federal level and the implications thereof.

Analysing results from access to information (ATI) requests and interviews across six federal Canadian departments, we identify similarities in how each securitises their operations. There are patterns in security practices, risk management techniques and assessments, and cooperation with other agencies to solicit, broker and manage information. These departments' operations reflect corporate security practices in pursuit of 'national interests.' In other words, while these security professionals share much with their municipal and provincial corporate security counterparts, at the federal level operations are under a central auspice: to secure and guard such information from persons challenging or threatening Canadian 'national interests' and 'national security.' This focus on national security (and in part terror) distinguishes corporate security personnel at the federal level in Canada from municipal or provincial corporate security counterparts. Such an effort involves extension of security and surveillance practices and networking across federal departments, which indicates that corporate security creep is accelerating.

To explore corporate security's intersection with national security at the federal level in Canada, we examine the qualifications and practices of corporate security personnel within these departments. We also investigate how department employees are required to increase security within the workplace, from employee searches and screening, to privacy passwords, threat assessments, and risk management strategies. These operations are conducted for the 'national interest' yet they also permit the 'creep' of corporate security in federal departments. Contributing to research on relationships that link 'security nodes' together, we use Dupont's (2014) notion of a security regime to interpret these findings.

First, we assess the corporate security model and how it creeps as a set of security policies and practices. We provide a conceptual framework by outlining how surveillance is crucial to corporate security efforts to promote national interests and national security. Second, we describe our research methods, including ATI requests. Next we examine the themes arising from these data. We analyse how 'national interests' and 'national security' are converging in unique ways. While these federal departments are encouraged to solicit, broker and manage information within their networks, simultaneously such federal departments must guard against intruders or outside agencies gathering knowledge of federal departments' operations. A key signifier in security discourse is "indeterminable danger" (Bell 2006, 149) that legitimises securitisation of federal department operations and extension of risk management. To strengthen 'national security,' departments survey one another to gather information for the 'national interest.' In conclusion, we discuss implications of our findings for research on corporate security, and reflect on the proposition that corporate security at the federal level of Canadian government is necessary to promote national interests and human freedom.

Corporate Security 'Creep'

Corporate security units in large private organisations have a long history, especially in North America. There are few, if any, major private corporations without an in-house corporate security unit and in recent years corporate security values, credentials, and practices have been migrating into government.

Whether corporate security entails guarding entrances and exits of buildings and lands, protecting CEOs or other VIPs, investigating or drug testing employees, safekeeping company secrets, or preventing corporate espionage, corporate security operates to protect and promote organisational goals (Button and George 1994; Nalla and Morash 2002; Borodzicz and Gibson 2006). Contrasting with contract security firms that only seek profits, as well as with the understanding of policing for the public good (Loader and Walker 2007; White 2012), the corporate security model is founded on centralised management of information, personnel, and physical security (Brooks 2013). It is most notably associated with the Ford Motor Company's corporate security unit (Weiss 2014) but beginning in the mid to late twentieth century it began creeping into the public sector (see Walby and Lippert 2015a).

Corporate security's gradual emergence in each level of government in Canada and the USA, including in federal departments, we term 'corporate security creep.' Developed in private corporations and uploaded into the workings of government, this policy transfer involves practices of asset protection, loss prevention, and employee surveillance. This policy transfer-as-creep is central to our inquiry here, as it is occurring in an imperceptible, unremitting manner. While in-house security is slightly altered to respond to each risk and threat assessment, the bigger picture is overlooked. As Walby and Lippert (2015b) contend, the result is a hybrid type of governance that is "neither purely public nor private, and which blends security and policing" (3) to the point where rethinking in-house security raises new questions concerning security technology and policy transfer from private to public sector (see also Meerts 2014; Williams 2014).

This creep means not only more federal departments and government personnel will be governed through corporate security but also governed through risk. Here security provision and risk management merge almost seamlessly. Federal departments and agencies address crises, such as global terrorism and cybercrime, through risk assessments founded on similar policies that have crept into departments, all the while legitimising the 'creep' as necessary 'for the nation's sake.' However, distinguishing between what is to be securitised (i.e. the nation's 'interests') and the securitising operations (i.e. 'national security' threats) is often difficult. Attention to the role of 'national interest' and 'national security' in federal agencies' policies permits us to observe how this pair of securitising signifiers extends corporate security creep.

Corporate Security and National Security in Context

The expansion of administrative surveillance was crucial to the rise of the nation-state (Giddens 1987). Surveillance remains integral to state power. No single factor has caused this expansion, nor does it emanate from a single point within the state apparatus. Rather, it is linked to several institutional agendas, including military conquest, risk management, and corporate security. Technological development has also led to new forms of state surveillance, as it has allowed for the routine collection and analysis of mass amounts of information (Haggerty and Ericson 2006; Tootell 2006). Corporate security creep further extends state surveillance capacities.

Yet not all surveillance is equal. Its form depends on the kind of department and the network of which it is a part. Dupont (2014) defines a "security regime" as "the convergence of internal and external forces and constraints that determine the conditions under which security is produced and exchanged by an organization" (265). Obviously this has implications for the type and intensity of surveillance. Dupont (2014) suggests that the security regime shapes a given organisation's security mandate, techniques used to fulfil that mandate, and how much that organisation collaborates with others. A range of internal and external forces and constraints shape corporate security units, though there is at least some variation by public and private sector (Walby and Lippert 2015b) and, in the public sector, by level of government. At the federal level of government corporate security units merge with national security trends and also become enrolled in the pursuit of national interest.

Corporate security is unique in partially involving surveillance turned inward on an organisation (Lippert and Walby 2012; Gill and Howell 2014). The extension of surveillance that modern government applies as much to internal civil servants and government ministries as to external criminalised persons deemed as threats. And there is something unique about surveillance conducted in the name of national security but carried out by corporate security personnel. Few concepts are more contentious and of such importance for the exercise of powers within federal departments than 'national security' and the related concept of 'national interest.' Affixing these discourses to any practice or policy is a significant act of securitisation. Few studies have been able to define what comprises a state's national interests (Cohen 1995) or its national security threats (Pearson 1988; Lustgarten and Leigh 1994; Heide et al. 2005; see Bell 2006 regarding both interests and security). Moreover, little research has investigated how federal intelligence agencies construct categories to classify national security threats (Monahan and Palmer 2009; Monaghan and

Walby 2012). Such notions appear to legitimise either national interests or national security and to depend on the ruling government (Lustgarten and Leigh 1994; Cohen 1995; Heide et al. 2005). Examining how much these notions are incorporated into securitising trends in federal departments provides an opportunity to assess how corporate security creep has permeated government departments and agencies within Canada, and how the intersection of corporate security and national security extends surveillance efforts in these agencies.

Threats to 'national security' have become frequently reported post-9/11 (de Larrinaga and Salter 2014), as intelligence gathering has become one of the most strategic processes of surveillance (Pozen 2005; Walsh and Miller 2015). In the USA federal agencies are encouraging one another to expand information sharing while simultaneously reducing transparency (Pozen 2005, 2010). In Canada this expansion is imminent with recent passage of the Anti-Terrorism Act (Bill C-51) (Forcese and Roach 2015; Forcese, this volume). The debate about secrecy and transparency has arisen in Canada, as successive governments beginning in the 1990s, first the Liberals, then the Conservatives and the Liberals once again, have tried to balance on that same national security tightrope, juggling tensions between freedom and privacy (Roy 2013, 2014). What constitutes Canada's 'national interest' is contested. The few studies examining this dilemma suggest the definition of national interest is open to interpretation by the current political governing body (Lustgarten and Leigh 1994; Cohen 1995). As Lustgarten and Leigh (1994) suggest, the hazards of conflating national interests and national security are real, because "giving national security so wide-ranging a meaning is potentially extraordinarily oppressive," and could erode the distinction between private and public spheres of social life (27). When corporate security creeps into the federal level, it enters these debates. At lower levels of government or in the less-scrutinised private sector, say in global corporations like Barrick Gold, however, it may not.[1]

---

[1] Barrick Gold corporate security units conduct security risk assessments on local communities and other entities construed as threats. They take steps to manage risks. They set up perimeters, key card access points, surveillance cameras, and physical and technology security features at their mining sites and offices. They establish control rooms to coordinate these practices. Corporate security units respond to what they call critical incidents including fraud, theft, bomb threats, and attempted robberies. They also investigate and monitor employees (Barrick Gold Corporation 2012).

Beyond the focus on security and surveillance, we argue that tethering categories such as national security and national interest to corporate security creates a unique security regime (Dupont 2014) compared to say provincial and municipal government in Canada where terrorism is less a priority. This regime requires greater surveillance and data and the electronic capabilities to gather, share, analyse, and process data flows across previously separate fiefdoms of public sector organisations. In this sense, during this past decade the emphasis on "joined up government, shared governance and interoperable computer systems" became intertwined with the security and surveillance apparatus of the public sector (Roy 2014, 4). Corporate security at the federal level entails these changes. National security and intelligence agencies in Canada have extended their reach since 9/11 and their surveillant targets have become such due more to suspicion than to reasonable, probable grounds (Bell 2006). We illustrate that one under-examined way this has happened is through corporate security.

Corporate security at the federal level is also unique in how it becomes tethered to the notion of human freedom of which liberal government is said to be the purveyor (Lippert and Walby 2016, 330). Bell's (2006) study of Canadian National Security policy illustrates how policy is mobilised through administrative practices and discourses that "take elusive risks to freedom … and safety of the population as an opportunity for action," and is only made possible through a generalised expansion of surveillance (149). It is because dangers to freedom are presented as a consequence of the threats to which Canada is 'supposedly subjected' that security becomes the solution "not only to the problem of *indeterminate danger*, but also to the problem of freedom" (ibid., 149, italics emphasised). The extent to which operations within such departments have been further securitised for 'the nation's sake' becomes important to investigate.

Methodology

Our research began with access to information (ATI) requests as a way of producing data about federal employees' job qualifications and daily tasks that incorporate the corporate security model. We made requests to Correctional Services Canada (CSC), Canadian Security Intelligence

Service (CSIS), Public Safety Canada, Indian and Northern Affairs Canada (INAC) (but recently renamed Aboriginal Affairs and Northern Development Canada), Department of Foreign Affairs, International Trade and Development (DFAITD), and Health Canada. Beyond investigating 'corporate security creep' and securitising political rhetoric, in this chapter we contribute to literature that seeks to incorporate ATI requests into security and policing research. ATI requests can be incorporated into research design since they provide access to documents not already comprising the public record. The implications of ATI requests are substantial as they can produce data that provide a critical perspective of federal departments and public organisations. Security and surveillance scholars have used the Canadian *Access to Information Act* and its legislation to aid in security and policing research (Walby and Monaghan 2010, 2011; Walby and Larsen 2012a,b; Walby and Lippert 2012).

Although an ethnography of government employees may provide a more in-depth understanding of organisational change and how personnel work (McDonald 2005), this data collection strategy can be easily blocked when examining security and policing agencies and their practices (see Walby and Lippert 2012, 2015b). Moreover, shadowing may only provide a glimpse of practices of government personnel. ATI requests are a viable means of producing textual data, and can reveal a scope of practices within government not otherwise visible. Without ATI, corporate security practices and trends would be difficult to study, given the lack of publicly accessible information about them.[2]

---

[2] We also encountered barriers during data collection. We submitted similar requests to numerous federal government departments, including the Department of National Defence and the Royal Canadian Mounted Police. The former's ATI Coordinator stalled the request claiming the Department of National Defence did not have a corporate security unit. We engaged in several tense conversations with the ATI Coordinator, noting that all federal government agencies that received the same request had so far indicated they had such a unit and would comply. Yet this ATI Coordinator continued to insist the Department of National Defence had no such corporate security unit, and indicated he wanted to close the file. We then located open source material, including policy and budget documents, on the Department of National Defence website that pointed to the existence of their corporate security unit. Upon receiving this material, the ATI Coordinator then chose an unusual course of action by asking us to contact a member of the corporate security unit to clarify search parameters. The unit representative then indicated the requested information was not formatted to fit the parameters of the search as per the original wording, and so asked for drastic alteration of the request. We complied and the representative eventually released some files outside of the ATI process but had effectively responded to the request in a way that was neither open nor

Our data include two interviews with corporate security personnel who were promised anonymity. Both were working as corporate security personnel in the federal government, but had previously worked in corporate security at other levels of government. These respondents elaborated upon similarities and differences among corporate security arrangements at various government levels in Canada.

Coding to locate common themes across the data occurred in two steps. First, open coding was used to identify themes. Second, axial (or focused) coding was performed to construct the subsequent analysis sections. Differences among government personnel's qualifications and job tasks were identified in open coding. Once core patterns and themes were identified, axial (or focused) coding was used to collate the data set. The purpose was to delineate relationships and emerging trends from such data (Strauss 1987; Walker and Myrick 2006), to which we now turn.

Corporate Security Practices in Federal Government Agencies

Examining ATI data across six federal Canadian departments (CSC, CSIS, Public Safety Canada, INAC, DFAITD, and Health Canada)[3] below we demonstrate how each securitises their operations, and how this involves security practices, risk management techniques, and information sharing and brokering. We highlight how corporate security has crept into these six departments and showcase how they have altered job summaries, qualifications and/or functions to further national interests and security aims.

---

forthcoming, and had disclosed information in a format ill-suited to our interests. These data from the Department of National Defence are incomplete, so we have not analysed them for this chapter. The Royal Canadian Mounted Police eventually released material but it was mostly redacted and exempted and so was not included in our analysis either.

[3] These data resulted from the following access to information requests (by ATI reference number): National Defence A-2013-01210; Foreign Affairs, Trade and Development Canada A-2013-01918; Canada Border Services Agency A-2013-09431; Correctional Service Canada A-2013-00369; Correctional Service Canada A-2013-00372; Environment Canada A-2014-00076; Royal Canadian Mounted Police A-2013-05815; Government of Canada Privy Council Office A-2014-00037. These are referenced in text by Department acronym. For additional information, please contact Kevin Walby.

Corporate security at the federal level is unique compared to other levels due to the source of directives, policies, and templates that shape it. Municipal-level corporate security often draws from outside, including private entities (such as the American Society for Industrial Security or ASIS International), for directives, policies, and templates (Walby and Lippert 2015b), at the federal level master texts such as the Treasury Board (TB) Policy on Government Security are harmonised with Directives on Departmental Security Management, creating standardisation absent from other levels of public sector corporate security.

Adhering to the Treasury Board Policy on Government Security (TBPGS) means federal corporate security units must perform audits and reach benchmarks every quarter. For instance, Treasury Board Policy on Government Security requires that all facilities meet a common minimum program (Facility Security Readiness Level 1). For some buildings security must meet levels 2–4. Security testing, training and procedures as well as safety implementation are to be based on TBPGS. The common minimum program must be tested and updated at least twice annually. TBPGS also compels corporate security units to create internal security business plans, with the rationale of enhancing "collaboration/sharing opportunities with other government departments and allies" (CSIS). Other policies such as Canada's Cyber Security Strategy govern the work of corporate security personnel at this level, whereas such standards are absent from public corporate security elsewhere. Operating at the federal level also subjects these employees to laws not otherwise present at municipal or provincial levels. This point was confirmed in an interview with a federal corporate security team member previously employed at the municipal level (Jimmy, federal corporate security manager). As well, CSIS internal security personnel are permanently bound to secrecy about their work under the *Security of Information Act* and can be prosecuted for releasing information about it. Another major difference between private sector corporate security and corporate security in the federal government is the standardised security classifications across the latter and the focus on national security (including terror) as a driver of corporate security practices.

Corporate security personnel at the federal level communicate when they participate in the Federal Association of Security Officials, the

Canadian Technical Security Conference, the Government Security Forum, and what was until recently called the National Capital Security Partners' Forum (NCSPF). The latter also organised an event entitled NCSPF: National Security versus Corporate Security in May 2012. In 2014 the NCSPF morphed into the Security Partners' Forum, and has become more national and global in its aspirations, as discussed below. The same personnel distribute information on Linked-In and other government communication platforms to share best practices and engage in benchmarking required by TB.

No matter where it operates, including in the Canadian federal government, corporate security requires a team. The work is distributed among security managers, in-house guards, information technology specialists, and security-related administrative assistants. Not unlike their municipal and provincial counterparts, federal corporate security managers must foster "a culture of security" (INAC) across the department. All employees are then trained to embrace this security culture but are also monitored because of it. Our data suggest security goals are increasingly entering security job descriptions. These include maintaining and/or developing department physical security, physical and electronic access control, and security policies, standards and expectations.

First, the responsibility to keep facilities secure is a prominent feature. Both CSIS and DFAITD, for example, stipulate that maintenance and repairs must be conducted to ensure and secure protection of facility and personal property, employees and visitors. The replacement of defective door controls, circuit boards, security seals, power supplies for intercom systems are among the types of repairs required for DFAITD surveillance projects. Developing physical security schemes arose in other federal departments, such as CSC, INAC and Public Safety Canada, which outlined key activities for ensuring a "safe and secure institutional environment" (CSC) by securing assets, information and the physical facilities from "unauthorized access, disclosure, modification or destruction" (Public Safety Canada). Both CSIS and INAC stipulate the necessity of conducting security and safety patrols, with security officers in both departments monitoring physical security through CCTV and alarm systems.

Second, information and asset protection is accomplished through physical and electronic access control. Physical access control includes inspections of locking devices, maintaining physical security zones and demarcating authorised areas for employees; instituting and policing visitor access controls, ID card access systems, and investigating irregularities with ID/access cards; safe keeping locks, keys and combinations, and overseeing combination resets when there is an "unacceptable increase in risk to personnel, information or assets" (INAC, 34). Securitising electronic access control means that security officers and managers monitor 911 interface and fire alarm systems, record and verify ID/access cards, and investigate irregular ID/access operations.

Finally, to strengthen current security measures, federal departments develop policies, standards and expectations of safety within their respective facilities and identify security trends and developments for future consideration. Within CSC, CSIS, INAC, and Health Canada measures are taken by guards, security analysts, and managers to monitor "[s]ecurity practices, methods and approaches" (CSC) for effectiveness and compliance with relevant department policy. Adherence to security policy is crucial within these measures, as ensuring and prioritising "safety, efficiency, reliability and operational availability" (CSIS) allows for security policies to be harmonised more coherently within a site. Such coherence produces faster responses to securitise departmental information and assets from security breaches. Especially within CSC, identifying key security, surveillance, and intelligence trends for future consideration is deemed essential for current security provision, as such trends benefit 'high profile' security/ surveillance projects (CSC). Indeed, identifying trends ensures that policies and standards reflect departmental interests (CSC). One such project is the INAC identification card project, which, according to INAC documents, "will protect government personnel, assets, information and operations through the use of an identification process which minimises or completely prevents access by unauthorised individuals, with possible malevolent intent, to department facilities" (INAC). Identification card projects are as old as corporate security itself (see Walby and Lippert 2015a), but when these projects are framed in corporate security terms to foster national interests and protect national security, they adopt a unique tenor compared to other levels of public corporate security.

These documents suggest that strengthening security practices within federal departments will ensure stronger preventative measures and a faster response to national security risks such as terrorism. If federal departments think security measures can only be strengthened through audits and assessments that discern cracks in the security façade, then knowing security leaks securitises federal departments while surveying future threats. For instance, in one department, threats include "terrorism, criminal activity, cyber-terrorism, foreign intelligence services, insider threats, natural disasters and demonstrations/picketing" (Public Safety Canada). Securitising buildings and assets for the nation's sake are articulated to explain how practices within federal departments' corporate security models will be further securitised. Yet little evidence of how the nation's interests are part and parcel of the physical security of these sites indicates a lack of transparency between federal departments' operating corporate security models and the public at large. This lack of transparency raises concerns over the secrecy that typifies federal government operations.

Department/Agency Cooperation and Corporate Security

Cooperation and securitisation have become high-ranking priorities within partnerships between federal departments and other agencies, as examined in the next section. Federal departments maintain multiple points of contact and dealings with these organisations, meaning they are increasingly keen on cooperation, information sharing, and knowledge brokering. Our data suggest in federal departments, specifically CSC, CSIS, INAC, Public Safety Canada, and Health Canada, there is cooperation with other public, private, federal, and international agencies distant from the political sphere, as well as talk of strengthening cooperation within home agencies. To maintain effective security and information channels, liaison with such agencies is needed, and efforts are made by federal departments to discuss security trends and developments, and "solicit cooperation for security projects" (CSC).

This type of corporate security trend reveals encounters with unique cooperation arrangements (for a further discussion regarding accountability and oversight issues within corporate security, see Walby and

Lippert 2015b). These are partially fostered by TBPGS that entails different types of work—such as knowledge or information work or physical and/or electronic security provisions—and requires close liaisons with other departments and partnering agencies to share information, relay research data and identify trends, and successes in detection/prevention/intervention practices. In this way, the common minimum program for corporate security across departments is continually tightened up. This knowledge brokering is developed through networks, and these departments hold themselves accountable for soliciting cooperation so that security concerns remain topical.

Information sharing fosters greater cooperation and collaboration, as exchanging views, relaying data, and identifying trends between partnering departments and agencies ensure transparent information channels. As a security practice, information sharing promotes security knowledge that assists departments in the development and securitisation of their site (Bigo 2002). As trained professionals, the security managers and analysts are better able to make security decisions with managers and analysts in other departments and agencies, as an increase in cooperation results in increased access to resources, such as "security intelligence reporting and threat assessments" within home and partnering agencies (Walby and Lippert 2015b, 53). At the same time, obtaining information requires the awareness of government personnel to obtain more information for management's needs, such as researching and reviewing institutional policies and practices of other Canadian partners and agencies.

Little is known about federal-level corporate security and international benchmarking. This information was not evident in the documents we analysed, but may have been exempted or redacted. Observing how partnering countries securitise may benefit the Canadian federal government in attempting to protect valuable information. Researching and reviewing others' security may reveal 'cracks' in their systems, which would advantage the Canadian government in securitisation against another country's arrangements. Arguably, policy transfers between agencies and countries would illustrate how the corporate security model creeps at both the domestic and international level. The security regime (Dupont 2014) we are describing seems to have fewer external drivers (e.g. ASIS, other countries) at this time and therefore may not transfer well across countries. In other words, the policy mobility of federal-level corporate security across countries, including to Australia, is likely low at this time. However, this may change as the Security Partners' Forum tries to foster communication across corporate security units, and across countries.

Corporate Security and Risk Management

At the level of practice, the 'creep' of security provisions and risk management is indistinguishable; the benefit of prying them apart—if possible—is limited. In terms of how national interests and values are upheld, the risks that become known through surveillance are increasingly drawing on more and more information flows. This information, in turn, must be stored and shared (Joshi et al. 2002; Loukidelis 2004) and in a networked world, security measures must reduce the risk of leaks as much as possible. Ensuring cooperating organisations and agencies that their information is safeguarded can only be accomplished through further securitising federal departments.

Invoking risk and threat assessments, for example, would guide federal departments in their calculations of risk necessary to detect, prevent, or manage threats. Within the data obtained from the CSC, Public Safety Canada, CSIS, Health Canada, and to a greater extent, INAC, there is mention of proactively assessing risk and vulnerability within their departments' operations. The job qualifications within INAC, including project, program, and service delivery managers instruct that the department's job positions are responsible for ensuring that "risk and security management strategies are in place" (INAC) as well as 'identifying relevant inputs' from Threat and Risk Assessment (TRA) to establish and strengthen security requirements (INAC). According to INAC, a TRA should incorporate a threat assessment that collects various "representative threat scenarios, indicating the asset, the threat event, the likelihood of the threat being realized, the impact if it succeeds, and the calculated exposure rating" (INAC). The TRA should also include a vulnerability and risk assessment, and a recommendation and action plan. A vulnerability assessment lists existing safeguards for "the subject assets and a statement about the vulnerabilities that need to be addressed" while a risk assessment provides a statement about "the probable consequences of going ahead without further risk mitigation" (INAC). Finally, an action plan reflects new safeguards to be deployed to "reduce the risks characterized in the Risk Assessment and a description of the risks and liabilities remaining after the planned safeguards have been deployed" (INAC).

Our data suggest federal departments ensure risk management strategies are implemented. For example, Public Safety Canada developed a "Corporate Security Risk Register" used to record and collate "risk information from separate entities and reports, and plans for how to respond to risks" (Public Safety Canada). Once risk assessment is complete, the department submits the plans to the government to respond to major identified corporate risks. It is because of this register that risks identified during 2011–2012 suggested that "enhancing national security by countering terrorism and improving information sharing" became the government's top priorities and strengthening risk management at the federal level (Public Safety Canada).

The intensification of risk management, which increases the prevalence of risk assessment practices such as the TRAs and the Corporate Security Risk Register, legitimises political rhetoric that affirms the risk to the national interest and "national security" (Public Safety Canada). As one INAC document notes, corporate security policy is based on "assessments of risks to the national interest and to the department's employees and assets" (INAC). Likewise, according to Health Canada documents, corporate security must undertake department-wide threat and risk assessments but also be concerned "with loss of sensitive information that could injure the National interest, the Department's reputation and its officials" (Public Health Canada). At the same time, Canada's national security policy orients itself to an "increasingly complex and dangerous threat environment," in which the prevalence of threat has become an imminent characteristic of society and that, as never before, there are multiple sources of threat to the Canadian public (PCO 2004, iii). This policy suggests that further security measures should be implemented to respond to the challenge of terrorism and other domestic and global threats to the Canadian population's safety and freedom. Enhancing national security would be capable "of responding proportionately to existing threats while adapting quickly to meet new threats *that may emerge*" (PCO 2004, 8, italics emphasised). We see how "supposedly indeterminable danger" (Bell 2006, 149) appears within security discourse to emphasise the Canadian government's justification for further securitisation of department operations and risk management.

Discussion and Conclusion

Dupont and Wood (2006) contend that security studies must explore the relationships that link 'security nodes' together, such as the connections among policing and criminal justice agencies, government and parliamentary bodies, and private interests. Contributing to this effort, we have examined corporate security nodes at the federal government level in Canada. We have shown how corporate security personnel look inward as much as outward, oversee access and egress to buildings, and deploy corporate in-house strategies. Thus they have much in common with corporate security found in lower levels of government. However, at the federal level, these personnel are assigned to national security concerns nonetheless. We have also shown how these units are subject to the Treasury Board Policy on Government Security among other protocols at the federal level that distinguishes their work from corporate security counterparts at lower levels of public service. One implication of our findings is that even with the focus on terror and threat these arrangements in practice have as much to do with corporate security as national security, and have more in common with what happens in numerous sites across several federal departments' jurisdiction than a national emergency.

Though these federal personnel engage in practices similar to their provincial and municipal counterparts, their federal level exposes them to laws and policies unique in the corporate security realm. And though corporate security counterparts at lower levels are not currently subject to these federal policies, they soon could be as the security regime of federal-level corporate security continues to extend. Part of the mandate of the CSC corporate security manager, for instance, is establishing "a consultative network with officials of federal, provincial, municipal and external organisations … [to] solicit cooperation and joint participation in high profile projects" (CSC). Passage of the Anti-Terrorism Act (Bill C-51) enhances this information sharing among corporate security units positioned at different levels of government (Forcese and Roach 2015; Forcese, this volume). As one respondent indicated, convergences with defence, intelligence, and other levels of government security are what these personnel are working towards. This is the purpose of the Security Partners' Forum, which was started by federal-level corporate security personnel in Canada but that now includes international members from the public sector corporate security at multiple levels.

Our analysis also has examined issues of surveillance and security, emphasising how corporate security models legitimise the further securitisation of national interests. The notion of national interests and indeed the threats that federal-level corporate security focuses upon remain nebulous and inherently political. The notions of national interests and national security are tethered to corporate security to create a unique security regime. We have used Dupont's (2014) notion of security regime to explore internal and external forces and constraints that shape corporate security in the federal public sector. Future research could explore whether the idea of security regime should be applied to individual nodes or entire security networks not only in Canada but also in other countries. Such an approach would examine how far a unique security regime can extend. We have used the notion of corporate security creep to capture how corporate security is extending at the federal level of government in Canada. Moreover, we have argued that ATI data are useful in exposing the process of corporate security creep within the public sector, and the role of corporate security in Canadian federal departments.

In the wake of 9/11, security serves as rubric for government operations and managing populations (Bell 2006). Yet in a liberal democracy, this arrangement raises a peculiar proposition: that the source of security and freedom is to be located in the federal government. In this way, corporate security is propped up as a purveyor of security but also freedom for Canadians. How security becomes promoted as a pathway to freedom must be questioned if future research is to explore how corporate security creep is permeating levels of government and, if necessary, how it might be halted.

References

Barrick Gold Corporation. 2012. *Security Management System.* Toronto.

Bell, Colleen. 2006. Surveillance Strategies and Populations of Risk: Biopolitical Governance in Canada's National Security Policy. *Security Dialogue* 37(2): 147–165.

Bigo, Didier. 2002. Security and Immigration: Toward a Critique of the Governmentality of the Unease. *Alternatives* 27(1): 63–92.

Borodzicz, Edward P., and Stevyn Gibson. 2006. Corporate Security Education: Towards Meeting the Challenge. *Security Journal* 19(3): 180–195.

Brooks, David. 2013. Corporate Security: Using Knowledge Categorization to Define a Practicing Body of Knowledge. *Asian Journal of Criminology* 8(2): 89–101.

Button, Mark, and Bruce George. 1994. Why Some Organizations Prefer In-House to Contract Security Staff. In *Crime at Work: Studies in Security and Crime Prevention*, ed. Martin Gill, 201–213. Leicester: Perpetuity Press.

Cohen, Andrew. 1995. Canada in the World: The Return of the National Interest. *Behind the Headlines* 52(4): 1–16.

Dalton, Dennis R. 2003. *Rethinking Corporate Security in the Post 9/11 Era: Issues and Strategies for Today's Global Business Community.* New York: Butterworth Heinemann.

de Larrinaga, M., and M. Salter. 2014. Cold CASE: A Manifesto for Canadian Critical Security Studies. *Critical Studies on Security* 2(1): 1–19.

Dupont, Benoît. 2014. Private Security Regimes: Conceptualizing the Forces that Shape the Private Delivery of Security. *Theoretical Criminology* 18(3): 263–281.

Dupont, Benoît, and Jennifer Wood. 2006. Conclusion: The Future of Democracy. In *Democracy, Society and the Governance of Security*, eds. Jennifer Wood and Benoît Dupont, 241–248. Cambridge: Cambridge University Press.

Forcese, Craig, and Kent Roach. 2015. Bill C-51 Moves Us One Step Closer to the End of Privacy. *Toronto Star*, February 17.

Giddens, Anthony. 1987. *The Nation-State and Violence.* London: Polity.

Gill, M., and C. Howell. 2014. Policing Organizations: The Role of the Corporate Security Function and the Implication for Suppliers. *International Journal of Police Science and Management* 16(1): 65–75.

Haggerty, Kevin D., and Richard V. Ericson. 2006. The New Politics of Surveillance and Visibility. In *The New Politics of Surveillance and Visibility*, eds. Kevin D. Haggerty and Richard V. Ericson, 3–25. Toronto: University of Toronto Press.

Heide, R. L., T. Grant, C. Ankersen, D. Roy, and J. Boileu. 2005. *Defining the National Interest: New Directions for Canadian Foreign Policy.* Centre for Security and Defense Studies: Carleton University. Conference Report.

Joshi, James B.D., Arif Ghafoor, and Walid G. Aref. 2002. Security and Privacy Challenges of a Digital Government. In *Advances in Digital Government: Technology, Human Factors, and Policy*, eds. William J. McIver and Ahmed K. Elmagarmid, 121–136. Boston: Kluwer Academic Publishers.

Lippert, Randy K., and Kevin Walby. 2012. Municipal Corporate Security and the Intensification of Urban Surveillance. *Surveillance & Society* 9(2): 310–320.

———. 2014. Municipal Corporate Security, Legal Knowledges, and the Urban Problem Space. *Law and Social Inquiry* 39(3): 720–739.

———. 2016. Governing Through Privacy: Authoritarian Liberalism, Law, and Privacy Knowledge. *Law, Culture and the Humanities* 12(2): 329–352.

Lippert, Randy K., Kevin Walby, and Rhys Steckle. 2013. Multiplicities of Corporate Security: Identifying Emerging Types and Trends. *Security Journal* 26(3): 206–221.

Loader, Ian, and Neil Walker. 2007. *Civilizing Society.* Cambridge, UK: Cambridge University Press.

Loukidelis, David. 2004. Identity, Privacy, Security: Can Technology Really Reconcile Them? Address by Privacy Commissioner of British Columbia, Victoria. www.oipc.bc.ca.

Lustgarten, Laurence, and Ian Leigh. 1994. *In from the Cold: National Security and Parliamentary Democracy.* Oxford: Clarendon Press.

McDonald, Seonaidh. 2005. Studying Actions in Context: A Qualitative Shadowing Method for Organizational Research. *Qualitative Research* 5(4): 455–473.

Meerts, Clarissa. 2014. Corporate Security: Governing through Private and Public Law. In *Corporate Security in the 21st Century: Theory and Practice in International Perspective*, eds. Kevin Walby and Randy K. Lippert, 97–115. Houndmills: Palgrave Macmillan.

Monaghan, Jeffrey, and Kevin Walby. 2012. Making Up 'Terror Identities': Security intelligence, Canada's Integrated Threat Assessment Centre and Social Movement Suppression. *Policing & Society* 22(2): 133–151.

Monahan, Torin, and Neal Palmer. 2009. The Emerging Politics of DHS Fusion Centers. *Security Dialogue* 40(6): 617–636.

Nalla, Mahesh, and Merry Morash. 2002. Assessing the Scope of Corporate Security: Common Practices and Relationships with Other Business Functions. *Security Journal* 15(3): 7–19.

Pearson, Geoffrey. 1988. CIIPS Working Paper #11—International Security and Canadian Interests: Report of a Working Group. *Canadian Institute for International Peace and Security*. Ottawa, Canada.

Petersen, Karen Lund. 2013. The Corporate Security Professional: A Hybrid Agent Between Corporate and National Security. *Security Journal* 26(3): 222–235.

———. 2014. The Politics of Corporate Security and the Translation of National Security. In *Corporate Security in the 21st Century: Theory and Practice in International Perspective*, eds. Kevin Walby and Randy K. Lippert, 78–96. Houndsmills: Palgrave Macmillan.

Pozen, David E. 2005. The Mosaic Theory, National Security, and Freedom of Information Act. *The Yale Law Journal* 115(3): 628–679.

——— 2010. Deep Secrecy. *The Stanford Law Review* 62: 257–340.

Privy Council Office (PCO). 2004. *Securing an Open Society: Canada's National Security Policy*. Ottawa: National Library of Canada.

Roy, Jeffrey. 2013. *From Machinery to Mobility: Government and Democracy in a Participative Age*. New York: Springer.

———. 2014. Secrecy, Security and Digital Literacy in an Era of Meta-Data: Why the Canadian Westminster Model Falls Short. *Intelligence and National Security* 31: 1–23.

Strauss, Anselm. 1987. *Qualitative Analysis for Social Scientists*. Cambridge: Cambridge University Press.

Tootell, Holly. 2006. The Application of Critical Social Theory to National Security Research. *Prometheus* 24(4): 405–411.

Walby, Kevin, and Mike Larsen. 2012a. Access to Information and Freedom of Information Requests: Neglected Means of Data Production in the Social Sciences. *Qualitative Inquiry* 18(1): 31–42.

———. 2012b. Getting at the Live Archive: On Access to Information Research in Canada. *Canadian Journal of Law and Society* 27(1): 623–634.

Walby, Kevin, and Randy K. Lippert. 2012. The New Keys to the City: Uploading Corporate Security and Threat Discourse into Canadian Municipal Governments. *Crime, Law and Social Change* 58(4): 437–455.

Walby, K., and R. Lippert. 2015a. Ford First? Corporate Security and the US Department of War's Plant Protection Service's Interior Organization Unit 1917–1918. *Labor History* 56(2): 117–135.

―――. 2015b. *Municipal Corporate Security in International Context*. London: Routledge.

Walby, Kevin, and Jeffrey Monaghan. 2010. Policing Proliferation: On the Militarization of Police and Atomic Energy Canada Limited's Nuclear Response Forces. *Canadian Journal of Criminology and Criminal Justice* 52(2): 117–145.

―――. 2011. Private Eyes and Public Order: Policing and Surveillance in the Suppression of Animal Rights Activists in Canada. *Social Movement Studies* 10(1): 21–37.

Walby, Kevin, Alex Luscombe, and Randy K. Lippert. 2014. Expertise and the Professionalization of Municipal Corporate Security in Canadian Cities. In *Corporate Security in the 21st Century: Theory and Practice in International Perspective*, eds. Kevin Walby and Randy K. Lippert, 116–133. Houndsmills: Palgrave Macmillan.

Walker, Diane, and Florence Myrick. 2006. Grounded Theory: An Exploration of Process and Procedure. *Qualitative Health Research* 16(4): 547–559.

Walsh, Patrick, and Seumas Miller. 2015. Rethinking 'Five Eyes' Security: Intelligence Collection Policies and Practice Post Snowden. *Intelligence and National Security* 31: 1–24.

Weiss, Robert. 2014. Corporate Security at Ford Motor Company: From the Great War to the Cold War. In *Corporate Security in the 21st Century: Theory and Practice in International Perspective*, eds. Kevin Walby and Randy K. Lippert, 17–38. Houndmills: Palgrave Macmillan.

White, Adam. 2012. The New Political Economy of Private Security. *Theoretical Criminology* 16(1): 85–101.

Williams, James. 2014. The Private Eyes of Corporate Culture: The Forensic Accounting and Corporate Investigation Industry and the Production of Corporate Financial Security. In *Corporate Security in the 21st Century: Theory and Practice in International Perspective*, eds. Kevin Walby and Randy K. Lippert, 56–77. Houndmills: Palgrave Macmillan.

Interviews

Federal Corporate Security Manager. 2014.

8

The 'Security of Security': Making Up the Australian Intelligence Community 1975–2015

Darren Palmer and Ian Warren

Introduction

The legal and institutional arrangements for Australian security and intelligence underwent major changes in the 1970s. Existing agencies were publicly acknowledged for the first time, new agencies were established, new powers of investigation and surveillance were introduced and an emergent 'intelligence community' was formed. As in Canada (and the USA), numerous 'crises' in Australian intelligence practices led to and informed various commissions of inquiry that made visible previously hidden intelligence institutions and associated surveillance practices. Subsequent inquiries, security and intelligence plans, national statements and reforms in Australia built upon these developments, indicative of a good measure of continuity in intelligence and surveillance arrangements. This chapter identifies how intelligence and security arrangements were

D. Palmer • I. Warren (✉)
Department of Criminology, Deakin University, Geelong, Victoria, Australia

© The Author(s) 2016
R. Lippert et al. (eds.), *National Security, Surveillance and Terror*,
DOI 10.1007/978-3-319-43243-4_8

'problematised' from the 1970s, and a new 'intelligence community' was created as an object of governing.

Governmentality and Security

This chapter uses a governmentality approach to explore the "making up" (Rose 1996, 328) of this new community as an object of government. Governmentality is concerned with understanding how "different sites" and "different regularities" have "distinctive modes of governance … which generate knowledge of subject populations in order to govern 'the conduct of conduct'" (Dupont and Pearce 2001, 125). It involves moving beyond an "institutional-centric" (Foucault 2009, 116) approach focused on the internal logic and operations of an institution, its component parts, organisational arrangements and the knowledge generated within the institution and in relation to other institutions. Instead, governmentality seeks to understand institutions from the outside, using a genealogical approach, "de-institutionalising and de-functionalising relations of power" in order to examine "the way they are formed, connect up with each other, develop, multiply, and are transformed on the basis of something other than themselves" (Foucault 2009, 119). Governmentality displaces the idea of "the state as a 'coherent entity'" or sovereign authority over a defined territory and seeks instead to look to the ways in which different "activities … become problematised and rethought and potentially modified" (Dupont and Pearce 2001, 126). It is that governing now is much more than the operation of the state and sovereignty over territory, and much more than its apparatuses and mechanisms of law and discipline: this new 'art of government' concerns the "right disposition of things" arranged "to a suitable end" (la Perriere, cited in Foucault 2009, 98) whereby "the analysis relocates 'the State' within an investigation of *problematics of government*" (Rose and Miller 1992, 174, emphasis original).

As Rose and Miller have argued, 'an analytic of the problematics of government' seeks to explore the different ways authorities "seek to shape the beliefs and conduct of others in desired directions" (Rose and Miller 1992, 175). This approach analyses the various "projects, plans and practices of those authorities," their justifications and the governmental technologies of "mundane programmes, calculations, techniques, apparatuses, documents and procedures" (Rose and Miller 1992, 175). In terms of the emergence of an intelligence community, the key technique of community coordination has been used to continually renew governmental strategies over the past 40 years (see also Jones, this volume). As with any community, there has been a sense of an always already dysfunctionality or pathologies, leading to further governmental strategies and techniques reaching ever-deeper into its features and formats. We approach these and subsequent developments as moments or events in a series of governmental shifts concerning the problematisations of the 'security of security' or how Australian intelligence apparatuses are governed. This idea of apparatuses sequent developments as *dispositif* of security developed in Foucault's *Security, Territory, Population* (2009) and is applied here to the arrangements of the institutions of security and intelligence.

While Foucault has been criticised for the lack of clarity concerning the dispositif of security in relation to sovereignty and discipline and the place of the dispositif of security in the post-9/11 context has been questioned (Bigo 2008), the central constituent parts of security consist of a shift in emphasis from control over territory (sovereignty) and control over space (discipline) to governing through shaping of the freedom of circulation. We suggest that there has been a realignment of security whereby both sovereignty and discipline operate with an ever-more stringent effort at the delineation between good and bad circulations. This is where the rise of surveillance in everyday life operates to enhance sovereign authority and disciplinary practices to enable a clearer demarcation and 'labeling' of the abnormal while at the same time the 'normal' are able to circulate freely as is 'normal' to 'our way of life.'

Finally, this also means that governing through the intelligence and security community cannot be viewed as a stable technique but rather something that is fluid and adjustable: an apparatus for generating the 'right disposition of things.' In these arrangements, security and intelligence remain a community but now one that has enhanced capacities for intelligence gathering that enjoys greater freedom in the circulation of information. In turn, these new-found capacities translate into the ability to allow the ongoing freedom of circulation for those remaining in the tightened or more circumscribed norm, a delineation subject to ongoing refinement along a continuum with more restrictive forms at one end and more expansive forms at the other. Security is centrifugal, reaching out into the everyday "opening, integrating and enlarging" (Bigo 2008, 97). The dispositif of security seeks to understand cases, events or a milieu not by isolating but by seeking to understand the norm, enhancing the mobility of things to enable a form of sorting against the norm. In this sense, the dispositif of security fosters movement, circulation and freedom built upon the liberty of freedom to move, to be mobile, albeit circumscribed by the identification of, and intervening upon abnormal movement. This is not the politics of exception or emergency but rather the identification of the abnormal in the circulation of things.

Applied to our focus on intelligence and security agencies, the 'security of security' involves the problematisation of the right arrangements concerning the freedom of circulation: how can the circulation of information within the security and intelligence community be arranged so as to facilitate or enable good circulation within the intelligence community while at the same time facilitating or enabling good circulation within the population? How can security and intelligence agencies meet governmental objectives while at the same time not overly encroaching upon the freedoms and liberties of the population? What is the right way for liberal government to govern national security mechanisms in ways that also protect freedom? We do not propose to answer these questions in an ahistorical, reductionist or teleological manner, but rather to locate them within particular 'problematisations' that shift the emphasis between the modalities of law, discipline and security (Foucault 2009, 4–6) to highlight profound shifts in governmental techniques over the past 40 years.

Below we explore the shifting governmental rationalities and techniques through the examination of open-source data on reviews of and statements concerning intelligence arrangements, drawing particularly on three key documents: the Hope Royal Commission on Intelligence and Security (RCIS) (Hope 1976); the Flood Report (2004); and the *Review of Australia's Counter-Terrorism Machinery* (Department of Prime Minister and Cabinet 2015). While we refer to several other reviews and reports on intelligence and security, the three reports represent the start or introduction of the idea of an intelligence community (Hope) as an object of government, a mid-period review that captures post-9/11 changes (Flood) and the final 2015 Review that provides us with the most recent detailed documentation of Australian intelligence and security arrangements. We do not address state and territory levels of government or "security beyond the state" (Abrahamsen and Williams 2009, 2011) or the broader continuum of counter-terrorism and policing networks (Palmer and Whelan 2014) (but see Jones and Walsh, this volume). Further, we do not claim this to be an exhaustive empirical history of the reviews of security and national intelligence, but rather schematic and selective use of reports that highlights the transformations in response to the question of how to govern national security intelligence apparatuses. As Rose and Miller (1992) suggest, studies of governing differ from traditional historical and sociological realism (and in this area we would add international relations and security studies) "eschew[ing] sociological realism and its burdens of explanation and causation" and instead focusing on "the ways in which authorities … have posed themselves" questions on how to govern (177).

This chapter proceeds by introducing the re-casting of security from an external to an internal focus, beginning 40 years ago. This responds to the perceived dual risks of the lack of intelligence capacity on the one hand, and the need to manage the risks associated with enhanced surveillance capacities on the other. In this process a 'community' is formed and governmental techniques are established to govern this community. The 'intelligence community' is an "imagined community" (Anderson 1983) that brings into existence sets of arrangements and practices to be governed through new techniques, and the creation of new administrative and interdependent bureaucracies. Intelligence arrangements have been problematised so that they are "made amenable to authoritative action *in terms of* features of communities and their strengths, cultures, pathologies" (Rose 1996, 331, emphasis original). While Rose was discussing a broader and more fundamental emergent shift from strategies of government based on 'the social' to those based on 'the community,' we regard the governmentalisation of the state as also shaping "the deliberations, strategies, tactics and devices employed by authorities for making up and acting upon" state intelligence agencies (Rose 1996, 328). This chapter explores this process of governing through community in the intelligence and security domain.

We conclude that today's intelligence and security assemblage permeates throughout Australian society, embedding surveillance in everyday life, culminating in reforms to the surveillance of metadata. However, we are not concerned with identifying the growth of 'big brother,' its panoptic and disciplinary powers or the Big Leviathan of Australia's security and intelligence arrangements, but rather the processes, procedures, knowledge and techniques that have shaped the making of the contemporary intelligence community (Collier 2009). Despite much of the analytical literature arguing that 9/11 represents a paradigmatic break so as to talk of pre- and post-9/11, the history of the past 40 years has been one of increasing the 'flows' and 'circulation' of surveillance capacities and information within and beyond an 'intelligence assemblage' that predates these events. Just as much of the Foucauldian and Deluezian literature on security and governing concerns itself with understanding the biopolitical logic of enhancing population mobilities while developing capacities to delineate between 'good' and 'bad' flows, so too has a similar process been at play in the domain of national security with important implications for understanding contemporary practices.

'Making Up' the Intelligence Community

Some 40 years ago, Australia's intelligence and security arrangements were problematised along two lines of inquiry: their adequacy in meeting changing geo-strategic conditions and the ability of different intelligence practitioners within and across existing and newly formed agencies to collaborate and coordinate with each other. The Hope Royal Commission on Intelligence and Security (RCIS) set the scene for these changes and challenges.

As Hope indicates, intelligence would no longer simply be part of defence and foreign affairs protecting the nation, but now would constitute its own domain of practice.

> In the past, intelligence has been believed to be of most relevance in the field of defence and related policy areas. It is, however, not only a matter of defence. More and more, intelligence is relevant to the formation of

national policies in a number of other areas; this is a trend that will continue. (Hope 1976, 3)[1]

The Hope RCIS is one of the most significant inquiries into intelligence and security in Australia's history, re-shaping the institutional assemblage of security and intelligence and informing a major recalibration of security and intelligence beyond the focus on Defence and Foreign Affairs and towards internal security risks.[2] It also took place in the broader international context of committees examining the operation of intelligence and security agencies for instance in Canada (Mackenzie 1969; McDonald 1979) and the USA (Rockefeller 1975; Church 1976) that similarly re-shaped the intelligence and security assemblages in those countries.

The RCIS was implemented by the newly elected Labor Government in 1972. Labor had a pre-election policy commitment to a fundamental examination of the history, functions, administration, coordination and future of security and intelligence agencies. The Royal Commission operated from 1974 to 1977 and found that not only was there a need to inwardly re-orient the directions of security and intelligence, but Commissioner Hope was also critical of their organisational arrangements and capacities: "The Australian intelligence community is fragmented, poorly coordinated and organised. The agencies lack proper guidance and direction" (RCIS (3rd Report) 1976, 4). In addition, Hope pointed to the "unnecessary secretiveness" (ibid., 5) of the intelligence community and made many recommendations for enhancing both internal and external accountability across the intelligence community as Australia needed to develop its own intelligence capacity rather than remain heavily reliant on intelligence partners (see Jones, this volume).

In Hope's review and criticism of Australian intelligence and security, we can identify an emergent shift in the ways of thinking about how to govern intelligence and security. This concern with "making up" (Rose and

---

[1] There were eight multi-volume reports of the Royal Commission with information now held and available from the National Archives of Australia which were used in researching this chapter. See http://www.naa.gov.au/collection/explore/security/royal-commisson/.

[2] This is not to suggest that the Hope Commission was fully progressive in dealing with the intelligence and security agencies and framework but that it was significant in terms of shaping developments in this field. For criticism see Cain (1994) and Hocking (1993, 2004).

Miller 1992, 174) the intelligence community has two important dimensions. First, in a literal sense Hope was naming intelligence agencies as an emergent community consisting of both extant institutions and newly recognised agencies to be formally incorporated into the community. The concept of an 'intelligence community' was first used in the USA in the Dulles Report (1949). The chairperson was subsequently appointed new Director of the CIA (Warner and McDonald 2005, iii). Hope deployed this concept in Australia. Further, the idea of a 'community' creates a sense of the benign community of entities but also a shared solidity of purpose. At the same time 'community' is wonderfully adaptive, seeming natural and providing means for delimiting membership of any group. Second, Hope was seeking ways to enable "a kind of regulated freedom" (ibid.) where newly formed and existing agencies were brought into being and reformed through new legislation that would clarify their roles and responsibilities, while ensuring the capacity to form a community. As Rose and Miller (1992) suggest, "law translates aspects of a governmental programme into mechanisms that establish, constrain or empower certain agents or entities and set some of the key terms of their deliberations … both legitimating and regulating at the same time" (189–190).

For the new intelligence community, a legislated mandate and powers, as well as purportedly enhanced accountability mechanisms, provides a basis for the legitimacy of the move of intelligence beyond defence. The problematic of governing intelligence was one of negotiating between the perceived need for peace-time intelligence and the limits to be placed on the emergent intelligence community due to concerns about the capacity for using the intelligence surveillance powers for overtly political (anti-left) purposes. In sum, if an intelligence capacity were to be formally developed, the problematic of governing concerned what institutional formats intelligence would take, how it would be governed and to what ends. The idea of a 'community' would be the form for arranging intelligence. How then to arrange the assemblage of institutions? For Hope, coordination would be the means of ensuring the right disposition of things, a governmental technique as a key not in the sense of a fixed notion of what coordination means and how it is to be achieved, but rather as a flexible and mutating 'prescription' that allows the 'community' to adapt to changing problematics and ongoing normalising interventions.

Hope wanted to enhance coordination to ensure the circulation or flow of intelligence information across the emergent security assemblage, while at the same time seeking ways to delineate between 'good' and 'bad' circulation. While dominant uses of Foucault and Delueze have been concerned with understanding how security and surveillance are increasingly directed at delineating between 'good' and 'bad' flows within the population, our focus is on how a parallel political rationality of security shaped governmental technologies to govern the Australian intelligence community and the ongoing concern with good and bad flows of information and people in a coordinated intelligence community. While governing mentalities are always already overlapping, in the Hope Royal Commission we can identify that disciplinary governmentality was intersecting with a security rationality. Security and intelligence had to be controlled and made accountable for breaches of laws and regulations and had to be more directed to enhance utility, but at the same time the utility of the intelligence community had to enhance the flow of good information. The disciplinary mechanisms that were developed included more clearly defined legal powers (1979), and later the introduction of an Inspector-General of Intelligence and Security (1987), and a Parliamentary Joint Committee on ASIO (the Australian Security Intelligence Organisation) (1988). By comparison, Canada also introduced an Inspector General from 1984 but abolished this position in 2012 and has never had a Parliamentary Committee dedicated solely to oversight of the intelligence community despite numerous recommendations to do so (for the early years see Whitaker 1992).[3]

Hope's approach to opening up security and intelligence information flows was to occur by enabling the participation of agencies beyond defence and foreign affairs through establishing a Permanent Heads

---

[3] Canada introduced a non-parliamentary Security Intelligence Review Committee (SIRC) (established under the *Canadian Security Intelligence Service Act* 1984) appointed by the Governor in Council, which examines issues concerning agency cooperation, and a similarly appointed independent statutory body (Communications Security Establishment Commissioner) to review legal compliance and receive complaints. Section 56 of the *CSIS Act* 1984 created a requirement for a comprehensive review after five years, which did recommend a parliamentary committee to oversee CSIS but government refusal at the time led to the introduction of a Sub-Committee of the Justice Committee of Parliament to review CISS and SIRC (see Samuels and Coad (1995, 48–49) on this and for their discussion of Australian committee meetings with this Canadian sub-committee in the mid-1990s).

Committee on Intelligence and Security involving agency heads and secretaries of relevant government departments. Thus problematic silos and
limited networks were opened up to the possibility of greater collaboration and coordination across government, which marked the beginnings
of the Australian security and intelligence assemblage.[4]

Two central issues emerged from the RCIS.[5] First, the security architecture was radically transformed. Second, the narrative concerning
the never-ending search for coordination, cooperation and collaboration was established. In terms of the former, the Commonwealth Police
Force became the Australia Police in 1975 and in 1979 became the
Australian Federal Police. In 1977 an additional intelligence analysis
agency, the Office of National Assessments (ONA) was created within
the Department of the Prime Minister and Cabinet, and in 1978 the
Defence Signals Directorate (DSD) was created and ASIO was given
important new investigative powers. This intelligence architecture would
largely remain 'stable' until after the turn of the century (a review of
Defence intelligence led to the Defence Intelligence Organisation, DIO
being introduced in 1990, see Hocking 2004; see Jones, this volume).

Hope's identification of the need for greater coordination and cooperation across the intelligence community involved clear delineations
between intelligence and policy formulation, intelligence gathering and
assessment, and security intelligence and law enforcement. A concern
with coordination was deemed central to Hope's critique of extant security and intelligence arrangements and, as shown below, remains a key
'problematisation' of intelligence and security arrangements and a narrative shaping ongoing reforms. There are two parts to this problematisa-

---

[4] It should be noted that the existence of some intelligence agencies had not been formally acknowledged to the public, including The Australian Signals Intelligence Service (ASIS) and DSD.
Similarly, Canada's equivalent to DSD, the Communications Security Establishment ('Canada' was
added in 2008) was established in 1946 but remained unknown until 1974 when a CBC documen-
tary disclosed 'The Fifth Estate.' It remains a key intelligence agency, located with the Department
of National Defence since 1975. The *Antiterrorism Act* 2001 (Bill C-36) refined and increased its
communication interception powers and in particular the ability to intercept domestic communications when this involves a party outside Canada. CSEC is a key agency in the Five Eyes information sharing agreement (see Walby and Anaïs 2012).

[5] We are not claiming that all of the changes were an immediate outcome of the RCIS but rather
that the RCIS (as well as Hope's subsequent *Protective Security Review* November, 1979) set out the
basis for architectural change.

tion. First, 'bad' cooperative and collaborative practices had been allowed to occur, such as the relationships between ASIO and state police Special Branches. Various media reports on Special Branch surveillance of political 'subversives' and a subsequent South Australian (SA) inquiry into the SA Police Special Branch (White 1977) led to the sacking of the SA Police Commissioner (see Hocking 2004, 55–69). This is an example of the liberal 'fear of fear' as political and community concerns with the overreach of surveillance and the 'bad' circulation of surveillance data led to limits being placed on intelligence and surveillance practices, such as the development of clearer provisions concerning collaboration with agencies outside the intelligence community via the new *ASIO Act* in 1979. Second, the new ONA (*ONA Act* 1977) was given a legislative mandate as a statutory authority to review international intelligence activities and to inform government of "any inadequacies in the nature, extent or … coordination of those activities" (s. 5(1)(d)). Coordination would now be overseen by a statutory agency. As will be seen below when examining the Flood Review (2004), the ONA was seen as 'failing' to ensure adequate flows and distribution of security information.

While the RCIS established the intelligence community and placed the issues of coordination and collaboration as key and ongoing problematics (similar concerns were identified in Canada during this period by the Office of Auditor General of Canada in 2003, 2004 and 2009: see Auditor General of Canada 2009 for an overview), they continued to be major issues documented in subsequent inquiries including:

- The *Protective Security Review* 1978–1979), which was commissioned following the bombing of the Sydney Hilton Hotel in February 1978 and examined the threat of terrorism in light of the need for enhanced commonwealth and state agency cooperation;
- Hope (1984), who followed his earlier inquiry to examine progress, as well as ongoing issues of coordination and accountability;
- The 1992 Richardson Review (cited in Samuels and Coad 1995, 5), which reviewed intelligence and security following the "disappearance of the strategic and ideological divide between East and West" and identified the need for "management and coordination arrangements … to be adjusted so that they could cope with the pressures of a more

diverse international environment" (Samuels and Coad 1995, 5). This was somewhat similar to the analysis of CSIS Director Ray Protti's (1992) review in Canada;

- Flood's (2004) *Report of the Inquiry into National Intelligence*, which examined coordination and oversight of the intelligence community in light of the false claims of Iraq's possession of weapons of mass destruction that were used, falsely, to support invasion by the 'coalition of the willing' (discussed in more detail in the next section);

- Smith's (2008) *Review of Homeland and Border Security* (with a noted change in terminology), which recommended against the introduction of a Homeland Security agency and highlighted the need for improvements in coordination and strategic planning (which led to);

- The *National Security Statement* (2008), which introduced the concept of the 'National Intelligence Community,' a unified national security budget and cancelled the previous Labor Government's preference for a Department of Homeland Security. This statement broadened the definition of security threats beyond the dominance of terrorism, and in particular focused on climate change as part of an 'all hazards approach' to security leading to an expansion of relevant agencies/departments and the introduction of the National Security Adviser located in the Department of Prime Minister and Cabinet alongside the ONA. As then Prime Minister Rudd stated: "Increasing complexity and interconnectedness is a fact of life in the modern, global environment. Classical distinctions between foreign and domestic, national and international, internal and external have become blurred" (Rudd 2008, 5);

- The *Counter-Terrorism White Paper* (Department of Prime Minister and Cabinet 2010), which lead to the introduction of the Counter-Terrorism Control Centre within ASIO to ensure multi-agency coordination; and

- Cornall and Black's (2011) *Independent Review of the Intelligence Community* (itself a product of the Flood Inquiry's recommendation that independent reviews occur every five to seven years), which focused on the 'traditional' 'six core agencies' recognised as intelligence community members, and pointed to the need for improved collaborations below senior management level and the continuation of expanded secondments across agencies to improve collaboration, an "evolution [that] *will take time*" (Cornall and Black 2011, 22, emphasis added).

This is not an exhaustive list of inquiries, reports and plans problematising intelligence community coordination, but is indicative of the manner in which the governmental technique of coordination remained central to governing Australia's intelligence and security apparatuses. We now turn to the first major report after the flurry of changes introduced post-9/11 (for details of these changes see Jones as well as Walsh, this volume).

Flood Report (2004)

The problematisation of the intelligence and security community's "strengths, cultures, pathologies" (Rose 1996, 331) had been a major concern post-9/11. As the US 9/11 Commission (National Commission on Terrorist Attacks Upon the United States 2004) highlighted, the coordination of the intelligence age was a major limitation on the capacity to prevent terrorism. Its final chapter called for "A Different Way of Organizing Government" that would be achieved through a 'unity of effort' and enhanced coordination of the 15 agency 'confederation' (see Chap. 13). At the same time in Australia, 'failing' coordination returned in the aftermath of the controversy over the 'intelligence failure' that blurred intelligence, information and policy in the backdrop to the invasion of Iraq. The Flood Inquiry was implemented to review the intelligence 'failure' associated with this and other recent events (the Fiji coup in May 2000, the Bali bombing in 2002, the rise of Jemaah Islamiya in Indonesia and allegations of a 'pro-Jakarta' bias within DIO and ONA, East Timor and Solomon Islands collapses 2000–2003) in terms of intelligence coordination.

As indicated above, since 1977 ONA had a legislative mandate as a statutory authority to review international intelligence activities and to inform government of "any inadequacies in the nature, extent or … coordination of those activities" (*ONA Act* s. 5(1)(d)). In investigating the intelligence failure, Flood did not identify any "evidence to suggest that ONA's judgment was influenced by policy or political considerations" (Flood 2004, 29, or with DIO's advice on Indonesia and East Timor, 2004, 48). However, Flood criticised ONA's role as overseer of coordination, suggesting that ONA lacked resources, its "coordination role" was "unclear"

(2004, 56), there was no mechanism for ensuring the intelligence community assisted ONA in enhancing coordination and, finally, that the legislation meant that in reviewing coordination ONA was reviewing itself (2004, 57). Further, the oversight of the Parliamentary Joint Committee on ASIO, ASIS and DSD (PJCAAD) did not have policy or operational oversight in its terms of reference (2004, 55). Other intelligence community agencies were also identified as requiring greater coordination efforts. Taken together, these concerns underpinned Flood's subsequent recommendations for introducing "a stronger coordination" (Flood 2004, 164) mandate for ONA via a Foreign Intelligence Coordination Committee (FICC). The FICC would be chaired by ONA and have representation drawn from all intelligence community heads, as well as senior public servants from the Departments of Prime Minister and Cabinet and Foreign Affairs (2004, 60–61) to overcome the "relatively informal arrangements for community coordination" (Flood 2004, 164, and see recommendations 6–8, at 181–182). In sum then, the 'failures' of intelligence and policy in the lead in to the Iraq war were not found to be the problem, but rather the 'strength of weak ties' (Granovetter 1973) was inadequate and limited in terms of enhancing and ensuring coordination.

Finally, addressing what he called 'Cross-Community Issues' (Flood 2004, 152), Flood highlighted several key areas for further development including recruitment, training, international collaboration and information technology coordination. Broader recruitment and skills would enhance the "sharing of expertise among agencies" and help "to build links with government department[s], think tanks and other repositories of analytical strength" (2004, 153). In addition, Flood recommended "secondments between agencies" (2004, 154), and "cross-cutting training" to be developed by the new FICC to form "a foundation for whole-of-government approaches to intelligence needs" (ibid.). Flood wanted intelligence relationships extended beyond the Five Eyes (though in the public report he only refers to the UK and USA) to identify ways of enhancing existing relationships with foreign intelligence partners as well as developing new opportunities for "increased cooperation" in Europe and the Middle East (2004, 156–157).

In sum, we can see the shifting programs and techniques to govern security and intelligence through a mentality of security. Flood moves between determining the right disposition for the oversight of coordination through to ensuring intelligence employees work in each others' agencies and share common knowledge to build common community culture and overcome idiosyncratic internal pathologies and divisions. Simultaneously, this structure moves back again to a 'whole-of-government' approach to security that finally looks outwards to developing new security relations beyond sovereign territory in Europe, as well as beyond the state's intelligence community to incorporate specialist Think Tanks and the private sector (Palmer and Whelan 2006).

Many changes occurred in the period following Flood that are beyond the scope of this chapter (see Walsh and Jones, this volume). However, one important development we need to document occurred in 2008 following the then Prime Minster Kevin Rudd's National Security Statement (Rudd 2008). Rudd announced that the FICC was being replaced by the National Intelligence Coordination Committee, to be chaired by the new National Security Advisor (Canada had appointed a National Security Advisor in 2004). The change in terminology, authority and relationships with other personnel and agencies was significant: a *Coordination Committee would oversee coordination* with the committee being chaired by a Prime Ministerial appointment located within the Department of Prime Minister and Cabinet rather than an independent statutory officer; and the coordination would now focus more on linking the 'foreign intelligence' dimensions of the intelligence community with the emergent national security assemblage that incorporated agencies beyond the Australian intelligence community.

Counter-Terrorism 2015

Our final 'moment' in the development of 'security of security' in the Australian intelligence community is the *Review of Australia's Counter-Terrorism Machinery* (Department of Prime Minister and Cabinet 2015). Several key features of the report are central to our analysis. First, the title refers to the 'machinery' of organisation, a Taylorist conceptualisation assuming 'production' can be delivered through rational planning and organisation that will deliver clear goals, activities, responsibilities and coordination. Usually, this approach is seen as best suited to stable environments and repetitive production. It is unclear how this metaphor fits with what the report indicates is a changing environment where "the threat of terrorism in Australia is rising and it is becoming harder to combat" (2015, iv), as a range of "significant challenges to national security … places unprecedented strain on agencies working in this field" (2015, 13). What is particularly stunning about this document is the manner in which it highlights the achievement of bringing together intelligence and law enforcement as a coordinated whole. No longer concerned with any pretence of delineation between intelligence security and policing, the Review identifies that prior to 2001, only 12 agencies were involved in Commonwealth counter-terrorism activities in only six of the identified functions: *Intelligence*; *Law Enforcement*; *Offshore Disruption*; *Border*; *Community Engagement*; and *International Engagement* (2015, 5 (see Chart 3)).[6] By 2014, existing agencies spread across the six functions became multi-functional and new agencies/departments were added totaling 24 members of the intelligence community. The counter-terrorism functions now included representatives from education and human and social services as part of the *community engagement* strategy, as well as defence, agriculture and the Maritime Safety Authority in *Border*, and Airservices Australia and the Commonwealth Department of Public Prosecutions in *Law Enforcement*.

In identifying "challenges and weakness" in the intelligence community, the Review found there had been a "rising tide" of threats, growing in complexity with many "suspects who were previously unknown to authorities" (2015, 18). While acknowledging that "[s]uccessive reviews have highlighted information sharing as critical," which "has improved in recent years, the problems are far from solved" (2015, 19–20). The Review used the interdiction of people seeking asylum on boats and either turning back boats or taking occupants into offshore detention centres, commonly known as Operation Sovereign Borders (OSB), as *the* model for effective leadership and coordination (2015, 22). Despite being widely criticised, achieving a desired "OSB effect" required strengthen-

---

[6] While some of these titles might be a little confusing such as 'Border,' we remain faithful to the actual text of the Review.

ing "existing coordination mechanisms" (ibid.).[7] However, like the earlier Smith Review (2008), the 2015 Review also rejected the need for a new US-style Department of Homeland Security or UK-style Department of Home Affairs. Instead, using the OSB model the Review recommended a single leader, namely a National Counter-Terrorism Coordinator (2015, 26). The Government agreed to these proposals in a media release on the day the Review was released (Prime Minister of Australia 2015) and the appointment was made on 25 May 2015. Australia now has a Coordinator of coordination in the intelligence assemblage.

Conclusion

Over the past 40 years in Australia, the coordination of intelligence and security has been a key governmental technology. While in the early part of this period coordination was concerned with 'declaring' and legislating the existence of various intelligence bodies to develop the capacity for 'making up' an emergent 'intelligence community,' subsequent efforts after 9/11 took on a more urgent and deeper search for techniques for enhancing coordination. Even the 'intelligence failures' of the invasion of Iraq were addressed in terms of the need to enhance the governing of coordination (Flood 2004). Most recently, the 2015 Review vested the role of coordination in a single authority on authority in the form of the National Counter-Terrorism Coordinator: a Coordinator of coordination.

While we have covered considerable territory documenting changes to the machinery of Australian national intelligence and security we accept that even more in-depth analysis of key programmatic texts would support claims in this chapter. Furthermore, there is a need to examine the interplay between the different levels of government, governments in different locations, and the always already failing governmental desires. Nonetheless, we argue that the past 40 years have witnessed a dramatic

---

[7] It should be noted that OSB has been severely criticised for its general inhumanity and immorality as well as its breach of international treaties, though offshore asylum hearing processes were found by the High Court to be legal.

shift in governing security by what we have referred to as the emergent 'security of security.' This is not to suggest that it has been an evolutionary process without any counter-tendencies, "failed securitizations" (Salter 2011, 125) or the constraining "liberalism of fear" (the fear of being fearful of government practice) that operates "in ways that can actually *inhibit* the processes of securitization" (Williams 2011, 454). We have instead documented key moments of shifting thoughts, plans and techniques on how to govern intelligence and security, resulting in the security of security based on opening up the capacities of intelligence to operate as a rationality of security whereby the barriers to the circulation of 'security goods' are opened up in favour of freedom of circulation and access to information across an ever-growing intelligence community.

Old barriers, such as those between law enforcement and intelligence, between 'domestic' and 'international,' have been broken down. Limits to the collection of information are continually withdrawn. This has culminated in the most recent requirements for all internet service providers to store all client metadata for two years and for this data to be accessible to 19 listed intelligence and law enforcement agencies without the 'unnecessary' barriers of slow and expensive warrant procedures (Warren 2015). Just as we started with the Hope Royal Commission admitting that unacknowledged security agencies were in existence and needed to be formally recognised and established as part of the Australian intelligence community, we now have the post-Snowden revelations of previously unknown security practices being recognised and legitimated through legislation (see also Forcese, this volume).

But a mentality of security comes to the fore that is way more than a sovereign act of declaration, more than the legitimation through law, and more than a disciplinary technique established to punish bad intelligence practices. This is not to suggest that security replaces discipline, but instead there is "a triangle: sovereignty, discipline, and governmental management" (Foucault 2009, 108). A pertinent recent example involves the introduction of the new Australian Border Force that has implemented a range of new disciplinary techniques for staff including targeted integrity testing, drug and alcohol testing, the power to suspend the *Fair Work Act* 2009 to enable termination for serious misconduct and the mandatory reporting of serious misconduct and criminal behaviour. This is one small example of how the mentality of government and apparatuses of security intersect with other mentalities rather than a neat succession of law-discipline-security (Foucault 2009, 10). There is therefore an interplay of these rationalities and associated mechanisms of power. 'Human security' is posited as requiring this free flow of good intelligence information across law enforcement and intelligence agencies to ensure the priority of what is now constructed as the most fundamental human right: pre-emptive security from insecurity. In the current period, the fear of governing too much and in a manner that limits freedom is answered by the elevation of freedom from insecurity as *the* governmental priority via the apparatuses of security, which is to be achieved by a Coordinator of community coordination.

References

Abrahamsen, Rita, and Michael C. Williams. 2009. Security Beyond the State: Global Security Assemblages in International Politics. *International Political Sociology* 3(1): 1–17.

———. 2011. *Security Beyond the State: Private Security in International Politics*. Cambridge: Cambridge University Press.

Anderson, Benedict. 1983. *Imagined Communities: Reflections on the Origin and Spread of Nationalism*. London: Verso.

Auditor General of Canada. 2009. *2009 March Report of the Auditor General of Canada*. Ottawa: Office of the Auditor General of Canada.

Bigo, Didier. 2008. Security: A Field Left Fallow. In *Foucault on Politics: Security and War*, ed. M. Dillon and A.W. Neal, 93–114. Basingstoke: Palgrave Macmillan.

Cain, Frank. 1994. *The Australian Security Intelligence Organization: An Unofficial History*. Abingdon, UK: Frank Cass.

Church, Frank. 1976. *(Chair) United States Senate Select Committee to Study Governmental Operations with Respect to Intelligence Activities*. Washington, DC: US Government Printing Office.

Collier, Stephen J. 2009. Topologies of Power: Foucault's Analysis of Political Government Beyond 'Governmentality'. *Theory, Culture and Society* 26(6): 76–108.

Cornall, Robert, and Rufus Black. 2011. *Independent Review of the Intelligence Community. Report*. Canberra: Commonwealth of Australia.

Department of Prime Minister and Cabinet. 2010. *Counter-Terrorism White Paper: Securing Australia/Protecting Our Community*. Canberra: Department of Prime Minister and Cabinet.

———. 2015. *Review of Australia's Counter-Terrorism Machinery*. Canberra: Commonwealth of Australia.

Dulles, Allen W., and William H. Jackson. 1949. *The Central Intelligence Agency and National Organization for Intelligence: A Report to the National Security Council*. 1 January. Approved for release per the Mori review through Historical Review Program at http://sttpml.org/wp-content/uploads/2014/04/CIA-Dulles-Jackson-Correa-RDP86B00269R000500040001-1.pdf.

Dupont, Danica, and Frank Pearce. 2001. Foucault Contra Foucault. *Theoretical Criminology* 5(2): 123–158.

Flood, Philip. (AO). 2004. *Report of the Inquiry into National Intelligence*. Canberra: Commonwealth of Australia.

Foucault, Michel. 2009. *Security, Territory, Population*. Basingstoke: Palgrave Macmillan.

Granovetter, Mark S. 1973. The Strength of Weak Ties. *American Journal of Sociology* 78(6): 1360–1380.

Hocking, Jenny. 1993. *Beyond Terrorism: The Development of the Australian Security State*. Sydney: Allen and Unwin.

———. 2004. *Terror Laws: ASIO, Counter-Terrorism and the Threat to Democracy*. Sydney: University of New South Wales Press.

Hope, Justice R. M. 1976. *Royal Commission on Intelligence and Security*. 3rd Report, 1 December 1976. Canberra: National Archives of Australia, Series No. A8908, 3B.

Hope, Justice R.M. 1979. *Protective Security Review (Unclassified)*. Canberra: Australian Government Publishing Service.

——— 1984. *Royal Commission on Australian Security Agencies*. Canberra: Australian Government Publishing Service.

Mackenzie, Maxwell W. 1969. Report of Canada Royal Commission on Security (Abridged). http://epe.lac-bac.gc.ca/100/200/301/pco-bcp/commissions-ef/mackenzie1969-eng/mackenzie1969-eng.pdf.

McDonald, Justice D. C. 1979. *Commission of Inquiry into Certain Activities of the Royal Canadian Mounted Police* (First Report: Security and Information). http://epe.lac-bac.gc.ca/100/200/301/pco-bcp/commissions-ef/mcdonald1979-81-eng/mcdonald1979-81-report1/mcdonald1979-81-report1-eng.pdf.

National Commission on Terrorist Attacks Upon the United States. 2004. Washington, DC: Government Printing Office.

Palmer, Darren, and Chad Whelan. 2006. Counter-Terrorism Across the Policing Continuum. *Police Practice and Research: An International Journal* 7(5): 449–465.

———. 2014. Policing and Networks in the Field of Counter-Terrorism. In *Political Violence, Terrorism and Counter-Terrorism*, eds. D. Lowe, A. Turk, and D. Das, 145–166. Boca Raton, FL: Taylor & Francis CRC Press.

Prime Minister of Australia. 2015. Review of Australia's Counter-Terrorism Machinery for a Safer Australia, Media Release, February 23. https://www.pm.gov.au/media/2015-02-23/review-australias-counter-terrorism-machinery-safer-australia-0.

Rockefeller, Nelson. 1975. (Chair) *President's Commission on CIA Activities Within the United States*. New York: Manor Books.

Rose, Nikolas. 1996. The Death of the Social? Re-Figuring the Territory of Government. *Economy and Society* 25(3): 327–356.

Rose, Nikolas, and Peter Miller. 1992. Political Power Beyond the State: The Problematics of Government. *The British Journal of Sociology* 43(2): 173–205.

Rudd, Kevin. 2008. The First National Security Statement to the Australian Parliament. Address by the Prime Minister of Australia, The Hon. Kevin Rudd MP, December 4. http://www.royalcommission.vic.gov.au/getdoc/596cc5ff-8a33-47eb-8d4a-9205131ebdd0/TEN.004.002.0437.pdf.

Salter, Mark. 2011. When Securitization Fails: The Hard Case of Counter-Terrorism Programs. In *Securitization Theory: How Security Problems Emerge and Dissolve*, ed. T. Balzacq, 116–131. London: Routledge.

Samuels, Gordon J., and Michael H. Coad. 1995. *Commission of Inquiry into the Australian Secret Intelligence Service. Report.* (Public Edition). Canberra: Australian Government Publishing Service.

Smith, Ric. 2008. *Report of the Review of Homeland and Border Security* (Summary and Conclusions). Canberra: Commonwealth of Australia. http://www.royalcommission.vic.gov.au/getdoc/0be3af5e-16eb-4ba5-93c0-b83cb3a55860/TEN.004.002.0431.pdf.

Walby, Kevin, and Seantel Anaïs. 2012. Communications Security Establishment Canada (CSEC), Structures of Secrecy, and Ministerial Authorization after September 11. *Canadian Journal of Law and Society* 27(3): 363–380.

Warner, Michael, and J. Kenneth McDonald. 2005. *US Intelligence Community Reform Studies Since 1947*. Washington, DC: Strategic Management Issues Office, Centre for the Study of Intelligence.

Warren, Ian. 2015. Surveillance, Criminal Law and Sovereignty. *Surveillance and Society* 13(2): 300–305.

Whitaker, Reg. 1992. The Politics of Security Intelligence Policy-Making in Canada: II 1984–91. *Intelligence and National Security* 7(2): 53–76.

White, Acting Justice. 1977. *Special Branch Security Records Report*. Adelaide: South Australian Government Printer.

Williams, Michael C. 2011. Securitization and the liberalism of fear. *Security Dialogue* 42(4–5): 453–463.

Legislation

Australian Security and Intelligence Organization Act. 1979.

Office of National Assessments Act. 1977.

9

Justifying Insecurity: Canada's Response to Terrorist Threat Circa 2015

Erin Gibbs Van Brunschot

Introduction

In October 2014, an individual on Canada's anti-terrorism radar killed a soldier in Quebec by running him down with a motor vehicle. Only two days later, Michael Zehaf-Bibeau shot and killed a soldier standing guard in Ottawa. Early commentary from Prime Minister Stephen Harper denounced these events as acts of terrorism. These acts, for the prime minister, provided confirmation of the increasing global threat terrorism posed. Earlier that month, the government had adopted a motion pledging Canada's continued support for the US-led coalition against the Islamic State of Iraq and the Levant (ISIL or, more commonly, ISIS or Islamic State of Iraq and Syria). The timing of the October 2014 attacks was immediately framed as evidence that the ISIS threat was real and provided further justification for enacting legislation that would significantly change the nature of how security is perceived and pursued in Canada.

E. Gibbs Van Brunschot (✉)
Department of Sociology, University of Calgary, Calgary, AB, Canada

© The Author(s) 2016
R. Lippert et al. (eds.), *National Security, Surveillance and Terror*,
DOI 10.1007/978-3-319-43243-4_9

In this chapter, I examine the socio-political context of these events of October 2014 along with the legislative response. I consider how it is that government representatives participate in framing 'terrorist events' in ways that bolster their positions, policies and agendas. These positions are not only assumed on the national stage, but also internationally. The governing party immediately used these events as an opportunity to justify Canada's position in the US-led coalition. The government's framing of these events as evidence of a global terrorist threat impacting Canadians 'at home' obscured alternative interpretations of these events based on, for example, mental illness and addiction. Further, these events provided an opportunity for exercising the government's recent 'terrorism one-trick pony,' that is, punitive responses to 'radicalisation' and terrorism, the result of which has significantly altered Canada's security landscape.

Post-9/11, prime ministers of Canada and Australia as well as heads of state elsewhere framed their messages of security in multiple ways, depending upon the nature of the audience and context (Gibbs Van Brunschot and Kennedy 2012). Their messages also varied given the immediacy of the perceived threat, the resources available to address the threat and the relationships which depended on and were validated and legitimated by mutual understandings of threats (Gibbs Van Brunschot and Kennedy 2008, 12). In what follows, I explore how it is that the events of October 2014 affirmed and confirmed, both domestically and abroad, Canada's place in the fight against terrorism. I begin by reviewing the legislative and global contexts that emerged post-9/11. This summary provides a national legislative context for the emergence of events in late 2014 and locates how the Canadian government had been prepared to deal with the threat of terrorism at the national level. I then consider the global socio-political environment and Canada's position in the vortex of managing international terrorist threat.

The Legislative Context

The Anti-Terrorism Act, 2001

Initial responses to 9/11 consisted of national and international condemnations of the attacks. In Canada, the *Anti-Terrorism Act (ATA)* was brought forward by then-Prime Minister Jean Chretien in 2001. After abbreviated discussion, the Act was passed quickly in the House of Commons by December. The *ATA* amended the *Criminal Code of Canada*, including definitions of 'terrorist activity'[1] and 'terrorist group.' While the definition of terrorist activity is considered broad (see also Forcese, this volume), provisions within the *ATA* included those "designed to ensure that activities related to lawful armed conflict under international law, advocacy, protest, dissent or work stoppage, or the mere expression of a political, ideological or religious belief ... will not be considered 'terrorist activity'" (Wispinski 2006, 2).

In addition to offences related to terrorist activity or terrorist group involvement, the *ATA* provided law enforcement with new tools to investigate the likelihood of terrorist involvement, including investigative hearings and preventive arrests. Information gathering provisions were impacted by the *ATA*, specifically with regard to the government's power to share information. As Wispinski (2006) notes, the *ATA* did not necessarily provide for enhanced data collection, but instead allowed the government to reduce public access to various types of data. The *ATA* also allowed listing terrorist entities in the *Criminal Code*. While being listed is not itself a crime, the consequences of associating with listed entities, financially or otherwise, is a criminal offence. The suppression of terrorist financing was dealt with directly in *ATA* through revisions to the *Proceeds of Crime (Money Laundering) Act* by ensuring that large or suspicious monetary transactions would be investigated for terrorist links. Importantly, the 2001 *ATA* included sunset and review provisions related to investigative hearings and preventive arrests. These provisions expired 31 December 2006.

Several bills (Bill C-17, Bill C-19 and Bill S-3) were introduced to extend the investigative and preventive arrest provisions, but these were not passed due to parliamentary sessions ending (Bird and Valiquet 2012). It was not until 2012 that Bill S-7 (*Combating Terrorism Act*) came into effect. This Act reinstated provisions regarding investigative hearings and preventive arrests and introduced new terrorism offences, including prohibiting individuals from leaving or attempting to leave Canada

---

[1] Section 83.01(1) CC defines terrorist activity "to include any act or omission committed inside or outside of Canada that, if committed in Canada, is one of the terrorist offences referred to in ten anti-terrorist international conventions into which Canada has entered. It is also defined to include a variety of other acts or omissions committed inside or outside of Canada, either partially or wholly, for political, religious or ideological purposes, causes or objectives" (Wispinski 2006, 2).

to participate in terrorist activity, increasing penalties for some terrorism offences (i.e. harbouring individuals who have committed terrorist activity), and amending definitions of 'special operational information' ensuring confidentiality of government sources of that information (Bird and Valiquet 2012, 1). Again, there are clauses in Bill S-7 that stipulate that the investigative hearing and preventive arrest clauses be subject to sunset clauses five years after the Bill takes effect (ending 2017), "unless the operation of those sections is extended by a resolution of both houses of Parliament" (Bird and Valiquet 2012, 13).

Smart Border Declaration (2001)

As noted above, securing the border between the USA and its neighbours was a high priority post-9/11. Commonly referred to as the world's longest undefended border, 9/11 called into question the essentially free-flow of people, goods and resources across the Canada–US border (see Muller as well as Pratt, this volume). The Smart Border Declaration (White House 2001) and its '30 point plan' addressed, broadly: the secure flow of people, the secure flow of goods, secure infrastructure and the coordination of information sharing (US Department of State 2002). Significant for our discussion are the assumptions that underlie these changes. First, the Smart Border Declaration assumes that borders extend beyond geopolitical physical borders by establishing procedures that may be initiated long before any actual border is crossed (Côté-Boucher 2008, 144). This means that the border is extended inward and outward. Crossings have to be planned well in advance to secure appropriate paperwork, for example, and surveillance of citizens and non-citizens within the borders of Canada and the USA is increased by agencies' increased ability to both share and generate intelligence (Côté-Boucher 2008, 144; see also Muller, this volume). Second, the 'diffuse border,' as Côté-Boucher (2008) explains, only monitors particular types of mobility. For example, certain types of migrants may be deemed threatening, while others (such as business travellers), are facilitated in their border crossings.

While Canada is influenced by national and international factors when developing legislation meant to address particular threats, how national threat is conceived is impacted by the broader international context as well as by the responses to threats by countries who share political and economic relationships. Before I examine the case of Zehaf-Bibeau in more detail, I describe the global context of threat and Canada's position relative to such threat. In particular, I remark upon the evolution of ISIS and the role of the USA to establish a global context within which the events of October 2014 were interpreted, defined and dealt with.

Canada, Iraq and Syria

As part of its effort to eliminate the terrorist threat of Al-Qaeda after 2001, in 2003 the USA, under President George Bush, ordered the invasion of Iraq. According to Filkins (2015), it was alleged that many former Iraqi army members were the foundation of the Iraq insurgency (as many as 250,000 men) against the USA. The USA left Iraq in 2011 in a 'relatively stable' state after nearly entirely defeating the Islamic State of Iraq (ISI—an outgrowth of Al-Qaeda). What remained of the insurgents was thought to be minimal (Filkins 2015). Later in 2011, however, Syria's Sunni majority challenged the governing Syrian dictatorship, led by Bashar al-Assad, resulting in chaos ("Sunni-Shia Divide" n.d., n.p.). As Filkins (2015) notes, after nearly "staggering toward the grave only months before," the leader of the Islamic State of Iraq, Abu Bakr al-Baghdadi, saw this as an opportunity and dispatched soldiers to fight with the Sunnis in Syria. These soldiers acquired followers in Syria to fight against the reigning Syrian government. In 2013, "ISI became the Islamic State of Iraq in Syria. ISIS was born" (Filkins 2015). In 2014, ISIS fighters took over parts of Northern and Western Iraq. This prompted the USA to return to the area and to begin bombing ISIS to assist Iraq.

Where is Canada in all of this? In their analysis of 'global counter-terror actor types,' Ilbiz and Curtis (2015) suggest there are three types of actors: trendsetters, trend followers and individual players. They identify the USA and UK as trendsetters, Canada and Australia as trend followers, and Russia and China as individual players. Trendsetters are characterised by qualities such as having "high levels of political and economic influence at the global level" and are often being targeted by terrorist groups

(Ilbiz and Curtis 2015, 43). Trend followers, in contrast, have lower levels of political and economic influence at a global level, are less likely to be targeted by terrorist organisations and tend to respond to global agendas rather than set them (Ilbiz and Curtis 2015, 44). Individual players are noted to have varying levels of economic and political influence at the global level, are seldom targeted by terrorists, and involve themselves in international responses where they see benefits for themselves.

As noted above, the definition of and response to threat may be influenced by the audience for whom actions are undertaken and with whom relationships must be maintained. As a trend follower, as well as an economic dependent, on 7 October 2014, the Canadian government adopted a motion supporting Canada's joining the US-led coalition against the Islamic State of Iraq and the Levant (ISIL).[2] The motion of support included: (1) recognising ISIL as a terrorist group; (2) recognising the threat that ISIL posed to people of the region; (3) recognition that without strong and direct force, ISIL will continue to pose a threat to international peace and security, including threatening Canada; (4) affirming Canada's interests in protecting innocent and vulnerable citizens of the region; (5) acknowledging the request of the government of Iraq for support against ISIL; (6) acknowledging the participation of Canada's friends and allies in an international coalition to fight ISIL; (7) and noting that the United Nations Security Council recognises the threat posed by international terrorism by passing Resolution 2178 (2014) (United Nations 2014). The motion also supported contributing Canadian military assets to fight against ISIL and not deploying ground troops.

Knowing the legislative and global contexts within which events occur provides insight into why both past and current events are interpreted as they are. Government responses, either in terms of legislative responses or motions seeking to address and frame national and global events, are a means of communicating with different types of audiences. In their analysis of how politicians talk about counter-terrorism, Chowdhury and

---

[2] The USA determined that the group that they were fighting is "ISIL" not "ISIS." While there is some speculation about why the acronym changed from ISIS to ISIL, it is considered by some to be a more direct translation of the Arabic name for this group of insurgents and may also denote an area much bigger than Syria (Fuller 2015).

Krebs (2010) note there are key audiences to whom politicians speak including, for example, other members of parliament, a national public, and international entities. Chowdhury and Krebs explain that public rhetoric is political and the key concept is legitimation, defined as "the articulation before key audiences of publicly acceptable reasons justifying concrete actions and policy positions" (2010, 127). Political talk is framed in ways that legitimise positions taken up by government. In Canada's case, joining the US-led coalition legitimated Canada's position not only as a trend follower but also as an ally of the more powerful USA and of the global cause of fighting terrorism.

October 2014, Martin Rouleau-Couture and Michael Zehaf-Bibeau

I now turn to the case of Michael Zehaf-Bibeau's Ottawa shooting and examine how government representatives framed this event for audiences to whom politicians spoke. I then examine how explanations for this event drew on the legislative and global contexts within which it occurred.

At the same time that the Canadian Parliament was approving the motion to denounce the Islamic State movement, RCMP was meeting with Martin Rouleau-Couture who had been monitored for the past four months. In July 2014, police had arrested Rouleau-Couture on his way to Turkey. Eleven days after his meetings with the RCMP ended, apparently due to lack of evidence regarding his intention to join a terrorist group, Rouleau-Couture ran over two soldiers at a strip mall in Saint-Jean-sur-Richelieu, Quebec: one soldier was injured and another was killed. Police fatally shot Rouleau-Couture. Media reports indicate that Rouleau-Couture's family had been alarmed about the change in his personality and had contacted the police a year earlier. Rouleau-Couture's Facebook page was said to have "extolled Islamic State violence, expressed anti-Semitic sentiments and denigrated Christianity" (Austen 2014, n.p.). In its coverage of this story, *The New York Times* headline read: "Hit-and-Run that Killed Canadian Soldier is called Terrorist Attack" (Austen 2014, n.p.). Stephen Blaney, Canada's Minister of Public Safety, is quoted as saying this "attack was 'clearly linked to terrorist ideology'" and was not the act of a mere criminal (Austen 2014, n.p.). Only two days later in Ottawa, Michael Zehaf-Bibeau killed an unarmed soldier at the National War Memorial before being shot dead on Parliament Hill. In their rush to fill the gaps to explain how this type of event could happen, the media were quick to report details about Zehaf-Bibeau's life, which I now summarise.

Born in Canada in October 1982, to a Canadian mother and Libyan father, Zehaf-Bibeau lived with his parents in Montreal and appeared to have an unremarkable school history, graduating in 1999. In 2001, at the age of 19, he was reportedly convicted of a number of crimes, both personal and property, and in 2004, was incarcerated for 60 days for possession of the drug PCP. It is not clear what Zehaf-Bibeau had been doing with his time between 2004 and 2009, but his relationship with his mother appeared to have nearly ended when he moved to British Columbia (BC) in 2009 and they became estranged for five years. It appears that once in BC, Zehaf-Bibeau began to practice Islam and developed a cocaine habit. Zehaf-Bibeau was reportedly unable to pay his rent by December of 2011 and was living on the streets in Burnaby. He went to the local RCMP detachment and confessed to a crime he claimed to have committed ten years ago, for which police had no information. Allegedly, Zehaf-Bibeau had hoped to be arrested to receive treatment for his addiction. While he reportedly saw a psychiatrist that night, he was soon released. Upon release, Zehaf-Bibeau attempted to rob a McDonald's restaurant brandishing a stick and was arrested and taken into custody. Another psychiatric assessment determined addiction was the issue, not mental illness. After being held in pre-trial custody for over 60 days, a third examination provided some evidence for a mood or bipolar disorder. At his trial, Zehaf-Bibeau pled guilty to the lesser charge of uttering a threat. The media speculate that Zehaf-Bibeau appeared to have addressed his addiction while incarcerated.

Upon release, Zehaf-Bibeau visited the mosque he previously attended and was subsequently expelled when caught with a stolen key to the facility. By 2014, Zehaf-Bibeau was reportedly living in Alberta and working in the oil fields. By the beginning of September, Zehaf-Bibeau was living at a homeless shelter in Vancouver and reportedly once again addicted to cocaine. While watching reports about ISIS, Zehaf-Bibeau would allegedly become outraged and claim the USA was the true terrorist (Friscolanti 2014). By mid-September, Zehaf-Bibeau checked out of the Vancouver shelter and indicated he was going to hitchhike East to sort out his delayed passport. Zehaf-Bibeau went to the Libyan embassy in Ottawa on 2 October 2014 to see about renewing an expired Libyan passport (he had visited there in 2007 with his father): "His bizarre demeanour and confusing answers raised enough red flags that an embassy official told him it would take at least three weeks to assess his request" (Friscolanti 2014). He had applied for his Canadian passport, but the application had been forwarded to the RCMP for a criminal background check. Zehaf-Bibeau was staying at an Ottawa shelter in the weeks prior to his death, and had contacted his mother six days before the shooting. They agreed to meet for lunch. His mother reports they talked about religion and of his plan to move to Saudi Arabia where people would share his convictions. He also talked to her about his belief that he was being tested by "shaytan," an Islamic term for devil, who was trying to tempt him.

Zehaf-Bibeau reportedly purchased a used car prior to visiting an aunt outside of Ottawa where he had once lived. It is suspected that Zehaf-Bibeau may have retrieved the rifle he used to kill the soldier from the property. On the morning of 22 October, Zehaf-Bibeau drove back to Ottawa and parked his vehicle to record the now infamous cellphone video. Minutes later, Zehaf-Bibeau shot and killed a Canadian solder. Fifteen minutes after entering Centre Block, Zehaf-Bibeau was shot dead though not before wounding an RCMP officer.

Post-MZB

Soon after the shooting, Prime Minister Harper and the opposition party leaders provided commentary that framed the events for the public. The prime minister delivered his address:

> *Fellow Canadians, in the days to come, we will learn more about the terrorist and any accomplices he may have had. But this week's events are a grim reminder that Canada is not immune to the types of terrorist attacks we have seen elsewhere around the world. But let there be no misunderstanding. We will not be intimi-*

dated. Canada will never be intimidated. In fact, this will lead us to strengthen our resolve and redouble our efforts and those of our national security agencies to take all necessary steps to identify and counter threats and keep Canada safe here at home, just as it will lead us to strengthen our resolve and redouble our efforts to work with our allies around the world and fight against the terrorist organizations who brutalise those in other countries with the hope of bringing their savagery to our shores. They will have no safe haven. (CBC 2014b)

Tom Mulcair, leader of the official opposition and the New Democratic Party, stated in his initial remarks: "*These acts were driven by hatred but also designed to drive us to hate. They will not. We will stand up, we will stand together. We will persevere, and we will prevail*" (CBC 2014b). Liberal Party Leader Justin Trudeau commented:

We will get answers to how and why this happened. They will be vital in preventing any future attack. And to our friends and fellow citizens in the Muslim community, Canadians know acts such as these committed in the name of Islam are an aberration of your faith. Continued mutual co-operation and respect will help prevent the influence of distorted ideological propaganda posing as religion. (CBC 2014b)

The prime minister is the only politician who immediately used the word 'terrorist' though little public information had been released about the offender's links to any terrorist group. While the prime minister was the first to suggest Zehaf-Bibeau was a terrorist, Trudeau indirectly suggested the perpetrator was Muslim. What is clear from the party leaders is that Canada was now seemingly facing a threat similar to that facing other countries around the globe. Harper stated that Canada would 'redouble' its national security efforts to ensure that Canada is safe and would continue to fight with allies against terrorism. Harper did not suggest that Zehaf-Bibeau was a criminal but rather a terrorist who, apparently, prompted and justified additional legislative methods of dealing with the threat of terrorism, both at home and abroad.

A week later Mulcair explained why he avoided using 'terrorism'; "I don't think we have enough evidence to use that word … When you look at the history of the individual involved you see a criminal act, of course" (CBC 2014a). Mulcair proceeded to explain that Zehaf-Bibeau's history of mental illness and attempts to receive care precluded using 'terrorist.' Mulcair stated: "fundamental difference between the horrific acts of a profoundly disturbed individual and organized terror" (CBC 2014a). This difference, he suggested, has profound implications for any legislative response. Prime Minister Harper's response to this commentary was that he felt there was "no contradiction in individuals who may have a series of personal financial and mental difficulties, and also be engaged in terrorist Jihadist activities" (CBC 2014a). Harper, in effect, dismissed the possibility these events could be framed as anything other than terrorism when he further stated, "we do not think it helps Canadians to do anything but address these matters head on, face them for what they are, and this government will take its responsibilities seriously and bring forward measures to protect the country" (CBC 2014b). The possibility this was a criminal act, a contributing cause of which may be mental illness, was rejected. Further, those who might consider or ask questions regarding other sources of motivation were delaying the efforts of government who had defined the reality for the public. Any consideration of other contributing factors was reduced to governmental and social irresponsibility.

The day after this event, RCMP Commissioner Bob Paulson confirmed that Zehaf-Bibeau was in Ottawa to sort out a passport issue and had been intending to fly to Syria (reportedly contradicting Zehaf-Bibeau's mother, who later stated he was headed to Saudi Arabia). Paulson indicated this passport issue may have motivated Zehaf-Bibeau, though it appears his passport was flagged only because of his criminal record. Paulson also indicated that Zehaf-Bibeau was not on the RCMP's list of high-risk travellers nor flagged for any national security issues, though he "may have held extremist beliefs" (Carlson 2014).

Enter Bill C-51, the Anti-Terrorism Act: January 2015

Although the *Combatting Terrorism Act* (Bill S-7) was effected in October 2014, Prime Minister Harper kept his promise to do more to fight terrorism. In January 2015, this resulted in the introduction of Bill C-51, which proposed significant changes to the powers of the Canadian Security and

Intelligence Service (CSIS) and an array of changes to laws related to terrorism. In their analysis of Bill C-51, Forcese and Roach (2015) detail changes of particular note, including allowing CSIS to "take measures, within or outside Canada, to reduce the threat" of terrorism (2015, 1; see also Forcese, this volume). They further noted these measures may, when authorised by a federal court, "contravene a right or freedom guaranteed by the Canadian Charter of Rights and Freedoms" (Forcese and Roach 2015, 1). A proposed amendment to the *Criminal Code* included making it an offence to "advocate and promote terrorism offenses in general" (Forcese and Roach 2015, 6), while another *Criminal Code* amendment allowed for the deletion of "terrorist propaganda from the internet" (Forcese and Roach 2015, 9). New legislation, the *New Security of Canada Information Sharing Act*, would allow sharing information among Government of Canada institutions for national security purposes. Other new legislation, the *New Secure Air Travel Act*, would prevent air travel among those who are suspected of travelling to engage in terrorism. Finally, there were amendments to the existing preventive detention recognisances addressed to lowering the threshold for detention and extending the detention periods.

The criticisms of Bill C-51 were widespread and immediate, coming from numerous sources: Canada's Privacy Commissioner, the Canadian Bar Association, former prime ministers and Supreme Court justices (CBC 2015) and academics, to name a few. In a letter dated 23 February 2015, several legal scholars[3] outlined major criticisms of Bill C-51, focusing on the Bill's implications for the *rule of law*, for constitutional and international rights and for democracy. First, they state the Bill's information sharing scope does not address protection of privacy and the exceptionally broad definition of terrorism makes a much wider range of legal activities potentially now fall within illegal boundaries. Second, they also note that the expanded definition of advocating and promoting terrorism 'in general' harmfully reduces freedom of speech. The letter questions how deradicalisation programmes might be impacted if the discussion cannot be frank but is now rather fettered by the possibility that the expression of views may be viewed as criminal. Social media forums, pres-

---

[3] This letter was signed by over 100 legal scholars in alphabetical order. As Jennie Abell is the first of this list of names, the letter is referenced as Abell et al. 2015.

ently sites where much information can be gathered, may be silenced due to the possibility of participants being charged. A third criticism is that the mandate of CSIS has now changed from an intelligence-gathering agency to an agency that is able to "actively intervene to disrupt activities by a potentially infinite range of unspecified measures" (Abell et al. 2015, 3). Bill C-51 allows for these new CSIS activities to contravene the *Charter of Rights*. The authors note that this constitutes a "complete misunderstanding of the role of judges in our legal system and constitutional order" (Abell et al. 2015, 3) in that rather than judges protecting rights and freedoms, Bill C-51 asks them to undermine protection of rights and freedoms by authorising warrants that purposely fail to protect citizens. A fourth criticism is that Bill C-51 fails to include any measures, or any focus on measures, proven to be effective against terrorist threats, such as working with communities in deradicalisation efforts (Abell et al. 2015, 4). Finally, the authors note that Bill C-51, unlike many similar previous legislative acts and bills, does not include any oversight or review functions. As Forcese and Roach (2015) also indicate, unlike other bills introduced to counter new threats, the lack of a sunset clause means that Bill C-51 becomes a permanent part of Canada's security structure—regardless of whether the threat is current or not. Other criticisms of Bill C-51 focus on the lowered threshold for detention. This means instead of law enforcement believing that there is a reasonable basis that an individual 'will' commit a terrorist act, 'may' replaces the word 'will.' As the academics' letter points out, the initial wording, 'will,' was established during a time of threat (post-9/11, 2001) that was arguably a context of more serious threat than what Canada currently faces from ISIS.

Despite the criticisms from a multitude of directions and many public protests, Bill C-51 was passed in the House of Commons by a vote of 183 to 96 on 6 May 2015.

The Video

Prior to shooting Corporal Nathan Cirillo, Zehaf-Bibeau was alone in his car, recording a video with his cell phone. In the video, released by the RCMP (in part) in March of 2015, Zehaf-Bibeau stated that Canada's participation in events in the Middle East made Canada his enemy: "this is in retaliation for Afghanistan and because Harper wants to send troops to Iraq" (Boutilier 2015).[4] He also stated: "Canada's officially become one of our enemies" and wanted to "hit some soldiers just to show that you're not even safe in your own land … so you gotta be careful" (Boutilier 2015). When released, the RCMP held back approximately 18 seconds of the video for further analysis. At its initial release, RCMP Commissioner Bob Paulson indicated that he believed that someone else was involved with Zehaf-Bibeau. He stated: "I wouldn't characterize it as a network, as it's commonly understood, but I am persuaded that he was influenced by other individuals towards these crimes. And so in that sense I'm of the view that there are other individuals involved" (Payton 2015). Paulson further added:

> It's not relevant to us, or our investigation, what kind of terrorist Zehaf-Bibeau was, or if he was a particularly intelligent, sophisticated, influential or personally disciplined terrorist … To us, it all turns on the evidence we collect which we compare against the statute. What was he doing and why was he doing it? (Payton 2015)

When the 18 seconds were later released in late May 2015, Zehaf-Bibeau is praying in Arabic for the first 13 seconds of the video and for the last five seconds. With new legislation in hand and after ten months of collecting evidence, as of August 2015, there have been no charges associated with this case, suggesting that this change in legislation may not have been as effective a means to address terrorist threat as had been proposed.

Where to from Here?

As the video indicates, Zehaf-Bibeau confirms he was inspired by and supported the insurgency in Iraq. When Prime Minister Harper first responded to this event, he immediately claimed that it (as well as the

---

[4] The quotations in this section come from the (entire) video shot by Zehaf-Bibeau which may be found at Boutilier (2015).

event two days earlier) was a terrorist attack. The information available to the prime minister on 22 October 2015 was likely limited, though it is unknown how early he may have been aware of the video where Zehaf-Bibeau declares his support of the insurgency. As occurred in post-9/11, and subsequently, prime ministers tend to condemn vociferously terrorist activity—and any activity that appears to be at all like terrorism (Gibbs Van Brunschot and Kennedy 2012). Chowdhury and Krebs (2010) suggest that there are multiple audiences for which political statements are made. At the national level, Canadian politicians (Harper, Mulcair and Trudeau) are speaking to citizens of Ottawa and Canada. Their commentary reflects that 'we' are in this together as Canadians and as citizens ('us Canadians,' 'we come together,' 'we will remember who we are').

Defining the situation as terrorism for the national audience, as Harper suggested, has a twofold appeal. First, responsibility for the attack is removed from the immediate context and from the governing body. By labelling Zehaf-Bibeau a terrorist, the assumption that the greatest security threats come from outside the country is essentially confirmed—although Zehaf-Bibeau may have been born in Canada, external evil (in the form of ISIS) appears to have caused his extremism. 'Real terrorism' is rarely associated with that which is ultimately 'homegrown.' Specifically, while terrorists may be born and raised in Canada, as in this case, what has turned them to terrorism has come from outside and from the already-declared nemesis. Associated with this point is that alternative explanations are effectively voided. If mental illness and addictions are reduced to terrorism, then responsibility again lies elsewhere and not with the individuals' country (which could otherwise be seen as failing to provide adequate social supports). Second, while blame is placed elsewhere, both the government and citizenry are prompted to unite against a common enemy. Prime Minister Harper's comments are revealing as Canada's (and the coalition's) fight is to prevent the enemy from bringing "their savagery to our shores" (CBC 2014b). The prime minister's fears appear to be supported by a recent survey which noted that while Canadians are divided with regard to how to deal with terrorist threats, the most prominent named terrorist group, ISIS, is seen as having no redeeming features and is viewed as condemnable (Leger 2014). Perhaps the best evidence that the public agreed that 'something must be done' about terrorism was the fact that Bill C-51 easily passed in the face of apparently ineffective protests against it.

Canadian politicians also speak to an international audience. In early October 2014, approximately two weeks prior to the Zehaf-Bibeau and Rouleau-Couture events, Prime Minister Harper had pledged Canada's support for the US-led coalition against ISIL. While the events in October were national, they provided the prime minister with a means to reiterate his position that Canada is at risk from internationally based threats and justified Canada's position as an ally in fighting ISIS. While this message is delivered to national audiences, there is global political capital gained for the prime minister following an event that justifies the international position he has taken. For example, Prime Minister Harper states: "[Ottawa shooting] *will lead us to strengthen our resolve and redouble our efforts to work with our allies around the world and fight against the terrorist organisations who brutalise those in other countries*" (*CBC* 2014b). Again, the declaration of a common worldwide enemy brings countries together in ways that would not otherwise be possible. For others in the coalition, this Canadian event serves to 'prove' the global threat of terrorism when even a country like Canada, which has little global influence in international affairs and is a follower, is the target of international terrorism. For the coalition, any attack against a member state provides continued evidence of terrorist threat and justification for the coalition's existence. While some members of the coalition may be more likely targets of terrorist attack, such as those playing leadership roles, membership in this coalition affirms a 'team mentality' with threats to be addressed (or condemned) collectively. Although some members will be weaker players, as is Canada, the team/coalition together address threats that challenge the team as a whole.

It has been noted that Zehaf-Bibeau was not on the RCMP's radicalism radar when he committed his crimes. While Zehaf-Bibeau's beliefs were in support of ISIS, he appears to have been supportive of the cause independent of any direct contact with other supporters. It remains unclear how the new legislation would identify a person like Zehaf-Bibeau as a risk any more than previous legislation. What is clear is that the net that Bill C-51 has cast is much wider given unclear definitions of what might be included in revisions such as advocating and promoting terrorism 'in general.'

The difficulty with the government's response is that issues reduced to the shorthand 'terrorism' are complex and require consideration of other dimensions—terrorist activity may be symptomatic of a confluence of factors. Regarding Zehaf-Bibeau, it appears that his life was complicated by addiction, mental illness and familial and social disenfranchisement. Although the prime minister stated that terrorism did not preclude the involvement of those who were either economically or mentally challenged, these factors appear central to the evolution of this event and require separate attention. Without a doubt, extremism that precedes involvement in terrorist activity must be addressed, as must other factors which are identified as giving rise to these activities. As Borum (2011a) observes, the term 'radicalisation' often serves as much to gloss over the complexity and range of ideologies as does the looseness of the term 'terrorism' gloss over a range of motivations and underlying issues. The relationship between 'radicalisation' and terrorism may, in fact, be tenuous: "most radicals did not (and do not) engage in terrorism, and many terrorists did not (and do not) 'radicalize' in any traditional sense" (Borum 2011a, 2).

In the aftermath of the Zehaf-Bibeau incident, references were made by media and the prime minister casting doubt that this was 'lone wolf' terrorism (Huffington Post 2014)—the idea that Zehaf-Bibeau did not act alone as originally suspected: "it's not necessarily the case that there was only one guy" (Huffington Post 2014). The 'lone-wolf strategy' was identified in 2010 by CIA Director, Leon Panetta, as being "the main threat to this country [US]" (as cited in Pantucci 2011, 3). While the definition of 'lone wolf' varies, it tends to refer to ideologically driven single individuals committing terrorist acts—essentially undermining the commonly held belief that terrorism is a group phenomenon although the individual may feel as though he is part of a group (Pantucci 2011, 2; see also Spaaij and Hamm 2015). Whether this was an instance of 'acting alone,' this case fails to befit the government's chosen response to terrorist threat.

As Zierhoffer (2014) makes clear, what is central to counter-terrorism is developing insight into how attacks are formulated and the elements that converge to produce a terrorist attack. Zierhoffer (2014) explains that the identification of threat is not something that can be left to law enforcement agencies but instead requires input from other experts and from the community. Perhaps it is in this regard that community input regarding the differences between extremism and radicalisation might best be sorted out—though this conversation appears less likely given the changes brought about by Bill C-51. While Bill C-51 attempts, for example, to outlaw the distribution of 'terrorist propaganda' including from the Internet, making this an offence seems unlikely to better detect or reveal those who might seek and absorb such information independently and without contact with those who post it (Zierhoffer 2014, 50). Current law enforcement strategies seem even less likely to be able to address, let alone prevent, someone moving from exposure to terrorist propaganda to acting on extremist beliefs.

Conclusion

While Bill C-51 has attempted to throw the legislative doors wide open to address terrorism offences 'in general,' whether the Bill facilitates evidence collection and impacts terrorism remains to be seen. Regardless of the outcome of this legislation, there is currency in the Canadian government communicating its stand against 'terrorism,' however conceived, and avoiding any critical evaluation of the language they use to describe these events. Nationally, the government appears to be doing something to address a proximate (though ultimately foreign) threat: criticisms of the legislation can be readily reframed as endangering public safety. Audiences, for the most part, believe they know what terrorism is and no audience is against public safety. Internationally, Canada is seen as a legitimate team player, having experience with terrorism and being able to present evidence of the seriousness with which this issue is addressed by way of legislation at home and participation abroad.

The challenge in preventing future incidents of terrorism requires greater understanding of the evolution of this phenomenon including the correlates of and precursors to this activity, such as identifying extremism as distinct from mental illness and addiction. Rather than conflating these issues into a reactive and punitive model, the challenge for counter-terrorism strategies will be to consider the confluence of factors that are associated with twenty-first century terrorist activity. While Zehaf-Bibeau supported ISIS, it is also clear that he was plagued by other factors that appear to have made terrorist activity a reasonable response. As Borum (2011b) observes, twentieth-century terrorism assumptions may no longer hold. Terrorism's link to specific groups and motivations may be far more nebulous in a global society that has greater access to ideas and people than ever before. Governments would do well to see terrorism as a tactic (Borum 2011a) and pay greater attention to the differences among those who use it, which may or may not include the mentally ill, addicted and 'radicalised,' for example, than to hold to a position that views terrorism as an indistinguishable 'enemy.'

References

Abell, Jennie et al. 2015. An Open Letter to Members of Parliament on Bill C-51, February 23. Posted to DocumentCloud, by Laura Payton, CBC News. https://www.documentcloud.org/documents/1678018-open-letter-on-bill-c-51.html. Accessed 15 June 2015.

Austen, Ian. 2014. Hit-and-Run That Killed Canadian Soldier Is Called Terrorist Attack, October 21. http://www.nytimes.com/2014/10/22/world/americas/canadian-soldier-run-down-in-what-officials-call-act-of-terror-dies.html?r=1. Accessed 1 Aug 2015.

Bird, Jennifer, and Dominique Valiquet. 2012. Legislative Summary of Bill S-7: An Act to amend the Criminal Code, the Canada Evidence Act and the Security of Information Act. Library of Parliament Research Publications, Publication Number 41-1-S7-E, pp. i–ii: 1–28.

Borum, Randy. 2011a. Rethinking Radicalization. *Journal of Strategic Security* 4(4): 1–6.

———. 2011b. Radicalization into Violent Extremism I: A Review of Social Science Theories. *Journal of Strategic Security* 4(4): 7–36.

Boutliler, Alex. 2015. RCMP Release Withheld 18 Seconds of Michael Zehaf-Bibeau's Cellphone Manifesto. http://www.thestar.com/news/canada/2015/05/29/ottawa-attacker-praises-allah-in-unedited-version-of-pre-shooting-video.html. Accessed 25 Oct 2015.

Carlson, Kathryn Blaze. 2014. Ottawa Suspect Tried to Get Passport to Go to Syria, October 23. http://www.theglobeandmail.com/news/national/mps-head-back-to-work-morning-after-ottawa-shooting/article21254540/. Accessed 1 June 2015.

CBC. 2014a. Ottawa Shooting: Stephen Harper Tells MPs He's Sorry He Left During Attack, October 29. http://www.cbc.ca/news/politics/ottawa-shooting-stephen-harper-tells-mps-he-s-sorry-he-left-during-attack-1.2816912. Accessed 1 June 2015.

———. 2014b. Ottawa Shooting: Harper, Mulcair, Trudeau Speak About Attack, October 23. http://www.cbc.ca/news/politics/ottawa-shooting-harper-mulcair-trudeau-speak-about-attack-1.2809530. Accessed 15 June 2015.

———. 2015. CSIS Oversight Urged by Ex-PMs as Conservatives Rush Bill C-51 Debate, February 19. http://www.cbc.ca/news/politics/csis-oversight-urged-by-ex-pms-as-conservatives-rush-bill-c-51-debate-1.2963179. Accessed 1 June 2015.

Chowdhury, Arjun, and Ronald R. Krebs. 2010. Talking About Terror: Counterterrorist Campaigns and the Logic of Representation. *European Journal of International Relations* 16: 125–150.

Côté-Boucher, Karine. 2008. The Diffuse Border: Intelligence-Sharing, Control and Confinement Along Canada's Smart Border. *Surveillance and Society* 5(2): 142–165.

Filkins, Dexter. 2015. Did George W. Bush Create ISIS? May 15. http://www.newyorker.com/news/news-desk/did-george-w-bush-create-isis. Accessed 1 June 2015.

Forcese, Craig, and Kent Roach. 2015. Proposed Amendments to Bill C-51, Anti-Terrorism Act 2015. *Social Science Research Network*. http://papers.ssrn.com/sol3/papers.cfm?abstract_id=2576202.

Friscolanti, Michael. 2014. Uncovering a Killer: Addict, Drifter, Walking Contradiction, October 30. http://www.macleans.ca/news/canada/michael-zehaf-bibeau-addict-drifter-walking-contradiction/. Accessed 1 June 2015.

Fuller, Jaime. 2015. The Fix: 'ISIS' vs. 'ISIL' vs. 'Islamic State': The Political Importance of a Much Debated Acronym. http://www.washingtonpost.com/blogs/the-fix/wp/2015/01/20/isis-vs-isil-vs-islamic-state-the-political-importance-of-a-much-debated-acronym-2/. Accessed 1 June 2015.

Gibbs Van Brunschot, Erin, and Leslie W. Kennedy. 2008. *Risk Balance and Security*. Los Angeles, CA: Sage Publications, Inc.

———. 2012. Contrasting Approaches to Terrorism: A Multi-National Comparison. *Journal of Conflict Studies* 29: 163–193.

Huffington Post. 2014. Stephen Harper's 'Lone Wolf' Comments Based on Arrest of Montreal Teen: PMO, December 18. http://www.huffingtonpost.

ca/2014/12/18/stephen-harpers-lone-wolf-pmo_n_6348996.html. Accessed 1 June 2015.

Ilbiz, Ethem, and Benjamin L. Curtis. 2015. Trendsetters, Trend Followers, and Individual Players: Obtaining Global Counterterror Actor Types from Proscribed Terror Lists. *Studies in Conflict & Terrorism* 38(1): 39–61.

Leger. 2014. Survey and Focus Groups—Fall 2014 (Executive Summary). Paper submitted to Privy Council Office. http://epe.lac-bac.gc.ca/100/200/301/pwgsc-tpsgc/por-ef/privy_council/2015/028-14-e/summary.pdf. Accessed 1 June 2015.

Pantucci, Raffaello. 2011. A Typology of Lone Wolves: Preliminary Analysis of Lone Islamist Terrorists. Report for the *International Centre for the Study of Radicalisation and Political Violence* (ICSR), 1–23.

Payton, Laura. 2015. Michael Zehaf-Bibeau Warns in Video: 'You Gotta be Careful,' March 6. http://www.cbc.ca/news/politics/michael-zehaf-bibeau-warns-in-video-you-gotta-be-careful-1.2984170. Accessed 1 June 2015.

Spaaij, Ramón, and Mark S. Hamm. 2015. Key Issues and Research Agendas in Lone Wolf Terrorism. *Studies in Conflict & Terrorism* 38(3): 167–178.

"Sunni-Shia Divide." n.d. Council on Foreign Relations. http://cfr.org. Accessed 1 June 2015.

United Nations Security Council. 2014. "Resolution 2178 (2014)." S/Res/2178. http://www.un.org/en/sc/ctc/docs/2015/SCR%202178_2014_EN.pdf. Accessed 25 Oct 2015.

US Department of State. 2002. Fact Sheet: The White House, Washington, DC, U.S.—Canada Smart Border/30 Point Action Plan Update. http://2001-2009.state.gov/p/wha/rls/fs/18128.htm. Accessed 25 Oct 2015.

White House. 2001. Action Plan for Creating a Secure and Smart Border. Office of Homeland Security. http://georgewbush-whitehouse.archives.gov/news/releases/2001/12/20011212-6.html. Accessed 25 Oct 2015.

Wispinski, Jennifer. 2006. The USA Patriot Act and Canada's Anti-Terrorism Act: Key Differences in Legislative Approaches. Paper prepared for Library of Parliament Canada. http://www.parl.gc.ca/content/lop/researchpublications/prb0583-e.htm#footnote56.

Zierhoffer, Diane M. 2014. Threat Assessment: Do Lone Terrorists Differ from Other Lone Offenders? *Journal of Strategic Security* 7(3): 48–62.

Part III

Introduction: National Security, Surveillance and Terror: Issues and Dilemmas

This final part comprises five chapters that focus on issues and dilemmas of national security, surveillance and terror. These include aspects of accountability, privacy, sovereignty and legitimacy common to both two countries.

The first chapter is focused on a new technology increasingly used in national security, surveillance and law enforcement in both countries: unmanned aerial devices (UAVs). Molnar and Parsons assert that the rapid pace implementation of this technology, as with many other surveillance technologies and practices, often means law and regulation are trying to catch up with ongoing technological development and refinement. Molnar and Parsons use Ericson's concept of 'counter-law' to explore how UAV regulation aligns with the notion of 'rule with law' rather than 'rule of law.' This suggests how recent legal developments have enhanced discretionary authority, weakened legal constraints or thresholds for decision-making and lessened accountability mechanisms. Applied to UAVs in Canada and Australia, the chapter identifies the diversity of UAV devices and the extensive use of UAVs in both countries both in a specific sense (individual targets) and in a general or 'diffuse' sense in which UAVs collect large amounts of non-targeted data. The authors then identify the permissiveness of surveillance laws and raise questions about the capacities of privacy laws to constrain use of UAVs and the dispersal of the data collected via UAVs, suggesting that privacy might indeed be a part of 'counter-law,' and 'privacy compliance' facilitates surveillance rather than protecting privacy and human rights.

Anna Pratt next interrogates jurisdiction and Canada-US Maritime Border Control. Jurisdiction is a focus for law enforcement in Canada, Australia, the USA and other countries and a growing issue in maritime security. This notion is explored through the Canada–US Shiprider program, a cross-border maritime enforcement program created to respond to criminality and security concerns along the shared maritime border by removing the international maritime boundary as an obstacle to law enforcement. Now formalised, Shiprider vessels can pursue and interdict other vessels, an arrangement that commenced a decade ago amidst crime and security concerns along the shared maritime border. The program removes the international maritime boundary and uses it as a portable resource that accompanies the 'ship-rider.' This matters in relation to Shiprider's operations in Coast Salish territories and in Akwesasne Mohawk territory where bi-national border enforcement strategies transect the jurisdictional patchwork of indigenous border nations. This chapter underscores that more than two nations are relevant to what happens in maritime security, thus complicating notions of national security in particular.

Benjamin Muller then confronts a related vital site of national security: the land border. Rather than a borderless arrangement with the USA, Muller asks whether the Canadian border is now like the checkpoints within a 100 miles of the US border, mostly found in that nation's southwest region. Examining the adoption of US-led mass surveillance, intensified information sharing with the USA (official and unofficial), and the uncritical embrace of identification and surveillance technologies such as biometrics and UAVs by the Government of Canada over the past decade, the chapter explores to what extent the Canada–US border has become an additional checkpoint in a series of nodes found throughout the USA.

The next chapter by David Martin Jones traces the evolution of Australia's national security apparatus operating through a tradition of 'managerial rationalism.' This argument is framed in relation to long-standing historical developments in Australian national security and emergency management that have sought to silence democratic criticism of government surveillance activities. Jones contends that contemporary approaches to managerial and executive oversight of myriad forms of domestic, military and law enforcement surveillance activity stems largely from the failure of these agencies to cooperate meaningfully with regional neighbours. For example, the Bali bombing highlighted the lack of inter-agency communication within Australia's intelligence community, and meaningful cooperation with Indonesia's security and law enforcement agencies. The net effect has been gradual expansion of Australia's domestic surveillance, security and emergency preparedness bureaucracy, which aims to prevent the radicalisation of young Australian Muslims and the more isolated occurrence of 'lone wolf' incidents. This has resulted in a crude form of pre-emption through the legal authorisation of greater domestic surveillance to restrict access to fundamentalist propaganda and other warning signs pointing to an impending national emergency. However, despite expanded funding for a wide range of domestic security and intelligence activities, it is virtually impossible to measure the impact of this form of 'managerial rationalism.' Jones indicates the contemporary approach resembles the equivalent processes introduced by Sir Robert Menzies in the immediate post-World War II period, to enhance Australia's national security and surveillance capacity against the actual and perceived threats presented by communism. Under its most recent iterations, there is evidence of increased Parliamentary and bureaucratic oversight of activities of Australia's national security agencies in attempting to combat a growing array of 'polymorphous threats.' However, Jones questions whether these approaches are adequate to strategically identify and pre-empt recognised national security risks, while domestic police surveillance activity has not been subjected to these accountability mechanisms.

It is fitting to complete the volume with a chapter by Tia Dafnos, Scott Thompson and Martin French that confronts the main themes of the volume: national security, surveillance and terror. This chapter explores the Indigenous refusal of Canada's colonial dream, providing an introductory account of protest manifest such as the *Idle No More* Movement. It argues post-1982 Aboriginal Rights and Self-Government policies have not led to Indigenous self-determination. Forms of Indigenous self-determination and Indigenous protest in the post-9/11 era have been recast as threats to critical infrastructure and are now integrated into the emergency management paradigm of national security. This continues the Canadian state's ongoing investment in surveillance of Indigenous peoples. Reflecting on Canada's Government Operations Centre, the chapter concludes with a critique of state surveillance of Indigenous protest, arguing that its rationales are being conceptualised not only through a lens of colonial pacification, but also through the war on terror.

Numerous other similarities are evident between the two countries in the preceding parts. The chapters in this final part do likewise, but they also underscore two key differences between Canada and Australia in relation to the volume's three themes. One is that the targeting of Indigenous peoples is more pronounced in Canada than in Australia in relation to national security, thus implying that the two countries are positioned differently in at least this respect. Thus, maritime security and the responses to protests are greatly shaped by this fact. The second is the sharing of a land border and existing in close maritime quarters with an economic and military superpower. Certainly Australia is in close proximity to China, and its economy serves a similar role as Canada's does for the USA. However, the former is not faced with the same security issues raised due to closer proximity and greater exchanges of populations.

10

Unmanned Aerial Vehicles (UAVs) and Law Enforcement in Australia and Canada: Governance Through 'Privacy' in an Era of Counter-Law?

Adam Molnar and Christopher Parsons

Introduction

In 2013, *Surveillance and Society* published a debate on the state of privacy knowledge and practices in the context of surveillance (Bennett 2011). The discussion was a scholarly trial of the limits and possibilities of privacy as a regime of governance and as a concept. This trial judged privacy as the dominant paradigm through which the more invasive aspects of emerging forms of surveillance were countered. However, privacy as a regime of governance, and as a set of policy instruments, operates within several legal practices that enable or restrain the use of surveillance devices. Attempts to enrich the lexicon of privacy (Roessler and

A. Molnar (✉)
Department of Criminology, Deakin University, Burwood, Victoria, Australia

C. Parsons
Munk School of Global Affairs, University of Toronto, Toronto, ON, Canada

© The Author(s) 2016   **225**
R. Lippert et al. (eds.), *National Security, Surveillance and Terror*,
DOI 10.1007/978-3-319-43243-4_10

Mokrosinska 2015), move beyond privacy altogether (Gilliom 2011), or supplement the 'harms' associated with privacy infringements (Parsons 2015a; Parsons et al. 2015), are gaining traction to critique and understand contemporary manifestations of surveillance-related harms.

This chapter contributes to the ongoing analyses of privacy by attending to the relationship between unmanned aerial vehicle (UAV)-facilitated surveillance and the *rule of law*. Specifically, the chapter explores the emergence and use of sensors attached to UAVs and considers how their use by law enforcement is governed through lawful authority and privacy protections in Australia and Canada. It also critically examines the extent to which current laws and regulations relating to UAV surveillance activities have been weakened through routine and systematic 'counterlaw' measures that involve the displacement of law and legal principles intended to uphold the original premises of the *rule of law*. Such conventions provide checks and balances on factors that undermine civil liberties, privacy, and social justice (Ericson 2007).

Scholarly research on domestic surveillance has thus far described relevant legislation in Western liberal democracies that apply to UAVs and compliance by civilian organisations, law enforcement, and the private sector (Bracken-Roche et al. 2014; Finn and Wright 2012; Parsons and Molnar 2013). This chapter moves beyond this discussion by exploring how expressions of 'counter-law' by lawful authorities for UAV surveillance, including privacy legislation, permit unnecessary and disproportionately arbitrary discretion to enforce 'the law.' As Austin (2015) notes, "surveillance activities can be 'lawful' in a narrow sense but still violate the rule of law in a more robust sense" (295).

The chapter proceeds in four sections. The first section discusses how the *rule of law* has been supplanted by *rule 'with' law* to determine lawful surveillance practices involving a series of counter-law measures. The second section describes the various ramifications of the technological environment of UAV. Better understanding of the ramifications of UAV-facilitated surveillance provides the background for understanding the full data collection capacities of UAVs, and how such collection occurs within an integrated technical and organisational setting. The third section introduces the current state of UAV surveillance activities by law enforcement and national security agencies in Australia and Canada, exploring the key institutional drivers of UAV-enabled surveillance and mapping the associated legal frameworks through which such surveillance is regulated in each jurisdiction by a constellation of privacy policies, technical possibilities, and safety regulations. The fourth section concludes by asserting that the current landscape of privacy law places few constraints on UAV-facilitated surveillance and points to the pitfalls of 'privacy' in this context. The chapter concludes by arguing that intrusive law enforcement surveillance practices might be more effectively considered as part of the systemic emergence and persistence of 'counter-law' measures that condition lawful practices of surveillance and intelligence more generally.

"Counter-Law", Rule with Law, and Privacy

In 2006, Richard Ericson proposed 'counter-law' to describe the relationship between law and the socio-technical practices of policing and security. 'Counter-law' comprises both "law against law" (Counter Law I) and "surveillance" (Counter Law II) (Ericson 2006, 6; 2007). "Law against law" attends to legal statutes and reinterpretations of existing forms of lawful authority that undermine traditional principles of the *rule of law* and the procedural administration of criminal justice. Put another way, through Counter Law I, law can be used by enforcement agencies to advance securitisation efforts through ever more expansive discretionary mandates. The most explicit examples of Counter Law I include various anti-terrorism laws that rely on vague legal definitions, weakened reasonableness thresholds to establish pre-emptive or pre-crime measures, and executive prerogative through ministerial authorisations, all of which redraw boundaries of legal permissiveness in ways that expand the legal mandates for law enforcement activity.

Counter Law II refers to strategies of surveillance and intelligence gathering through the use of technologies that have emerged as routine and systematic measures to mitigate perceptions of risk and enhance public safety. Both Counter Law I and Counter Law II express a mutually constitutive relationship in the fields of national security and policing. Counter Law II affords enhanced identification practices through surveillance measures that adhere to the mandates afforded through Counter Law I. Counter-law transformations, taken as a whole, constitute a punitive pre-crime policing apparatus that is "transformed into an institution of suspicion, discriminatory practices, invasion of privacy, denial of rights, and exclusion" (Ericson 2006, 7).

Counter Law I has almost exclusively been understood as an 'offensive' expansion of policing and intelligence powers. Counter Law I is supplemented, however, by the deliberate weakening of privacy and data protection legislation. This occurs at the same time as, and often in response to, the aggressive expansions of discretionary law enforcement surveillance powers by governments. The weakening of privacy manifests in retracting previously assured legal guarantees combined with failures to expand or deepen existing accountability mechanisms (Parsons 2015b).

Bowling and Sheptycki (2015) have termed this 'post-legal' space as a field of *rule with law*. Drawing on Robert Reiner's (2010) analytical dualism of the 'black letter of the law' (law doctrine) and the 'blue letter of the law' (operational discretion), Bowling and Sheptycki call for a deeper appreciation of how 'blue letter law' is a form of 'living law' that is revealed in the actual practices of policing. The legal permissiveness of 'black letter law,' which is often subject to transformations vis-à-vis Counter Law I, creates possibilities for police and national security discretion to exert 'the blue letter of the law' to expand, rather than constrain, arbitrary discretionary enforcement powers. For our purposes, it is helpful to adapt this framework in an era of ubiquitous computing and intelligence-led policing technologies.

The black letter law establishes the space within which blue letter law thrives. Whenever blue letter law encounters 'hard limits' on active powers, subsequent efforts to reform Counter Law I often arise to facilitate broader discretionary surveillance. Bowling and Sheptycki conclude, like Ericson, that the emergence of a wide remit for 'blue letter law' redraws the legal boundaries of discretionary authority and that weakens democratic accountability, transparency, and oversight: *rule of law* becomes *rule with law* (Bowling and Sheptycki 2015).

The analysis below sheds light onto how the surveillance ramifications of UAV surveillance in contemporary law enforcement compound the force of Counter Law II. It provides a backdrop for analysing how the technical capacities and information sharing capabilities afford by UAVs are, to greater or lesser extents, subject to legal authorisation and regulatory controls in Australia and Canada.

UAV Surveillance in Law Enforcement

Police, security intelligence, military, and border patrol agencies have recognised UAVs can significantly reduce the costs of reconnaissance and intelligence collection in urban environments and border zones, to enhance emergency responses, public safety, and crowd control monitoring (United States Government Accountability Office 2012). To this end, Canadian authorities have considered using UAVs for a range of operations, including locating survivors during natural disasters, and photographing crime scenes (Parsons and Molnar 2013). The value of UAVs comes from their ability to be fitted with different technological payloads, each of which collects different kinds of data. In this way UAVs become 'force multipliers' for existing surveillance technologies (particularly when their use can span multiple agencies across many legal jurisdictions).[1] The range of surveillance technologies that can be mounted on UAVs to enhance existing policing practices include:

- High Definition zoom lenses that can be integrated with analytics software;
- Thermal Imaging, night vision, radar and LIDAR (light radar) technologies;
- Facial or 'soft biometric recognition' technologies;
- Wireless information communication technologies;
- Automated-licence plate recognition (ALPR);
- Modular telecommunication/cyber interception hardware and software such as Identity Mobile Subscriber Identity (IMSI) catchers and 'off-the-shelf' remote controlled hacking technologies.

A UAV's payload is enhanced by its aerial capabilities, including how long it can remain airborne, its manoeuverability, and peak altitude. Moreover, police operations are partially dictated by the UAV's size. Strategic UAVs are large fixed-wing aircrafts that reach altitudes of 20,000 metres and offer persistent intelligence collection. They are most

---

[1] For this reason UAV surveillance will not supplant more efficient modes of terrestrial intelligence-collection, such as accessing stored telecommunications data.

commonly deployed in military operations to monitor foreign conflict zones by tracking suspicious vehicles, observing buildings and transport routes, or detecting actions associated with the deployment of improvised explosive devices. Google and Facebook are developing strategic UAVs that boast persistent aerial capabilities. For example, Google's UAV is larger than a Boeing 767 and uses solar power to stay aloft for months, years, and eventually, indefinitely (Barr and Albergotti 2014). By contrast, micro and mini UAVs, which generally range from the size of a person's palm to several feet in diameter, are designed for agile manoeuverability at low altitudes, enabling them to navigate urban infrastructure.

A fixed-wing strategic UAV with wide-angle persistent high-power zoom lens can capture broad swathes of high-resolution moving imagery in urban environments. This data can be integrated with analytics software for enhanced 'on the fly' crime control tracking. By contrast, a fixed-wing UAV with signals intelligence capabilities or a mini UAV with telecommunication interception technology can perform a near-undetectable 'fly-over' of a target area to conduct data collection operations. Each type of UAV is a significant 'force multiplier' that can accommodate a range of surveillance operations because of the capacity to collect data from persistent, and potentially undetectable, aerial vantage points using such a broad range of technological payloads.

Framing the Surveillance Ramifications of UAV Use in Law Enforcement

UAVs share attributes with other surveillance technologies used by law enforcement agencies for pre- and post-crime security operations, such as closed-circuit television (CCTV) video surveillance or Automated Licence Plate Recognition (ALPR) for traffic surveillance. In line with surveillance technologies generally, UAVs disaggregate people "into a series of discrete informational flows which are stabilised and captured according to pre-established classificatory criteria" (Haggerty and Ericson 2000, 2). Prior to a criminal offence, UAVs can monitor and gather basic data on individuals, groups, and objects within a normalised social environment. Any deviations from the norm, identified as 'risky,' 'dangerous,' or 'suspicious' identities or actions, can then be singled out for further investigation. UAVs can also gather imagery or other information after a crime has occurred. Investigators can use aerial-based sensors to recompose crime scenes or collect forms of data normally unavailable to land-based officers.

However, UAV-facilitated surveillance introduces several legal tensions in the collection of data. The first involves the tension between surveillance and privacy, which occurs through the highly specific *and* diffuse collection of data from aerial vantage points. Such surveillance is *specific* because the device attempts to isolate particular targets, but is also *diffuse* because the collection includes a large amount of data collected 'incidentally' on otherwise innocent or 'non-deviant' groups and environments. When 'incidental' information constitutes 'personally identifiable information,' such as a person's face at a specific location, a mobile device's unique identifier that is linked to personally identifying subscriber data, or even heat emissions from a building which can infer whether and when its owner is present, it raises serious concerns about over-collection through UAV-facilitated surveillance.

The second tension is between data collection and the wider organisational information sharing practices common in law enforcement. UAV-facilitated surveillance operates under laws that regulate reasonableness relative to the intrusiveness and proportionality of information collection. After data is collected, it is subject to various legal and policy requirements that mandate how and where such information can be handled, retained, disclosed, or otherwise acted upon. Consequently, there may be significant variations between point-of-collection constraints versus the subsequent sharing of collected data within and across law enforcement and security agencies.

The use of UAVs by law enforcement agencies is indirectly constrained by aviation safety requirements. Australia's Civil Aviation Safety Authority (CASA) and Transport Canada (TC) are similar to other civil aviation bodies in Europe, and the US Federal Aviation Authority (FAA), which all insist that privacy issues are beyond their regulatory scope (Klan 2014). Despite this, civil aviation authorities are influencing the geographic distribution of UAVs by restricting their use over highly populated urban areas where the risk of human injury or death associated with failure or accident is heightened while authorising their use over less densely populated rural areas. The result is citizens in urban centres enjoy more privacy from restricted uses of UAVs by law enforcement agencies compared to citizens in rural regions. Assuming UAV technologies become more reliable and safer they will likely be permitted to fly over urban centres more frequently. Therefore, the privacy afforded by safety rationales will presumably diminish as the vehicles become less prone to failure or accident.

Governance and Regulatory Landscapes in Australia and Canada

UAVs and Law Enforcement in Australia

In Australia, UAVs have been championed by law enforcement and national security agencies. The Ministry of Defence plans to spend AUD $3 billion to provide up to seven UAVs for maritime border patrol (see Pratt, this volume) and aerial signals intelligence monitoring (Stewart 2014). Australian law enforcement agencies also use UAVs for improved 'situational awareness' during high-risk emergency response operations (Cowan 2014). Discovering how many UAVs are possessed and used by Australian law enforcement agencies is challenging because authorities are not statutorily required to disclose such information. Moreover, counter-law exceptions in the *Privacy Act* as well as the national *Freedom of Information* (FOI) *Act* stymie researchers' abilities to determine UAV use(s) by Australian authorities. For instance, under Sect. 37 of the *FOI Act*, agencies do not have to disclose their use of surveillance technologies if disclosure would or is "reasonably likely to[,] prejudice the effectiveness of those methods" (*Freedom of Information Act* 1982, s. 37). Such secrecy provisions are central to authorising surveillance while lawfully denying citizens' abilities to understand it. It is also a prime example of a Counter Law I measure that redraws black letter law to facilitate a broadening of law enforcement operations that rely on surveillance measures while shrinking opportunity for public accountability. In any case, media reports (Bochenski 2015) and public committee evidence (Parliament of the Commonwealth of Australia 2014) have revealed UAVs are rapidly being adopted into law enforcement and national security practices.

Authorising Law Enforcement Use of UAV Surveillance

Both federal and state jurisdictions can authorise the use of UAV surveillance in Australia. Section 37 of the 2004 federal *Surveillance Devices Act* (SDA) (Cth) allows several agencies including the Australian Federal Police (AFP) and Australian Crime Commission (ACC) to use 'optical surveillance devices' without warrant. Even when a technological payload involves video collection, this does not require a judicial warrant to record activities or objects in a public space, regardless of whether 'incidental' data collection will likely occur. The sole restriction found in Sect. 37 regarding optical surveillance devices is that there be "no entry to premises without permission and no interference with any vehicle or thing" (*SDA* 2004, s. 37). Per this language, it is difficult to imagine a scenario where federal authorities will need a warrant to authorise video UAV surveillance. Furthermore, the breadth of high-definition video, infrared, thermal imaging, and other radar optical payloads that can be affixed to UAVs do not entail "entry into premises" or "interference with a vehicle or thing" (ibid.). Similarly, at the state level, Western Australia, Victoria, Northern Territory, and New South Wales passed their own Surveillance Devices Acts between 1998 and 2007. These provide a wide remit of lawful authority to deploy optical surveillance devices in public places without judicial oversight.

While the AFP has unfettered power to deploy UAV surveillance technologies, they appear to be pursuing partnerships to access military UAV sensor information. The AFP has stated that relying on Australian Defence Force (ADF) UAVs offers a "unique advantage" to carry out "covert" domestic law enforcement functions (Dorling 2014). The legal permissiveness for Australian police or military to deploy UAVs creates expansive conditions for the aerial surveillance of Australian citizens. The federal *SDA* constitutes an expression of counter-law because it enables discretionary and warrantless use of visual imaging technologies to track Australian citizens. In fact, the federal and state SDAs are forms of counter-law, insofar as they allow law enforcement agencies to publicly assert that their actions are lawful while citizens forego any substantive privacy protections under equivalent Freedom Of Information (FOI) requirements.[2]

Australian Privacy Law as "Rule with Law" and UAV Surveillance

Australian privacy laws are "multi-layered, fragmented and inconsistent" (ALRC 2008). The primary legal instrument is the Australian *Privacy Act* (Cth) (1988), which regulates all public-sector and law enforcement organisations. The *Privacy Act* has been subsequently subdivided into the more digestible Australian Privacy Principles (APPs) (OAIC 2014). Australia's information privacy laws, like most Western polities, apply only to 'personal information.' The Act protects "information collected about an individual whose identity is apparent, or can reasonably be ascertained, from the information or opinion" (ALRC 2008, s. 36). The extent to which personal information captured through UAV surveillance falls within these terms is unclear, because case law does not offer much guidance; Australian common law has yet to clarify what constitutes 'core' biographical or inherently personal information and 'extraneous' information. Without these basic divisions being reified in case law it is challenging to determine whether UAV-based surveillance engages legally circumscribed privacy protections involving personal information.

In any case, even if the APPs were to apply to 'personal information' intercepted by UAVs certain organisations, acts and practices are exempt. Exempted organisations include intelligence-gathering and national security organisations such as the Australian Security Intelligence Organisation (ASIO), the ACC, the Australian Signals Directorate (ASD) and the Ministry of Defence. While the AFP, the Australian Customs Service, and CrimTrac, the national information sharing service for Australia's law enforcement, and national security agencies (OAIC 2015) are all covered by the *Privacy Act* and the APPs, these organisations also enjoy considerable exemptions. Two in particular are worth noting. APP 6.2 permits

---

[2] Making matters worse, warranting processes under the *Surveillance Devices Act* place relatively weak limitations on subsequent disclosures of the collected information.

using or disclosing personal information if it is "required or authorized under the law," or if it is "reasonably necessary for enforcement of the criminal law or of a law imposing a pecuniary penalty, or for the protection of the public revenue" (ALRC 2008, s. 37). Exceptions are also widespread at state and territory level. The majority of state laws allow law enforcement agencies to disclose information if it is believed this is reasonably necessary "for the prevention, detection, investigation, prosecution or publish [sic] of criminal offences or breaches of a law imposing a penalty or sanction" (Butler 2014, 464). Even when an organisation is subject to the APPs but lacks a specific exemption, there is considerable legal latitude because the APPs offer no clear or direct guidance on the relationship between UAVs and their collection of personal information. The result is that even agencies that must comply with the APPs have no explicitly articulated limits on the use of optical sensors attached to UAVs.

The *Privacy Act* exceptions function as forms of Counter Law I by expanding the 'blue letter' scope for broader information sharing between law enforcement agencies, given that collected data can be communicated "where it relates, or appears to relate, to the performance of the functions of the relevant agency" (Smith 2012, 3). In addition, various 'black letter laws' authorise these expanded 'blue letter' measures. For example, Sect. 19(1) of the *ASIO Act* establishes a lawful framework for ASIO to collaborate with federal and state law enforcement agencies and other national security organisations. Such collaboration is permissible so long as the head of the partnering agency has requested the cooperation. Further, Sect. 8(1)(bf) of the *Federal Police Act* of 1979 authorises the AFP to coordinate with domestic and foreign law enforcement and national security agencies. The AFP can also partner with the private sector under Sect. 35 of the *Federal Police Act* to "engage persons as consultants, or independent contractors, to perform services" (*Federal Police Act* 1979, s. 35). Similarly, changes in the *National Security Legislation Amendment Bill* (No. 1) (2014) gave ASIO 'employees' the same lawful authority as ASIO 'officials.' The result is that private contractors can work under state direction and enjoy legal protections while conducting otherwise illegal surveillance activities. These amendments, in aggregate, provide nearly unfettered legal authority for private sector UAV operators to gather and manage data on behalf of the Australian law enforcement community.

The compliance requirements outlined in the various SDAs and the APPs also constitute 'black letter law' for police and national security intelligence collection. *Even if* the APPs applied to UAV-enabled surveillance, a series of exemptions and legal obscurities in Australian privacy law limit meaningful restrictions on arbitrary operational discretion regarding the collection and sharing of personal information. These exemptions and obscurities are prime examples of privacy-inflected Counter Law I that redraw the substantive boundaries of privacy protections in Australia while upholding a façade of 'lawfulness' for surveillance by another name. These exceptions are a fig leaf that hides massive expansions of aerial surveillance and data sharing beneath the guise of lawful compliance with 'privacy protections' for Australian law enforcement agencies that are not fully exempt from the APPs. In effect, Australian law enforcement and security agencies can maintain that their aerial surveillance and data-sharing practices are lawfully authorised and compliant with privacy law despite the relative lack of meaningful protection under the APPs. CASA requirements provide the largest, and a very indirect, restriction of the government's surveillance-motivated UAV operations. A 400-foot flying restriction is placed on domestic law enforcement agencies, even though police insist their UAVs are currently limited in their capacity to provide ongoing covert surveillance. CASA also requires a persistent 'line-of-sight' for any given UAV in operation at all times. However, CASA insists it has no regulatory legitimacy in dealing with privacy issues (Klan 2014) even though it has established rules that affect the use of UAVs and, thus, how they might infringe upon Australians' privacy. As aerial technologies develop, it is highly probable that civil aviation safety restrictions will be lifted. This could potentially remove constraints on Counter Law II to further the use of UAVs as systematic instruments for urban surveillance and policing.

UAVs and Law Enforcement in Canada

The Royal Canadian Mounted Police (RCMP) has investigated the use of UAVs for its operational and strategic purposes since 2005. As of 2012, the RCMP boasted a total of approximately 17 UAV platforms and 60 vehicles in use (RCMP 2014; Quan 2014). The classes range from smaller mini-UAV 'quadcopters' to larger fixed-wing UAVs capable of "long endurance flights" (Quan 2014). The numbers of devices, classes, and expected uses for UAVs by law enforcement in Canada are all growing.

The RCMP maintains it does not deviate from TC's scope of authorised uses for UAVs. These include traffic collision reconstruction investigations, support for emergency response and search and rescue, chemical, biological, radiological, nuclear and high-yield explosive (CBRNE) situations, and major crime scene investigations (Parsons and Molnar 2013; RCMP 2014). In spite of these limitations, the RCMP is exploring expanded uses for UAVs including aerial traffic surveillance, reconnaissance missions during hostage scenarios, and major event security (Quan 2014). The formal RCMP policy position on UAVs also states they "may be used as an investigative aid when there is no expectation of privacy or when required judicial authorizations have been obtained" (Quan 2014). However, as recently as 2014, the RCMP insisted that UAVs "shall not be used for surveillance of persons or vehicles except in exigent circumstances where there is an imminent risk to life or safety" (RCMP 2014).

Federal, provincial, and municipal policy forums have largely driven the UAV policies of Canadian law enforcement agencies. Here we focus on federal policy forums. At the federal level, the RCMP is the primary institutional driver of UAV operations for policing operations in Canada. The National Unmanned Aerial Systems Working Group (NUASWG) provides most guidance on UAVs that is taken up by the RCMP. The group includes representatives from nearly all RCMP divisions as well as individuals from Federal and International Operations (FIO) and the RCMP's Ottawa "Tech Ops" arm, as well as CAP.[3] The RCMP has designated the NUASWG as a group of "subject matter experts" that are "required to assist with the development of National Policy with respect to the purchase and use of UAS systems in Canada" (RCMP 2014).

Surveillance is contentious in the NUASWG. Some members fear that if UAVs are used for surveillance "the program could suffer nega-

---

[3] CAP was identified only in abbreviated form in the obtained RCMP internal documents and, given this, we cannot provide its full definition or RCMP affiliation.

tive public opinion to the point where it could affect UAS operations" (RCMP 2014). However, the next sentence of the NUASWG meeting minutes notes that fixed-wing aircrafts "with proper equipment to conduct surveillance" are also "available"[4] to RCMP Border Integrity and the Special O unit (RCMP 2014). The Border Integrity unit includes both Canada and US border-control services, while the Special O unit is the RCMP's "elite and highly specialized covert surveillance unit" (RCMP 2015).

However, the RCMP's present UAV-based surveillance capacities are excess of its position as outlined in its public media policy and a letter it wrote to the Office of the Privacy Commissioner. In that letter, the RCMP insisted it was "not presently utilising these systems in [a surveillance] capacity" (RCMP 2014). The deployment of devices under the Border Integrity and Special O mandate also appears to violate the mandated scope of allowable applications set forth by TC, which explicitly excludes surveillance activities.

The RCMP is seeking expert legal opinion on UAV-facilitated surveillance and is discussing how to encourage TC to lift its flight restrictions to expand how the RCMP conducts UAV-based aerial surveillance. The lawful authority governing UAV surveillance technologies in Canada is also somewhat unclear. Specifically, it is not evident how the information captured from UAV sensors will be officially interpreted under the *Charter of Rights and Freedoms* (hereafter, the *Charter*) and the federal *Privacy Act*. However, previous rulings concerning rights to privacy in public spaces, and the use of police helicopters to search property or track vehicles, informs the normative and legal boundaries of UAV surveillance in Canada.

Authorising Law Enforcement Use of UAV Surveillance

The lawful authority of UAV surveillance in Canada is principally regulated through federal statutes including the *Privacy Act*, TC's civil aviation safety

---

[4] It is unclear exactly whether "available" refers to strict ownership or whether vehicles are tasked from the USA, Defence, or another source.

standards, and the *Charter*.[5] The *Privacy Act* requires federal government institutions to comply with rules governing the collection, use, disclosure, retention, and disposal of any recorded information "about an identifiable individual" (*Privacy Act* 1985). The boundary for *Charter* violations often rests upon the concepts of reasonableness and proportionality that determine whether 'core biographical' information has been collected. To complicate matters, *R. v. Spencer* (2014) reified a right to public anonymity that shields individuals from unwarranted law enforcement intrusion into private affairs. However, the implications of *Spencer* are unclear in relation to UAV-enabled surveillance. What is abundantly clear however is that by December 2014, the RCMP did not consider its UAV operations as necessarily falling under the auspice of the *Privacy Act* (Quan 2014).

Any federal institution that plans to collect, amend, or alter personal information for bureaucratic or administrative purposes must complete a Privacy Impact Assessment (PIA) to evaluate the appropriateness of the proposed activity. As of 2014, the RCMP had not conducted PIAs for its UAV operations (RCMP 2014). This may indicate that authorities believe data collected through UAVs involves *non*-personally identifiable information. If true, the RCMP's UAV operations would not be seen by the RCMP and other law enforcement agencies as even potentially violating the reasonable expectations of privacy of Canadian citizens. Interpreting the technology as an aid to improve general 'situational awareness,' that is to provide a wider survey of the environment to assist operations, could be used to insulate law enforcement from criticisms that their practices pose an invasion of Canadians' personal privacy and *Charter* rights (Parsons and Molnar 2013). Law enforcement authorities might also try to insulate their operations from obligations under the *Privacy Act* by designating their UAV use as non-targeted surveillance, or as the collection of information that sidesteps any gathering about specifically designated person or persons. The RCMP is seemingly testing the boundaries of aerial surveillance collection in the courts, a process that will go unchecked in Australia given the limited or non-application of the APPs and a concomitant absence of a formal bill of rights.

---

[5] Provincial and municipal law enforcement agencies are also subject to provincial legislation and regulations in addition to the federal requirements, though we do not deal with these in detail.

UAV Regulation and the Courts

Court rulings provide guidance to law enforcement and subsequent judicial proceedings about how different uses of surveillance systems cohere with the *Privacy Act* and protected rights under the *Charter*. The Supreme Court of Canada (SCC) has written that privacy is "an essential component of what it means to be free" and has established the *Privacy Act* is a quasi-constitutional document (*R. v. Dyment* 1988). Despite this acknowledgement, the stultifying force of the *Charter* as a check on UAV-enabled surveillance appears conflicted. In particular, two cases stand out as key precedents that furnish the black and blue letters of lawful UAV surveillance. In *R. v. Tessling* (2004), the Supreme Court "examined the constitutionality of the police conducting warrantless searches of private dwelling houses using infra red technology during the course of criminal investigations" (CCLA 2004). The infrared sensors detected heat emanating freely beyond the defendant's home. Given that the sensor detected a property that did not reveal core biographical details about any individuals, and was not found to affect the dignity, integrity, and autonomy of the individual, the defendant had no reasonable expectation of privacy. On this basis, it was ruled that no unwarranted search occurred. However, the *Tessling* precedent is unclear about whether any further applications of UAV monitoring that rely on infrared technology will necessarily violate the privacy rights of Canadians.

In *R. v. Wise* (1992), the SCC concluded that tracking a vehicle along a public roadway raises concerns under Sect. 8 of the *Charter*. This outcome indicates that persistent aerial surveillance *could* amount to a violation of protections against unreasonable search and seizure of individuals moving through public space. The issue could hinge on whether there are restrictions against collecting data through 'the haystack' method versus accessing the data and performing targeted analysis. In the provincial context, a decision by the Office of the Information and Privacy Commissioner of British Columbia on ALPR, established limits on the mass surveillance and retention of personal identifiers during routine law enforcement patrols in that province (BCIPC 2012; Parsons et al. 2012). Interestingly, the same rulings may not directly apply to information detected through sensor technologies that are interpreted as not collecting or being explicitly linked to personally identifiable information.

Much like Australia, Canada's aviation safety requirements present the most forceful constraint on law enforcement uses of UAVs. The RCMP must remain compliant with TC's mandated scope of acceptable applications in order to fly a UAV. This limits the scope of RCMP applications to "Collision Reconstruction, Major Crime Scenes, Search and Rescue, Hazardous Material scenes and ERT [Emergency Response Team] calls for service" (RCMP 2014). In spite of this civil aviation requirement, the RCMP is negotiating with TC to expand the range of applications on "the issue of surveillance" (RCMP 2014). However, this restriction on the RCMP does not affect all government agencies.

TC has excluded the Department of National Defence from civilian oversight and regulation regarding UAV deployments in Canada. The consequence is one set of airspace regulations for civilian operators and another for military operators. As domestic law enforcement bodies collaborate across agencies, including the Canadian Forces involved in domestic initiatives, this bifurcation of airspace and the authorities operating within it opens the door to information sharing arrangements that let the military collect data to share with domestic agencies. While the military will operate per its mandates and objects, and thus may not always fly to assist domestic authorities, the integration of intelligence-collection systems in the federal government may serve as the rationale for more domestic military UAV flights. In effect, the Canadian military does not suffer from the same black letter restrictions that fetter the RCMP when dealing with TC.

The black letter of information sharing amongst Canadian law enforcement, defence, and intelligence agencies is now a seemingly unfettered blue letter scope under Bill C-51. The Security of Canada Information Sharing Act (SCISA) contained within C-51 authorises information sharing across government for purposes associated with any "activity that undermines the security of Canada" (Parliament of Canada 2015). These authorisations extend well beyond national security provisions to include any investigative purpose involving "public safety" and the "economic or financial stability of Canada" (Parliament of Canada 2015). The Bill (which became in late 2015 the *Anti-terrorism Act*) permits 17 institutions and departments to share information[6] "in accordance with the law … to any person, for any purpose" (Parliament of Canada 2015; Geist 2015). This provision undermines any other restrictions under the *Privacy Act* that might curtail UAV surveillance.[7] The new Act creates such an ambiguous zone of 'black letter' law that social actors can exploit, leaving 'blue letter' law as the real delimiter of information collection and sharing. Like their Australian counterparts, Canadian law enforcement agencies can insist that aerial surveillance and data-sharing practices remain privacy compliant. While the *Charter* provides at least some semblance of pushback on the blue letter of UAV operations, privacy laws, when they apply, predominantly function as fig leaves meant to secure public support for 'lawful' surveillance without actually providing significant protection to Canadian residents and citizens.

Conclusion: What's Left of Privacy in an Era of Counter-Law?

Scholars and practitioners are grappling with how anti-terrorism laws in Western democracies have widened the scope for police and national security operations in the absence of adequate accountability and parliamentary oversight (see Forcese, this volume). The implications of these laws are even more ambiguous, because government authorities often deploy new technologies secretly and without fulsome public consultation. Some scholars have looked to counter-law to explain how this trend provides further powers in the hands of law enforcement after 9/11 by way of overly vague legal definitions, a general lowering of reasonableness thresholds to justify greater information collection, and the centralisation of

---

[6] The Bill identifies the following 17 institutions and departments: Canadian Border Services Agency; Canada Revenue Agency; Canadian Armed Forces; Canadian Food Inspection Agency; Canadian Nuclear Safety Commission; Canadian Security Intelligence Services; Canadian Communication Security Establishment (CSE); Citizen and Immigration; Finance, Foreign Affairs Trade and Development; Health; National Defence; Public Safety; Transport Canada; FINTRAC; Public Health Agency; Royal Canadian Mounted Police. This list can expand or contract under ministerial authorisation.

[7] For a review of how *PIPEDA* applies to UAV surveillance in Canada, see Bracken-Roche et al. 2014.

discretionary executive decision-making authority in ways that place further pressure on human rights, civil liberties, and privacy (Ericson 2007).

While this chapter has focused on UAV-facilitated surveillance through a systematic comparison of Australian and Canadian 'black letter' and 'blue letter' laws, its discussion carries broader implications for debates concerning 'lawful' domestic law enforcement operations that feature technology-led strategies of surveillance. The general expansion of discretionary law enforcement powers enhanced by new technologies threatens the very *rule of law* itself. These developments must be understood as part of a broader trend where discretionary powers are extended while systematic privacy protections and accountability mechanisms atrophy (Parsons 2015b). This trend is part of a wider set of rational and systematic practices that have also simultaneously eroded the existence of substantive privacy protections and accountability processes (Parsons 2015b).

Counter-law provides a way to view and critique the erosion of substantive privacy rights. Our comparison of privacy law in Australia and Canada reflects a broader trend about the role that weak privacy law plays in an era of counter-law. 'Privacy' is not immune to exploitation by state authorities to further warrantless and expansionary police surveillance powers that are meant to 'secure' social order without accompanying transparency, oversight, or accountability measures. When privacy is exploited in such a way, it becomes merely another legal tool for policing and security agencies to broaden unacceptable state intrusions into private life. More broadly, when various forms of law, including privacy law, authorise warrantless surveillance activities instead of imposing judicially scrutinised limits on these activities, then the *rule of law* is distorted and replaced by *rule with law* (Bowling and Sheptycki 2015). Echoing Lippert and Walby (2016) privacy law risks "becoming less a barrier to government power and more an instrument of its exercise" (3) as technology-inflected 'black letter' and 'blue letter' counter law develops and unfolds.

Future research on the relationship between surveillance and *rule of law* must explore how mechanisms of transparency, accountability, and oversight are implicated in the encroachments of Counter Law I and II. Such work should focus on whether the hollowing out of privacy protections and the limitations of effective review and oversight bodies in liberal democracies are creating a 'post-legal' space for the use of arbitrary and exceptional discretionary powers determined by law enforcement and security agencies themselves. If such a space of exceptionality is emerging, we must also critically address the effectiveness of non-governmental advocacy groups in repelling expansions in Counter Law I and II and enhancing privacy protections. If restrictions are not successfully (re) imposed on authorities vis-à-vis strengthened privacy laws and oversight systems, we are forced to inquire whether black and blue letter law will continue to swallow the *rule of law* altogether to ensure 'privacy compliance' merely signals the continued impoverishment of this and other fundamental human rights.

References

Austin, Lisa M. 2015. Lawful Illegality: What Snowden Has Taught Us about the Legal Infrastructure of the Surveillance State. In *Law, Privacy and Surveillance in Canada in the Post-Snowden Era*, ed. Michael Geist, 103–126. Ottawa: University of Ottawa Press.

Australian Law Review Commission. 2008, August 12. *For Your Information: Australian Privacy Law and Practice* (ALRC Report 108). Canberra: ALRC. http://www.oaic.gov.au/privacy/privacy-resources/privacy-fact-sheets/other/privacy-fact-sheet-17-australian-privacy-principles.

Barr, Alistair and Reed Albergotti. 2014. Google to Buy Titan Aerospace as Web Giants Battle for Air Superiority. *The Wall Street Journal*. http://online.wsj.com/news/articles/SB10001424052702304117904579501701702936522. Accessed 23 May 2014.

Bennett, C.J. 2011. In Defence of Privacy: The Concept and the Regime. *Surveillance & Society* 8(4): 485–496.

Bochenski, Natalie. 2015. Queensland Police Recruit Drones in Forensic First. *Brisbane Times*, May 28. http://www.brisbanetimes.com.au/. Accessed 11 July 2015.

Bowling, Ben, and James Sheptycki. 2015. Global Policing and Transnational Rule with Law. *Transnational Legal Theory* 6(1): 141–173.

Bracken-Roche, Ciara , David Lyon, Mark James Mansour, Adam Molnar, Alana Saulnier, and Scott Thompson. 2014. *Surveillance Drones: Privacy Implications of the Spread of Unmanned Aerial Vehicles (UAVs) in Canada*. A Report to the Office of the Privacy Commissioner of Canada. Kingston: Surveillance Studies Centre, Queen's University.

British Columbia Office of the Information and Privacy Commissioner. 2012, November 15. *Use of Automated License Plate Recognition Technology by the Victoria Police Department: Investigation Report F12-04*. Victoria: BCOIPC. https://www.oipc.bc.ca/investigation-reports/1480. Accessed 13 July 2015.

Butler, Des. 2014. The Dawn of the Age of the Drones: An Australian Privacy Law Perspective. *UNSW Law Journal* 37(2): 434–470.

Canadian Civil Liberties Association. 2004, March 24. *R. v. Tessling*: Police Searches with Infra-Red Camera. Toronto: Canadian Civil Liberties Association. http://ccla.org/2004/03/24/r-v-tessling-police-searches-with-infra-red-cameras/. Accessed 24 Sep 2013.

Cowan, Paris. 2014. Qld Police Drone Options Take Off. *IT News*, March 24. http://www.itnews.com.au/News/375818,qld-police-drone-operations-take-off.aspx. Accessed 14 July 2015.

Dorling, Philip. 2014. Federal Police Want to Use Military Drones to Spy on Australians from the Sky. *The Sydney Morning Herald*, February 11. http://www.smh.com.au/. Accessed 12 July 2015.

Ericson, Richard V. 2006. Security, Surveillance and Counter-Law. *Criminal Justice Matters* 68(1): 6–7.

———. 2007. *Crime in an Insecure World*. Cambridge: Polity.

Finn, Rachel L., and David Wright. 2012. Unmanned Aircraft Systems: Surveillance, Ethics and Privacy in Civil Applications. *Computer Law and Security Review* 28: 184–194.

Geist, Michael. 2015. Why Watching the Watchers Isn't Enough: Canadian Surveillance Law in the Post-Snowden Era. In *Law, Privacy and Surveillance in Canada in the Post-Snowden Era*, ed. Michael Geist, 225–256. Ottawa: University of Ottawa Press.

Gilliom, John. 2011. A Response to Bennett's 'in Defence of Privacy. *Surveillance & Society* 8(4): 500–504.

Haggerty, Kevin D., and Richard V. Ericson. 2000. The Surveillant Assemblage. *British Journal of Sociology* 51(4): 605–622.

Klan, Anthony. 2014. CASA Rejects Drone Control Role. *The Australian*, March 7. http://www.theaustralian.com.au/business/aviation/casa-rejects-drone-control-role/story-e6frg95x-1226847372175. Accessed 22 July 2015.

Lippert, R., and K. Walby. 2016. Governing Through Privacy: Authoritarian Liberalism, Law, and Privacy Knowledge. *Law Culture and the Humanities* 12(2): 329–352.

Office of the Australian Information Commissioner (OAIC). 2014. Privacy fact sheet 17: Australian Privacy Principles. OAIC Website. http://www.oaic.gov.au/. Accessed 23 July 2015.

————. 2015. Which Law Enforcement Agencies Are Covered by the Privacy Act? OAIC Website http://www.oaic.gov.au/. Accessed 12 Aug 2015.

Parliament of Canada. 2015. Bill C-51, *Anti-Terrorism Act*. 2nd Session, 41st Parliament, 20 January (1st reading). http://www.parl.gc.ca/House Publications/Publication.aspx?DocId=6932136&Col=1&File=4.

Parliament of the Commonwealth of Australia. 2014. *Report: Eyes in the Sky, Inquiry into Drones and the Regulation of Air Safety and Privacy*. Canberra: House of Representatives Standing Committee on Social Policy and Legal Affairs, 14 July. Accessed Aug 2014.

Parsons, Christopher. 2015a. Beyond Privacy: Articulating the Broader Harms of Pervasive Mass Surveillance. *Media and Communication* 3(3): 1–11.

————. 2015b. *The Governance of Telecommunications Surveillance: How Opaque and Unaccountable Practices and Policies Threaten Canadians*. Telecom Transparency Project. http://www.telecomtransparency.org/release-the-governance-of-telecommunications-surveillance/. Accessed 12 July 2015.

Parsons, Christopher and Adam Molnar. 2013. *Watching Below: Dimensions of Surveillance-by-UAVs in Canada*. Block G Privacy and Security Report. Toronto. http://www.blockg.ca/portfolio.

Parsons, Christopher, Colin Bennett, and Adam Molnar. 2015. Privacy, Surveillance, and the Democratic Potential of the Social Web. In *Social Dimensions of Privacy: Interdisciplinary Perspectives*, eds. Beate Roessler and Dorota Mokrosinksa, 202–222. Cambridge, UK: Cambridge University Press.

Parsons, Christopher, Joseph Savirimuthu, Rob Wipond, and Kevin McArthur. 2012. ANPR: Code and Rhetorics of Compliance. *European Journal of Law and Technology* 3(3). http://ejlt.org/article/view/164/256.

Quan, Douglas. 2014. RCMP Drone Expansion Comes with Hefty Price Tag, Prompts Concerns of 'Mission Creep.' *National Post*, December 31. http://news.nationalpost.com/news/canada/rcmp-drone-expansion-comes-with-hefty-price-tag-prompts-concerns-of-mission-creep. Accessed 11 July 2015.

RCMP. 2014. *Access to Information Request*, A-2013-06427.

RCMP "O" Division Fact Sheet. RCMP Website. Date Modified 2015-08-06. http://www.rcmp-grc.gc.ca/on/about-apropos/fs-fd-eng.htm. Accessed 10 July 2015.

Reiner, Robert. 2010. *The Politics of the Police*. 4th ed. Oxford: Oxford University Press.

Roessler, Beate, and Dorota Mokrosinska, eds. 2015. *Social Dimensions of Privacy: Interdisciplinary Perspectives*. Cambridge, UK: Cambridge University Press.

Smith, Stephen Francis. 2012, October 2. Australian Minister of Defence: Rules to Protect the Privacy of Australians. http://www.defence.gov.au/AGO/library/ago-privacy-rules.pdf. Accessed 23 June 2015.

Stewart, Cameron. 2014. $3bn plan for drone force to patrol our borders. *The Australian*, February 15. http://www.theaustralian.com.au/. Accessed 12 July 2015.

United States Government Accountability Office. 2012. *Unmanned Aircraft Systems: Measuring Progress and Addressing Potential Privacy Concerns Would Facilitate Integration into the National Airspace System.* Report to the Congressional Requestors, GAO-12-981, September. http://www.gao.gov/assets/650/648348.pdf. Accessed 24 Aug 2015.

Legislation

Australian Federal Police Act 1979 (Cth). http://www.austlii.edu.au/au/legis/cth/consol_act/afpa1979225/. Accessed 12 July 2015.

Freedom of Information Act 1982 (Cth) s.37. http://www.austlii.edu.au/au/legis/cth/consol_act/foia1982222/s37.html. Accessed 12 Aug 2015.

Privacy Act, RSC 1985, c. P-21. http://laws-lois.justice.gc.ca/eng/acts/P-21. Accessed 12 July 2015.

Surveillance Devices Act 2004 (Cth). http://www.austlii.edu.au/au/legis/cth/consol_act/sda2004210/. Accessed 12 July 2015.

Cases

R. v. Dyment. 1988. 2 SCR 417 at 427. http://scc-csc.lexum.com/scc-csc/scc-csc/en/item/375/index.do. Accessed 10 July 2015.

R. v. Tessling. 2004. SCC 67 at 55. http://scc-csc.lexum.com/scc-csc/scc-csc/en/item/2183/index.do. Accessed 9 July 2014.

R. v. Spencer. 2014. 2 SCR 212. https://scc-csc.lexum.com/scc-csc/scc-csc/en/item/14233/index.do. Accessed 8 July 2015.

R. v. Wise. 1992. 1 SCR 527. http://scc.lexum.org/en/1992/1992scr1-527/1992scr1-527.html. Accessed 6 July 2015.

11

The Canada–US Shiprider Programme, Jurisdiction and the Crime–Security Nexus

Anna C. Pratt

A few years ago the US Coast Guard snapped a photo of a Great Lakes smuggler smiling at their camera with his middle finger in the air, "flipping us the bird," as one frustrated officer defined his contemptuous gesture. The smart-ass smuggler knew the Coast Guard was powerless to retaliate. They had pursued him at high speeds, but he had managed to make it into Canadian waters—and he knew exactly where the borderline was ... So the Coast Guard, observing the rules of national sovereignty, was unable to pursue this guy, and he knew it. (Kenny 2007)

In our language and the way it is passed down, the line of what is now known as the International Border belongs to somebody else. It wasn't meant for Kanienkehaka or the Mohawk Nation or any of the Six Nations. We understand that much. (Grand Chief of Akwesasne, Michael Kanentakeron Mitchell, quoted in *Mitchell v. M.N.R.* SCC 2001)

A.C. Pratt (✉)
Department of Social Science, York University, Toronto, ON, Canada

© The Author(s) 2016   **249**
R. Lippert et al. (eds.), *National Security, Surveillance and Terror*,
DOI 10.1007/978-3-319-43243-4_11

Introduction

The often-repeated tale of the cocky criminal flipping the United States Coast Guard (USCG) the bird while speeding across the international border beyond the reach of US law enforcement authorities neatly captures the scenario that the Canada–US Cross Border Maritime Law Enforcement programme, known as Shiprider, aims to prevent. Deeply embedded in and enabled by the crime–security nexus (Pratt 2005, 2012), Shiprider aims to facilitate bi-national cross-border maritime law enforcement through an unprecedented reconfiguration of jurisdictional practices that effectively "removes the international maritime boundary as a barrier to law enforcement" (Government of Canada 2014). Following Ford (1999), rather than an abstract legal construct or a kind of container in which enforcement practices occur, territorial jurisdiction can be helpfully understood as a 'bundle' of productive practices that converge at the intersections of law, space and time. This approach invites us to examine specific jurisdictional practices in local contexts.

This chapter focuses upon the past and planned operations and effects of Shiprider in the waterways that flow through Akwesasne Mohawk Territory, commonly identified as a particularly high-risk crime zone by law enforcement authorities, government officials and the media (MacLeod 2014; Hataley and Leuprecht 2013; Dickson-Gilmore 2002). Here, Shiprider's reconfiguration of jurisdictional practices takes on further significance in the context of an unceded indigenous territory—a border nation (Starks et al. 2011) cleaved by an international border, where local communities contend with and continue to contest imposed settler boundaries (Hele 2008; Luna-Firebaugh 2002, 2005; Starks et al. 2011). The land and marinescape of Akwesasne is widely characterised as a 'jurisdictional nightmare' by Canadian policy officials, enforcement authorities and local communities alike (Hataley and Leuprecht 2013; Mitchell 2012). While the specific enforcement successes of Shiprider are yet to be demonstrated, I argue Shiprider is a key player in the "jurisdictional games" (Valverde 2015) that stitch together and effectively assert the primacy of nation-statehood and its connections among national sovereignty, territory and jurisdiction (Ford 2011).

This chapter unfolds in five parts. First, I describe the Shiprider programme and its novel reconfiguration of maritime jurisdictional practices and provide some background information about its emergence in the shared waterways along the Canada–US international border. Second, I consider how, at the level of policy, Shiprider's reconfiguration of jurisdictional practices is enabled by the crime–security nexus, a concept referring to the conflation of crime and public safety with national security concerns through the spectre of organised crime. The third section details how this crime–security nexus has had particularly extensive effects in Akwesasne Mohawk Territory, itself shaped by a bundle of intersecting and contested jurisdictional regimes and practices. While Shiprider's origins and objectives are embedded in this nexus, the fourth section proposes these patrols in Akwesasne waterways stand poised to govern much more than crime and national security. This chapter closes with reflections on the effects of Shiprider as a key player in jurisdictional games (Valverde 2015) occurring on the land and marinescapes of Akwesasne Mohawk Territory.

Shiprider and the Reconfiguration of Territorial Jurisdiction in the Maritime Environment

The bi-national Shiprider programme was introduced to respond to cross-border crime and security concerns along the shared Canada–US maritime border (Government of Canada and Government of United States 2009). This strategy re-crafts maritime border enforcement through the deployment of a radical reconfiguration of jurisdictional practices that disturbs the traditional connections among territory, sovereignty and authority in unprecedented ways. This was underlined in 2011 by Michael Zigayer, Senior Counsel for the Department of Justice, Canada, when asked about the Shiprider Framework Agreement: "Senator, this particular treaty is unprecedented; it does not exist anywhere else on the planet" (Canada Standing Senate Committee on National Security and Defence 2011).

Shiprider vessels are jointly crewed by designated and specially trained Royal Canadian Mounted Police (RCMP) officers and USCG officers with authority to enforce *both* Canadian and American laws on *either side* of the international border under the host country's direction and laws. Specifically, under the Canadian *RCMP Act* (1985), US officers are designated as supernumerary special constables in Canada and enjoy the same enforcement powers as RCMP officers. In turn, though not entirely equivalently, Canadian officers are designated as US Customs officers working with the US Coast Guard, under the enforcement authority of the *US Code of Federal Regulations* (2015).

The precise geographic location of the mapped international border still matters, but not in the usual way. Instead of enabling or restricting a nation's sovereign enforcement operations to the territory that it envelops, the geographic borderline operates more like a switch that determines which sovereign nation is the 'host' and, therefore, which nation's legal regimes will be enforced. This means that whereas under traditional jurisdictional border practices maritime law enforcement authorities previously had to stop and if possible 'hand off' a pursuit at the border, a Shiprider vessel can now pursue and interdict vessels with 'seamless continuity' across the border: "The Shiprider program removes the international maritime boundary as a barrier to law enforcement by enabling seamless and continuous enforcement and security operations across the Canada-US border" (Government of Canada 2014). This is explained further by Sgt Jock Wadley of the RCMP Border Integrity programme:

> In effect, it is a force multiplier for both agencies where if we look at the coastline where we are working here. Criminals are not bound by the line in the water that we call the border. They can run the border at will. They can use the border to hide behind; whereas, we, as law enforcement agencies for each country, are required to stop at the border. Without the Shiprider program … once someone crosses the border, we cease our activity. With the Shiprider program, we can follow it to its conclusion. (RCMP 2010)

Shiprider thus introduces an extraordinarily novel step in the "jurisdictional tango" (Ford 1999) of maritime border control that thoroughly reconfigures relations among territory, sovereignty and authority. Instead of a bundle of practices that continually makes and remakes a territorially defined contiguous 'seam' that envelops the sovereign nation and enables enforcement authority within its territorially defined jurisdiction, Shiprider repackages jurisdictional practices and authority into a portable and mobile resource that travels through space and time with the individual ship *riders* within, across and beyond the territorial border. Simultaneously, sovereignty assumes a kind of mobile and convertible quality like a cloak to be cast on and off by ship riders as they enter different national territories. The portability of authority and this shape-shifting sovereignty across international boundaries produce borders that resemble less of a contiguous 'seam' and more of a flexible zone as fluid and pliable as the water below.

Background

Shiprider was first introduced as an 'Integrated Maritime Security Operation' in the shared Detroit River waterway between Windsor, Ontario, and Detroit, Michigan, to respond to security concerns during the 2005 Superbowl XL held in Detroit. These arrangements were formalised through a memorandum of understanding. In 2007, the Canada–US Shiprider programme was piloted as 'proof of concept' for 60 days on the St Lawrence Seaway in the Cornwall, Ontario/Massena, New York, border area and on the West Coast in the Straits of Juan de Fuca between British Columbia and Washington State—the waterways that flow through Akwesasne Mohawk Territory in the east and the Salish Sea in the west. The *Shiprider 2007 Impact Evaluation Report* concluded that Shiprider was an important 'force-multiplier' that will facilitate more economical and effective cross-border law enforcement in the face of mounting cross-border criminal and security threats. In 2009, the Canadian Public Safety Minister and the US Homeland Secretary signed the *Shiprider Framework Agreement* (Government of Canada and Government of United States 2009). In 2010, Shiprider operated during the Winter Games in Vancouver and during the G8/G20 Summits in Toronto. The 2011 *Canada–US Beyond the Border Action Plan* called for regularisation of Shiprider by September 2012 as well as its eventual extension on to land.

After the legislation twice failed to pass in Canada due to the pro-
roguing of Parliament in 2009, and its dissolution for the 2011 federal
election, Shiprider quietly became law in 2012 with the passage of the
Integrated Cross-Border Law Enforcement Operations Act, which was deeply
buried within the federal Conservative Party's 452-page omnibus *Jobs,
Growth and Economic Prosperity Act*. In 2013, Shiprider was formalised,
and at the time of writing in August 2015 there are now two full-time
Shiprider operations, one in the Windsor, Ontario/Detroit, Michigan,
waterway and one in Surrey, British Columbia/Blaine Washington.
Two more will be introduced in 2015/2016 at locations based on "joint
threat and risk assessments" (Public Safety Canada 2014). According to
a senior RCMP officer, these will operate in the St Lawrence Seaway
near Cornwall, Ontario/Massena, New York, and in the Kingston area
(RCMP Interview 2014b).

Shiprider and the Crime–Security Nexus

The regularisation of Shiprider was a key part of the 2011 *Canada–US
Beyond the Border Action Plan*, which followed the 2011 Canada–US declaration entitled *Beyond the Border: A Shared Vision for Perimeter Security
and Economic Competitiveness*. Yet, Shiprider is mandated to cover all
forms of cross-border criminality including activities associated with
organised crime groups (RCMP 2014a). This is underpinned by a crime–
security nexus that involves two simultaneous processes emerging since
the mid-1990s: the redefinition of a host of criminal activities as threats
to national security through the spectre of organised crime, and the historically unprecedented expansion of national security to include criminal
threats to the economy and public safety (Pratt 2005, 2014a). This development repositions what might otherwise be considered a host of 'ordinary' crime threats to local public safety (drugs, guns, violence) as national,
transnational and international threats to national security (organised,
transnational crime and links to terrorist groups) and the state, conceived
in economic rather than political terms. From the outset, Shiprider was
introduced to target intersecting crime–security threats along the shared
maritime border. As explained in the *2007 Impact Evaluation Report*:

Canada and the United States share responsibility for their contiguous (Great Lakes/St. Lawrence Seaway) and near-coastal border waters and are increasing on-water patrols to enhance their capacity to intercept and board vessels which may pose threats to either nation. A coordinated and integrated approach to marine security along the Canada-US border is vital to protecting the integrity of the border and the national security of both nations. *The enhancement of the marine security partnership will further each nation's respective abilities to detect and prevent criminal activities which may endanger their economic and national security interests.* (RCMP 2008, 10, emphasis added)

This elasticity of security is again highlighted in the 2006 *Proof of Concept Evaluation*, which notes that while the prevention of terrorist attacks is obviously an important national security objective, "cross-border criminality—e.g. the smuggling of drugs, illegal aliens, weapons and other 'commodities' pose an equally dangerous threat to the peace and security of both nations" (RCMP 2006, 10). In 2007, 1200 hours of joint integrated patrols and 187 boardings in the Cornwall area resulted in seizures of 1290 kgs of Bulk Fine Cut Tobacco, 1,280,400 Contraband cigarettes, 47 kgs of Marihuana, several boats, and several arrests were made related to these seizures (RCMP 2008, 17). It is in the shadow of the crime–security nexus that these metrics could be deemed a success.

In Canada, the RCMP was deemed to be 'uniquely positioned' to undertake the Shiprider initiative due to its expertise in these overlapping domains:

The RCMP involvement stems from the fact as Canada's National Police force it is mandated with the responsibility of protecting Canada's borders from criminal incursions and threats. The RCMP's role in Canadian marine security is to enforce the laws that deal with national security, organised crime, and other federal statutes such as those involving smuggling, illegal drugs and immigration. Shiprider falls squarely within the scope of those activities aimed at protecting and enhancing Canada's border integrity. (RCMP 2008, 16)

The kinds of cross-border criminal activities targeted by Shiprider include the "illicit drug trade, migrant smuggling, trafficking of firearms, the smuggling of counterfeit goods and money, and terrorism" (Government of Canada and Government of United States 2009). The enforcement urgency associated with these criminal activities is made that much more compelling by reference to the entrenched involvement of organised crime in these activities. As noted in 2011 by Senator Roméo Dallaire, "The success of the Shiprider program is mainly due to the fact that it meets a real need in the marine sector, particularly with respect to the ongoing obligation to intervene in illegal cross-border activities carried out by organized crime groups" (Canada Debates of the Senate 2011). Even in the absence of official statistics on the nature and extent of organised crime groups in cross-border criminal activity (RCMP 2006, 11), it is this increasing threat, as suggested by "anecdotal evidence" (ibid., 15), that is definitive for Shiprider. According to Bob Paulson, then deputy commissioner of the RCMP, there are

> national security-based threats that come from both countries into each other's country and from the world in general. However, the lion's share of the manifesting of the threat is the organized crime threat, the transborder shipment of contraband and all the things associated with organized crime, such as drugs, predominantly; weapons; tobacco; etcetera. (Canada Senate Standing Committee on National Security and Defence 2011)

The anticipated long-term results of Shiprider are as striking as the nature of the threats: "an increased impact on organised crime; reduced threat of terrorists; and a safer more secure society and economy" (RCMP 2006, 6). The spectre of organised crime effectively links crime and national security concerns and provides powerful justification for enhanced and novel transnational maritime enforcement practices such as Shiprider. The close intersections of crime and security and the connections mobilised between multiple scales of governance, local to national and transnational, are displayed in this diagram from *Securing an Open Society: Canada's National Security Policy* (Privy Council 2004, 3), which neatly depicts with arrows a self-validating continuum of overlapping circles of threats posed to the security of Individuals, Society/State and International System, as well as a parallel continuum that depicts a hierarchy of scales of Responsibility for Action, from the Individual through to the International Community (Fig. 11.1).

Fig. 11.1 Security Threats and Responsibility for Action Chart. Reproduced in accordance with fair use principles from this public government document: Privy Council Office Canada 2004. *Securing an Open Society: Canada's National Security Policy*. Available here: http://publications.gc.ca/collections/Collection/CP22-77-2004E.pdf

Beyond Bi-National Parameters: Shiprider Patrols in Akwesasne Mohawk Territory

The Canada–US Shiprider programme points to a novel bi-national deployment of jurisdictional practices in the shadow of the crime–security nexus, within a shifting topography of border control. These practices might appear to be, as suggested by Saskia Sassen (2008) and others, beginning to escape "from their earlier frame within distinctive national regimes" (Walters 2009, 2). However, Shiprider has important implications for jurisdictions beyond bi-national parameters. While Shiprider reconfigures maritime jurisdictional practices in ways that begin to decouple sovereign authority and national territories, it operates in waterways that flow through First Nations' territories. In these local operations, Shiprider asserts the regimes of *both* nations rather than escaping the regimes of any one.

Shiprider was piloted on the West Coast and now permanently operates in the Juan de Fuca Strait and the Georgia Basin, waterways that flow through the Salish Sea and surrounding basin. Here, the traditional territory of Coast Salish peoples covers 72,000 sq km, and in 1848 it was divided by the international boundary between Canada and the USA that many Coast Salish people still refuse to recognise (Miller 2012). Further east, the Shiprider programme was piloted in the waters of the St Lawrence Seaway that flow through Akwesasne Mohawk Territory, where it is slated to be unrolled on a permanent basis in 2015–2016. In stark contrast to the language of seamless continuity, here 140 km of waterway flow around about 432 islands through Canada, the USA, the provinces of Ontario, Quebec, the state of New York, multiple municipalities as well as 80 sq km of unceded territory of the Akwesasne Mohawk Nation, which extends across the St Lawrence River and the international border to include the St Regis Mohawk Reservation in New York State. While often represented in policy and in mass media as a kind of 'lawless black hole' (Gunter 2009; Kershaw 2006), this region is actually thoroughly intersected by a host of deeply contested socio-spatial boundaries, legal and quasi-legal regimes and jurisdictional practices. Here, diverse national, sub-national and transnational authorities, including both the elected and the traditional First Nations' governing bodies, operate at different, overlapping and sometimes conflicting scales. The Mohawk Council of Akwesasne is the elected system of government imposed by the Canadian Government in 1899. It is made up of three geographic and administrative districts, Tsi:Snaihne (Snye, Quebec), Kana:takon (St Regis, Quebec), and Kawehno:ke (Cornwall Island, Ontario), governed by 12 District Chiefs and one Grand Chief. In addition to the imposed electoral system of government, the Mohawk Nation Council of Chiefs is the traditional governing authority of the Mohawk Nation located in Akwesasne. The Mohawk Nation consists of eight communities spread across New York, Ontario and Quebec and is a part of the Haudenosaunee Confederacy which is made up of six nations: Mohawk, Oneida, Onondaga, Cayuga, Seneca and Tuscarora. In Akwesasne ("where the partridge drums"), indigenous understandings of sovereignty, jurisdiction and land pre-date the Western legal ones that were forcibly imposed with along with reserves and the Band system (McNeil 2007). Akwesasne is indeed "the nexus of a dizzying array of borders within borders and cultures within cultures," where residents "have to contend with regulations and government structures from their community, the Mohawk Nation, the confederacy, three states, and two countries" (Allen 2006), as well as multiple linguistic-ethnic divisions including Canadian Francophones and Anglophones, American Anglophones and different Mohawk dialects (Busatta 2015).

It is axiomatic that wherever there are borders and customs, there will be smuggling. As explained by George-Kanentiio, in Akwesasne, "smuggling was a way of life along the river long before, and long after, prohibition" (George-Kanentiio 2006, 27). In this "contested jurisdiction border community" (Jamieson 1998, 259) geography, economy and environmental degradation have further fuelled the market for legal and illegal forms of cross-border trade. Akwesasne Mohawk Territory is variously represented in policy, scholarship and the media as the 'contraband capital of Canada' and a 'jurisdictional nightmare' for law enforcement, especially in relation to the smuggling of tobacco, guns, drugs and people and connections to organised crime (Blackwell 2010; Kershaw 2006; Jamieson 1998; Daudelin et al. 2013). The representation of Akwesasne as a 'high-risk' cross-border crime zone (MacLeod 2014), a view which merges easily with the historical criminalisation of indigenous people in Canada, received a further boost after the 2001 terrorist attacks in the USA fuelled fortifications of Akwesasne as a gaping 'black hole' in border security (Kershaw 2006; Spencer 2011; Grand Chief Mitchell interview April 2015).

The convergence of the domains of crime and security has had particularly extensive effects in Akwesasne. There are no less than 17 national, sub-national, international and First Nations' enforcement agencies at work, including, for example, Cornwall Community Police Service, the Ontario Provincial Police, the Cornwall detachment of the RCMP, the RCMP Anti-Contraband Force, Sûreté de Quebec, Akwesasne Mohawk Police, the CBSA, New York State Police, Saint Regis Mohawk Tribal Police, the US Coast Guard, US Customs and Border Protection, US Immigration and Customs Enforcement. There are also joint policing initiatives formed since 1996 including the Cornwall Regional Taskforce, the Akwesasne Partnership Initiative and Canada–US Integrated Border Enforcement Teams (IBETS). In 2014, the RCMP announced plans to create a 92-million-dollar border integrity technology enhancement project that will target more than 100 'high-risk' cross-border crime zones spanning 700 km of Eastern Canada including the land and marinescapes of Akwesasne. As explained by RCMP Assistant Commissioner Joe Oliver:

> The concept involves employing unattended ground sensors, cameras, radar, license plate readers, both covert and overt, to detect suspicious activity in high-risk areas along the border ... What we're hoping to achieve is a reduction in cross-border criminality and enhancement of our national security. (MacLeod 2014)

The reaction of the Mohawk Council of Akwesasne was swift, denouncing the RCMP surveillance web as "an attack on not only our sovereignty; but also on our human rights, mobility rights and privacy rights" (Mohawk Council of Akwesasne 2014).

Whither Sovereignty?

While controversial and one-sided, Shiprider agreements between the US and Caribbean and Latin American nations have proliferated since the early 1990s (Brown 1997; Ferguson 2012; Robinson 2009; Watson 2003), and USCG and RCMP authorities reassure that this Shiprider agreement is fully reciprocal and leaves the sovereignty of both nations intact (USCG Interview 2014, 2015; RCMP Interview 2014a, b). Nonetheless, the steady expansion and securitisation of increasingly integrated Canada–US border policies since the 1990s has been variously regarded as signalling the erosion of sovereignty or the emergence of 'new,' 'merged,' 'shared' or 'dispersed' forms of sovereignty, effectively "conceding sovereignty to gain sovereignty" (Kent 2011, 803). Advocacy groups such as the Council of Canadians, Canadian Civil Liberties Association, American Civil Liberties Union and Privacy International regard Shiprider as a threat to Canadian and US sovereignty that extends and connects the crime and security mandates of both nations and raises troubling questions about accountability, privacy and information sharing, due process and civil rights (Kitchen and Rygiel 2015). A classified cable released by WikiLeaks records that as early as 2005 Government of

Canada officials had already been interested in the Shiprider programme for several years, but had "not been able to get beyond the political fear over sovereignty or a prospective incident involving a high profile arrest or shooting of a Canadian citizen by an American officer" (WikiLeaks 2005). The even more controversial land-based version of Shiprider (called 'Next Gen') was apparently put on hold largely due to substantial public and political concerns about Canadian sovereignty. Senior officers in the RCMP and the USCG working at policy headquarters in Ottawa indicated that they had "moved too fast" with Next Gen and that "baby steps" were needed, presumably to slowly acclimatise Canadians to the presence of American enforcement officers in Canadian territory (RCMP Interview 2014a, b, 2015; USCG Interview 2014).

One such step was taken at the time of writing in March 2015 when Canada and the USA signed the *Canada–US Customs Preclearance Agreement*, which will allow the USA to establish customs facilities on the Canadian side of the border at highway checkpoints, bus depots, train stations and marine terminals. The agreement allows US Customs and Border Patrol (CBP) officers (who are law enforcement officers, unlike Canada Border Services Agency (CBSA) officers) to work in Canada and carry firearms and includes a reciprocal provision to allow CBSA officers to work in the USA. Interestingly, this agreement preserves the immunity of CBP officers working in Canada from Canadian prosecution (Chown Oved 2015). The same senior RCMP and USCG officers interviewed in the summer of 2014 explained the Canadian refusal to extend the same immunity to US CBP Shiprider officers was a deal-breaker that resulted in withdrawal of CBP from the Shiprider programme (RCMP Interview 2014a, b; USCG Interview 2014).

The government response to concerns about the whittling away of Canadian sovereignty is steeped in cynicism and clearly exhibits the jurisdictional games at play. In an extraordinary exchange in the Standing Senate Committee on National Security and Defence, Michael Zigayer, Senior Counsel, Department of Justice Canada, responded to a question about Shiprider's impact on Canadian sovereignty by reassuring that Shiprider's training programme and designation actually *transforms* US officers *into* Canadian ones when in Canadian territory, which effectively enhances rather than diminishes Canadian sovereignty:

[W]e are actually enhancing Canadian sovereignty by putting more Canadian law enforcement officers in these shared waters. When you designate an American Coast Guard officer or the New York State Police or any of the American partners on the other side, you designate him or her as a Canadian peace officer. You have increased the number of Canadian officers patrolling. I would argue that we have enhanced Canadian sovereignty by enhancing the protection of Canada. (Canada Standing Senate Committee on National Security and Defence 2011)

This argument that Shiprider fortifies Canadian sovereignty through its shape-shifting jurisdictional practices resonates strongly with the experiences and concerns of indigenous communities. While the Council of Canadians and others may fret that Shiprider represents a serious threat to Canadian sovereignty, from the often-neglected perspective of the elected and the traditional leadership of the Akwesasne Mohawk people, Canadian sovereignty is indeed being effectively strengthened rather than eroded (Oka and Ayers 2012).

'There Is No Border'

Ray: *That's Canada.*
Lila: *That's Mohawk land—the Res is on both sides of the river.*
Ray: *What about the border patrol?*
Lila: *There is no border.*
       (Frozen River 2008)

The Mohawk understanding that 'there is no border' contrasts sharply with the law enforcement perspective that there is "a *hole* in the international border":

The border meanders through the communities and small concrete markers on the side of the road or in the bush are the only indication of the shifting line. The border travels through residential areas (and in some cases through houses) and through fields and bush. From an international perspective this makes it extremely difficult to enforce … some sense of border between Canada and the United States. For the people of Akwesasne this is not an issue, as both the north and south sections are regarded as being part and parcel of the same Mohawk territory. The reality is that Akwesasne represents a hole in the international border through which people and goods (legal and illegal) travel virtually at will. (RCMP 2008, 24)

As recounted by Mohawk historian Darren Bonaparte, when the border between the USA and Canada was drawn through their land, the Mohawk people of Akwesasne were told that it would not affect them, that it was "20 feet above their heads" and applied only to non-natives. Instead, "[H]istory has shown that border was actually about four inches above the ground, just high enough to trip the average Mohawk as he walked from one part of his community to the other" (Bonaparte 1999, 1). The Mohawk people of Akwesasne have long "refused to consent to colonial mappings and occupations of their territory" (Simpson 2008, 195). As explained by Chief Lorraine White of the St Regis Council of Chiefs, "[t]he border was imposed on us by others, and it truly became a dividing line, clearly segmenting and differentiating our community ... But we have always maintained that we're one people" (quoted in Allen 2006).

In 1997, the Federal Court of Canada upheld the rights of Akwesasne Grand Chief Michael Mitchell under the *Treaty of Amity, Commerce, and Navigation of 1794* (the 'Jay Treaty') to cross the international border without paying duty on household and commercial goods. In his testimony before the Supreme Court of Canada, which ultimately overturned the Federal Court decision, Mitchell explained that the international border imposed on Mohawk territory "wasn't meant for [the] Kanienkehaka or the Mohawk Nation":

So, when our people in Akwesasne today say this border was not intended for us, they have an understanding in historical terms of the interpretation of those promises. In our language and the way it is passed down, the line of what is now known as the International Border belongs to somebody else. It wasn't meant for Kanienkehaka or the Mohawk Nation or any of the Six Nations. We understand that much. (quoted in *Mitchell v. M.N.R.* 2001, paras. 117–118)

The *2007 RCMP Evaluation Report* concedes that "Shiprider did not get off to a good start in Akwesasne" (24). The pilot took place in Akwesasne with neither prior consultation with Mohawk leaders nor participation of the Akwesasne Mohawk Police. Shiprider vessels were vandalised and shot at (RCMP Interview 2014a). According to the traditional governing body, the Mohawk Nation Council of Chiefs, this was an assault on the sovereignty of the Mohawk Nation (Mohawk Nation Council of Chiefs 2011). Shiprider, as elaborated by Brian David, Acting Grand Chief of the Mohawk Council of Akwesasne, raises many critical questions for the Mohawk people of Akwesasne:

> How will the police distinguish the good people in Akwesasne from the not-too-good people in Akwesasne? How will these activities disturb some of the customary traditional patterns we have in the river system, like fishing or trapping … How does this dovetail into some of the rights we have already established in the Supreme Court of Canada and those that we have under way? How does this dovetail into the direction that our community is moving with its nation-building initiative—the self-government negotiations with Canada? (Canada Debates of the Senate 2011)

While the 2007 Shiprider pilots were nonetheless deemed a resounding success due to their enforcement potential, the *RCMP Impact Evaluation Report* was clear on the need to "consult and engage" the Aboriginal communities of Akwesasne and St Regis "in the development of any future initiative in this geographic area" (RCMP 2008, 6). In interviews, RCMP officers related they had "made a mistake" in how they had introduced Shiprider in the St Lawrence waterways (RCMP Interview 2014b) and that "since the pilot … we haven't done anything in that area yet. A lot of outreach and things need to be done before we can go into that area" (RCMP Interview 2014a).

The RCMP and USCG officers have been unwavering in their position that Shiprider has no specific mandate to target the contraband tobacco trade or First Nations' communities. But this claim may be little more than legitimation of the programme among the Akwesasne Mohawk community. In Senate Committee meetings and Parliamentary debates that preceded the legalisation of Shiprider in 2012, the connections between the smuggling of contraband tobacco, organised criminal activities and Akwesasne Mohawk territory were key justifications offered by enforcement officials for its expansion. In September 2014, the Standing Committee on Legal and Constitutional Affairs heard submissions on Bill

C-10, the *Tackling Contraband Tobacco Act* that became law in November 2014. The specific connections between Akwesasne, cigarette smuggling and organised crime dominated the justifications for the bill's criminalisation of trafficking in contraband tobacco. Further, as claimed by Trevor Bhupsingh, Director General of the Law Enforcement and Border Strategies Directorate at Public Safety Canada, Shiprider is an example of an integrated enforcement partnership between Canadian and US law enforcement "that [is] helping us with the contraband tobacco initiative … along the water boundary between the Canada and the US border" (Canada Proceedings of the Standing Senate Committee on Legal and Constitutional Affairs 2014).

By early 2015, it appears that outreach is well underway. Grand Chief Michael Mitchell of the Mohawk Council recounted in April 2015:

> We actually had a meeting on Shiprider with the policing organisations of both the United States and Canada … so it's fairly recent, and they could not be better behaved police officers—polite, accommodating. You know, I ripped into them and they just took it: 'you're right, we know we should have consulted, we should have done this, we should have done that. However, you know going forward,' and I said 'No. Going forward we're going to patrol our waters. We're going to make up what is the marine patrol Shiprider. We'll determine the kind of partnerships we're going to need.' And I was testing the water you might say. And they were agreeing, they were agreeing with everything that I'm saying and all: … 'it should be your people that are going to be patrolling and we'll provide the equipment.'… The ones that came were kind of like the department heads of the RCMP and Homeland Security and then US border patrol and US Coast Guard and New York State Troopers, US Customs and Immigration were there. Pretty big table and all we did was ask to meet with a few of them on this matter but they all came and they're tripping on each other trying to be gracious and accommodating. (Grand Chief Mitchell interview April 2015)

Grand Chief Michael Mitchell is hopeful about how the Shiprider programme will be rolled out in Akwesasne:

> They all said, 'because this thing is not going to be a success without you.' So they're saying, 'it's your territory it's your waters and all and we have to come and appreciate that.' So …we're promised to have a major involvement, play

a major part manpower wise, equipment wise and the concern for the community. I said, 'there's going to have to be a large effort in consulting the community members [to let them know] that this program is there for their protection as well. If it's just the interest of the US and Canada there's going to be resistance. You have to clarify that we're really protecting [Akwesasne's] borders first.' Yes, we ain't through with that you know. There must be some way we can put something like that together. I began to see they really didn't have that plan but they sure jumped on it … I have some confidence that we will have major involvement. (Grand Chief Mitchell interview April 2015)

Conclusion

The crime–security nexus and its effective blending of crime and security concerns in relation to 'the state' provide the dominant justification at the level of national policy for Shiprider's extraordinary reconfiguration of jurisdictional practices in maritime cross-border law enforcement. At this scale, the resonance of the bi-national, cross-border Shiprider programme with expansive processes and tensions of globalisation and securitisation are striking. Shiprider provides another example of emergent transnational security arrangements as well as the efforts taken at the same time to negotiate and protect national sovereignty interests. This includes privacy and accountability measures but also the restriction by law of Shiprider patrols to "shared waterways," defined further as "undisputed areas of the sea or internal waters along the international boundary between the United States and Canada" (Government of Canada and Government of the US 2009). Effectively erasing the entrenched history of colonialism, dispossession and ongoing indigenous struggles for 'land and life' (LaDuke 1999), Shiprider's legislators and policy-makers were thinking only of border disputes between the participating nation-states, such as Canada and the USA in the Arctic over the Northwest Passage, in the Beaufort Sea or over the sovereignty of the tiny Machias Seal Island in the Bay of Fundy. Not even a footnote is provided to explain the omission of indigenous struggles for land and nationhood in its definition of 'disputed areas.'

While Shiprider may certainly display globalising and securitising qualities, neither of these broad paradigms shed much light on its operations and effects in local contexts. While Shiprider's projected enforce-ment outcomes in relation to cross-border crime/security threats are yet to be fully demonstrated (RCMP Interview 2014a), the significance and effect of Shiprider extend well beyond crime control and enforcement metrics. As argued by Audra Simpson, smuggling has long provided the occasion for the assertion, defence and contestation of different versions of sovereignty through the deployment of jurisdiction (Simpson 2008). This resonates strongly with the introduction of Shiprider in Akwesasne Mohawk Territory, where the crime–security nexus justifies the assertion and prioritisation of national and bi-national sovereign jurisdictions. The jurisdictional tango (Ford 1999) performed here on native land, redraws the connections between national sovereignty, jurisdiction and territory and reaffirms "the ordering of indigenous people in space" (Ford 2011, 1). Shiprider's unprecedented reconfiguration of jurisdictional practices and its erasures, enactments and effects represent a new step in the 'juris-dictional tango' performed in the complicated land and marinescapes of Akwesasne Mohawk Territory. While the dance step may be new, the tune strikes some familiar chords.

References

Allen, Kristina. 2006. Homeland Insecurity. *Cultural Survival Quarterly: Two Countries, One People* 30(3). http://www.culturalsurvival.org/publications/cultural-survivalquarterly/united-states/homeland-insecurity.

Blackwell, Tom. 2010. Contraband Capital; The Akwesasne Mohawk Reserve Is a Smuggling Conduit, Police Say. *National Post*, September 22.

Bonaparte, Darren. 1999. A Line on a Map: A Mohawk Perspective on the International Border at Akwesasne. *Wampum Chronicles: Contemporary Issues: Border Crossing Rights.* http://www.wampumchronicles.com/bordercrossing.html. Accessed 19 Aug 2015.

Brown, Kathy. 1997. The Shiprider Model: An Analysis of the US Proposed Agreement Concerning Maritime Counter-Drug Operations in Its Wider Legal Context. *Contemporary Caribbean Legal Issues* 1: 1–80.

Busatta, Sandra. 2015. The Akwesasne Mohawk at the Margin of the State. In *Nationalisms and Identities Among Indigenous Peoples: Case Studies from Across North America*, eds. Martina Neuburger and Peter Dörrenbächer, 47–67. Oxford: Peter Lang International Academic Publishers.

Canada. 2011. *Debates of the Senate (Hansard)*. 3rd Session, 40th Parliament, Volume 147, Issue 91, March 3.

Canada. Parliament. 2011. Standing Senate Committee on National Security and Defence. *Proceedings of the Standing Senate Committee on National Security and Defence*. Issue 11, Evidence-February 14.

———. 2014. *Proceedings of the Standing Senate Committee on Legal and Constitutional Affairs*. Issue 17, Evidence-September 25.

Chown Oved, Marco. 2015. Could Armed U.S., Border Guards be Coming to Union Station? *thestar.com*, April 19. http://www.thestar.com/news/gta/2015/04/19/could-armed-us-border-guards-be-coming-to-union-station.html. Accessed 19 Aug 2015.

Daudelin, Jean, Stephanie Soiffer, and Jeff Willows. 2013. Border Integrity, Illicit Tobacco and Canada's Security. *National Security Strategy for Canada Series*. Macdonald Laurier Institute.

Dickson-Gilmore, E. Jane. 2002. *Communities, Contraband and Conflict: Considering Restorative Responses to Repairing the Harms Implicit in Smuggling in the Akwesasne Mohawk Nation*. Report by the Research and Evaluation Branch – Community, Contract and Aboriginal Policing Services Directorate, Royal Canadian Mounted Police (RCMP), Ottawa.

Ferguson, Tyrone. 2012. Shiprider Revisited: Security and Transnational Crime in the Caribbean. *Caribbean Dialogue: A Journal of Contemporary Caribbean Issue* 8(4): 29–48.

Ford, Richard. 1999. Law's Territory (A History of Jurisdiction). *Michigan Law Review* 97(4): 843–930.

Ford, Lisa. 2011. *Settler Sovereignty: Jurisdiction and Indigenous People in America and Australia, 1788–1836*. Boston: Harvard Historical Studies 166.

George-Kanentiio, Douglas M. 2006. *Iroquois on Fire: A Voice from Mohawk Nation*. Westport, CT: Praeger Publishers.

Government of Canada. 2014. *Beyond the Border Action Plan News*. Spring. http://actionplan.gc.ca/en/content/beyond-border-action-plan-news-spring-2014. Accessed 19 Aug 2015.

Government of Canada/Government of the United States. 2009. *Framework Agreement on Integrated Cross-Border Maritime Law Enforcement Operations Between The Government of Canada and The Government of the United States of America*. Public Safety Canada. http://www.publicsafety.gc.ca/cnt/rsrcs/pblctns/frmwrk-grmnt-ntgrtd-crss-brdr/index-eng.aspx. Accessed 19 Aug 2015.

Gunter, Lorne. 2009. Say No to Mohawkistan. *National Post*, July 10.

Hataley, Todd, and Christian Leuprecht. 2013. Organized Crime Beyond the Border. *National Security Strategy for Canada Series*. Ottawa: Macdonald-Laurier Institute, April.

Hele, Karl S., ed. 2008. *Lines Drawn Upon the Water: First Nations and the Great Lakes Borders and Borderland*. Waterloo, ON: Wilfrid Laurier Press.

Indian Country Today. 2008. Coast Salish leaders Commit to Environmental Action, March 10. http://indiancountrytodaymedianetwork.com/2008/03/10/coast-salish-leaders-commit-environmental-action-92353. Accessed 19 Aug 2015.

Jamieson, Ruth. 1998. Contested Jurisdiction Border Communities' and Cross-Border Crime—The Case of Akwesasne. *Crime, Law and Social Change* 30(3): 259–272.

Kenny, Colin. 2007. Joint Defence on the Great Lakes: Time to Sink or Swim. *Ottawa Citizen*, November 9.

Kent, Jonathan. 2011. Border Bargains and the "New" Sovereignty: Canada–US Border Policies from 2001 to 2005 in Perspective. *Geopolitics* 16(4): 793–818.

Kershaw, Sarah. 2006. Drug Traffickers Find Haven in Shadows of Indian Country. *New York Times*, February 19.

Kitchen, Veronica, and Kimberly Rygiel. 2015. Integrated Security Networks: Less, Not More, Accountability. In *Putting the State on Trial: The Policing of Protest During the G20 Summit*, eds. Margaret E. Beare, Nathalie Des Rosiers, and Abigail C. Deshman, 148–167. Vancouver: UBC Press.

LaDuke, Winona. 1999. *All Our Relations: Native Struggles for Land and Life*. Cambridge: South End Press.

Luna-Firebaugh, Eileen. 2002. The Border Crossed Us: Border Crossing Issues of the Indigenous Peoples of the Americas. *Wicazo Sa Review* 17(1): 159–181.

———. 2005. Contemporary and Comparative Perspectives on the Rights of Indigenous Peoples: 'Att Hascu' Am O 'I-Oi?' What Direction Should We Take?: The Desert People's Approach to the Militarization of the Border. *Washington University Journal of Law & Policy* 19: 339–353.

MacLeod, Ian. 2014. RCMP Reveals Details of its $92-Million Plan to Erect a 700 Kilometer Surveillance Fence Along the US Border. *National Post*, November 4.

McNeil, Kent. 2007. The Jurisdiction of Inherent Right Aboriginal Governments. Research Paper, National Centre for First Nations Governance.

Miller, Bruce Granville. 2012. Life on the Hardened Border. *American Indian Culture and Research Journal* 36(2): 23–45.

Mitchell, Michael Kanentakeron. 2012. Irresponsible Statements. Letter to the Editor, *Standard-Freeholdercom,* January 6. http://www.standard-freeholder.com/2012/01/06/letters-to-the-editor-irresponsible-statements. Accessed 19 Aug 2015.

Mohawk Council of Akwesasne. 2014. *Mohawk Council of Akwesasne Press Release* Kentenhko:wa/November 14.

Mohawk Nation Council of Chiefs. 2011. Letter to the Editor. *Indian Times,* March 10.

Oka, Cynthia Dewi, and Alison J. Ayers. 2012. At the Gates of Fortress North' America: Race-Ing the SPP and its Political Subject. *Studies in Political Economy* 86: 23–53.

Pratt, Anna. 2005. *Securing Borders: Detention and Deportation in Canada.* Vancouver: University of British Colombia Press.

———. 2012. Immigration Penality and the Crime-Security Nexus. In *Canadian Criminal Justice Policy: A Contemporary Reader,* eds. Karim Ismaili, Jane Sprott, and Kim Varma, 273–297. Oxford: Oxford University Press.

———. 2014a. Wanted by the Canada Border Services Agency. In *Criminalization, Representation, Regulation: Thinking Differently About Crime,* eds. Deborah Brok, Amanda Glasbeek, and Carmela Murdocca, 285–326. Toronto: University of Toronto Press.

Privy Council Office Canada. 2004. *Securing an Open Society: Canada's National Security Policy.* http://publications.gc.ca/collections/Collection/CP22-77-2004E.pdf. Accessed 19 Aug 2015.

Public Safety Canada. 2014. *Public Safety Canada 2014–15: Report on Plans and Priorities 2014–15.* Her Majesty the Queen in Right of Canada, Cat. No.: PS1-8/2014E-PDF. http://www.publicsafety.gc.ca/cnt/rsrcs/pblctns/rprt-plns-prrts-2014-15/rprt-plns-prrts-2014-15-eng.pdf. Accessed 19 Aug 2015.

Robinson, LCDR W. Brian 2009. You Want Authority With That? How I Learned to Stop Worrying and Love Shipriders. *The Coast Guard Journal of Safety and Security at Sea Proceedings of the Marine Safety and Security Council.* Summer, 62–68. https://www.uscg.mil/proceedings/archive/2009/Vol66_No2_Sum2009.pdf. Accessed 19 Aug 2015.

Royal Canadian Mounted Police. 2006. Evaluation. *Detroit-Windsor Shiprider Pilot September 12–25,* 2005 Proof of Concept Evaluation, January 10.

———. 2008. Internal Audit, Evaluation and Review Services Evaluation Directorate. *Shiprider* 2007 *Impact Evaluation Final Report,* October 15.

———. 2010. Canada–US Shiprider—Transcript. Olympic Shiprider Pilot: Pegasus Video. http://www.rcmp-grc.gc.ca/ibet-eipf/shiprider-video-transcript-eng.htm. Accessed 19 Aug 2015.

Sassen, Saskia. 2008. The World's Third Spaces. *openDemocracy: Free Thinking for the World*, January 8. https://www.opendemocracy.net/article/the_world_s_third_spaces. Accessed 19 Aug 2015.

Simpson, Audra. 2008. Subjects of Sovereignty: Indigeneity, The Revenue Rule and Juridics of Failed Consent. *Law and Contemporary Problems* 71(3): 191–215.

Spencer, Bree. 2011. Akwesasne: A Complex Challenge to US Northern Border Security. *The National Strategy Forum Review* 20(3). https://nationalstrategy.wordpress.com/2011/07/19/breeding-grounds-for-terrorism-and-transnational-crime/. Accessed 19 Aug 2015.

Starks, Rachel Rose, Jen McCormack, and Stephen Cornell. 2011. *Native Nations and US Borders: Challenges to Indigenous Culture, Citizenship, and Security*. Tucson, AZ: University of Arizona.

Valverde, Mariana. 2015. *Chronotopes of Law: Jurisdiction, Scale and Governance*. New York: Routledge.

Walters, William. 2009. National, Global, Zonal: Rethinking the Securitization of Mobility. Paper prepared for the International Studies Association, Annual Meetings, New York City. 14–18 February 2009.

Watson, Hilbourne. 2003. The 'Shiprider Solution' and Post-Cold War Imperialism: Beyond Ontologies of State Sovereignty in the Caribbean. In *Living at the Borderlines: Issues in Carribbean Sovereignty and Development*, eds. Cynthia Barrow-Giles and Don G. Marshal, 226–274. Kingston, Jamaica: Ian Randle Publishers.

WikiLeaks. 2005. Canada Gives Positive Soundings on Great Lakes Shiprider. Cable: 05Ottawa2344_a, 2005 August 3, 20: 54. https://www.wikileaks.org/plusd/cables/05OTTAWA2344_a.html. Accessed 19 Aug 2015.

Interviews

RCMP. 2014a. Interview. Ottawa, Canada, July.

———. 2014b. Interview. Ottawa, Canada, July.

USCG. 2014. Interview. Ottawa, Canada. July.

———. 2015. Interview. Seattle, Washington, US. May.

Grand Chief Michael Kanentakeron Mitchell. Interview. Toronto, Canada. April.

Film

Frozen River. 2008. Written and Directed by Courtney Hunt. Sony Pictures
Classics.

Legislation and Case Law

Integrated Cross Border Law Enforcement Act S.C. 2012, c. 19, s. 368.
Jobs, Growth and Economic Prosperity Act S.C. 2012, c.19.
Royal Canadian Mounted Police Act [RCMP Act] R.S.C., 1985, c. R-10.
Tackling Contraband Tobacco Act S.C. 2014, c.23.
US Code of Federal Regulations Electronic Code of Federal Regulations. Current
as of August 17, 2015. http://www.ecfr.gov/cgi-bin/ECFR?page=browse.
Accessed 19 Aug 2015.
Mitchell v. M.N.R. 2001 SCC 33.

12

Intelligence and National Security: Australian Dilemmas Post-9/11

David Martin Jones

Introduction

Since 2001, expenditure on the security services has increased exponentially in Western democracies, particularly amongst the Five Eyes (FVEY): the UK, the USA, Canada, Australia and New Zealand. This has occurred in conjunction with the expansion of counter-terror laws. Yet somewhat problematically the phenomenon of Islamist-inspired violence and how it recruits amongst the Western diaspora has become more difficult since the removal of Osama bin Laden and most of the core leadership of Al Qaeda in the first decade of the twenty-first century. In Australia and Canada, the decisions of successive governments of differing political complexions to maintain laws that many libertarians see curtailing free speech have coincided with new surveillance laws to police the Internet and the growing use of social media as a jihadist recruiting tool. It was

D.M. Jones (✉)
School of Political Science, University of Queensland, Brisbane, Queensland, Australia

© The Author(s) 2016   **273**
R. Lippert et al. (eds.), *National Security, Surveillance and Terror*,
DOI 10.1007/978-3-319-43243-4_12

widely advertised that the decision not to proceed against controversial speech act laws in Australia was to maintain community harmony. (This is a strikingly similar view to that advocated by soft authoritarian regimes like Singapore in order to maintain religious harmony in multicultural societies.) At the same time, Muslim communities feel targeted by the extension of new laws that breech social media privacy.

This chapter examines the evolving Western managerialist approach to security using Australia as a case study. It argues that the growth and proliferation of security agencies since 2001 has not facilitated greater internal security but rather worryingly undermines the notion of the political. Consequently, it fails to take seriously the Western state's own political self-understanding that emerged in the wake of the collapse of European Christendom. In an updated version of the national interest this would allow for a serious interrogation of Islamist radicalism and its appeal without requiring the growing legislative tyranny of a security state.

Intelligence and National Security: Australian Dilemmas

Australia, like Canada, suffers from the anxiety of a British constitutional legacy and its adaptation over time to the contingent experience of internal and external threats. Both countries' responses to 9/11 witnessed the expansion of counter-terror legislation and counter-terror establishments to address Al Qaeda and the emergence of the Global Jihad Movement (GJM). In both countries, this development of the security state has sparked an unresolved debate over the character of surveillance, the accountability of domestic security services and the threat they posed to civil liberties in a constitutional democracy. Attending to the Australian case sheds an interesting light on the evolution of national security post-9/11. It involves, inter alia, a proliferation of legislation, government expenditure and the expansion of agencies involved in national security. This has not necessarily proved the most efficient or the most prudent way to address the threat of global jihadism and leaderless resistance.

The Evolution of Australian Intelligence

From the foundation of a modern security service in 1949 under the Cold War auspices of MI5 to the expansion of the concept of security after 2001, the practice of national security has periodically troubled Australia's liberal democratic ethos. From 2002 to 2010 successive governments promulgated 45 new security laws, all bar one dealing with counter-terrorism. The foundation of the Islamic State (IS) in June 2014 and foreign fighter recruitment to its army from Australia's Lebanese community reinforced this legislative tendency. It also posed a dilemma for Australia's political conscience. During 2014, the government passed a *Counter Terrorism Amendment Act* to respond to urgent operational requirements and introduced legislation to amend the *Telecommunications (Interceptions and Access) Act* and address the phenomenon of recruitment to IS. Finally, after attacks on Melbourne police officers and Man Haman Monis' lone-actor attack in Sydney's Martin Place in December 2014, the federal government's 2015 *Review of Australia's Counter Terrorism Machinery* proposed a dedicated national security department with ministerial oversight.

This development of an Australian counter-terror bureaucracy post-2001 sits uneasily with an understanding of social contract and consent that seeks to guarantee habeas corpus, maintain a distinction between the public and private spheres and guarantee freedom of speech as self-regarding and central to the principle of democratic liberty. Both Liberal and Labour governments have approved, or failed to amend, legislation that curtails freedom of speech whilst elaborating and participating in a machinery of electronic surveillance that has received widespread international condemnation and incurred damaging leaks. Former NSA contractor and whistle-blower Edward Snowden observed the scale of the USA, UK, Canada, Australia and New Zealand or Five Eyes (FVEY) supranational intelligence-gathering organisation that "doesn't answer to the known laws of its own countries" (Snowden 2014).

Part of the goal of this chapter is to trace how an Australian national security dilemma has evolved since 1942. It traces the manner in which the state's recent legislative response to the problem posed by internal and external security threats has expanded the national security state.

Enhanced security has important social and political ramifications and has implications both for constitutional accountability and confidentiality. The chapter argues that security legislation is too often reactive and responds to a well-established Australian tradition of managerial rationalism. The chapter further considers what alternative political understandings might provide legislative guidance without either undermining a prudential concern with national security or eroding Australia's continuing commitment to constitutional democratic practice.

The Evolution of Australian Security

Over the post-Second World War period, the maintenance of national security and the evolution and practice of an Australian Intelligence Community (AIC) has raised questions concerning its necessity and sustainability. More precisely, the extent of "terrorist organisations" willing to engage in "an action … with the intention of advancing a political, religious or ideological cause and with the intention of coercing … the government," as the *Security Legislation Amendment (Terrorism) Act* 2002 puts it, together with the constitutional oversight of those agencies charged with detecting and deterring them has occasioned an enduring political debate. Moreover, in the last decade, the proliferation of legislation and the expansion of the nation's security espiocracy have exacerbated this sometimes vitriolic debate concerning the limits of political freedom and the necessity of surveillance.

The pursuit of national security, especially since 2001, has exposed a paradox at the core of modern Australian democracy, namely, that the practice of political freedom might entail proscribing those dedicated to subverting it by violent means. Prior to the "exceptional" first decade of the twenty-first century, successive Australian governments showed a lack of conviction about the "need for security and intelligence organizations" combined with "public apathy on the part of most Australians and hostility to them from a minority" (Templeton 1977, 6). This "resulted not in less spying but simply in less efficient spying" that only exacerbated this paradox (Templeton 1977, 6). The development of a distinctive Australian perception of national security in the geopolitical aftermath of the Cold War continues to shape the character of Australian intelligence and the conduct of the organisations comprising the AIC. The fact that a report by the *Independent National Security Legislation Monitor*, called for sweeping changes to the "unnecessary, disproportionate and ineffective" Australian anti-terror laws introduced since 2002, served only to highlight the central constitutional paradox that has always confronted Australian intelligence-gathering (Blackbourn 2013).

To explore the problem of AIC accountability further, we first need to consider the contingent manner in which a centralised national security architecture developed after the Second World War. The anxiety of influence exerted a peculiar hold over the Australian perception of national security. More precisely, the strategic interests of the UK and the USA profoundly influenced the structure and philosophy of the AIC from its inception.

At the behest of the British Counter Espionage Service the Australian Commonwealth established its first Special Intelligence Bureau in 1916. In the inter-war period, the Commonwealth Investigation Branch of the Commonwealth Police (CIB) assumed responsibility for political surveillance. Fear of communist subversion after 1917, and of Soviet espionage after 1945, meant that the Communist Party of Australia (CPA) aligned with Moscow from 1922 to 1989, constituting an enduring focus of surveillance. The government proscribed the party between 1940 and 1942 and again in 1950. In the 1920s, the CIB also paid desultory attention to Japanese espionage. Yet, as Jacqueline Templeton observed in her history of *The Australian Intelligence and Security Services 1900–1950*, the collection of secret intelligence lacked both a clear "policy and defined objectives" (Templeton 1977). Moreover, even when "certain requirements were laid down at a national level, there was no firm central control over the operation of the services at a local level" (Templeton 1977, 6). The problem of central control versus local autonomy within a federal system, as well as competition between agencies as the espiocracy evolved, represents a further enduring tension in Australian security organisation.

Thus, in 1949, under pressure from its allies, the UK and the USA, the Labour government of Ben Chiffley agreed to the creation of an Australian Secret Intelligence Organisation (ASIO) to address Soviet espionage in Canberra. Subsequently, in 1952, the Liberal government of

Robert Menzies secretly approved the formation of the Australian Secret Intelligence Service (ASIS) to gather information abroad about threats to Australian security.

An analogous secrecy pervaded the evolution of intelligence-gathering services linked to the Australian armed forces and housed within the Ministry of Defence over the same period. The Defence Signals Bureau (1947, renamed the Defence Signals Directorate in 1978) operated clandestinely under the umbrella of the UK, USA, Canada and New Zealand signals intelligence agreement. Analogously, the Defence Imagery and Geospatial Organization (DIGO) and the Defence Intelligence Organisation (formerly the Joint Intelligence Organization) (DIO) also date from the Cold War and were allied to suspicions of Soviet war in the Asia Pacific theatre at the end of the Second World War and the KGB's penetration of Australia's government revealed by the Venona transcripts (Ball and Horner 1998). After 1949, the DIO came to distance itself from the assessment and intelligence-gathering activities of the civilian intelligence organisations, ASIO and ASIS. This reflected a growing suspicion within the Ministry of Defence concerning the activities of ASIO and ASIS.

Intramural tensions between the services led to Justice Robert Hope's *Royal Commission on the Intelligence Services*, which reported in 1977 that the AIC was both "fragmented and poorly coordinated" (Hope 1976, 34). To remedy this, the Liberal government of Malcolm Fraser established the Office of National Assessments (ONA) in 1977. In contrast with the allied influence involved in the creation of the other security agencies, the ONA is a distinctive organisation that seeks to exercise an oversight role, housing a small staff of analysts reporting directly to the prime minister.

Following the Royal Commission's findings, the government also created the office of the Inspector-General of Intelligence and Security (IGIS) and the National Security Committee of the Cabinet (NSC), also in 1977, to exercise some form of political accountability. According to Gyngell and Wesley (2004), the Hope Royal Commission "improved oversight, and lines of accountability through individual ministers and cabinet were made much clearer" (145). From this perspective, the story of Australian intelligence is one of evolving accountability, where a security architecture created by administrative fiat, often in conditions of great secrecy, becomes subject to public scrutiny over time. As Gyngell and Wesley contend:

> The period from the first Hope Royal Commission Report in 1977 through his second report in 1984 to the Gordon Samuels and Michael Codd Commission of Inquiry into ASIS in 1995 and the Intelligence Services Act 2001 was a story of the gradual integration of the intelligence services into the Australian policy process, a growing movement to accountability and greater transparency. (Gyngell and Wesley 2004, 149)

Ironically, although the *Security Intelligence Act* 2001 and its various amendments after 2001 enhanced ASIO's power to issue control orders, search orders and warrants for preventative detention, the legislation also established the Parliamentary Joint Committee on Intelligence and Security (PJCIS) to review the administration and expenditure of ASIO, ASIS, DIGO, DIG, Defence Signals Directorate (DSD) and ONA and make recommendations to the relevant ministry. In other words, as the powers of the security agencies expanded and their personnel and expenditure grew dramatically after 2002, so too did parliamentary oversight of the AIC. This process culminated in the creation in 2010 of the office of *Independent National Security Legislation Monitor* to examine counter-terror legislation, whilst the similarly independent Office of Inspector of Intelligence and Security reports annually on the "legality and propriety of intelligence agencies' extended activities" (Thom 2014, 6). This constitutional accountability of an expanded state surveillance machinery is little discussed but has significance for the conduct of surveillance and how the AIC has addressed internal threats and foreign fighter recruitment since 9/11.

9/11, Bali and the Transformation of National Security Architecture

9/11, the Bali bombing of October 2002 and the London attack of July 2005, together represented an important psychological threshold for the perception of national security and the Australian response to its evolving dilemmas. Indeed, piecing together the evolving relationship between the

Indonesian terror franchise Jemaah Islamiyah (JI), the Philippine Abu Sayyaf Group and Al Qaeda globally between 1985 and 2002, it is evident that both Australian and regional intelligence and police services exhibited a marked degree of complacency about the nature and extent of the regional Islamist threat (Martin Jones and Smith 2012). Even after the Bali bombing, Australian police and the AIC denied any connection between JI and Al Qaeda. In January 2003, Australian police sources even maintained that "there is nothing concrete to link al-Qaeda to the [Bali] bombings" (*The Australian* 2003a). Eventually, in February, it was officially, but somewhat obscurely, admitted that "until the events of October 12" JI was "an unknown quantity" (*The Australian* 2003b).

In many ways, the scale of the intelligence failure across the region reflected a wider inter-governmental complacency towards the spread of Islamic extremism prior to the Bali bombing, which consistently underestimated the nature and extent of the threat. Indeed, Australian security analysts were asserting a week before the Bali attack that "the tendency is still to overplay [the terror] threat" (Dupont 2002, 8).

After Bali, however, the AIC, the wider community and the media accepted, in principle, the proposition that terrorism had shifted from a nuisance criminal behaviour to the primary national security focus. In the aftermath of the joint Australia–Indonesia police and intelligence effort to find and arrest the Bali bombers, together with the regular discovery of plots to attack Australian infrastructure between 2003 and 2014, it appeared that Australia needed an overarching national security strategy to counter transnational terrorism with domestic implications.[1] It was assumed that a national strategy would more clearly define the threat to Australia, identify the key long-term trends in terrorist activity and offer policy and intelligence responses.

However, following a series of further attacks against Australian interests in Southeast Asia in 2004, the Department of Foreign affairs and Trade (DFAT) produced a white paper on transnational terrorism. It

---

[1] Beginning with the Willie Brigitte Faheem Lhodi plot in 2003 to attack infrastructure targets through the Benbrika plot in 2005, and the Holdsworthy Barracks plot in 2009, to the arrests in Brisbane and Sydney in October 2014 and the lone wolf attack in Martin's Place in 2014, what is now termed the Global Jihadist Movement (GJM) has posed difficulties both internationally and nationally for Australian security.

advocated a three-pronged response: build effective operational-level cooperation; help other countries develop and strengthen their capabilities to fight terrorism; and build political will amongst governments to combat terrorism (DFAT 2004, 77). It also led to the appointment of a counter-terrorism ambassador within DFAT to coordinate collaboration between Australian agencies and international partners.

After Bali, transnational terrorism became the defining issue in Australia's domestic and foreign relations. It also affected the practice of intelligence collection. After 2002, Australian diplomacy attempted to secure greater cooperation with Southeast Asia across the full range of political, military and development assistance sectors. Between 2002 and 2010, Australia negotiated separate bilateral memoranda of understanding on counter-terrorism cooperation with Asian and Pacific countries, co-hosted four ministerial regional summits and provided more than AUS $100 million in aid projects to assist regional counter-terrorism efforts. This notwithstanding, Australia's participation in the Iraq War in 2003 exacerbated the internal and external terror threat to Australian interests. Moreover, after 2006, the emerging threat from an online jihadist movement calling for global resistance to the *kuffar* rendered the potential terror threat more protean and unpredictable. Both ASIO's 2007 and 2008 reports to Parliament identified the "threat of terrorism" (ASIO 2007, 3) and "violent jihadist" activity as the organisation's chief concern (ASIO 2008, 3). This was further exacerbated after June 2014 by the emergence of Islamic State and its attraction to a disaffected Lebanese Sunni Muslim diasporic community in Australia.

The intersection and exploitation of localised grievances and separatist movements in Southeast Asia combined with globalised Islamist ideology poses a complex array of challenges. The direct challenge to Australia has two separate, but overlapping dimensions. The first is the immediacy of the threat. As the 2005 ASIO annual report notes, there had been at least one aborted, disrupted or actual terrorist attack against Australians or Australian interests every year since 2000 (ASIO 2005). A decade later, the government's *Review of Australia's Counter-Terrorism Machinery* found

The threat posed by global Islamist terrorism is growing and becoming more diverse. Perhaps the most striking example of this growth is evident in the Iraq-Syria conflict zone. Here, the lethal convergence of ideological attraction and the geographical accessibility of the conflict has drawn foreign fighters on an unprecedented scale. (Department of Prime Minister and Cabinet 2015, 10)

Indeed, as the review further observed, "the conflict in this region has seen the creation of a new generation of increasingly capable, mobile, and digitally-connected terrorists with the ability to disseminate their extreme ideology around the world" (Department of Prime Minister and Cabinet 2015, 10).

Intelligence Resourcing and the Changing Nature of Terrorism Post-2001

After 2001, Western counter-terrorism efforts disrupted, but did not destroy, the structure and organisation of transnational jihadist networks. In fact, from the drawdown of US troops in Iraq commencing in 2009 to the announcement of a new caliphate or Islamic State in June 2014 witnessed "an apparent evolution in terrorist tactics [that] is also dramatically altering our threat landscape: terrorist groups are increasingly encouraging random lone actor attacks" (Department of Prime Minister and Cabinet 2015, 10). With the erosion of the leadership of Al Qaeda and the assassination of Osama bin Laden in 2011, jihadism became protean and leaderless, making its penetration by intelligence agencies more difficult. Suicide attacks that employed 'clean skins' reduced the chances of detection. As the London bombings in July 2005 and the proliferation of lone-actor attacks in Boston, London, Montreal, Ottawa,[2] Sydney and Paris between 2012 and 2015 demonstrated, home-grown radicals can quickly become agents of global jihad. Moreover, Internet use by Islamic terrorist groups places a high premium on assessing this type of open-source information. However, the allied intelligence community has so far failed to respond effectively to this virtual battleground, as the rise

---

[2] Lone actor attacks in Montreal on 20 October 2014 and on the war memorial in Ottawa on 22 October 2014 were responsible for the death of three Canadian servicemen. See http://edition.cnn.com/2014/10/22/world/americas/canada-ottawa-shooting/.

of the Islamic State and its online recruitment and leaderless resistance strategies testify.

In this context, a younger generation of Muslims from migrant communities in Sydney, Melbourne and Brisbane were from 2010 increasingly susceptible to the appeal of third-generation jihadism promulgated via the social media strategy of the Global Jihadist Movement (GJM). After the wars in Iraq and Afghanistan, a younger and social-media-savvy group of Islamist thinkers, with extensive experience of the West, recognised that the global confrontation between a purified Islam and the *jahiliyyah*, or infidel West, needed to be conducted with greater sophistication. They also recognised that the global movement required dual jihadist strategies: an intensification of violence in the Middle East after the withdrawal of US forces in 2011 and a more amorphous transnational and leaderless resistance such as that practised in Sydney in December 2014, Paris in January 2015 and the failed Anzac Day plot in April 2015 (Hegghammer 2010; Burke and Mark 2015). Although security services and the Western media hasten to dismiss as lone wolves or 'stray dogs' the actors in recent attacks in Boston, Ottawa, Sydney or Paris, these attacks serve a wider strategic and ideological purpose, reflecting the philosophy of the more important jihadist tacticians since 9/11: Abu Musab al-Suri, author of the much-translated *Call to Global Islamic Resistance* (2005); Abu Bakr Naji, author of *The Management of Savagery: The Most Critical Stage Through Which the Ummah Will Pass* (2004), a virtual blueprint for building a caliphate and a guiding text of Islamic State's leaders; and Anwar al-Awlaki, the US citizen of Yemeni background who was the leading figure in al-Qaeda on the Arabian Peninsula until he was killed by a US drone strike in 2011. Their adaptation for a global audience of Islamism's apocalyptic political vision informs the thinking of Islamic State.

Al-Suri's *Call to Global Islamic Resistance*, published online, sought spontaneous, self-radicalised actions "which will wear down the enemy and prepare the ground for waging war on open fronts ... without confrontation in the field and seizing control of the land, we cannot establish an (Islamic) state, the strategic goal of the resistance" (Maher 2015, 245; Meleagrou-Hitchens 2015, 77). Al-Awlaki adapted extracts from this long tract for *Inspire*, the English online journal that recalibrated the strategy and made jihad hip for young Muslim diaspora in the West. The former boxer, male stripper, Salafist convert and Sydney sheikh Feiz Mohammed facilitated this development after al-Awlaki's death. Feiz exercised a notable influence over the Tsaernev brothers responsible for the attack on the Boston marathon in 2013. The leaderless resistance abroad that al-Awlaki and al-Suri envisaged and which Islamic State promotes with an estimated 90,000 posts a day for 'generation jihad,' complements the 'management of savagery' within the protean Islamic State.

The AIC's Response to Global Jihadism

In Australia, responsibility for open-source collection on the Internet and other media shifted from DFAT to ONA following the recommendations of the 2004 Flood Inquiry. Although ONA has increased the pool of analysts working on open-source collection, it cannot track even a small percentage of the estimated 4800 terrorist websites, let alone the social media posts used by Islamic extremists.

Notwithstanding evident intelligence failings post-2001, and the AIC's glacial and bureaucratic response to the latest ebullition of global jihadism, successive governments have nevertheless invested heavily in the AIC as the principal tool to combat transnational and home-grown terrorism, as well as the emergence of the new social-media-driven threat. As the 2015 *Review of Australia's Counter Terrorism Machinery* observed:

> In Australia, from 2001–2002 to 2013–2014, Australian Security Intelligence Organisation (ASIO) was increased more than fivefold; that of the Office of National Assessments (ONA) almost quadrupled; for the Australian Secret Intelligence Service (ASIS) it more than tripled and for the Australian Federal Police (AFP) it more than doubled. (Department of Prime Minister and Cabinet 2015, 3)

Meanwhile recruitment to the AIC also rose dramatically. ASIO's staff increased from 600 officers in 2002 to 1900 by the close of the decade (Neighbour 2014). Although the level of AIC funding fell a little after the Labour government's review of counter-terrorism in 2010, awareness of the threat posed by Islamic State saw Tony Abbott's Liberal Government increase it by a further AUS $634 million in 2014 (Department of Prime Minister and Cabinet 2015, 7). This investment represents a significant long-term commitment to placing intelligence security at the forefront of the government response to the new risk environment.

Yet somewhat problematically, as a 2008 Australian Strategic Policy Institute report observed, "there is no systematic way to examine public expenditures on counter-terrorism" (Ergas et al. 2008, 17). Despite the formation of a National Threat Assessment Centre in 2003 and a Counter-Terrorism Control Centre in 2010 as well as the application of efficiency dividends to the AIC after 2010, measurement of AIC effectiveness remains rudimentary.

Law, Freedom and Counter-Terror: A Misconceived Debate

At the same time the intelligence agencies enjoyed a boom in resourcing, the Howard Government between 2002 and 2007 controversially amended the law governing terrorism to facilitate its pre-emption, as well as granting special powers to the Australian Federal Police (AFP) via amendments to the *Australian Federal Police Act* 2004. As Hocking (2004) observed, "organizationally the events of September 11 also set in train a steady expansion in the domestic counter-terrorism institutional machinery, an expansion heightened by the bombings in Bali" (195). The government's proposals were essentially two-fold: the expansion of ASIO's powers by yet another amendment to the *ASIO Act*, and new laws to combat the specific crime of terrorism. The *Security Legislation Amendment (Terrorism) Act* 2002 introduced specified offences of terrorism into Australian federal criminal law. A terrorist act was defined as

> an action or threat of action … done with the intention of advancing a political, religious or ideological cause and with the intention of coercing or influencing by intimidation, the government of the Commonwealth or State or Territory … or intimidating the public. (Hocking 2004, 202)

The 2002 Act further identified a range of ancillary offences relating to connections with proscribed organisations. Under the new legislation, moreover, the Attorney General, and not the judiciary, decides whether an organisation "planning assisting in or fostering the doing of a terrorist act" should be proscribed (Hocking 2004, 202).

Together with a legal definition of terror and its ancillary prescriptions and penalties, the government altered the *ASIO Act* to enhance "the powers of ASIO to investigate terrorism offences," which entailed the power to detain individuals and to conduct coercive interrogations under strict control orders (ibid.). Reporting on the *ASIO Legislation Amendment (Terrorism) Bill* 2002, the Parliamentary Joint Committee on ASIO, ASIS and DSD considered it "one of the most controversial pieces of legislation considered by Parliament in recent times" that would "undermine key legal rights" (ibid.).

The proposed anti-terror measures evoked a chorus of academic, media and legal disapproval. For civil libertarians, moving ASIO into "the arena of pre-emptive security policing" represented an "unprecedented" assault on the rule of law (Hocking 2003). Equally significantly, the 2002 legislation reversed an earlier approach to political violence that refused political credibility to groups or individuals having recourse to violence in the name of an ideological abstraction. The 1984 *ASIO Act* treated politically motivated violence as an offence at common law. The concept of terrorism, constitutional lawyers averred, was imprecise (Hocking 2004, 202).

Criticism of the legislation focused upon how it eroded democratic rights like freedom of association and habeas corpus. Critics observed that the executive proscription of political, religious and ideological organisations evoked memories of the Menzies Government's attempts to proscribe the Communist Party in 1950. Hocking (2004) considered the anti-terror laws "carried profound implications for freedom of political association and political expression. The new crime of membership of a terrorist organization … institutionalizes … guilt by association" (202). Following extensive review, amended legislation in 2003 gave additional powers to ASIO, but included parliamentary oversight. In 2005, the government introduced further legislation,

> including new ASIO powers to coercively question persons under warrant in relation to terrorism offences and AFP powers to seek preventative

detention orders to prevent an imminent terrorist attack and/or the loss of vital information immediately after a terrorist act. (Hocking 2004, 16; Department of Prime Minister and Cabinet 2015, 7)

Despite academic, legal and media condemnation of the "enactment of a vast body of national security law" (Lynch et al. 2015, 2), the threat Australia's security agencies faced was one not easily curtailed without expanding or at least redefining ASIO's power to act pre-emptively against groups prepared to undertake suicide attacks. Indeed, ASIO employed the new legislation to foil attacks on Australian targets. In June 2006, Faheem Khalid Lodhi was sentenced for planning terrorist acts in Sydney. More dramatically, in November 2005, ASIO in conjunction with Federal, Victorian and New South Wales police, arrested 18 Muslim men in Sydney and Melbourne planning attacks on the Melbourne Cricket Ground (MCG) and the Crown Casino. The subsequent trial of 12 of those arrested in *Operation Pendennis* resulted in six convictions under the new laws in September 2008.

Nevertheless, the application and expansion of this legislation to cover telecommunications intercepts since 2014 remains politically contentious. The case of Australian/Egyptian citizen Mamdouh Habib notably reinforced a cosmopolitan elite suspicion about the AIC approach to counter-terrorism and its collusion with the CIA. The CIA had detained Habib in Pakistan in October 2001 on the grounds that he had prior knowledge of the 9/11 attacks on New York and Washington. Although Habib's case was not directly related to the new laws, his rendition to Cairo in November 2001 occurred before his internment at Guantanamo Bay. After his release in 2005, Habib claimed that ASIO and AFP officers were present during his enhanced interrogation in Cairo and were complicit in a process that involved cruel and inhumane treatment. In March 2006, 'Jihad' Jack Thomas was sentenced to five years in prison for receiving funds from a terrorist organisation, yet on appeal the case was dismissed. In 2007, an ASIO and AFP case against medical student Izhar ul-Haque also collapsed. Most devastating for the enforcement of new counter-terror laws was the AFP's detention and arrest of Dr Mohamed Haneef for his alleged role in failed attacks on a London nightclub and Glasgow airport in July 2007.

However, all these cases were subject to independent scrutiny by the office of the Inspector-General of Intelligence and Security (IGIS), which has taken its constitutional responsibility seriously. Under *The Inspector-General of Intelligence and Security Act* 1986, the Inspector-General has the power to require attendance of witnesses, take sworn evidence, retain documents and enter Australian intelligence agencies' premises. In other words, these cases of apparent abuse were subject to legal oversight.

The cases of Habib, ul-Haque and Haneef raised public concern but also showed the IGIS actively examining claims that ASIO and ASIS acted extrajudicially in the wake of 9/11 and the new security powers vested in them. In 2011, the current Inspector-General, Vivienne Thom, conducted a detailed investigation into the *Habib* case and found that neither ASIO nor AFP officers were involved in his transfer to Cairo or attended his interrogation. Thom's report did, however, find that both ASIO and AFP needed clearer guidelines about providing information to foreign governments about Australian citizens and should "ascertain that the interviewee would not be subject to cruel, inhumane or degrading treatment" (Thom 2011, 12).

The IGIS also investigated the circumstances surrounding the interrogation and prosecution of Izhar ul-Haque in 2007. ASIO and AFP officers suspected ul-Haque's involvement in the Faheem Khalid Lohdi and Willie Brigitte plot to commit a terrorist act in Sydney in 2003. In 2006, Lohdi received a 20-year sentence for three terror-related offences. Yet, the New South Wales Supreme Court dismissed charges against ul-Haque, a known associate of Lohdi, in 2007, and criticised two ASIO officers for their 'oppressive conduct.' The IGIS investigation found that there was no evidence to support the claim of "false imprisonment" or "unlawful detention" (IGIS 2008, 40). What the IGIS did consider problematic, however, was the lack of coordination between ASIO and the AFP in their conduct of the ul-Haque investigation. In particular, the then IGIS, Ian Carnell, considered that ASIO displayed a "lack of confidence" in sharing information with the police and failed to communicate its operational plan to the "relevant police authority" (ibid., 42).

A similar breakdown in communication between agencies also occurred in the case of Dr Mohamed Haneef. AFP officers arrested Haneef at Brisbane airport in July 2007 in connection with a failed terrorist attack on Glasgow International Airport that involved his second cousins Kafeel and Sabeel Ahmed. Held in solitary confinement for 12 days under the *Anti-Terrorism Act* 2005, Haneef was eventually released without charge. The subsequent inquiry into the *Haneef* case led by former New South Wales Justice John Clarke QC (ibid., 20) found the evidence against Haneef was 'completely deficient' and that ASIO had informed the AFP that there was no evidence to suggest Haneef was 'guilty of anything.' Ultimately, Clarke concluded that AFP Commander, Ramzi Jabhar, manager of Counter-Terrorism Domestic, had "lost objectivity" and was unable to see that the evidence he regarded "as highly incriminating amounted to very little" (Clarke 2008, 20). Clarke recommended that Parliament implement oversight of the AFP and reform the counter-terror legislation. Similarly, the Street review of the AFP counter-terror practice identified a failure of "interoperability between the AFP and its national security partners" (Street 2008, iv). This deficiency stemmed from three sources: firstly, the conflict between the intelligence-gathering function of the security agencies and the evidence-gathering of police; secondly, the problem of confidentiality in terms of intelligence-gathering versus the constitutional requirement of accountability; and thirdly the tendency of different security agencies to "silo" information that the Flood Report into the Australian intelligence agencies had previously highlighted (Flood 2004, 174). Arrest and detention on the grounds of pre-emption continues to divide public opinion about the utility of the counter-terror legislation and the political and security roles that the AFP has assumed since the government granted it special powers and an enhanced counter-terror mandate without adequate parliamentary oversight since 2004.

The Flood Report and Its Aftermath: The Continuing Problem of AIC Coordination

Despite AIC's expanding powers and the widespread criticism of their potential misuse and threat to liberal democracy, it had become evident as early as 2003 that the AIC had a credibility problem as a result of 'sexing up' evidence concerning Saddam Hussein's possession of weapons of mass destruction, and uncritically following UK and US intelligence assessments that persuaded the Howard Government to join the US-led 'Coalition of the Willing.' The resignation of ONA analyst Andrew Wilkie on the eve of the Iraq War in protest at the 'unbalanced' use of intelligence highlighted what appeared to be a government propensity to use information selectively to justify policy decisions (Wilkie 2004).

In an atmosphere of growing scepticism about the legitimate use of secret intelligence, and on the recommendation of a parliamentary inquiry into the quality and effectiveness of Australian intelligence, the government appointed Philip Flood to assess the Australian intelligence agencies in 2004. Flood's report depicted an overworked, under-resourced intelligence community lacking strategic direction. Flood nevertheless found that ONA and DIO Iraq assessments had not been politically managed.

Nevertheless, Flood identified a number of weaknesses in the AIC. In particular, he revealed a culture that uncritically accepted preconceptions governing both assumptions and sources (Flood 2004, 174). Flood recommended a renewed focus on analytic techniques and improved command of foreign languages. Flood also emphasised the need to maintain a distinction between the detached activity of intelligence collection and the demands of policy making, by broadening ONA's charter to embrace a new Foreign Intelligence Co-ordination Committee chaired by ONA and including ASIO and the AFP. Subsequently, the government introduced the National Threat Assessment Centre (NTAC), an all-agency coordination body for filtering intelligence data as a 'refinement' to existing bureaucratic structures. The NTAC, however, fails to address the structural problem posed by information silos within and between agencies (Brew 2003, 1). In 2010, a new Counter-Terror Control Centre adumbrated the NTAC. Yet, as the Clarke report on the *Haneef* case intimated, the call for 'better coordination' and integration became a stock rhetorical response to the complex problem of understanding and addressing the evolving nature of asymmetric threats. Indeed, despite cosmetic adjustments, the Flood inquiry produced a better-resourced and larger AIC, but one that still resembled and acted in a remarkably similar way to that which existed before 2001.

In 2007, the new Labour government of Kevin Rudd proposed a radical review of national security. Rudd commissioned Ric Smith, a former

Defence Department bureaucrat, to conduct a Homeland and Border Security Review in February 2008. However, the review delivered little that was innovative. Incorporating the review findings in the *First National Security Statement* in December 2008, Kevin Rudd accepted Smith's recommendation that Australia avoid the US model of a Department of Homeland Security. Predictably, Rudd opted instead for "a new level of leadership, direction and coordination" of "the existing community of relatively small, separate agencies" (Rudd 2008, 8). Rather than contemplating radical reform to the Cold War structure of security intelligence, Rudd created a new office of the National Security Adviser within the prime minister's department, but separate from ONA, to provide strategic direction and support a "whole-of-government national security policy" (Rudd 2008, 8). To facilitate this 'integrated approach,' Rudd also announced the new crisis coordination centre (CTCC) and founded a national security college to inculcate security executives in the whole-of-government approach.

The national security statement summated prevailing orthodoxies about improving coordination. Where the review did innovate was by extending the definition of security to embrace both new Labour ideology and the expansion of the Canberra bureaucracy. Thus the statement proposed climate change as "a most fundamental national security challenge for the long term future" (Rudd 2008, 4). The Labour government's predilection for stretching the already contested concept of national security to embrace fashionable elite enthusiasms only further confused the already far-from-detached pursuit of strategic intelligence.

The emergence of Islamic State in 2014 and the lone-actor attacks in Melbourne and Sydney coinciding with Tony Abbott's new Liberal government (2013–2015) saw further calls for a review of security as well as the promulgation of new laws to address the phenomenon of foreign fighter recruitment and online radicalisation. Yet despite the Rudd and Gillard Government's creation of the new office of National Security Adviser to provide strategic direction to the disparate agencies in the AIC after 2010, and the Abbott Government's decision to create a new Counter-Terrorism Ministry in the wake of the Sydney attack in December 2014, problems of confidentiality, coordination and information sharing between the various agencies, and in particular between ASIO and the AFP, remain. It is this together with a tendency to proliferate agencies, anti-terror laws and special powers rather than a problem of accountability that is an enduring problem for the AIC. As we have seen, Parliament through the JCIS and IGIS exercises a reasonable degree of oversight over the core security agencies.

The organisation that is least politically accountable, however, is the AFP counter-terror force. Since 2001, the AFP has assumed an enhanced domestic and international counter-terror role. Significantly, in 2011, the *Parliamentary Joint Committee on Intelligence and Security Review of Administration and Expenditure* (2011, 35) recommended that its oversight power be extended to include the AFP. The government failed to support this recommendation on the grounds that the AFP was a law enforcement agency and not part of the AIC.

Herein lies the rub. As terrorism acquired a specific legal definition under the terms of *The Security Legislation Amendment (Terrorism) Act* 2002, its pre-emption assumed a political purpose. Yet, as Justice Sir Victor Windeyer observed in 1979, the best safeguard against new terrors lay in the rigorous enforcement of criminal law rather than making new laws about terrorism. Policing a political or ideological action necessarily politicises the police and engages the AFP in the world of security rather than law enforcement. To ensure greater accountability in an age of increased surveillance, the weakness in Australian oversight lies not in the realm of security agencies but in policing. Thus, since 1977 a series of royal commissions have rendered ASIO, ASIS, ONA and DIO accountable to Parliament. By contrast, since 2004 state and federal governments have extended the counter-terror role of the police forces of the seven Australian states and especially the AFP without according these forces a similar level of constitutional oversight. Thus, the Victorian, Queensland, New South Wales and Australian Federal Police forces have assumed an increasingly political counter-terror role without corresponding political accountability. Their oversight and coordination with the security agencies presents a distinctive managerial and constitutional problem. This problem is further complicated by legislation that responds to events, and is handicapped by an unnecessary proliferation of agencies that are mutually suspicious, sclerotically bureaucratic and insulated by different cultural practices.

Conclusion

Australia has traditionally sought security through alliance, which has left its imprint upon the structure and philosophy of national security and the intelligence required to sustain it. There also has been sometimes acerbic debate focused upon what Australian security should entail and the powers granted to agencies to sustain it. Political disagreement about both the external and internal nature of threats and a constantly changing risk environment exacerbate this security intelligence dilemma and distort the assessment and intelligence-collection process.

A number of enduring dilemmas emerge from the history of the essentially contested and increasingly politicised concept of Australian national security. Firstly, the national security debate increasingly required legal accountability and parliamentary oversight of all security agencies as the sine qua non of political democracy. From 1997 to 2004, a number of royal commissions established a political and legal structure rendering Australian security agencies constitutionally more accountable.

The problem is that to be effective intelligence requires confidentiality, or secrecy, "not just to protect sensitive intelligence sources, but also to protect fearless analysis" (McLennan 1995, 81). As former ONA analyst A.D. McLennan observed "it would be hard for minister to walk away from complicating intelligence judgments, were they public knowledge" (ibid.). In an era of asymmetric violence and intense media scrutiny, maintaining confidentiality and detachment has become increasingly difficult. Moreover, the evolution of new polymorphous threats like contemporary jihadism renders particularly vivid the irresoluble constitutional dilemma concerning the relationship between the prudential pursuit of security and the safeguarding of democratic rights and abstract notions of justice. This dilemma will continue to preoccupy those engaged with assessing Australian intelligence and national security.

Secondly, the evolution of the AIC also demonstrates the uncertain and shifting international environment in which agencies operate. From the formation of ASIO to the creation of the new National Security Adviser, the various Australian agencies represent partial responses to very different security dilemmas. As a result, there exists a tendency to overlapping jurisdictions and institutional sclerosis where agencies immured in a structure designed for Cold War contingencies fail to adapt to new exigencies, like the rapid evolution of the GJM via social media. This is evident in the Australian response to the new leaderless resistance promulgated by al-Awlaki and Sydney sheikhs like Feiz Mohammad. Nor do the preoccupations of successive Labour and Coalition governments between 2002 and 2015, with piecemeal reform and improving coordination and cooperation across the AIC, necessarily address the silo mentality that goes with the territory of bureaucratically entrenched practice over time.

Somewhat differently, the penchant of the media, academe, common lawyers and a cosmopolitan elite for focusing the debate on counter-terrorism laws in terms of a universal attack on civil liberties help comprehend the political character of a specific threat to democracy like that posed by the GJM. This means that the often histrionic debate over counter-terror laws precludes attention to the recurrent threat posed to the integrity and constitutional stability of a political democracy from espionage and subversion—the threats, of course, that ASIO, ASIS, DIO and DSD were founded to combat. The price of freedom requires both eternal vigilance and confidentiality. Currently, and notwithstanding the threat posed by online recruitment to jihad, Chinese espionage activity in Australia exceeds that of the Soviet Union during the Cold War, but public awareness about this threat to national security is minimal.

Finally, having elevated intelligence to the forefront of allied counter-terrorism efforts, there is an expectation amongst the public that new funding, integrated approaches, strategic frameworks and risk-based analysis will prevent the next 9/11. Such expectations are of course unrealistic. Intelligence remains an imprecise activity, liable to political distortion. The history of Australian security intelligence bears eloquent testimony to this imprecision.

References

ASIO. 2005. *Report to Parliament 2004–2005*. Canberra: Commonwealth of Australia.
———. 2007. *Report to Parliament 2006–2007*. Canberra: Commonwealth of Australia.

————. 2008. *Report to Parliament 2007–2008*. Canberra: Commonwealth of Australia.

Ball, Desmond, and David M. Horner. 1998. *Breaking the Codes Australia's KGB Network 1944–1950*. Sydney: Allen and Unwin.

Blackbourn, Jessie. 2013. Independent Review of Australian Anti-Terrorism Laws: An Effective Oversight Mechanism? *Oxford Human Rights Hub*, July.

Brew, N. 2003. *The New National Threat Assessment Centre* (Research Note No. 23). Canberra: Australian Parliamentary Library, December 1. http://www.aph.gov.au/Library/pubs/RN/2003-04/04rn23.htm.

Burke, Jason, and Monica Mark. 2015. Al-Qaida in Yemen Uses Video to Claim Responsibility for Charlie Hebdo Attack. *Guardian*, January 14. http://www.theguardian.com/world/2015/jan/14/al-qaida-claims-responsibility-charlie-hebdo-attack-paris.

Clarke, Sir John. 2008. *Report of the Inquiry into the Case of Dr Mohamed Hanee*, vol 1. Canberra: Attorney General's Department.

Department of Foreign Affairs and Trade (DFAT). 2004. *Transnational Terrorism: The Threat to Australia*. Canberra: Australian Government Printing Service.

Department of Prime Minister and Cabinet. 2015. *Review of Review of Australia's Counter-Terrorism Machinery*. Canberra: Commonwealth of Australia.

Dupont, A. 2002. Quoted in *Far Eastern Economic Review*, October 2.

Ergas, Henry, Scott Hook, Carl J. Ungerer, and Mark Stewart. 2008. *The Intelligence Reform Agenda*. Australian Strategic Policy Institute, November.

Flood, Philip. 2004. *Report of the Inquiry into the Australian Intelligence Agencies*. Canberra: Australian Government Printing Service, July.

Gyngell, Allan, and Michael Wesley. 2004. *Making Australian Foreign Policy*. Oxford: Oxford University Press.

Hegghammer, Thomas. 2010. The Case for Chasing Awlaki. *Foreign Policy*, November 24. http://foreignpolicy.com/2010/11/24/the-case-for-chasing-al-awlaki/.

Hocking, Jenny. 2003. Counter-Terrorism and the Criminalisation of Politics: Australia's new Security Powers of Detention, Proscription and Control. *Australian Journal of Politics and History* 49(3): 355–371.

————. 2004. *Terror Laws: ASIO, Counter-Terrorism and the Threat to Democracy*. Sydney: UNSW Press.

Hope, Robert M. 1976. *Report of the Royal Commission on Intelligence and Security* (3rd Report). Canberra: Australian Government Printing Service.

Inspector General of Intelligence and Security (IGIS). 2008. *Report of the Inquiry into the Actions Taken by ASIO in 2003 in Respect of Mr Izhar Ul-Haque and Other Related Matters*. Canberra: IGIS.

Lynch, Andrew, Nicola McGarrity, and George Williams. 2015. *Inside Australia's Anti-Terrorism Laws and Trials*. Sydney: New South Publishing.

Maher, S. 2015. *A Genealogy of Salafi Jihadism: The History of an Idea*. Unpublished PhD thesis, King's College, University of London, London.

Martin Jones, David, and Michael L.R. Smith. 2012. Ideology, Networks and Political Religion: Structure and Agency in Jemaah Islamiyah's Small World. *Politics, Religion and Ideology* 13(4): 473–493.

McLennan, A.D. 1995. National Intelligence Assessment: Australia's Experience. *Intelligence and National Security* 10(4): 71–91.

Meleagrou-Hitchens, A. 2015. *The Global Jihad Movement in the West: A Study of Anwar Al-Awlaki and His Followers in the Context of Homegrown Radicalisation and the Global Jihadist Western Recruitment Strategy*. Unpublished PhD thesis, Kings College, University of London, London.

Neighbour, Sally. 2014. Hidden Agendas. *The Monthly*.

Parliamentary Joint Committee on Intelligence and Security. 2011. *Review of Administration and Expenditure*. Canberra: Commonwealth of Australia.

Rudd, Kevin. 2008. *The First National Security Statement to the Parliament*, December 4. www.pm.gov.au/media/speech_0659cfm.

Snowden, Edward. 2014. Interview Transcript. *Norddeutscher Rudfunk*, January 26.

Street, Sir Laurence. 2008. *The Street Review: A Review of Interoperability Between the AFP and its National Security Partners*. Canberra: Attorney General's Department.

Templeton, Jacqueline. 1977. *Report of the Royal Commission on Intelligence and Security Australian Intelligence and Security Services 1900–1950* (7th Report). Canberra: Australian Government Printing Service.

The Australian. 2003a. January 25–26.

———. 2003b. February 15–16.

Thom, Vivienne. 2011. *IGIS Annual Report 2010–11*. Canberra: Commonwealth of Australia.

———. 2014. *IGIS Annual Report 2013–14*. Canberra: Commonwealth of Australia.

Wilkie, Andrew. 2004. *Axis of Deceit*. Sydney: Black Ink.

13

The Day the Border Died? The Canadian Border as Checkpoint in an Age of Hemispheric Security and Surveillance

Benjamin J. Muller

Globalisation, Security, Borders

At the end of the post-1989 decade, Thomas Friedman's 1999 triumphalist treatise, *The Lexus and the Olive Tree: Understanding Globalization*, celebrated a borderless dreamscape in which neoliberal and predominantly American principles were victorious global norms. While 9/11

Many thanks for the careful and engaged readings and comments of earlier drafts of this chapter from Randy K. Lippert, Darren Palmer, Kevin Walby and Ian Warner, all of whom helped enrich this argument. I also wish to express thanks to Thomas N. Cooke for his careful reading and suggestions on an earlier draft of this chapter. Also, special thanks to Javier Duran and the Confluencenter for Creative Inquiry at the University of Arizona, for essential research support and the necessary time and space to see this project through.

B.J. Muller (✉)
Department of Political Science, Kings University College, Western University, London, ON, Canada

© The Author(s) 2016   **297**
R. Lippert et al. (eds.), *National Security, Surveillance and Terror*,
DOI 10.1007/978-3-319-43243-4_13

forced some re-examination of this post-1989 euphoria, not least claims related to the end of history and the triumph of liberal democracy (see Fukuyama 1992), there were nonetheless continued moves towards ubiquitous deepening and widening global integration. There were also similar moves in Europe and greater levels of free trade in North America among Canada, the USA and Mexico, namely the consideration of the Security and Prosperity Partnership in North America in 2012 and earlier moves towards increasing cooperation in both security and defence as well as asylum and migration in the EU. Together these claims suggest borders were transforming, relocating and dislocating. During this period, borders reclaimed relevance within academic literature and in politics and policy circles (see Donnan and Wilson 1999), but 9/11 also accelerated pre-existing trends towards exceptionalism (Agamben 1998, 2004) and the securitisation of migration vis-à-vis borders (Huysmans 2000).

Bilateral and increasingly trilateral cooperation and coordination evolved in North America throughout the post-1989 period, drawing on smaller successful cooperative strategies of earlier decades (notably environmental regulations related to acid rain and coordinated clean-up of the Great Lakes. On matters related to coordinated governance strategies, see Larner and Walters 2002). Although nothing close to the Schengenland experience of Fortress Europe (at least not immediately), deeper collaborative and coordinated strategies towards common Canada–US border management accelerated post-9/11. One strategy was the short-lived Security and Prosperity Partnership (SPP) among USA, Canada and Mexico, which because of the changing nature of this trilateral relationship, not least the emergence of overwhelming border security and migration concerns, became a story of failure rather than success (see Gilbert 2007). Coalescing ideas about using risk management in border security, a shared fetishisation of identification and surveillance technologies and even of biopolitical norms (Muller 2008; Salter 2009) led to Canada setting up new and similar institutions. It also led to pursuing markedly similar practices[1] in border security and accompanying commitments to 'identity management' (see Muller 2008, 2009). Despite persistent negative

---

[1] In aviation security the American Transportation Security Authority (TSA) and the Canada Air Transport Security Authority (CATSA) took different approaches to security. The TSA placed greater emphasis on individuals, relying on profiling and pre-screening, whereas CATSA placed greater emphasis on objects. For an engaging critical discussion of this, see Salter 2009.

rhetoric about alleged insecurities at the Canada–US border from various secretaries of the US Department of Homeland Security (see CBC 2009), these security practices became dominant features of the North American relationship, but with marked differences in the US-border strategy in practice along its northern versus its southern border.

In an age of normalised exceptional (bio)power (Agamben 2004), alongside pre-existing commitments to neoliberal globalisation, interrogating the resiliency, existence and even location of the Canadian border is not esoteric. At a minimum, borders are bilateral spaces/places requiring if not coordination or cooperation, then at least actions and reactions, sometimes resulting in military stand-offs, demilitarised zones or even war. Articulated historically as the liminal space of the political, particularly in the realm of International Relations (IR), the border is framed by dominant discourses of world politics as the line separating order and disorder, anarchy and sovereignty, justice and immorality and so on (Muller 2008; Vaughan-Williams 2009; Walker 1993). The Canada–US border wears the moniker of the world's 'longest undefended border.' While always a misleading appraisal, this label has come under greater scrutiny since 9/11, for which the immediate US response, although brief, was to completely seal the Canada–US border. Subsequent strategies also have involved intensified securitisation and militarisation of the Canada–US border, more akin to the troubling escalation of security and technology along the Mexican–US border (Andreas 2005; Heyman and Campbell 2012). The analysis that follows considers the contemporary trajectory of exceptionalism and biopolitics together with the fetishisation of surveillance and identification technologies within so-called hemispheric border security strategies in North America. The chapter asks to what extent the Canadian border has become more analogous to an interior US border checkpoint, much like those proliferating throughout the Northern and Southern US borderlands. I provide an analysis of the reliance on checkpoints in the Arizona–Sonoran borderland, the space of many infamous approaches to border security, not least SB 1070.[2] It is with this particular experience of border security management in mind that I then consider

---

[2] Among other things, Senate Bill 1070 created in spring 2010 allowed for racial profiling by State law enforcement, challenging federal jurisdiction, not to mention other aspects of the US Constitution. See also Muller 2013.

the (non)existence of the southern Canadian border,[3] particularly in the context of US-led mass surveillance, information-sharing, and institutional and strategic isomorphism in North American border security.

A significant challenge throughout literature on exceptionalism is its relative hopelessness or the extent to which it does not allow for meaningful political agency or alternatives to the amplification and acceleration of executive power these analyses describe. Although limited, some attention is paid to this issue (Lemke 2005). As such, the chapter critically considers the ramifications of the alleged 'death' of the Canadian border, its transformation towards a checkpoint through technological fetishism and sovereign exceptionalism. Moreover, taking stock of the challenges posed by the border as checkpoint thesis, the chapter contemplates examples of citizen engagement and forms of civic oversight in the contested checkpoints in Southern Arizona as possibilities for alternative forms of border politics at the dynamic Canada–US border and borderlands. Although not the primary focus of this analysis, a deserving mention is what might be termed counter-performances, wherein the state narratives of centralised power, conceptions of (in)security and threat, as well as otherness, clash with the lived experiences of the borders and borderlands. These counter-performances challenge the dominant narratives of border insecurity and counter the specific accounts of history, culture and identity that state border security strategies wish to instil that run counter to the lived experiences of borderlands.

It is worth considering the concept of exceptionalism more explicitly before moving further. Exceptionalism, for the sake of this analysis, in the first instance simply refers to the increasing concentration of executive sovereign power and the related decline of forms of judicial and legislative oversight. Often associated with enhanced discretionary sovereign power exercised in times of war, exceptionalism has slowly emerged as a norm of governance, in a trajectory that according to some begins well before 9/11 (Agamben 2004). While this sort of discretionary sovereign power always has been common at the border, as a broader norm *away* from the border, exceptional politics has certainly accelerated in post-

---

[3] It is important to refer specifically to the southern Canadian border, as the northern border throughout the Arctic involves a range of international interests and various states, and it is arguably more contested and undergoing a retrenchment markedly different from the trends along the Canada–US border.

9/11 (see Muller 2009). Evidenced in both Canada and the USA by exceptional anti-terrorist legislation (i.e. USA *Patriot Act* and Canada's Bill C-36 which led to widespread changes to the *Criminal Code* as well as citizenship and immigration arrangements; see also Forcese, this volume), various executive orders and enhanced powers in the Cabinet and Prime Minister's Office, changes to the issuing of warrants and the coupling of security threats with immigration and refugee policy is increasingly commonplace (specifically regarding migration, Australia is often referred to as the high-water mark of exceptional, securitised politics, evidenced most clearly by the "No Way" anti-migrant government campaign (see Chambers and Jones, both this volume)).[4] These strategies continually enhance executive power while limiting oversight, and allow for 'exceptional' politics and policies, which over time can become the norm. While there are many examples, the Arizona checkpoints provide a particularly cogent one. These checkpoints are both extraterritorial, in so far as they are not located at the physical border, and attempt to exercise discretionary sovereign power as though they were located there vis-à-vis a federal authority. This makes them a poignant example of exceptionalism. As such, this forms a critical access point to the exceptional and changing nature of borders generally, and the contemporary dynamics of the Canadian border, in light of US trends, pressures and incentives. The checkpoint strategy in Arizona, and to a lesser extent across the USA, not only indicates the USA's embrace of extraterritorial exceptionalism. Together with a panoply of strategies, it also highlights the overall change to the norm of examination in border management to a norm of surveillance and suspicion. Such normative changes to border security are most keenly felt by Canadian officials, as indicated by the post-9/11 institutional changes in Canada that were largely in lockstep with US changes.

This chapter focuses on three issues. First, it examines the general tendency towards a reliance upon, even fetishisation of surveillance and identification technologies in border security management. Often led by USA, the (over)commitment to surveillance and security and its alleged benefits is not unique to the USA (see Muller 2013), which is considered

---

[4] As part of the Operation Sovereign Borders, the Government of Australia released a controversial advertising campaign "No Way."

here with reference to the checkpoint strategy used by US Border Patrol in Arizona. These particular strategies occur within a broader context of exceptional politics. After some discussion of this general tendency and the checkpoint analogy, the chapter considers the *Beyond the Border Agreement*, which attempts to skirt jurisdictional and legal differences between Canada and the USA, embracing a normalisation of the exception that contributes to a potential erasure of the border, in the same manner that it bypasses oversight. While implementation of some aspects of the agreement are for constitutional reasons relatively unlikely (see also Jochelson and Doerksen, this volume), the celebration and codification of this particular political imaginary is nonetheless important, indicating which limits of the political imagination remain resilient and which seem incredibly pliable. Finally, the chapter examines an instance in which a Canadian resident was denied access to the USA on the basis of non-transparent information-sharing between the two states and exposed deeply troubling biopolitical politics of exclusion on the basis of mental illness. The focus here draws on Foucault's notions of biopolitics from both his earlier and later works (Foucault 1978, 2010). The intention is to invoke the constellation of politics that focuses both on the body and notions of health and illness, normality and abnormality, but also considers more neoliberal regulatory aspects of population management, which focuses on a statistical and risk analytics both in constructing the category of 'population,' but also in rendering that category as a *thing* that is manageable (see also Salter 2015). This cogent metaphor of border-as-checkpoint emphasises the co-commitment to surveillance and exceptional authority in border security, but also the deep biopolitical dimensions of exceptional power, and how the location, nature and character of the Canadian border is undergoing significant change.

Beyond the Border: Surveillance and Theatres of Insecurity

In an amusement park in the central Mexican state of Hidalgo, *Parque EcoAlberto*, visitors are offered what the American public broadcaster PBS referred to as the "thrills and chills of illegal border crossing" (Zhorov and Fronteras 2013). The objective of the park is to dissuade potential migrants from deciding to make the perilous trip. Actors playing *coyotes* or smugglers wear balaclavas and focus on the horrific conditions of the desert. A slow death by exposure and hypothermia, and being preyed on by scavengers of the desert, is bizarrely converted into the so-called thrills and chills of the often fatal if not near-death experiences of undocumented crossings of the Mexico–US border. As other observers noted, turning the perilous crossing into a fun theme park adventure might not have the intended outcome of dissuading would-be migrants (de Hinojosa 2013). Although not part of the *Beyond the Border Action Plan (BtB)*, one can imagine the proliferation of border amusement parks, also known as pre-clearance programmes, (re)training migrants, tourists and travellers about not only the natural environment's hazards, but also the allowable tax exemptions, duties and even border crossing etiquette. Indeed, the experience of enrolling into registered/trusted traveller programmes, such as NEXUS (the trusted traveller programme used on the Canada–US border) or SENTRI (the Mexico–US border equivalent), provides some level of training and disciplining for enrollees (Muller 2010).[5] The harmonisation and coordination slated to roll out in the pages of *BtB* not only necessitates greater bilateral coordination with law and border enforcement, surveillance and data sharing, as well as immigration and asylum policies, but a shared vision of an emerging North American homeland, which is less likely to spontaneously emerge in the manner desired by policy makers. Not only is the internationalisation of exceptional law and policy problematic (as noted by many contributors to this volume), but how divergent political cultures must coalesce for successful integration is often disregarded completely. An alleged shared commitment to surveillance and identification technologies in border security management, together with particular bilateral or shared policy strategies, contributes to not only similar border strategies, but even a redesign of the space and character of citizenship itself (see Muller 2010)

---

[5] As part of my work as visiting research fellow at the Border Policy Research Institute at Western Washington University in 2008, I enrolled in the NEXUS programme, paying close attention to the differential roles of the US and Canadian officials in the process, tracking the time and the daily experience of crossing the border four to five times per week over five months.

not unlike how the experience at *Parque EcoAlberto* is designed to retrain would-be migrants.

The *BtB*, released in December 2011, progressively increases the level of integrated bilateral cooperation and coordination in border security management between Canada and the USA. The action plan suggests shared risk assessment, shared standards for biometrics, and increased information-sharing in various areas, common entry/exit strategies, together with sharing data on "third country nationals," harmonising cargo (pre)screening, and enhancing a range of integrated border enforcement programmes such as "Shiprider" (see Pratt, this volume), which on land adopts the guise of Integrated Border Enforcement Teams (IBETs). Not surprisingly, the promise of efficiency and streamlined travel and mobility, together with a shared fetishisation for new identification and surveillance technologies by both respective federal governments has helped many proposed provisions move forward with minimal delays. As Spitzer notes, the relationship between market fetishisation and security/insecurity is an intimate one (Spitzer 1987). By turning insecurity into a permanent condition, capitalism renders the security commodity qualitatively different from other commodities, as the use-value comes to be replaced with risk calculations and faith. In other words, the hope that the CCTV camera, for example, deters and/or secures is all one has to hold on to, as the extent to which it succeeds is indeterminate. This is because the threat itself is often unseen and unpredictable (Mooers 2014, 120). However, provisions for shared border enforcement, proposing to allow law enforcement agents to act outside their national jurisdiction, have seen its share of delays. The idea of armed US law enforcement personnel entering Canada to enforce US law, exempt from Canadian law, raises serious questions about accountability, transparency and responsibility (see Pratt, this volume). And although it has become increasingly clear that border enforcement of the sort envisioned in the agreement is likely not to emerge in the near- to medium-term future (Hataley 2010), the agreement nonetheless provides a particular articulation of the political imagination when it comes to securing the border. Beyond obvious questions of sovereign jurisdiction, it is important to note the significant differences between respective laws of search and seizure, and the extent to which this dramatically enhances and expands the discretionary or exceptional power of the state. Typically reserved in Canada for the border itself, under the Border Search Exception in US criminal law, warrantless searches and seizures can take place at international borders or within a 'reasonable distance' from the border, which is defined under US law as 100 miles from the border, and has in many cases been liberally interpreted since 9/11. If transferred to Canada, this implicates a significant portion of the Canadian population. To what extent do these proposed plans necessitate a proliferation of spaces/places of discretionary power? Therefore, might this proposed cooperation imply or necessitate an internationalisation of exceptional sovereign power? Is this a convincing example of how 'border policies' contribute to shifts towards exceptional sovereign power in far broader areas of society and politics? The simple answer to many of these questions might be 'no', in that one cannot imagine boots-on-the-ground futures, where US Border Patrol vehicles patrol Canadian territories. However, as stories such as the infamous case of Maher Arar (Koblanck 2010) together with Edward Snowden's revelations and WikiLeaks demonstrate, personal data and information already freely criss-crosses the Canada–US border with ease, regularly subjected to different jurisdictions, laws, norms and security cultures. Later this chapter considers troubling instances of these information transfers with consequences to mobility, but before that, a look at other aspects of the Canada–US border relationship is necessary.

One prominent myth about Canada–US border relations is the oft-quoted label, 'the longest undefended border in the world'. Even those with cursory knowledge of Canadian–US relations, past and present, quickly realise the extent to which this is misleading. From the obvious macro-examples of the War of 1812 to micro-examples like the Pig War in 1859 in the San Juan Islands off the coast of Vancouver Island, border relations have been anything but genteel for most of the past two centuries. It was only a decade before the Pig War that Democratic presidential candidate James Polk used the election slogan 'Fifty-four Forty or Fight,' in reference to the parallel 54°40′ north, far above the agreed-upon 49th parallel, which came to be the Canada–US border decided in that region through the Oregon Treaty of 1846. This rather thin slice of history helps underscore that the construction of the modern sovereign nation-state is a synthetic exercise based on convincing storytelling. The same is true for the alleged possibility (and desirability) of a common North American homeland fostered in the *BtB*. Moreover, while the specific provisions of *BtB* are targeting enhanced coordination and integration in North American border management, they are within what has been termed "Borderworld" (Hodge 2011; Muller 2013).

The amplification of identification and surveillance technologies in contemporary border security has emerged globally, based on a model of US responses to 9/11 and the Global War on Terror. These technologies, particularly biometrics and body surveillance, have been represented as elegant resolutions to the problem of enhanced securitised and militarised borders within global neoliberal free markets. Furthermore, these technologies have emerged within a context of not only long-held commitments to unrestricted discretionary sovereign power at the border, even in Western liberal democracies, but also a post-9/11 environment of enhanced exceptional sovereign power writ large vis-à-vis various pieces of anti-terrorist legislation. Under conditions of exceptional power, related statutory changes become the norm, and clandestine operations of intelligence agencies are persistently enhanced. It is within this global environment that *BtB* emerges, making the notion of US border enforcement agents operating on Canadian soil with impunity no less questionable or unlikely.

Revealed through WikiLeaks and by former CIA employee and NSA contractor Edward Snowden, the level of clandestine cooperation and coordination across borders by intelligence agencies and law enforcement is staggering (see Bauman et al. 2014). Under such conditions, can the possibility of US agents operating with impunity in Canada be as far-fetched as some detractors of *BtB* suggest? In this contemporary 'borderworld,' a vast array of techniques and technologies are similar across the world's borderlands; in fact, borders and borderlands are increasingly rearticulated as exceptional techno-spaces. The reliance on biometrics and logics that are both coexistent and co-constitutive of these technologies and the categorisations they enable also have enabled prolific reliance upon them. The related preoccupation with 'identity verification,' or authentication, as an essential part of border management and security, as well as the ubiquitous escalation of discretionary state power have all become benchmarks in this emerging 'borderworld.' As such, these are crucial factors in the productive concealment of the politics of contemporary securitising and criminalising trends in border security (see Muller 2013). While the notion of increased on-the-ground coordination and cooperation among Canadian and US border enforcement agents envisaged in the *BtB* might seem far-fetched, it is less so when considered within a global context of border security norms and benchmarks, the epistemic communities, private corporate actors and so-called managers of unease who populate this political space (see Bigo 2002; also see Walby, Lippert and Gacek, this volume), determined to promote a particular model of border security management globally.[6] The question is not to what extent is the sort of proliferation of bordering practices and exceptional sovereign power envisaged in *BtB* possible within the trilateral or even bilateral context of North America, but instead to what extent *can* these global trends, in many cases motivated by both public and private US interests, be thwarted in the context of Canada–US border relations?

Checkpoints, Risks, Desert(ed) Borders

When confronting checkpoints in the southern Arizona desert, one finds a particularly visceral dimension to Nick Vaughan-Williams' (2009) statement that "the border is not where it is supposed to be" (1). Predominantly introduced in 2007–2008, these checkpoints are extraterritorial, exceptional, unexpected and generally unwelcome. As noted earlier, exceptionalism refers to a particular constellation of amplified and intensified state power, which is traditionally more ubiquitous at the limits of the political community, namely the border. However, specific dimensions of the US border security strategy in Arizona vis-à-vis the checkpoints brings such mechanisms *inside*, contributing to a general proliferation and normalisation of exceptionalism.

The checkpoints met with much local resistance, particularly at the checkpoint near Arivaca in south-western Arizona, and range in size,

---

[6] For a particularly persuasive and instructive example of the commonalities of identification technologies, norms and best practices, and the role of similar individuals and interests globally, the comparative account of national identity card strategies is apt, see Bennett and Lyon 2008.

B.J. Muller

scale and alleged impermanence, from small trailers to large-scale, well-staffed, covered, technologically advanced sites that mimic the official border crossings at the geographical border (it is worth noting that the existence of these extraterritorial border checkpoints problematise not simply the articulation of state power, but also the (dis)location of the territorial border itself). Whereas Mountz (2011) has exposed the extent to which checkpoints in the northern US borderlands are more 'mobile' and reflect the state's capacity to appear and disappear, those in the southern USA, particularly near Tucson, Arizona, are relatively stable and permanent. Although still a part of what Mountz refers to as the mobility of state power (2011, 318), there is something more deeply material and permanent, a flagrant expression of the exception as the norm throughout the southern US borderlands, where the temporary becomes permanent. Among the largest examples of this temporary (exceptional) *cum* permanent (norm) is the checkpoint in the north-bound I-19 highway south of Tucson, which appears as a border crossing in its own right. Still framed within discourses of temporality, the I-19 crossing is nonetheless equipped with licence plate cameras, sensors, CCTV cameras, Border Patrol K9 units, in addition to Border Patrol trailers, all under the cover of a large, arched roof. Careful not to raise the ire of local residents, Border Patrol agents at most checkpoints simply ask whether or not one is a US citizen. The Arivaca residents group 'People Helping People in the Border Zone'[7] claim, based on their own informal studies and reports of the checkpoint near Arivaca (see Lieberman 2014; Santos 2014), that this is coupled with racial profiling, which has a significant negative impact on the large number of Hispanic local residents. Local NGOs and citizen and individual initiatives often using social media, as well as local and national media, have given voice to a range of forms of resistance, almost as old as the checkpoints themselves.

One particular route to Arivaca from Tucson passes the San Xavier del Bac mission. On land belonging to the Tohono O'odham nation, the San Xavier mission is a powerful symbol of the complexity, fluidity and hybridity of the borderland, which the political imagination underpinning the logic of checkpoints directly undermines. Dating from the

[7] (http://phparivaca.org/).

late 1700s, the San Xavier mission is, among other things, an important legacy of Spanish colonialism in the region. Situated in a landscape that for thousands of years has been a trade corridor for the Tohono O'odham people and the Yaqui First Nations, the mission is central to local identities. Following Mexican independence in 1821, the San Xavier Mission was situated in Mexico. Shortly after the Treaty of Guadalupe Hidalgo of 1848, the Peace Treaty that ended the Mexican–American War (1846–1848), the Gadsden Purchase of 1854 placed the mission inside of US territory. The mission now sits on one of the larger Native American reservations of the Tohono O'odham people, and remains a destination site for many local Catholics, including Hispanic Americans, Caucasians, Yaqui and Tohono O'odham people. To a great extent, this site symbolises the overlapping identities and histories of mobility and the extent to which this particular space, even the urban space of Tuscon, is anything but 'American' and mono-cultural in the more pejorative sense. For example, Thomas E. Sheridan's account of the history of the Mexican community in Tucson in his book *Los Tucsonenses* emphasises both the extent to which the city of Tucson was a 'Mexican' community prior to the arrival of Anglo settlers and throughout the early twentieth century Mexicans made up the majority of the population, vibrant with Mexican entrepreneurs and politicians that made Tucson a particularly successful commercial centre in the South-west (Sheridan 1992). Moreover, Sheridan's account disrupts attempts to over-code this history by portraying Tucson as an Anglo-American city, in which Mexicans are rendered 'others,' rationalising draconian and intolerant legislation, at its zenith in something like Senate Bill 1070. This is one dimension of the borderland, but there are others, equally messy and complicated.

What the mission represents is the counter-narrative to the imagination of the borderland represented in the politics of the checkpoint. Reconstituted as a hostile space, the border necessitates discretionary sovereign power to not only maintain a security (and even military) response to a specific articulation of migration and trafficking problems, but also to exhibit an overt performance of the state and its politics in the liminal space of the borderland. These strategies are deployed in a borderland that not only has a long history of movement and mobility of all sorts, but in the relatively recent past has been a site of deep contestation about the location of the limit and the line, most notably articulated through the politics of the Gadsden Purchase of 30 December 1853. Similarly, in spite of the relatively resilient imaginations of the Canada–US border as an undefended, friendly space, there is nonetheless a perceived need to (re)assert state power, and articulations of exceptional power related to imaginations of threat, risk and uncertainty, promoting performances of nationhood over the often resilient borderland identities. As such, the Canadian border is increasingly perceived as an additional checkpoint for US national security, framed in 'hemispheric' terms. In some instances, this logic is articulated through policy strategies and cooperation and coordination among border institutions in Canada and the USA; in other cases, it is articulated through the longer-term transition of biopolitical norms, practices and commitments to particular understandings of (in) security, threat and the capacities of particular identification and surveillance technologies.

(Dis)appearance of the Canada–US Border and the Biopolitical Checkpoint

Considering the extent to which the Canadian border increasingly functions as a checkpoint as a part of US border security and surveillance, a pre-clearance, pre-assessment zone, there is both an appearance and simultaneous disappearance of the Canada–US border. This befits the so-called multi-lane strategy of contemporary border security and surveillance, which goes hand-in-glove with identity management, a reliance on technologies for authentication and verification of identity, to make the border less visible for some and more apparent for others. This (dis) appearance of the border also sits well with the proposed strategy in the *Beyond the Border* agreement. On the one hand, the border slips into the background and a unified, hemispheric strategy emerges, which was already set into motion with the Western Hemisphere Travel Initiative (WHTI). On the other hand, the border reanimates stories of mobility in the borderlands, as movement of any sort becomes unimaginable in the border's absence, thus challenging directly the border's fluidity and hybridity, and reifying lines, limits and boundaries. This all happens similar to the way the checkpoints throughout the Sonoran borderlands challenge the imagination of that borderland represented by the San Xavier mission.

Part of the story of the (dis)appearance of the Canada–US border can be told through the experience of particular individuals. One such story is Maher Arar's. An innocent victim of clandestine information-sharing between Canada and the USA, a profile based on assumptions formed from collected pieces of information made him appear sinister, leading to extraordinary rendition, torture, a costly public inquiry and even more costly exoneration (Centre for Constitutional Rights 2015). However, a less well-known victim of the (dis)appearance of the Canada–US border is Ellen Richardson, whose November 2013 attempt to cross into the USA was denied.

In November 2013, Richardson attempted to board a US-bound flight from Pearson International Airport in Toronto, Canada, and was denied entry by US Customs and Border Protection (CBP). At first glance, the story already merits attention as it demonstrates the power of the extraterritorial border, now *normal* in most Canadian airports, where armed US CBP and Immigration and Customs Enforcement (ICE) work to maintain an extraterritorial US border crossing or a checkpoint in Canada, not altogether different from the so-called temporary checkpoints spotting the Sonoran borderlands in Southern Arizona. In this particular case, Richardson was denied entry on the basis of records relating to hospitalisation for clinical depression in June 2012 (Babbage 2013). In an exceptional exercise of biopower, Richardson was told to ascertain "medical clearance" by one of three Toronto doctors, whose assessments are accepted by the Department of Homeland Security (Babbage 2013). In 2001, Richardson attempted suicide by jumping off a bridge, and sustained injuries, requiring years of physical and mental rehabilitation, and according to her psychiatrist she has improved markedly (Babbage 2013). Consistent with US policy, Richardson was denied entry on the basis of having a "past physical or mental disorder, with associated harmful behaviour that is likely to recur or lead to other harmful behaviour" (USCIS Policy Manual n.d., Vol. 8: Chap. 7; US Immigration and Nationality Act n.d., Sect. 212). While the biopolitical aspects of the US policy are certainly worth engaging critically (see Solomon 2013), what is equally or more interesting here is how US authorities ascertained this personal medical information about Richardson.

Federal law allows the Canadian government to transfer personal information outside Canada, but the conditions for such a transfer remain relatively unclear. As a rule, health records are not transferred to US authorities, which fails to explain why Richardson (and according to the New Democratic Party Health Critic (Babbage 2013) and a *New York Times* Op-ed (Solomon 2013), several others), was denied entry on her November 2013 trip to the USA. According to the CBP official, a systems check on Richardson revealed a 2012 hospitalisation for mental illness (Hauch 2013). Again, disallowing entry to the USA for mental illness, in this case clinical depression, raises serious questions about the nature of the biopolitical state, particularly in light of the fact that the Centre for Disease Control and Depression estimates one in ten US residents suffer from depression (Solomon 2013). According to the Canadian Mental Health Association, 20 per cent of Canadians will suffer from mental illness during their lifetime (CMHA 2015). The decision of Canadian officials to share mental health information with US officials denies entry to Canadians and also accepts US Immigration and Nationality biopolitical norms regarding mental health. As with many categories of immigration and asylum, the Canadian border often both functions and is treated as a checkpoint for US authorities, a site of pre-clearance, a gasket between the outside and the inside—which is by no means to suggest this limit does not also act as a similar line of enforcement for Canadian standards. Already since the introduction of WHTI in 2009, Canadians and US citizens require a passport of other WHTI compliant government-issued ID in order to enter the USA, and as a result, the Canadian border was simply compelled to operate with similar standards, lest US citizens become trapped in Canada, unable to re-enter the USA.

WHTI laid the groundwork for the so-called multi-lane strategy at the Canada–US border, where various categories of more and less 'trusted' or registered travellers faced differential treatment when crossing the border. What is clear from the story of Ellen Richardson's failed crossing, and other similar stories, is the extent to which a broader array of biopolitical categories is also applied. As Foucault shows in *Madness and Civilization*, the mad and the insane found themselves on the list of security threats for a very long time, already clearly so in the fourteenth century (Foucault 1989). Moreover, madness and insanity became "acts of sovereign reason" (Foucault 1989, ix), which, in Richardson's case, is exercised by the petty sovereign of the border guard. Foucault's account also demonstrates how "madmen" were denied access to certain rites and spaces, while allowed continued access to others, but nonetheless occupied a "liminal" position (Foucault 1989, 8). Treating the liminal at the limit (the border) is of particular interest. In much the same way as liberal democracies tend to conceal the discretionary power of sovereignty in the everyday; such exercises of discretionary sovereign power are evident at the border, or the liminal space of the political. At the limit, sovereign decisions and differentiations are common and made more intense when dealing with liminal categories. When standing in a security queue at the airport, for example, humour can be determined by the sovereign to be dangerous; similarly, mental illness is deemed threatening in the same manner as the amorphous 'terrorist,' in part due to the unpredictability. Although trusted and registered categories have grown, categories of suspicion seem to have proliferated far more rapidly in the liminal space of the border.

Conclusions

The Canadian State remains sovereign. However, to declare absolute sovereignty on the part of any state in an age of globalised commerce, capital and labour flows, and rapid data transfers through information and communication technologies is problematic. The long-standing bilateral relationship between Canada and the USA, while subject to fluctuations, has generally strengthened over time, particularly in collective border management. Post-9/11, a combination of cooperation and coercion has left the Canadian border more and more similar to a US border checkpoint, not dissimilar to the checkpoints found throughout southern Arizona in the Sonoran borderlands. Anything but absent, the presence of US border 'pre-clearance' crossings at most major Canadian airports, along with coordinated law enforcement and increasingly similar normative approaches to migration, asylum and even refugee health, contributes to how the Canadian border operates more and more as a gasket for US border security. The discourses of 'North America perimeter' and 'Western Hemisphere,' together with increasing institutional similarities (and in some cases even shared assumptions governing said institutions), indicate the increasing challenge for bespoke border security management. As the erstwhile Minister of Citizenship and Immigration Canada (CIC) Denis Coderre noted at a 2003 CIC conference, "the biometrics train has already left the station" (CIC 2003, 21), indicating something between a commitment to these identification technologies, and capitulation to the dominance of these technologies as an industry standard in border security. Contextualised within a shared understanding of exceptionalism, and the supposed need for heightened and intensified sovereign power at a time of enhanced threat and insecurity, in a move towards a more 'seamless' hemispheric border management in North America, the Canadian border is increasingly similar to a US border checkpoint.

The Canadian border may not have died, though certainly its slow but steady transformation towards a US border checkpoint raises serious challenges for civic engagement, let alone forms of political oversight. While members of the political community in Canada might ascribe to certain norms, politics and interests, the border itself becomes more akin to the biopolitical norms of the USA, particularly in terms of imaginations of danger, threat, (in)security and potential exceptions and exclusions. As such, the accounts of the Arizona checkpoints and metaphorical comparisons to the Canada–US border, along with anecdotes of exclusion by US authorities, are far more than interesting. Rather, they are instructive examples of the nature and operation of contemporary Canada–US border security management, and potential ways for action and engagement, similar to those present in the Sonoran borderlands. Not only are NGOs and forms of civic engagement possible and potentially effective, counter-performances that underscore the extent to which the borderland is a space of fluid and mobile identities, contestations and re-imaginations, and not fixed state imaginaries, can have lasting impact. While there are many examples to draw upon, certainly the civic buildings straddling the physical Canada–US border in the towns of Derby Line, Vermont and Stanstead, Quebec, as well as the community members who use them, provide everyday challenges and counter-performances to the account of a divided community forwarded by national imaginaries. Manifest in border facilities, security technologies, and the routinised use of identification cards and passports, as a tourist and traveller, particularly a so-called casual crosser, we might also challenge these narratives of uncertainty, risk, danger and (in)security that the Canadian border as checkpoint increasingly manifests.

References

Agamben, Giorgio. 1998. *Homo Sacer: Sovereign Power and Bare Life*. Stanford, CA: Stanford University Press.

———. 2004. *State of Exception*. Chicago: University of Chicago Press.

Andreas, Peter. 2005. The Mexicanization of the US–Canada Border: Asymmetric Interdependence in a Changing Security Context. *International Journal* 60(2): 449–462.

Babbage, Maria. 2013. US Border's Canadian Health Records Access Of 'Great Concern' to Privacy Watchdog. *The Canadian Press, Huffington Post*, November 29. http://www.huffingtonpost.ca/2013/11/29/us-border-canadian-health-records_n_4360984.html. Accessed 12 Jan 2015.

Bauman, Zygmunt, Didier Bigo, Paulo Esteves, Elspeth Guild, Vivienne Jabri, David Lyon, and R.B.J. Walker. 2014. After Snowden: Rethinking the Impact of Surveillance. *International Political Sociology* 8(2): 121–144.

Bennett, Colin, and David Lyon. 2008. *Playing the Identity Card: Surveillance, Security and Identification in Global Perspective*. London: Routledge.

Bigo, Didier. 2002. Security and Immigration: Toward a Critique of the Governmentality of Unease. *Alternatives: Global, Local, Political* 27: 63–92.

Canadian Broadcasting Corporation. 2009. Canada more Lax than U.S. About Whom it Lets in, Napolitano Says, April 21.

Canadian Mental Health Association. 2015. CMHA Fast facts. http://www.cmha.ca/media/fast-facts-about-mental-illness/#.VZtd6edhRec. Accessed 25 Sep 2015.

Centre for Constitutional Rights. 2015. The Story of Maher Arar: Rendition to Torture. https://ccrjustice.org/sites/default/files/assets/rendition%20to%20torture%20report.pdf. Accessed 29 June 2015.

Citizenship and Immigration Canada (CIC). 2003. *Biometrics: Implications and Applications for Citizenship and Immigration*, Forum Report, 7–8 October 2003, Ottawa, ON, Canada.

Donnan, Hastings, and Thomas Wilson. 1999. *Borders: Frontiers of Identity, Nation and State*. London: Bloomsbury Academic.

Foucault, Michel. 1978. *The History of Sexuality, Vol. 1: An Introduction*. New York: Vintage Books.

———. 1989. *Madness and Civilization: A History of Insanity in the Age of Reason*. London: Routledge.

———. 2010. *The Birth of Biopolitics: Lectures at the Collège de France, 1978–1979*. New York: Picador.

Fukuyama, Francis. 1992. *The End of History and the Last Man*. New York: The Free Press.

Gilbert, Emily. 2007. Leaky Borders and Solid Citizens: Governing Security, Prosperity and Quality of Life in a North American Partnership. *Antipode* 39(1): 77–98.

Hataley, Todd. 2010. Re-Conceptions of National Security in an Age of Terrorism: Implications for Federal Policing in Canada. In *Locating Global Order: American Power and Canadian Security after 9/11*, eds. Bruno Charbonneau and Wayne S. Cox, 183–199. Vancouver: UBC Press.

Hauch, Valerie. 2013. Disabled Woman Denied Entry to US After Agent Cites Supposedly Private Medical Details. *The Toronto Star*, November 23. http://www.thestar.com/news/gta/2013/11/28/disabled_woman_denied_entry_to_us_after_agent_cites_supposedly_private_medical_details.html. Accessed 12 Jan 2015.

Heyman, Josiah, and Howard Campbell. 2012. The Militarization of the United States-Mexico Border Region. *Revista de Estudos Universitários* 38(1): 75–94.

de Hinojosa, Alana. 2013. Fake Border-Crossing Amusement Park Mocks Immigrant Experience. *AlterNet*, July 3. http://www.alternet.org/immigration/fake-border-crossing-amusement-park-makes-mockery-immigrant-experience. Accessed 21 Oct 2013.

Hodge, Roger D. 2011. How the US Is Reengineering Homeland Security on the Borders. *Popular Science*, December. http://www.popsci.com/technology/article/2011-12/how-us-reengineering-homeland-security-borders. Accessed 24 Jan 2012.

Huysmans, Jef. 2000. The European Union and the Securitization of Migration. *Journal of Common Market Studies* 38(5): 751–777.

Koblanck, M. 2010. Special Delivery: The Multilateral Politics of Extraordinary Rendition. In *Mapping Transatlantic Security Relations: The EU, Canada and the War on Terror*, ed. M. Salter, 11–27. London: Routledge.

Larner, Wendy, and William Walters. 2002. The Political Rationality of the "New Regionalism": Toward a Genealogy of the Region. *Theory & Society* 31(3): 391–432.

Lemke, Thomas. 2005. A Zone of Indistinction: A Critique of Giorgio Agamben's Con-Cept of Biopolitics. *Critical Practice Studies* 7(1): 3–13.

Lieberman, Amy. 2014. Arizona's Checkpoint Rebellion. *Slate*, July 20. http://www.slate.com/articles/news_and_politics/politics/2014/07/arizona_immigration_checkpoint_criticism_border_patrol_harasses_people_and.html. Accessed 25 Sep 2014.

Mooers, Colin. 2014. *Imperial Subjects: Citizenship in an Age of Crisis and Empire*. New York: Bloomsbury.

Mountz, Alison. 2011. Specters at the Port of Entry: Understanding State Mobilities Through and Ontology of Exclusion. *Mobilities* 6(3): 317–334.

Muller, Benjamin J. 2008. Securing the Political Imagination: Popular Culture, the Security Dispositif and the Biometric State. *Security Dialogue* 39(2–3): 199–220.

——— 2009. *Security, Risk and the Biometric State: Governing Borders and Bodies*. London: Routledge.

——— 2010. Unsafe at Any Speed? Borders, Mobility and 'Safe Citizenship'. *Citizenship Studies* 14(1): 75–88.

——— 2013. Borderworld: Biometrics, AVATAR, and Global Criminalization. In *Globalisation and the Challenge to Criminology*, ed. Francis Pakes, 129–145. London: Routledge.

Salter, Mark B. 2009. Rethinking Aviation Security Screening. In *Protecting Airline Passengers in the Age of Terrorism*, eds. Paul Seidenstat and Francis X. Splane. Westport, CT: Praeger.

———, ed. 2015. *Making Things International: Circuits and Motion*. University of Minnesota Press: Minneapolis, MN.

Santos, Fernanda. 2014. Border Patrol Scrutiny Stirs Anger in Arizona Town. *New York Times*, June 27. http://www.nytimes.com/2014/06/28/us/border-patrol-scrutiny-stirs-anger-in-arizona-town.html?_r=0. Accessed 24 Sep 2014.

Sheridan, Thomas. 1992. *Los Tucsonenses: The Mexican Community in Tucson, 1854–1941*. Tucson, AZ: University of Arizona Press.

Solomon, Andrew. 2013. Shameful Profiling of the Mentally Ill. *The New York Times*, December 7.

Spitzer, Steven. 1987. Security and Control in Capitalist Societies: The Fetishism of Security and the Secret Thereof. In *Transcarceration: Essays in the Sociology of Social Control*, eds. J. Lowman, R. Menzies, and T. Palyis, 43–58. Brookfield, VT: Gower Publishing.

US Citizenship and Immigration Services Policy Manual. n.d. USCIS. http://www.uscis.gov/policymanual/HTML/PolicyManual.html. Accessed 12 Jan 2015.

US Immigration and Nationality Act, Department of Homeland Security. n.d. http://www.uscis.gov/iframe/ilink/docView/SLB/HTML/SLB/act.html. Accessed 12 Jan 2015.

Vaughan-Williams, Nick. 2009. *Border Politics: The Limits of Sovereign Power*. Edinburgh: Edinburgh University Press.

Walker, Rob B.J. 1993. *Inside/Outside: International Relations as Political Theory*. Cambridge: Cambridge University Press.

Zhorov, Irina, and Fronteras. 2013. Mexican Amusement Park Offers Fake Border Crossing Attraction. *PBS Newshour*, June 24. http://www.pbs.org/newshour/rundown/fake-border-crossing-is-amusement-park-attraction/. Accessed 21 Oct 2013.

14

Surveillance and the Colonial Dream: Canada's Surveillance of Indigenous Self-Determination

Tia Dafnos, Scott Thompson, and Martin French

[The 1995 slaying of Dudley George by the Ontario Provincial Police] stands as only one case study among many that demonstrates the risk posed to [First Nations] by legislation that gives heightened powers to police, narrows the civil rights of those involved in legitimate dissent and protest activities, and limits or suspends the civil rights of those perceived by the government to be involved in 'terrorist' activities ... the repeated characterization of [First Nations] peoples as insurgents in the past justifies our grave concerns about the risk of anti-terrorism legislation harming our

T. Dafnos (✉)
Department of Sociology, University of New Brunswick, Fredericton, NB, Canada

S. Thompson
Department of Sociology, Queens University, Kingston, ON, Canada

M. French
Department of Sociology and Anthropology, Concordia University, Montreal, QC, Canada

© The Author(s) 2016   **319**
R. Lippert et al. (eds.), *National Security, Surveillance and Terror*,
DOI 10.1007/978-3-319-43243-4_14

most basic rights. (Matthew Coon Come 2001, then National Chief of the Assembly of First Nations)[1]

Bill C-51 [Canada's new anti-terrorism legislation, creates] conditions where our people will be labelled as threats—threats to critical infrastructure or the economic stability of Canada—when asserting their individual or collective rights as [First Nations] citizens. This is not an abstract argument for our people. (Perry Bellegarde 2015, National Chief of the Assembly of First Nations)[2]

In 2001, and again in 2015, significant legislative developments designed to respond to the spectre of terrorism transformed Canada's national security and surveillance apparatuses. The first of these developments, which occurred in the wake of 9/11, was the 'massive and hastily drafted *Antiterrorism Act* (Bill C-36),' which 'included new legal concepts' like 'preventative arrests' and 'broad motive-based crimes for participation in or support for terrorist groups' (Roach 2003, 8). The second, more contemporary development is a response to two separate attacks against Canadian Forces members, and an incident in which an assailant discharged a gun within Canada's parliament buildings (see Van Brunschot, this volume). Quickly characterised by Canada's prime minister as "a grim reminder that Canada is not immune to the types of terrorist attacks we have seen elsewhere around the world" (Chase 2014), these events were leveraged by the Conservative federal government to justify new legislation that further expands Canada's surveillance and security apparatuses. As in 2001, experts and stakeholders have expressed concern about Canada's latest antiterror legislation. Critiques have focused on, among other issues, the amorphous definition of terrorism and the lack of transparency and oversight of organisations—like the Communications Security Establishment (CSE) and the Canadian Security Intelligence Service (CSIS)—equipped with new powers to identify and disrupt suspected terrorist activity.

---

[1] Coon Come, M. Statement Made Before the Standing Committee on Justice and Human Rights, [Concerning Bill C-36], Thursday, November 1, 2001. Online at: http://www.parl.gc.ca/HousePublications/Publication.aspx?Pub=CommitteeMeetingEvidence&Acronym=JUST&Mee=41&Language=e&Mode=1&Parl=37&Ses=1.

[2] Bellegarde, P. Statement Made Before the Standing Committee on Public Safety and National Security [Concerning Bill C-51], Thursday, March 12, 2015. Online at: http://www.parl.gc.ca/HousePublications/Publication.aspx?DocId=7876601&Language=E&Mode=1&Parl=41&Ses=2.

As the above epigraphs indicate, the Assembly of First Nations (AFN) has been a staunch critic of the legislatively-driven expansion of these surveillance and security apparatuses.[3] In 2001, and again in 2015, AFN leaders expressed concern about the potential of Canada's antiterrorism measures to criminalise self-determining Indigenous communities. The AFN situates the expansion of Canada's security and surveillance apparatuses in the long history of colonialism. From this perspective, Canada's national security initiatives represent a continuation of the 'colonial dream' that envisions the 'pacification, containment, and demobilization' of Indigenous communities (Simpson 2014, 127; see also Deloria 2004). The presence of self-determining Indigenous peoples always has been troublesome for the settler state[4] and, perhaps, has always represented an unspoken rationale for the long-standing effort to control Indigenous identity. Yet, inasmuch as recent developments represent a continuity of long-standing colonial anxieties about Indigenous self-determination, they also reconfigure institutional roles and practices, thereby intensifying the scrutiny of Indigenous communities.

Currently, surveillance and control efforts occur within the emergency management paradigm of national security (Dafnos 2013). Within this paradigm, assertions of Indigenous self-determination and jurisdiction are commonly conceptualised as potential threats to critical infrastructure. To illustrate this conceptualisation and its consequences, in what follows we detail some recent institutional mutations and surveillance activities.

We first describe the ideology of the colonial dream and its connection to the surveillance and pacification of Indigenous communities. We explore historical features of British colonial governance practices, which, via the concept of colonial emergency, provide the context for our discussion of present-day surveillance apparatuses. Next we provide a genealogy of twenty-first century developments in Canadian national security legislation and policy. This allows us to sketch the rise of the emergency

---

[3] The AFN is a national advocacy organisation representing First Nation citizens and communities (http://www.afn.ca/index.php/en/about-afn/description-of-the-afn).

[4] Settler states are colonial formations that assert territorial and political sovereignty through the expropriation of land and the suppression of Indigenous peoples and their social-political formations.

management paradigm of national security, and the concomitant fixation in law and policy upon securing critical infrastructure. We then describe some of the complex apparatuses that monitor Indigenous expressions of self-determination in Canada. Although capacities and effects of these institutions and processes are dynamic, our mapping efforts detail key organisational actors, thereby providing signposts for future empirical research. We conclude our chapter with a discussion of implications of these developments for how expressions of Indigenous self-determination fit within the developing emergency management paradigm and its conceptualisation of threats to the state.

The 'Colonial Dream': Surveillance as a Mode of Colonial Governance

The concept of the colonial dream, articulated by historian Philip Deloria, is useful for thinking critically about the settler-state's surveillance of Indigenous communities. Fundamental to this dream has been an ideology of pacification, which, Deloria argues, bridged:

> between the most powerful expectations of the eighteenth and nineteenth centuries—violence and Indian disappearance—and those of the twentieth, which clustered around various forms of primitivism. On the one hand, pacification rearticulated the vanishing-Indian ideology of the mid-nineteenth century, which erased white acts of dispossession and generously mourned the fact that Indians were disappearing naturally. [...] On the other hand, pacification also rendered Indians safe, thereby opening up their lives and lands to the visitations of various breeds of primitivists. (Deloria 2004, 50)

The ideology of pacification, and the 'colonial dream of fixity, control, visibility, productivity, and most important, docility,' were, of course, never fully realised (ibid., 27). But they provided an impetus for the development of an extensive surveillance assemblage, including tribal rolls that 'recorded individuals, along with pertinent demographic information,' church records that noted familial relations, ration-disbursement records that tracked food consumption, agency records that noted infractions, property, character, education and employment history, as well as allotment records that mapped individuals and families in space and sought to make Indigenous peoples 'intimately visible to the colonial bureaucracy' (ibid., 26).

Taking up Deloria's description of the colonial dream in her critique of the Canadian government's mapping and occupation of Mohawk territory, Simpson notes that 'historical practices of state surveillance' still profoundly shape contemporary social relations, via an ideology of pacification (Simpson 2014, 127). 'In order to be actualized in the present,' she writes, 'this dream requires that Indigenous economic activities be watched, that there be a state police presence in their community, and that Indians be passive in the face of this surveillance, regulation, scrutiny, and possible intervention' (ibid.). Deloria's analysis, developed by Simpson, clarifies both the connectedness of current surveillance apparatuses with the extension of long-standing colonial desires into the present through the settler-state's surveillance. When we speak of surveillance as a mode of colonial governance, we invoke both the past system of colonial subjugation, and what Simpson describes as the contemporary reality 'of colonialism's ongoing existence and simultaneous failure' (ibid., 7).

What is vital here is the relationship between surveillance and the dream of pacification. Pacification is an ongoing process, aimed at producing a specific 'peace' through 'civilising' political and legal strategies to capture 'hearts and minds' and through military dominance (Neocleous 2010). Pacification entails destructive and constitutive practices towards producing capitalist-colonial order. This is most contingent on the displacement and containment of Indigenous peoples and social systems that stand in the way of capitalist modes of production (Alfred 2005).

Scholars have described the connection between various pacification projects and surveillance (e.g. Neocleous 2010). As a key object of the contemporary colonial dream, pacification is inscribed into the process of classifying Indigenous subjectivities as risks to be watched and policed (Dafnos 2013). Surveillance apparatuses equate self-determining Indigenous subjectivities with risks often within terrorism discourses. To understand what the incorporation of critical infrastructure security into everyday government practices means, we situate the current moment within continuing histories of the colonial dream of instilling 'proper' productive practices within Indigenous communities and land bases, and the adoption of the political mechanism of colonial emergency to exert authority over Indigenous sovereignty. After discussing these colonial rationalities, this chapter demonstrates how surveillance, the emergency management paradigm, and the colonial dream converge within the Canadian polity.

The Colonial Regulation of Productive Practice

Historical North American colonial governance practices regarding Indigenous peoples stem primarily from British imperial conceptualisations of order, race struggle, and productivity. Within imperial rationalities, the superiority of British productive practices was asserted through the concept of 'social efficiency,' a term tied to social Darwinism and race struggle literatures, which links racial and cultural superiority to the capacity of specific peoples to most efficiently use natural and human resources. British superiority in social efficiency was evidenced by the capacity of the British race to expand into new territories and subdue 'primitive' races, and this efficiency argument was used to justify colonial expansion and the subjugation of others to British rule (Hobson [1938] 2005, 155). As Deherme (cited in Conklin) claimed:

> the most important result of colonization is to increase world productivity. [...] The earth belongs to humanity. It belongs to those who know best how to develop it, increase its wealth and in the process augment it, beatify it and elevate humanity. Colonization is the propagation of the highest form of civilization yet conceived and realized. (Conklin [1908] 1997, 56)

Colonisation was rarely understood by colonisers as oppressive or self-serving; rather, it was viewed as liberating, since it supposedly re-ordered modes of production of 'lesser' cultures, rendering them compatible with 'proper,' more 'efficient,' British forms. In this way, social efficiency arguments worked as 'the chief moral support' of colonialism (Grant 1890, 29) and the commercial exploitation of colonies.

Indigenous peoples complicated this deluded vision of colonial social efficiency. They were viewed as posing a significant risk through their 'disordered' political structures and 'inefficient' productive practices (Hobson [1902] 2005, 118, 122). British imperialism conceptualised it as the duty, even the burden, of colonialist governments to convert the native land and labour power into rightful 'proper' British productive forms. As a result, any independence of Indigenous peoples, or claims to land or self-governance found to be incompatible with British productive practices, were deemed direct risks to the prosperity of all and the success of the entire colonial project (Hobson [1902] 2005).

As the productive practices of the North American colonies shifted in the 1830s, from one with a reliance on Indigenous extraction of goods for trade and export to one in which Europeans sought to permanently settle land and directly supply markets with agricultural products, fish and other goods, 'the rights and ways of life of the Aboriginal people on whose lands this new economic activity was to take place' were re-defined as 'impediments to productive development' (*Royal Commission on Aboriginal Peoples* 1996, 115). With this productive shift, Indigenous peoples were seen less and less 'as nations worthy of consideration in the political councils of the now secure British colonies,' and more as 'an unproductive draw on the public purse' in need of colonial governance and education as to how to fit their land and labour into new economic practices (Ibid.). Soon after, passage of the *Gradual Civilization Act* and later the *Indian Act*, gave officials legal control over Indigenous lands and resources and confined 'Indians' to reserves 'out of the way of development' (Craik 2004, 168). It is not insignificant that, with this increasing perception of Indigenous incompatibility with economic activity, the commercial use of Indigenous lands made the disruption of economic supply chains a key form of political action (Cowen 2014; Pasternak 2013). It is useful to situate the settler-state's contemporary response to this form of political action in relation to a key mechanism of British imperial rule, the colonial emergency, which underlies more diffuse anxieties motivating the colonial dream.

Colonial Emergency

The 'colonial emergency' is a political mechanism of managing threats to imperial power based on the 'prerogative power' of executive authority and with legal foundations in martial law within British political-legal theory. These political-legal mechanisms are based on the power to declare a 'state of exception' (Agamben 2005). Conceptually and discursively, the 'exception,' and specific mechanisms such as 'emergency measures' or 'martial law,' are defined by opposition to the 'norm' and more concretely, to the *rule of law*. The state's use of coercive interventions or omissions aimed at the elimination of threats is legitimated by security logics to defend the body-politic and nation-state sovereignty. As Rifkin (2009), Morgensen (2011) and others have emphasised, the principle of 'state of exception' in Western legal systems emerged out of colonialism and the elimination of Indigenous nations.

The concept of 'emergency' allowed liberal democratic states to maintain the authoritarian 'prerogative power' of rulers in a legal form consistent with principles of liberalism (Neocleous 2008). This prerogative emergency power had been instrumental to British imperialism to assert control through political and coercive means (see Hussain 2003; Furedi 1993; Neocleous 2008) and had been transferred to colonial and post-colonial governments through 'emergency law' (Hussain 2003). Importantly, Furedi (1993) points out that 'emergencies' were not always *reactive* responses to uprisings or unrest, but were also 'pre-planned attempts at the political management of anti-colonial forces' (90). The exercise of emergency and prerogative power therefore relies on continuous surveillance of Aboriginal peoples.

The British Crown transferred prerogative power to the Canadian state through the 1867 *British North America Act*. Sect. 91 invested the federal government with authority to make laws in the interests of 'Peace, Order, and Good Government,' including 'extraordinary measures to deal with emergencies' (Valverde 2006, 78). British colonial prerogative power in governing Indigenous peoples was also transferred through Sect. 91(24), as responsibility for 'Indians and lands reserved for Indians' (Valverde 2006). Williamson (2009) describes Sect. 91(24) as a 'constitutionalized state of exception' that makes it 'both natural and expected that Indians receive differential treatment' (73).

Through this constitutionalised 'exception,' 'exceptional' use of settler-state power vis-à-vis Indigenous peoples is normalised. This has been evident in the contemporary national security assemblage in which the entwined concerns of 'proper' land use and the settler-state's assertion of political-territorial sovereignty coalesce to secure critical infrastructure.

(Re)Defining Risks to the Settler State: Emergency Management Paradigm of National Security

The emergency management paradigm of national security reflects a conceptual and institutional-bureaucratic *convergence* of emergency preparedness and national security functions of the state (Dunn Cavelty and Kristensen 2008). This convergence revolves around the common object of securing critical infrastructure from natural and 'human-induced' (i.e. accidents, terrorism, and 'civil unrest') threats. It is in the conceptualisation of 'critical infrastructure' that the historical colonial dream meets the reality of today's national security practice, though it is also exactly where these national security practices directly conflict with Indigenous sovereignty. In this way, critical infrastructure is the embodiment of the state's definition of 'proper' land use, while its 'critical' status opens the door to state exertion of emergency powers and measures to *ensure* the continuance of this form of productive practice. Where Indigenous sovereignty ensures the Indigenous right to choose how land is allocated, resources are used, and supply chains established, this vision of national security works to ensure that state-determined land allocation, resource use, and supply chains take primacy at all costs. Importantly, where visions of land allocation, resource use, and the maintenance of supply chains do not directly align, acts of Indigenous sovereignty are pitted against acts of national security. Canada's shift to a 'critical infrastructure' focus has thus intensified the potential for conflict between Indigenous sovereignty and national security actors.

As in Australia (as well as the USA, UK, and New Zealand), the intensification and concretisation of the emergency management paradigm in Canada occurred in the early 2000s with the introduction of new policies, funding, and legislation in the post-9/11 political climate. This has blurred the distinction between protest and security risk. For example, although the 2001 *Anti-terrorism Act*'s definition of terrorist activity explicitly excludes 'advocacy, protest, dissent or stoppage of work that is not intended to result in' 'serious bodily harm,' endangerment of life, or 'serious risk to health or safety of the public or any segment of the public,' as expressed by Matthew Coon Come in the epigraph above, direct actions such as blockades could be constructed as potential disruptions that could pose risks to safety.[5] And, although the 2001 legislation did not use the term, the definition of terrorist activity centres on threats to 'critical infrastructure.' Indeed, in subsequent policy initiatives, securing critical infrastructure would emerge as an explicit concern.

The 2004 National Security Policy (NSP), for example, provided the groundwork for an 'integrated security system,' to 'prepare for and respond to a range of security threats, including terrorist attacks, outbreaks of infectious diseases, natural disasters, cyber-attacks on critical infrastructure and domestic extremism' (Government of Canada 2004). Towards the interconnected objectives of enhancing state intelligence capacity and establishing an emergency management framework (Government of Canada 2004), core NSP initiatives included the establishment of the Integrated Threat Assessment Centre (ITAC) within CSIS, the development of a new Emergency Management Framework, and the creation of a Critical Infrastructure Strategy and Action Plan. As discussed in the following section, these policy frameworks have enabled new surveillance practices.

Object of Security: Critical Infrastructure

The 2009 'National Strategy for Critical Infrastructure' policy defines 'critical infrastructure' as 'processes, systems, facilities, technologies, networks, assets and services essential to the health, safety, security or economic well-being of Canadians and the effective functioning of government' (Public Safety Canada 2009, 2). Ten sectors are identified as comprising Canada's critical infrastructure: energy and utilities, finance, food, transportation, government, information and communication technology, health, water, safety and manufacturing (Public Safety Canada 2009). The actual *or potential* disruption of critical infrastructure is defined as a national security threat because it is described as essential

---

[5] Coon Come, M. Statement Made Before the Standing Committee on Justice and Human Rights, [Concerning Bill C-36], Thursday, November 1, 2001.

to the functioning of the state and well-being of the population. At the same time, over 85 per cent of critical infrastructure is privately owned and operated. This emphasis is similar to Australia (Palmer and Whelan 2006) and makes the security of critical infrastructure not just a biopolitical concern with the health and safety of population, but also links, as reflected in Public Safety Canada's definition, the functioning of the state to the economic security of private corporations. This finds practical expression as the safeguarding of processes and facilities that produce profits for owner-operators and shareholders.

Consistent with trends in the USA, UK, and Australia (Palmer and Whelan 2006), the Canadian Government adopted what is defined as an 'all-hazards' approach in its 2007 *Emergency Management Act (EMA)*. The *EMA* requires each federal department to manage its own 'risk environment' consisting of the department itself and the sector under its administration. The Critical Infrastructure Action Plan designates a lead department for each of the ten sectors (see also Walby and Lippert, this volume). For these departments, emergency management is aimed at ensuring the 'resilience' of material and circulatory infrastructures. The all-hazards approach of the *EMA* adopts a model of emergency management based on four pillars: mitigation, preparedness, response, and recovery.

Distinguishing the *EMA* from previous models of emergency preparedness is its emphasis on whole-of-government coordination, reflecting the priorities of the National Security Policy. The *EMA* model emphasises greater information-and-intelligence sharing among state and corporate institutions through both formal and informal mechanisms. This is intended to increase the ability to predict risks and thus to prevent or to mitigate threats through a coordinated response. The logics of the all-hazards emergency management framework of national security create insatiable demands for constant *situational awareness*, and in this way push for both the proliferation of information and intelligence production activities, as well as new and more effective mechanisms to enable the circulation of information and intelligence.[6] The breadth of the 'all-hazards'

---

[6] The concept of situational awareness first became popular in the context of air safety. It has typically implied perception of spatial and temporal elements in the physical environment. With Hier and Walby (2014), and others, we are primarily interested here in its recent problematic application to crowd management and emergency response.

approach reflects a definitional and structural expansion of governance through the mechanism of emergency.

Echoing the logic of the 'colonial emergency,' these practices and mechanisms work in distinct ways as the monitoring of Indigenous peoples as an *'exceptional' population* is seen to be *normalised*. Indigenous peoples and whole communities may be directly implicated within this framework as 'threats to national security' in two primary contexts: where 'critical infrastructure' is located on or near First Nations communities, or when the assertion of rights and jurisdiction creates *insecurities* for the state and corporations. Whether through legal challenges or direct actions such as blockades, historically successful forms of Indigenous activism have worked to directly and indirectly impact what has been defined as critical infrastructure, especially in the energy and utilities, manufacturing, and transportation sectors. In this way, the folding of private owner-operators into emergency management effectively conceptualises indigenous threats to colonialist 'proper' development not simply as 'backwards' or 'inefficient,' but also within discourses and institutionalised responses of emergency.

Key Actors in the Contemporary "Critical Infrastructure" Surveillance Assemblage

Below we chart the expansion of post-9/11 surveillance apparatuses, which can be conceptualised in terms of the interfacing of two sets of state actors. One set consists of law enforcement and national security agencies, and the other consists of government departments, which, although they do not have formal law enforcement mandates, are folded into the national security assemblage via emergency management of critical infrastructure. In this paradigm, a third set of actors is being incorporated into the assemblage: the private owner-operators of critical infrastructure. These three sets of actors are inter- and intra-connected via information and intelligence sharing. We highlight how these institutions, processes, and infrastructures work as *colonial* institutions of pacification.

The Law Enforcement-Security Actors

Below we detail three key law-enforcement-security organisational actors: CSIS' Integrated Threat Assessment Centre (ITAC), the Royal Canadian Mounted Police (RCMP), and regional-local police forces. The expansion and entanglement of these actors has intensified within the emergency management paradigm.

CSIS and the Integrated Terrorism Assessment Centre

Housed within CSIS, ITAC was established in 2004 as part of Canada's National Security Policy. ITAC reflects efforts to facilitate and increase intelligence production and sharing in the vein of 'fusion centres' in the USA (cf. Monahan and Regan 2012). Renamed the Integrated Terrorism Assessment Centre in June 2011, ITAC centralises the collection and analysis of national security intelligence from partner agencies such as the RCMP, the CSE, and other government departments, including Aboriginal Affairs and Northern Development Canada (AANDC). ITAC produces threat assessments, which are intended as 'integrated analyses of the intent and capability of terrorists to carry out attacks' (ITAC n.d.). These reports are disseminated to partners, emergency responders, and the private sector.

In 2007, ITAC produced regular assessments about the National Day of Action (NDA).[7] AANDC representatives were embedded within ITAC before and during the NDA to facilitate information sharing. These threat assessments note that, while peaceful protest is legitimate in democratic societies, 'Aboriginal protests' *could* become a national security concern 'where there is a threat of politically motivated violence or where protests threaten the functioning of critical infrastructure' (ITAC 2007). Throughout 2007 and 2008, ITAC produced multiple reports on 'Aboriginal protest' focusing on potential for 'violence' and/or critical infrastructure disruption, and the possi-

---

[7] The 29 June 2007 National Day of Action was organised to raise awareness. Over 50 demonstrations (among other events) occurred across Canada, including five blockades not endorsed by the AFN.

bility of sparking wider mobilisations. 'Aboriginal communities' and warrior societies have also been discussed in ITAC's 2010 and 2012 'Bi-annual Update[s] on the Threat from Terrorists and Extremists' under 'domestic-issue-based extremism,' because of the enduring issues of sovereignty and land claims coupled with periodic advocacy of 'violence' (ITAC 2010). These reports effectively blur 'categories of "terrorism" and "extremism," by which "extremism" becomes a catch-all for a host of groups associated with civil disobedience and direct action' (Monaghan and Walby 2012a, 144; see also Monaghan and Walby 2012b).

RCMP: The Aboriginal JIG and the Critical Infrastructure Intelligence Team

After 9/11, the bulk of new federal funding for national security went to the RCMP. The RCMP's return to national security investigations and its concerns with critical infrastructure have had several implications for Indigenous activism. One implication was the creation, in 2007, of an Aboriginal Joint Intelligence Group (JIG) within the RCMP's Criminal Intelligence Directorate. The Aboriginal JIG was mandated to "produce and disseminate intelligence concerning conflict and issues associated with Aboriginal communities" (RCMP 2009a, 5). The intent of the Aboriginal JIG was to develop an information-intelligence sharing network with partners including CSIS, the Ontario Provincial Police, Sûreté Sûreté du Québec, Natural Resources Canada and AANDC. Among its activities, the Aboriginal JIG produced weekly Situation Reports, and annual 'Communities of Concern' reports which included profiles of several Indigenous communities with specific ongoing or potential conflicts that could lead to 'civil disobedience and unrest' including 'grievances pertaining to land claims, treaty disputes, environmental issues, economic and sovereignty disputes, internal conflict and social issues' (RCMP 2009b). These reports reflect the centrality of critical infrastructure for surveillance practices. They include maps coupled with community profiles that clearly mark their relationship with and proximity to critical infrastructure points such as railways, electricity transmission towers, and highways. By 2009, these reports were being disseminated to approximately 450 'partners.'

The Aboriginal JIG was officially disbanded in November 2009 and monitoring of Indigenous protests involving threats to critical infrastructure became the full responsibility of the RCMP's National Security Criminal Investigations' Critical Infrastructure Intelligence Team (CIIT). The CIIT developed, as part of the broader Critical Infrastructure Strategy, a Critical Infrastructure Criminal Intelligence (CICI) programme, and was tasked with monitoring threats to infrastructure and developing partnerships with private owner-operators of critical infrastructure.

As of 2014, the CIIT engages in ongoing 'monitoring' of six critical infrastructure sectors: energy and utilities, transportation, finance, government, information and communication technology, and manufacturing (Murphy 2014). With the majority of critical infrastructure being privately owned-operated, the CIIT's monitoring is significantly dependent on the participation of corporate third parties, which are both 'clients' (recipients of intelligence) and sources of information and intelligence (RCMP 2007). Recognition of this dependency has led the RCMP to actively pursue partnerships. A key mechanism facilitating exchange of information and intelligence among law enforcement, government agencies and private sector actors is the Suspicious Incident Reporting (SIR) system. The SIR is a web-based portal, and critical infrastructure owner-operators have access to system information and the ability to contribute/report 'suspicious incidents' relating to their infrastructure and operations. These intelligence products are developed by sector-specific CIIT analysts based on the information provided by owner-operators; they are then disseminated to law enforcement, emergency management partners, and the owner-operators.

Ostensibly, the SIR does not target Indigenous communities, activists, and protests. However, in practice, information gathering on Indigenous communities, activists and protests does occur. For example, in 2013, a SIR file was created after the National Energy Board raised concerns about the security of hearings and possible threats to board members. Despite the lack of any intelligence showing possible threats, monitoring was initiated because of 'sustained opposition to the Canadian petroleum and pipeline industry' and by the fact that protest actions have previously occurred (Millar 2013; for a discussion of similar, tenuously justified instances of surveillance initiation within the SIR, see Dafnos 2015).

Other key components of the RCMP's National Security programme are Integrated National Security Enforcement Teams (INSETs), composed of representatives from multiple law enforcement and government agencies, which facilitate information-intelligence sharing and joint 'counter-terrorism' activities. INSETs have been established in Vancouver, Toronto, Ottawa and Montreal, and, reflecting energy sector concerns about threats to the oil sands industry, Edmonton. In 2002 and 2005, INSET operations targeted members of the West Coast Warrior Society. While no one was charged with offences, these *disruptive* operations contributed to the Society disbanding in 2005 (Young 2005).

Front-Line Policing: The 'Eyes and Ears' of Surveillance

With the emphasis on intelligence sharing, a key piece in the national security assemblage is front-line policing that collects information in the course of everyday activities. As former OPP Commissioner Julian Fantino stated during a parliamentary hearing in 2007, at the root of an intelligence apparatus are "[f]ront-line officers plugged in at the community level through contacts and relationships [who] represent a well-trained human radar system such that, if properly trained and resourced, can detect and report suspicious persons and activities that might constitute potential terrorist threats" (Parliament of Canada 2007). This logic has particular implications for the policing of activism.

Many policing initiatives have been introduced since the late 1990s that emphasise trust and relationship-building with activists and Indigenous communities. A major objective of these liaison or outreach initiatives is to encourage communication among police, communities, and protest organisers. While this may be effective for de-escalating police responses, it also involves obtaining information that, because of reporting requirements, feeds into situational awareness of the broader national security and surveillance apparatuses (Dafnos 2013).

Emergency Management Actors

In addition to the law-enforcement security organisational actors, it is crucial to detail the operations of emergency management actors, which do not have a law-enforcement mandate, but are nevertheless integral to monitoring indigenous expressions of self-determination. As with our discussion of the law-enforcement security actors, our description below is not exhaustive but focuses on prime movers: the AANDC and the GOC.

AANDC: The Indian Agent 2.0

The Indian Agent once represented the surveillant face of the Indian Affairs bureaucracy.[8] Today, the Indian Agent no longer exists, but the surveillant activities of the bureaucracy have been intensified by the logics of the 'all-hazards' emergency management paradigm.

In the proliferating emergency management framework of national security, AANDC has had a central role as both 'subject matter expert' for other agencies, and as a major source of information about Indigenous communities and their activism. Under the 2007 *Emergency Management Act*, AANDC was required to implement the all-hazards approach to managing risks to the department and risks affecting and *emanating* from First Nations reserve communities. According to its National Emergency Management Plan, 'all-hazards' is 'dependent on the situation' but includes all 'issues of civil unrest.' AANDC's Emergency and Issues Management Directorate (EIMD) has defined the scope of its monitoring to include 'civil unrest' that occurs *outside* reserve communities and outside AANDC's jurisdiction because 'the outcomes of these events have a direct impact on First Nations and, by extension, on the Department' (INAC 2010, 18, 32). In the circular logic of emergency management, 'civil unrest' is ostensibly categorised as an *issue*; 'issues' are situations that if escalated 'could become an emergency by definition' (AANDC 2011, 3).

---

[8] 'Indian Affairs' refers to the institutional bureaucracy established by the federal government to 'manage' Indigenous peoples. This bureaucracy has been renamed several times. It is currently called Indigenous and Northern Affairs Canada. At the time of writing it was called Aboriginal Affairs and Northern Development Canada (AANDC).

The catalyst for formalisation of AANDC's EIMD in 2007 was the impending National Day of Action, which, as discussed above, heightened demands for situational awareness through continuous monitoring and reporting to facilitate strategic law enforcement and government responses. The Emergency Operations Centre of the EIMD at AANDC national headquarters produces 'situational awareness' in the form of situation reports, notifications, weekly, weekend, and/or 'hotspots' summary reports. The most common types of events in these reports are forest fires, flooding, and 'civil unrest.' Unlike the RCMP and CSIS, AANDC monitoring is not limited to people or activities where there is a perceived criminal activity or national security dimension. There are therefore a much wider range of 'issues,' and thus, communities captured in EIMD monitoring (see Diabo and Pasternak 2011).

EIMD reports are compiled from information collected by AANDC regional offices by EIMD employees through open source monitoring, and from 'partners,' including other government departments and law-enforcement agencies through their own monitoring activities. These reports are disseminated throughout the AANDC bureaucracy to keep officials updated on emerging and ongoing matters, as well as to inform decision-making. Reports are also disseminated to external partners, including the Assembly of First Nations, Transport Canada, Justice Canada, The Privy Council Office, CSIS, the RCMP, provincial police forces and the Government Operations Centre.

Government Operations Centre

A central mechanism of integrated emergency management is the Government Operations Centre (GOC), housed in Public Safety Canada. The GOC is the hub for situational awareness relating to critical infrastructure threats. It collects intelligence from law enforcement and emergency management agencies, federal and provincial government departments, and other 'stakeholders.' In turn, GOC reports to these partners, with the aim of producing constant national-level situational awareness to support whole-of-government responses to issues and emergencies.

Despite GOC's insistence that activities are solely concerned with critical infrastructure threats, this is countered by their monitoring of activities where an emergency or critical infrastructure dimension is non-existent (Dafnos 2015). While concerns about rail, highway, or road blockades could be justified as falling under the GOC purview using the emergency management logic, events such as 'teach-ins' (grassroots meetings designed to raise awareness and to develop strategies to address political issues) reflect the political interests underlying this kind of 'monitoring.'

In June 2014, the GOC circulated a memo to federal departments and partner agencies requesting assistance in 'compiling a comprehensive listing of all known demonstrations which will occur either in your geographical area or that may touch on your mandate' (reported in Pugliese 2014). This information would then be disseminated by GOC to partners, with sensitive information reserved for the production of GOC Situational Awareness reports. Documents released under the *Access to Information Act* in 2014 show that the majority of protests reported to the GOC were related to Indigenous or environmental activism. Considering the extent of its monitoring, it is not surprising that AANDC is the main source of reporting to the GOC about Indigenous protests.

Conclusions

The introduction of Bill C-51 will further shape the development of these national security apparatuses. It is important, however, to situate the contemporary assemblage in the ongoing settler-colonial project of pacification, which works to suppress social–political–economic forms deemed obstructive to constituting a 'proper' capitalist-colonial formation. The increased surveillance of Indigenous communities and activists can be contextualised by the implementation of an emergency management paradigm of national security concerned with the protection of critical infrastructure, and the economic prioritisation of specific forms of natural resource extraction and commercial exploitation.

While the emergency management paradigm of national security has implications for civil dissent generally, it is especially significant for

Indigenous struggles because the assertion of self-determination fundamentally challenges the settler-state's claim to sovereignty. The potential for disruption of critical infrastructure has become the primary explicit rationale of police forces, intelligence agencies, government departments and private corporations for their surveillance of Indigenous communities, groups, and individuals. With the explicit identification of critical infrastructure as a primary object of national security, these practices are *rationalised and depoliticised* through the logics of safety, 'proper' development, and emergency management.

Additionally, as federal and provincial governments prioritise increasingly expansive policies of resource development, they have growing potential to conflict with acts of Indigenous sovereignty. This policy orientation stresses the centrality of Canada's natural resource sector, which constitutes 14 percent of Canada's economy (Natural Resources Canada 2014), and reasserts the risk of further conflict between acts of Indigenous sovereignty and national security. More than two-thirds of all rail and marine shipments in Canada are natural resource products (ibid.). The circulation of these products, which ties together circuits traversing energy, manufacturing, and transportation infrastructures, epitomises the capitalist-colonial settler-state's preoccupation with land use and resource extraction as central commercial and national security priorities. Such circuits of extraction also represent a key site for assertions of Indigenous rights and jurisdiction.

The settler-state's attempt to rationalise and depoliticise its colonial dream through burgeoning, secretive critical infrastructure surveillance apparatuses is problematic, not only because it pits Indigenous self-determination against national security, but also because of its allocation of policing resources to the surveillance of Indigenous groups. In stark contrast with the vast state resources deployed in securing conditions amenable to accumulation has been an utter disavowal of the state's responsibility to provide security for Indigenous women or to investigate their deaths and disappearances (Simpson 2014). This is evidenced by the scandalously high number of unsolved cases of missing and murdered Indigenous women and girls,[9] to which the Canadian federal government pays

---

[9] See, for example: http://www.cbc.ca/missingandmurdered/.

lip-service while simultaneously devoting its security resources elsewhere. This circumstance makes clear the violence inherent in the colonial dream and the ideology of pacification.

References

Aboriginal Affairs and Northern Development Canada. 2011. *Aboriginal Affairs and Northern Development Canada (AANDC) National Emergency Management Plan.* Ottawa: Public Works and Government Services Canada.

Agamben, Giorgio. 2005. *State of Exception.* Chicago: University of Chicago Press.

Alfred, Taiaiake. 2005. *Wasáse: Indigenous Pathways of Action and Freedom.* Peterborough: Broadview Press.

Chase, Steven. 2014. Prime Minister Labels Shootings as 'Terrorist' Acts. *The Globe and Mail*, October 22. http://www.theglobeandmail.com/news/national/in-national-address-prime-minister-labels-shootings-as-terrorist-acts/article21252133/#dashboard/follows/.

Conklin, Alice L. 1997. *A Mission to Civilize.* Stanford, CA: Stanford University Press.

Cowen, Deborah. 2014. *The Deadly Life of Logistics: Mapping Violence in Global Trade.* Minneapolis, MN: University of Minnesota Press.

Craik, Brian. 2004. The Importance of Working Together: Exclusions, Conflicts and Participation in James Bay, Quebec. In *In the Way of Development: Indigenous Peoples, Life Projects and Globalization*, eds. Mario Blaser, Harvey A. Feit, and Glenn McRae, 166–186. Ottawa: Zed Books.

Dafnos, Tia. 2013. Pacification and Indigenous Struggles in Canada. *Socialist Studies* 9(2): 57–77.

———. 2015. First Nations in the Crosshairs: As Canada Moves to Protect Resource Exploitation, Agencies Accelerate Spying on Indigenous Activist. *Canadian Dimension* 49(2). https://canadiandimension.com/articles/view/first-nations-in-the-crosshairs.

Deloria, Philip J. 2004. *Indians in Unexpected Places.* Lawrence: University of Kansas Press.

Diabo, Russell, and Shiri Pasternak. 2011. First Nations Under Surveillance. *The First Nations Strategic Bulletin*, January–May. http://rabble.ca/sites/rabble/files/FNSB%20Jan%20May%2011.pdf.

Dunn Cavelty, Myriam, and Kristian Søby Kristensen. 2008. *Securing 'the Homeland': Critical Infrastructure, Risk and (In)security.* New York: Routledge.

Furedi, Frank. 1993. Creating a Breathing Space: The Political Management of Colonial Emergencies. *Journal of Imperial and Commonwealth History* 21(3): 89–106.

Government of Canada. 2004. Securing an Open Society. Public Safety Canada. https://www.publicsafety.gc.ca/cnt/ntnl-scrt/scrng-eng.aspx.

Grant, George. 1890. *Canada and the Canadian Question: A Review*. Toronto: Imperial Federation League in Canada, C. Blackett Robinson.

Hier, Sean P., and Kevin Walby. 2014. Policy Mutations, Compliance, Myths, and Redeployable Special Event Public Camera Surveillance in Canada. *Sociology* 48(1): 150–166.

Hobson, J. 2005. *Imperialism: A Study*. New York: Cossimo.

Hussain, Nasser. 2003. *The Jurisprudence of Emergency: Colonialism and the Rule of Law*. Ann Arbour, MI: University of Michigan Press.

Indian and Northern Affairs Canada. 2010. *Final Report—Evaluation of the Emergency Management Assistance Program*. http://www.aadnc-aandc.gc.ca/eng/1100100011392/1100100011397.

Integrated Threat Assessment Centre [ITAC]. n.d. About ITAC. http://www.itac.gc.ca/bt/index-en.php.

Integrated Threat Assessment Centre [ITAC]. 2007. Threat Assessment: Aboriginal Protests—Summer 2007 (07/30). Obtained through ATI request 117-2008-123, May 11.

———. 2010. Canada: Biannual Update on the Threat from Terrorists and Extremists (10/151-E). Obtained through informal ATI request 117-2012-95, December 30.

Millar, Matthew. 2013. Harper Government's Extensive Spying on Anti-Oilsands Groups Revealed in FOIs. *Vancouver Observer*, November 19. http://www.vancouverobserver.com/politics/harper-governments-extensive-spying-anti-oilsands-groups-revealed-fois?page=0%2C0.

Monaghan, Jeffrey, and Kevin Walby. 2012a. 'Making Up 'Terror Identities': Security Intelligence and Canada's Integrated Threat Assessment Centre. *Policing & Society* 22(2): 133–151.

———. 2012b. 'They Attacked the City': Security Intelligence, the Sociology of Protest Policing, and the Anarchist Threat at the 2010 Toronto G20 Summit. *Current Sociology* 60(5): 653–671.

Monahan, Torin, and Priscilla M. Regan. 2012. Zones of Opacity: Data Fusion in Post-9/11 Security Organizations. *Canadian Journal of Law and Society* 27(3): 301–317.

Morgensen, Scott L. 2011. The Biopolitics of Settler Colonialism: Right Here, Right Now. *Settler Colonial Studies* 1: 52–76.

Murphy, Nicole. 2014. RCMP Critical Infrastructure Intelligence Team: An Overview. *IR3: Infrastructure Resilience Risk Reporter* 1(1): 7–11. http://carleton.ca/irrg/wp-content/uploads/IRRR-Vol1Issue1-April2014.pdf.

Natural Resources Canada. 2014. Key Facts and Figures on the Natural Resources Sector. http://www.nrcan.gc.ca/publications/key-facts/16013.

Neocleous, Mark. 2008. *Critique of Security*. Montreal: McGill-Queen's University Press.

———. 2010. War as Peace, Peace as Pacification. *Radical Philosophy* 159: 8–17.

Palmer, Darren, and Chad Whelan. 2006. Counter-Terrorism Across the Policing Continuum. *Police Practice and Research* 7(5): 449–465.

Parliament of Canada. 2007. Proceedings of the Standing Committee on National Security and Defence. Issue 17 – Evidence – Meeting of June 18. http://www.parl.gc.ca/Content/SEN/Committee/391/defe/17evb-e.htm.

Pasternak, Shiri. 2013. The Economics of Insurgency: Thoughts on Idle No More and Critical Infrastructure. *The Media Co-op*, January 14. http://www.mediacoop.ca/story/economics-insurgency/15610.

Public Safety Canada. 2009. *National Strategy for Critical Infrastructure*. Ottawa: Government of Canada.

Pugliese, David. 2014. Government Orders Federal Departments to Keep Tabs on All Demonstrations Across Country. *Globe and Mail*, June 4. http://ottawacitizen.com/news/politics/government-orders-federal-departments-to-keep-tabs-on-all-demonstrations-across-country.

Rifkin, Mark. 2009. Indigenizing Agamben: Rethinking Sovereignty in Light of the 'Peculiar' Status of Native Peoples. *Cultural Critique* 73: 88–124.

Roach, Kent. 2003. *September 11: Consequences for Canada*. Montreal, Kingston: McGill-Queen's University Press.

Royal Canadian Mounted Police [RCMP]. 2007. Briefing Note to Deputy Commissioner, 4 June 2007. Obtained through ATI request GA-3951-3-00060.

———. 2009a. RCMP Criminal Intelligence: Aboriginal Joint Intelligence Group. Aboriginal Communities, Issues, Events and Concerns 2009/10. Obtained through ATI request A-2011-06291.

———. 2009b. NAPS 2009 POWPM. Obtained through ATI request GA-3951-3-03434/11, March 3.

Royal Commission on Aboriginal Peoples. 1996. *Report of the Royal Commission on Aboriginal Peoples*. Ottawa: The Commission. http://www.collectionscanada.gc.ca/webarchives/20071115053257/http://www.ainc-inac.gc.ca/ch/rcap/sg/sgmm_e.html.

Simpson, Audra. 2014. *Mohawk Interruptus: Political Life Across the Borders of Settler States*. Durham, NC: Duke University Press.

Valverde, Mariana. 2006. 'Peace, Order and Good Government': Policelike Powers in Postcolonial Perspective. In *The New Police Science: Police Power in Domestic and International Governance*, eds. Markus D. Dubber and Mariana Valverde, 73–106. Stanford, CA: Stanford University Press.

Williamson, Tara. 2009. The Edges of Exception: Implications for Indigenous Liberation in Canada. *Appeal* 14: 68–83.

Young, George. 2005. Can Warrior Societies Survive in a Post 9/11 World? *Windspeaker* 23(6): 28. http://www.ammsa.com/publications/windspeaker/can-warrior-societies-survive-post-911-world-0.

Index

Note: Page numbers with "n" denote notes.

© The Author(s) 2016
R. Lippert et al. (eds.), *National Security, Surveillance and Terror*,
DOI 10.1007/978-3-319-43243-4

CPI Antony Rowe
Chippenham, UK
2018-12-05 16:50